INFLUENCES ON PARENT BEHAVIOR

STANFORD STUDIES IN PSYCHOLOGY

Editors

Robert R. Sears
Leon Festinger
Douglas H. Lawrence

INFLUENCES ON PARENT BEHAVIOR

Lois Meek Stolz

Tavistock Publications

First published in Great Britain in 1967
by Tavistock Publications Limited
11 New Fetter Lane, London E.C.4

Printed in the United States of America

To

Herbert Rowell Stolz

Who has helped many achieve understanding
and satisfaction in the arduous
adventure of parenthood

Preface

The study reported here describes the influences on child-rearing as perceived by 78 parents. The interviews used in the study were conducted during the spring of 1958, as a basis for an experimental investigation of the communication of information about child care. We believed that an evaluation of the effect of any specific influence on child-rearing required consideration of other influences simultaneously impinging upon the parent. Originally, we expected to develop from the interviews only an outline of the causes of parental behavior, but the results proved so rewarding that I undertook the task of analysis as a separate project.

In the collection and analysis of data for this study, a number of people have been involved, each of whom has contributed in one way or another. To them all, I am deeply grateful.

Participants in the formulation of plans for the interviews included Robert R. Sears and Wilbur Schramm (co-directors of the communication and child care project), A. Kimball Romney, Louise Shedd Barker, J. Stacey Adams, Richard Carter, and Lois Meek Stolz.

Celia Barker Lottridge assisted in preparing a preliminary outline of values, beliefs, and other influences on parent behavior.

Louise Shedd Barker made the initial home contacts and established relations with the parents that brought a high degree of cooperation. I am grateful to the parents who gave time to contribute to a study that they hoped would be useful to other parents. The interviews were conducted by Louise Shedd Barker, A. Kimball Romney, Ruth T. Storey, Elizabeth Rapp Tukey, O. Walters, and Lois Meek Stolz. Celia Barker Lottridge and

Alice Hitchcock checked the content of the interviews as data collection proceeded. Grace A. Barron set up the filing system and supervised the transcribing of the tape-recorded interviews. Her organizing ability contributed greatly to the smooth running of the project.

I wish to express particular thanks to those who performed various tasks connected with the analysis of data. Martin Moloff, William Burns, Ruth Terrell, and Michael Levine coded interview data. Eleanor Walker Willemsen and Lynette Kohn Friedrich rated residences and occupations of parents. Eleanor Walker Willemsen, Jay Siegel, Jerry and Nancy Wiggins, John Caffrey, and Janet Beavin assisted with the intricacies of machine computations. Ruth Lancaster served as general assistant and did a multitude of indispensable tasks. Her accuracy and amiability were great assets—especially in recurring crises. Mrs. Lida Price typed the final manuscript with unusual skill and Mrs. Elizabeth Musser and Mrs. Catherine Phinney did valiant work on earlier drafts.

For counsel and direction in the statistical treatment of data, I am deeply indebted to my friend John Wilder Tukey of Princeton University, and to the late Sidney Siegel. My warm appreciation goes to Alberta Engvall Siegel, who helped with difficult problems in the analysis, and also contributed greatly to the improvement of the manuscript. Mary Cover Jones read the first draft, and the revision profited by her comments.

To my husband, Herbert Rowell Stolz, I owe a long-standing debt for his wise counsel and his generous assistance, as well as his patience.

This study was partially supported by grant number 3M-9122-(c) from the National Institute of Mental Health.

L.M.S.

Stanford University
October 15, 1965

Contents

INFLUENCES ON
PARENT BEHAVIOR

I

The Study

During the past twenty years students of child development have become less interested in describing children's behavior and more interested in identifying the causes underlying their behavior. Recent studies have sought these causes, for example, in the parents' child-rearing practices or in behavior settings. This study opens up another area in the sequence, namely, the causes of parents' behavior. It is a systematic description of the influences that motivate or press a parent to use one procedure rather than another in bringing up his child. It is an inquiry into why parents raise their children the way they do—or, more precisely, an inquiry into the influences on child-rearing behavior as revealed in interviews with parents.

Every study of the practices of parents in the United States has shown that they bring up their children in diverse ways. One study of child rearing concludes, "The commonest phrase in this book is 'The mothers varied widely' " (Sears *et al.*, 1957, p. 467). Differences in practices have been found among mothers in the same community, mothers of the same age, mothers of similar social position, mothers of the same religion, mothers of similar ethnic background. The few available studies of fathers also indicate great variety in paternal child-rearing practices (Stolz *et al.*, 1954; Block, 1955). In this study we attempt to describe the influences that cause such differences among parents.

To our knowledge no previous study has attempted to describe the variety of influences modifying the practices of parents. Some antecedents of parental behavior have been identified in previous investigations of home atmospheres (Baldwin, Kalhorn, and

Breese, 1945), behavior settings (Barker and Wright, 1955), the use of communication sources (Hoeflin, 1954), independently measured personality characteristics of fathers (Block, 1955), extrapolated personality characteristics of mothers (Sears *et al.*, 1957), and wartime separation of fathers and children (Stolz *et al.*, 1954). Such investigations have focused on one, or at most a few, of the causes of child-rearing practices.

The Antecedents of Parental Behavior

Probably every parental practice has a history of influences behind it. Some of these influences are subtle and occur without conscious attention, some repressed, some partly forgotten, some conscious, vivid, and well-remembered. In this study, which is based on interviews, we shall consider only conscious influences and those partly forgotten but easily recalled, not the repressed or unconscious ones. We have considered personality variables only to the extent that parents introduced them as explanations of their behavior. According to Brim (1959, p. 61), some clinical writings imply that there is very little in parent role performance other than the playing out of unconscious desires acquired in childhood. However this may be, we have felt it worthwhile to study those areas where the parent has some latitude in choosing his behavior, and to discover what influences his choices.

We assume that a parent's child-rearing behavior flows from his values and beliefs, interacting with his personality characteristics, in a situation involving his child. We also assume that other influences operate as possible stresses to initiate, direct, reinforce, or inhibit parental behavior. Such modifications may come from past experiences (for example, in the Army), from other members of the family (for example, the spouse), from changes in the behavior setting (for example, moving from a farm to the city), or from a communication source (for example, a book for parents). The sequence, the pattern, and the weighting of influences on behavior will differ for different parents.

Values. Underlying the beliefs and practices of a parent are the values he holds: what he wants for himself and for his children, what he holds dear or abhors. Value statements express a relation between an object or event and an evaluative term such as "good," "bad," "desirable," "important" (Whiting and Child, 1953, pp. 28–29). Here are some value statements from our interviews:

> Individuality in children is worth preserving.
>
> We tell them they don't get room and board for nothing. Their daddy has to work, their mommy has to work, so they should do their share.
>
> I always have been conscious of good food. . . . I feel like to me eating is the most important thing in the world.

We use the term "values" to include the goals of parents, the roles they approve of for parents, and their aspirations for their children, as well as the behavior they seek to inculcate. Words such as *want, desire, should, ought, good, worth,* and *important* are key words for identifying values.

Beliefs. Behind every practice is some belief that instigates or justifies it. Beliefs are of two kinds. One kind is instrumental: it asserts that a relation exists between an act and a goal. Such a belief states that a certain cause leads to a certain effect, to some valued or disvalued outcome (Whiting and Child, 1953, p. 28). For example:

> As children grow older, if they continue to masturbate, it's probably due to lack of affection on the parents' part because then the children feel sort of unloved or unwanted.
>
> I think going to Sunday School makes a difference as far as learning to share things with other children and getting along with other children prior to going to regular public school.
>
> The children obey my husband more quickly than they do me because they respect a man more, and they don't see him as much, and he doesn't give them as many directions as I do.

The other kind of belief is descriptive. It assigns some attribute or quality to an object or event. For example:

> The first few months an infant gets so fussy and wants to be carried all the time; I think this is only part of growing up, I guess a stage of childhood.
>
> It seems to be a feminine characteristic for little girls to be interested in horses.

You don't really know until you practice; this is the best way to learn anything. And as you make mistakes and learn to do a thing differently, like putting on diapers wrong or something.

Other influences. We are concerned here with the broad range of motivations or stresses directly related to parenthood. These include the parent's previous experiences—both as a child and as an adult—in his family of orientation (his own parents and siblings) and in the community. They also include his experiences in his family of procreation (his own spouse and his children). We also include here what Barker calls "behavior settings," such as being in a restaurant for dinner, getting ready to go to bed, or having guests in the home (Barker and Wright, 1954). Here are a few examples illustrating this wide range of influences:

I think it's unfair to punish children unless they know why they're being punished. I know that it happened to me, being the eldest of three, and having a very strict father. He just didn't wait for an explanation. I was there and I was the oldest and I was responsible. I felt very strongly that on many occasions when I was blamed for something, he should at least have listened to my side. I'm just sort of determined that I should like to know what has happened before I punish my children.

We began having birthday parties for our children when they were very little. The wife wanted them. I could leave birthday parties completely off, as far as I'm concerned, but knowing how the children feel about them, I go along with it. I would never suggest a birthday party. She always suggests them, and I just sort of go along.

I come home at the end of the day, and I'm thinking about other things, and I may be tired, and I hear some hassling among the children, and my wife is tired and upset, and [Da 6.8] has aggravated her; well, then I just take off right at the peak and go after her [Da 6.8]. I really shouldn't get into this because it's between [Da 6.8] and her mother, but I do.

Finally, there are the influences that come from communication sources: from books and magazines, from television, from friends and relatives, from doctors, ministers, teachers. In addition, there are more subtle influences: what the Joneses do, what the school expects, how things are done at the hospital during the lying-in period.

Parents vary in their vulnerability to these sources. Some are eager for information about child-rearing, and actively seek out answers to their questions. Others, although interested, are often critical about what they read or hear on the subject. A few make little use of the communication network, feeling strongly that no one can tell a parent how to raise his child. Some excerpts:

At first this nursery school didn't seem like the answer to all my problems, and it was only toward the end of the second year that I even began to understand what they were talking about—began to understand what ideas I wanted to accept and which were right.

We've become very good friends with the principal of the elementary school. We sit in the evenings and have some pretty nice conversations with him, and we pick up some good ideas from him. He's a person who's had training in dealing with children.

There were articles in the magazines that said that children would get a complex if you spanked them. And I took it very seriously for a while, but then I decided I couldn't live in a house with a child like that, doing anything he pleased. I didn't have enough patience, I am afraid.

Relation to practices. We have made no attempt in this study to relate parental values, beliefs, and other influences to specific child-rearing practices. First things first: parental values, beliefs, and other influences must be described before they can be related to specific practices, just as in previous research parental practices were described before they were related to child behavior. We see this study as focusing on phase 2 of a four-phase sequence: (1) the situation, calling forth (2) the pertinent values, beliefs, and other influences, leading to (3) the parental practice, determining (4) the child's behavior.

Procedures of the Study

With the foregoing general assumptions in mind, we began to construct an outline of influences on parent behavior for our interviews by analyzing interviews that had been carried out for two previous research projects, one in the area of Palo Alto, California (Stolz *et al.*, 1954), the other in Newton, Massachusetts (Sears *et al.*, 1957). From the Palo Alto project we had about 200 interviews with parents of children under eight years old: three to five interviews each with 38 fathers, and two interviews each with 38 mothers. From the Newton project we had some 300 single interviews with mothers of five-year-olds. Although both studies focused on the relation of parents' attitudes and practices to their children's behavior, they also yielded some data on the causes of the parents' behavior. The preliminary outline based on these interviews was supplemented with material that seemed appropriate for parents of infants and adolescents.

We had to settle several points of methodology before we could begin interviewing parents. First, we decided to take the parents into our confidence, telling them what we were seeking and asking them for their help. (The alternative was to go at it indirectly, leading them to discuss their child-rearing practices but not divulging what we were really after.) The decision seems to have been wise. Sometimes a parent said, "Heavens, I haven't the slightest idea why I do what I do." But when we said, "Perhaps we can help you find out," he invariably expressed interest. Many parents thought about the causes of their behavior between interviews, and came to the next interview with helpful and revealing examples to discuss. Also it was easier for the interviewer not to be burdened with secrecy concerning his purpose.

Second, we decided to collect data from both the mother and father in each family, and thus to interview parents only when both agreed to cooperate. Fathers and mothers were to be interviewed separately by different staff members. Interviewers were not to discuss interviews with each other while data were being collected, and parents were to be reassured about this if necessary. Mothers and fathers were free to discuss anything they wished about the study with each other or anyone else. In fact, a respondent often brought in revealing examples after a discussion with his or her spouse.

Third, we estimated that we would need approximately four one-hour interviews with each parent, and we so informed the parents. We realized that some would have much more to contribute than others, and we planned to adjust accordingly. If interviews beyond the fourth seemed likely to yield rich rewards, and if the parent was willing, we would continue our sessions;

if the interviews were not yielding new material, we would stop earlier in the series.

Fourth, we prepared a guide for the interviews. It consisted of four parts: (1) the exploratory interview; (2) specific areas for intensive investigation; (3) a checklist of values, beliefs, and other influences; and (4) the family data form.

The exploratory interview was semi-structured, designed to let the parent discuss whatever areas of behavior had the most meaning for him. We assumed that such a procedure would insure high motivation for recalling behavior, and for searching for influences to account for it. The suggestions to the interviewer emphasized the desirability of inquiring into the instigation and direction of change if the parent reported any changes in his goals, beliefs, or practices, and of using any "problem" with a child or "critical incident" in the family to investigate any seeking for information from communication sources.

We wished to investigate two areas with all parents: one family setting (the evening meal) and one behavior system (obedience). If a parent began to discuss either of these topics during the exploratory interview, the interviewer could move directly into the more specific questions. We saw the exploratory and the intensive interviews as interweaving, rather than as two separate parts of the interview sessions.

The checklist was a device to help interviewers keep track of the material they were eliciting and the areas that still needed investigating. It was based on our preliminary outline of values, beliefs, and other influences.

The data form had three sections for recording data: on the parents' families, on the parents themselves, and on their children. We considered it important not to ask these factual questions (age, birthplace, education, etc.) until the last session, for two reasons. First, we did not wish to set a pattern of question-and-answer sessions with the interviewer taking the initiative. Second, we did not wish to appear invasive, at least not until we had made friends with the respondent and had already obtained our primary data.

At the first session, the interviewer explained the purpose of the study, the respondent's importance as a coworker, the working of the tape recorder, and the steps taken to ensure that the interviews would be confidential. In the typed interviews no names appear: the respondent is represented by a case number (as Mo 6 or Fa 2), reference to a wife or husband is indicated only by "spouse," and children's names are changed to symbols of sex and age (for example, a son eight and a half years old is indicated as So 8.5). Discussion always began with a concrete incident, the interaction of parent and child, but it was the interviewer's job to lead the parent to explore the causes underlying his behavior. Early in the study, we played back and discussed tapes of interview sessions in an effort to point out missed cues or to learn from especially well-handled episodes.

Six of us, four women and two men,* conducted the interviews. All were well qualified for the task, both by academic preparation and by experience in either research interviewing or professional interviewing. All were faculty or staff members at Stanford University.

At the initial home contact with the parents, each parent was asked if he preferred a man or woman interviewer. If a preference was expressed, we honored it in assigning personnel; if not, we assigned on the basis of schedule load. The four women interviewers conducted sessions with 34 mothers and 13 fathers; the two men conducted sessions with 5 mothers and 26 fathers.

Plan of the Report

We describe the respondents in Chapter II, and the method of analysis in Chapter III. Chapters IV through XI describe the influences on parental practices analyzed from the interviews. They include values of parents for themselves as parents, and for their children; beliefs of parents related to child-rearing; characteristics of parents, characteristics and behavior of children, spouse interaction, and parent-child interaction; behavior settings; past experiences of parents; and use of communication sources. In describing each category of influences we consider

* Our plan had been to have the same number of men and women, but one staff member left the study when it was too late to find another man for the job.

the emphasis given to the influence, the differences between matched mothers and fathers, and the relation of various influences to certain demographic variables. We also report how the parents' use of communication sources on child-rearing is related to some of the other influences on their behavior. In Chapter XII we discuss some implications of the study for future research and for those professionals who communicate information or advice to parents.

II

The Families

In order to make our study of the influences on parental behavior as inclusive as possible, we selected a group of families that would give us a wide range of diversity on certain demographic variables: age of parents; length of marriage; number, age, and sex distribution of children; national, religious, educational, occupational, and social background; degree of social mobility; and residence. Because of the limitations of the study, we were not able to obtain an adequate probability sample of the population on each of these items. However, we did succeed in finding 39 families that provided the diversity we were looking for. We had large, small, and average-sized families. We had young parents and old parents, relatively new marriages and mature marriages, completed families and expanding families. There were families of all boys, families of all girls, and families with both. Some of them had only one child; others had six or seven. And the variability was as great in other respects; for example, in education of parents, occupation of father, religious background, social position, and social mobility.

Method of Selection

We found the families in several ways: through agencies such as the Stanford Nursery Schools and the County Agricultural Agency; by visiting certain neighborhoods; and by following up suggestions from a pediatrician, a minister, and acquaintances. We were careful to include both families who were connected with community organizations and families who were not. After we had decided tentatively that a particular family was different enough from those we had already selected, we telephoned the parents at home. We explained that Stanford University was making a study of families, and that we would like to call on both parents to describe it and to see if they would be interested in participating. We insisted that we must see both parents at the same time, because both would be asked to participate, and we wanted to be sure that both were really interested.

Next a staff member called on the family at their convenience, usually in the evening after dinner. We considered this visit extremely important, for three reasons. First, it provided an opportunity to explain the purpose of the study, the contribution we believed it would make to other families in the future, and the obligations participation in it would impose on the families involved. Second, it gave us an opportunity to judge whether the parents were likely to continue cooperating for the necessary number of interviews. And third, during this visit to the home, the only one in most cases, the staff member gathered information that was later useful to the interviewer. We believe that the cordial and candid relations established during the first visit were directly reflected later in the parents' promptness in keeping appointments, and in their earnest efforts to be helpful.

Only seven families refused to participate, either over the phone or before the first interview, and their reasons seemed generally reasonable—illness, travel, heavy work load. Two families were dropped after one interview with each mother, because by then it had become obvious that it would be impossible to interview the fathers. One was an alcoholic; the other was usually away from home seeking employment.

Age, Marriage, and Children

At the beginning of the interviews, the mothers ranged in age from 20 to 46 years, with a mean of 32.9 years. The fathers ranged in age from 23 to 57 years, with a mean of 35.3 years. At the time of marriage, the mothers' ages varied from 17 to 31 years (mean, 23.3 years), the fathers' ages from 16 to 41 years (mean, 25.4 years). The length of marriage ranged from two to 16 years (mean, 10.1

years). In the "youngest" family the father was 23, the mother 20; they had been married two years, and their only child was a boy of eight and a half months. At the other extreme, in the "oldest" family, the father was 57, the mother 46; they had been married 16 years and had two children, a boy almost 14 and a girl 12.

Altogether there were 111 children in the 39 families: 54 boys and 57 girls. Six families had one child each; 11 families had two children; another 11 had three; seven had four; three had five; and one had seven. The median family had three children, with 22 families having either two or three children. Four of the couples with one child each had been married for only two or three years; the other two had been married for ten years.

Ten families had boys only and eight had girls only; the rest had both boys and girls. The boys' ages ranged from eight months to 13.9 years, the girls' from eight months to 13.2 years (see Table A.1 in Appendix A).

Twenty families reported that their family was complete; ten families hoped to have more children. In the remaining nine, the father and mother did not agree. But these statements must be taken with at least a grain of salt; in one family where both parents stated they expected no more children, the mother became pregnant shortly after our interviews ended.

Cultural Background of the Families

National background. All the parents who contributed data to the study were born in the United States except for one father, who had been here 20 years, and one couple, both born in England, who had been here five years. From the birthplaces of the parents of the respondents, we can form some idea of the cultural backgrounds of the respondents (see Appendix Table A.2). In 18 families the parents of both the father and the mother had been born in this country. Three of these families were Negro, and two were Jewish. In five families only one parent of one respondent had been born outside the United States. In eight families half of the parents of the respondents had been born outside the United States. In the remaining eight families all four parents of respondents had been born abroad. Appendix Table

A.2 shows the wide diversity in places of birth of the parents of the respondents.

Religion. The 39 families reported affiliations with 14 different religious groups. In 28 families husband and wife were of the same religion. Of these families, 12 couples were Protestant (Unitarian, Congregational, Episcopal, Presbyterian, Methodist, Baptist, Christian Science, and Assembly of God), eight couples were Catholic, three were Jewish, two were Buddhist, one was Mormon, and in two families neither parent had any religious preference. In the remaining 11 families the husband and wife were of different religions. Two wives went to their husbands' church, two husbands to their wives' church. One husband, a Protestant of Methodist parents, was taking instructions in Catholicism, his wife's religion. In the other six families, husband and wife belonged to different religious groups.

We sought to measure each family's consistency in religion by giving a point for each different religion held by the mother, the father, and each of their parents. The maximum possible score is 6 (a different religion for each person), but the highest we actually recorded is 4.5:*

Score	1.0	1.5	2.0	2.5	3.0	3.5	4.0	4.5
No. of families	11	1	1	4	11	7	3	1

Of the eleven families that were consistently of the same religion for two generations (score 1.0), four were Catholic, three were Jewish, two were Baptist, one was Mormon, and one was Buddhist. The average score is 2.5, which indicates a mixture of religious backgrounds in most of the families.

Education. The educational level of the respondents was rated on a seven-point scale (Hollingshead and Redlich, 1958, p. 391). The respondents were above average in education, both mothers and fathers on the average having had some college education. However, among both mothers and fathers, the range extended from those who had not gone beyond elementary school to those who held higher university degrees (see Appendix Table A.3).

* A score of 1.0 indicates the same religion for husband, wife, and all four of their parents. A half-point was given for a change of religion or for attending a different church.

We found that parents who had not gone beyond the sixth grade were not useful subjects for this research. They were unable to verbalize their ideas or, sometimes, to grasp what we were trying to do. Because of these and other factors, they did not keep appointments. The two families we had to drop from the study belonged to this group. One was a Negro family from Louisiana in which the father had had only a fifth-grade education and the mother "some high school." The other family was of Mexican background, born in Texas; the parents had each had about three years of schooling.

The two parents had comparable education in only eight families. In 17 families the father's education exceeded the mother's; in 14 the mother's exceeded the father's. On the average, fathers had .13 of a year more education than mothers.

Occupation of fathers. Among the fathers many occupations could be found: physician, professor, engineer, store clerk, safety superintendent, teacher, day laborer, nurseryman, farmer. The occupational level of the fathers was rated on a seven-point scale prepared by Hollingshead (Hollingshead, n.d.; Hollingshead and Redlich, 1958, pp. 390–91). Although the distribution includes all seven levels, it is skewed toward the upper end, with 59 per cent above the midpoint of the scale and 28 per cent below, the average rating being 3.26 (see Appendix Table A.4).

Residence. We selected the families from the residential area contiguous to Stanford University, 35 miles south of San Francisco. This area sprawls over much of the peninsula, and includes several towns whose boundaries exist only on a map; country-like sections that extend for ten miles beyond the towns toward the hills, and even some farming land. The residences of the families varied greatly: one family lived in a small old house attached to a greenhouse where the father worked, another in a deteriorating section just off the main highway, two on farms, and one in an attractive modern house on a half acre in a "select" neighborhood.

We had difficulty in rating houses, not only because of their variability, but also because of the rapid expansion of the area since World War II; there were many new tract houses, and in some neighborhoods elaborate and expensive houses had been built next to old modest ones. We began rating by using Warner's scale of house type (Warner *et al.*, 1949, pp. 149–50), but found that this scale, developed for a large urban center in the East, was not suitable for a fast-growing California community. We therefore developed a revised six-point scale that seemed more appropriate (see Appendix Table A.5). The houses were rated by two workers who did not know the families (agreement, $r = .84$). Where there was disagreement, as there was in 13 cases, the final rating was based on a conference at the house. No house was rated excellent, five were rated very good, eight were rated good, 18 fair, six poor, and two very poor.

Social position. We made several assessments of social position. We first used the social-class score developed by Hollingshead: residence score multiplied by 6, plus education score multiplied by 5, plus occupation score multiplied by 9. Next we transposed these scores into social-class levels I-V, according to Hollingshead's scheme (Hollingshead and Redlich, 1958, pp. 387–97). We also used a three-point scale—upper, middle, working (lower) —on which each respondent rated himself at the close of the interview. In addition, we devised a score for social mobility by subtracting a limited socioeconomic score for the family of procreation (2 × occupation score + 1 education score) from a similar score for the family of orientation.

Some of the relations between these various measures of social status are worth reporting. For this group of parents, the limited socioeconomic score is as satisfactory as the more complex score ($r = .96$), and is easier to obtain. However, we used the limited score only for obtaining the social mobility score. The parents' self-appraisals of their social position do not correlate well with the Hollingshead levels, the mothers' being especially divergent ($r = .42$ for mothers; $r = .68$ for fathers). One might suppose that mothers would be more self-conscious about social status and more inclined to upgrade their status. However, fourteen of these mothers rated themselves lower than Hollingshead's score, and only eight rated themselves higher. Fathers were even more conservative, 23 rating themselves lower and six rating themselves higher.

This sample of families had scores in social position from 26 to 114,* out of a possible range of 20 to 134. The distribution of their scores is compared below with the distribution of scores in a sample of families living in the industrial community of New Haven, Connecticut.†

	I	II	III	IV	V
Social level scores	(20–31)	(32–55)	(56–86)	(87–115)	(116–134)
Study sample	5.1%	38.5%	28.2%	28.2%	—
New Haven sample	2.7	9.8	18.9	48.4	20.2

Whether these families constitute a fair sample of the community around Stanford University is difficult to say, since no pertinent survey of the community has been made. However, one can be assured that in this community a higher percentage of families fall into social-class levels I, II, and III, and a lower percentage into levels IV and V, than in New Haven.

On the whole the families we studied had moved upward on the social ladder. Their social mobility scores‡ are distributed as follows:

From	+16	+10	+4	0	−1	−5
To	+11	+5	+1	0	−4	−11
Mothers	4	9	16	0	6	4
Fathers	3	11	12	2	10	1

Only 11 fathers have scores below those of their own fathers, while 26 have scores above, the range being from +16 to —6, and the mean +3.0. Age is probably a factor influencing some of the negative scores; for example, two of the three youngest fathers have negative scores. However, the median test reveals no statistically significant difference between the mobility scores of the older and the younger fathers. A larger number of mothers than fathers had moved upward, only 10 having negative scores but 29 having positive scores. However, the average mobility score for mothers is slightly lower, 2.9, and the range slightly larger, from +13 to —11. In 16 couples the father gained more than the mother in social mobility; in 17 the father gained less than the

* The two families in level V (116–134) had to be dropped from the study.

† The New Haven sample is from Hollingshead and Redlich, 1958, p. 395.

‡ Mobility score was computed as the respondent's limited socioeconomic score less that of his father. A score of zero indicates no change in mobility.

mother; in five the parents made equal gains; and in one the parents had equal losses. The limited socioeconomic score of the respondents' fathers does not correlate highly with either the socioeconomic score of fathers ($r = .42$) or that of mothers ($r = .37$).

Interrelations of Demographic Variables

In Table 2.1 we present the intercorrelations of the scores for mothers and for fathers on seven demographic variables.*

Age of parent. The older parents (both fathers and mothers) preponderantly had the older children. Older mothers tend to be more highly educated, and to have higher social position. Older fathers show the same tendencies, but not as strongly.

Number of children in family. Parents with larger families tend to have the older children, but this relationship is not as strong as one might expect. Families with high consistency in religion for two generations appear to show a slight tendency to have the larger families, as do mothers of lower educational level.

Educational level of parent. More highly educated fathers show a tendency to come from families of low consistency in religion. They are definitely of higher social position, but this relation is partly due to the fact that fathers' ratings on education contribute 22.9 per cent of the score on family social position. More highly educated mothers (who are likely to be older, as previously stated) are also of higher social position, but the relationship is not as strong as it is for fathers, because it is the father's education, not the mother's, that determines part of the score for the family's social position.

Social position and social mobility. The parents of higher social position are not only the older parents, and those with higher education, but also those who come from families with lower consistency in religion. Mothers of higher social position tend to be more highly mobile, and fathers show a tendency in the same direction. In addition, fathers of higher mobility tend to have older children and are of higher educational level.

* All correlations in this study were obtained by the Pearson Product Moment formula.

TABLE 2.1. *Intercorrelations between Demographic Variables*

(Correlations for fathers above diagonal; correlations for mothers below)

Variable	*Age of parent*	*Number of children*	*Age of oldest child*	*Consistency in religion*[f]	*Education level*[f]	*Social position*[f]	*Social mobility*
Age of parent ..	*	–.02	.63[e]	.05	.21	.34[b]	.24
No. of children	–.01	*	.35[b]	.27[a]	–.14	–.20	.14
Age of oldest child	.63[e]	.35[b]	*	.17	–.12	–.03	.33[b]
Consistency in religion[f]	.04	.27[a]	.17	*	–.40[c]	–.40[c]	–.05
Educational level[f]	.45[d]	–.27[a]	–.03	–.12	*	.86[e]	.30[a]
Social position[f]	.39[c]	–.20	–.03	–.40[c]	.55[e]	*	.28[a]
Social mobility	.14	–.05	–.15	–.20	.14	.40[c]	*

[a] $p < .10$; [b] $p < .05$; [c] $p < .02$; [d] $p < .01$; [e] $p < .001$.

[f] On these three variables a high score indicates a low rating. We therefore reversed the scales for the correlations.

CASE SUMMARIES

We have tried to show by analysis of certain demographic variables the wide range of variability represented by the 78 parents contributing to this study. It was important to have such variability if we were to chart the major influences on mothers' and fathers' behavior toward their children. However, analysis of this type cannot reveal the parents' individuality. At the close of each series of interviews, the interviewer wrote a summary of his impressions of the case. These impressions, added to the demographic data, give a vivid picture of the men and women who contributed to the study. Two of these summaries, slightly edited, are given here.

Case 1. One of the children in this family had attended the Stanford Nursery School, and the parents willingly consented to cooperate in the study. One wonders now how this ever happened; the father left for work at six in the morning and returned home at seven in the evening; the mother cared for a horse, a cow, and chickens, as well as four children ranging in age from three to twelve. But cooperate they did, the father sometimes staying until ten-thirty or eleven o'clock at night.

The mother was a vigorous, sturdily built woman of 37 years. She always came to the interviews in a hurry, looking hastily put together but in attractive clothes. Her manner was serious, but she showed real humor, including the ability to laugh at herself. She was eager to talk and to be accurate and honest.

The father was just over forty-two, a tall good-looking man, conservatively dressed and neatly groomed. His crewcut hair gave him a youthful appearance. His expression was pleasant, straightforward, and alert, without being tense. He spoke precisely in a pleasant well-modulated voice, selecting his words carefully for exact meaning. In interviews, he was relaxed but eager to search for the material we wanted, and gave the impression of trying to help in every way he could.

This couple had been married 13 years ago, when the father was 28 and the mother 24. This was a marriage of the east and the west coast; the father met the mother when he was in war work. The first two of their four children were born while the father was doing graduate work.

Both parents come from English stock; each had a parent who was born in England. Their background was Episcopalian, but they did not now belong to any denomination, although the father was interested in the Unitarian point of view.

They were both college graduates, the father having an advanced degree. For the preceding three years, he had worked in the research division of an industrial company.

They lived on the top of a low hill six miles from town, among a small group of houses with acreage, in the midst of dairy farms. They had three acres, with outbuildings for the horse, cow, and chickens. The father and mother had built the house themselves. This was a difficult house to rate, and one on which the raters disagreed between 3 and 4. The furnishings were adequate but somewhat worn with use; the pictures on the wall were modern. The impression one got was of a family-centered home whose emphasis was on cultural activity rather than decoration: an open piano with scattered music sheets, an easel, children's books, records, a violin and viola, a child's drawing. The house was clean; its untidiness was that created by six energetic people.

Their social-position score places this family in Class II (score 38 in a range from 32 to 55). This agrees with the mother's self-rating but is lower than the father's self-rating of upper-class. Actually they were upper-middle class in education, in father's occupation, and in their intellectual and cultural interests. However, they did not fit the upper-middle-class pattern in their consumption habits, their manner of living, or their value system, having purposely broken from the stereotype. They lived in the country because they wanted to live as they pleased, rather than as neighbors decreed. They developed a way of life on their hilltop that reflected their own values: for the mother, especially, the participation of all members of the family in productivity; for the father, the opportunity for each to fulfill his need to be creative.

Both parents had been socially mobile, but the mother much more so than the father. The mother's mobility score is +13, the father's +7. Both of the father's parents were professional people (in the arts), even though they had less formal education than their son. The mother's parents, on the other hand, had finished only a few grades in elementary school, and were both working people.

There were four children in the family: two sons (11.9 and 7.4 years) and two daughters (10.5 and 3.3 years). The oldest son was showing signs of independence, of wanting to break away from the close-knit family, and this was causing some concern, especially to the mother. The oldest girl had artistic talents, which pleased her parents. Both parents were deeply interested in their children, and in developing a home atmosphere stimulating to cultural activities.

Case 6. The mother in this family heard of our study at a sewing class in the neighborhood, and she and her husband agreed to cooperate when approached. She was a short, plump woman of 35, with the black hair and sparkling eyes of her Spanish mother. Her face was alert, pleasant, happy-looking. As she talked there were many smiles and some laughter. Her dress was always neat and fresh.

Her 35-year-old husband was lean, of medium height, with a pale face and a relaxed but reasonably animated expression. He was somewhat shy and hesitant. He did not express himself easily in words, whereas his wife was a great talker. They had been married 16 years, and were one of the oldest families in the study.

They had two children, a boy 10.7 years old and a girl 8 years old. The boy was quiet, obedient, and, in general, cooperative and well-behaved. The girl was boisterous, gay, self-willed, whining and pouting at times, full of mischief, and clever at manipulating her father. After the children the mother's main interest was her house; the father's was his job and garden.

All four of their parents were foreign-born. The mother had a German father and a Spanish mother; the father's parents were both Italian. The family was all Catholic except for the mother's father, who was either "nothing or Lutheran."

Both mother and father were high school graduates, but the father had received some additional technical training in the Service. The father held a job at a nearby factory as supervisor of safety regulations. His promotion to this position occurred during the interviews, and was an important event because of the increased social status it brought him. He now had his name on his office door, a symbol whose importance even his older brother recognized.

The family had lived in a new tract house for the preceding two years. Both father and mother were proud of this house, since it marked a distinct improvement over their previous residence in a large city. They had a large yard (about a quarter acre) that the father took great pride in, having "landscaped" it himself. The furniture was new, but rather scanty.

They owned a radio and television, on which they listened to the news, but otherwise the programs were chosen by the children. During the day the mother sometimes watched "soap operas," which she then discussed with a neighbor whom she admired and emulated. They subscribed to *Better Homes and Gardens* (for interior decoration and recipes), to *The National Geographic*, and to *Time*. The last two were read by the father, but the mother only looked at the pictures occasionally. They also got the daily local newspaper.

This was a socially mobile family. Compared to their parents, this father and mother were better educated, the father had a better job, and they lived in a much better house with better furniture. The mother was quite conscious of this change in social position, saying that she was now in the middle class but had grown up in a working-class family. She talked about changing the way she served her meals because she had admired a neighbor's serving meals in a certain way. She chuckled over the discomfiture of her father-in-law when this new style was introduced; she had told him emphatically, "From now on, in this house, the vegetables will be on the side table." Her husband was not as conscious of a change in social position, stating that his was a working-class family like his parents'. However, he reported with some pride his own better education and better job. Actually the father had risen in the social scale 9 points, whereas his wife had risen 4 points. Their social position is in Class III, with a score of 80 in a range of 56 to 86. The mother's family was Class IV, whereas the father's was Class V.

One can see from the above case summaries of two typically diverse families that each family in the sample presented a matrix of characteristics different from that of any other family. Our task, then, was to uncover the variety of influences that affected the behavior of these different parents in their relations with their children.

III
The Interview Data

When the interviewing was over, we found that we had amassed 8,862 double-spaced typewritten pages of transcript. The transcripts of the interviews with mothers, who contributed 55.9 per cent of the material, ranged in length from 34 to 262 pages (mean, 127.1). The fathers' transcripts ranged from 37 to 201 pages (mean, 100.1).

This difference is one we expected, since it was easier for most of the mothers to arrange time for the interviews. The fathers often had to squeeze interview sessions into a crowded schedule, coming late at night and tired after a long day, or early in the morning and anxious to get to their jobs. Some of the mothers welcomed the interviews as a release from the loneliness of housekeeping and as a chance to talk about their major concern, the rearing of their children. Although it is sometimes said that women talk more than men, 12 of the fathers we interviewed talked more than their respective wives.

Categorizing the Content of the Interviews

We first had to identify in the transcripts the data that had to be coded. We designated the unit to be considered an *element of discussion,* that is, a discussion by the parent, at one place in the interview, of one practice or one value or one belief and its related influences. The second step was to categorize each element into the appropriate value, belief, or other influences for which purpose we revised and expanded the outline developed as a guide for the interviews. Specific directions for categorizing were developed after preliminary experience in coding.

Reliability. After the directions for coding were prepared, a reliability check was run; two coders, M and B, made independent codings of 12 single interview sessions with six mothers and six fathers. The reliability (percentage agreement)* for the identification of elements ranges from 88.1 to 97.4 per cent (mean, 93.1). The reliability for differentiation of elements into values, beliefs, and other influences is also high (see Table 3.1).

TABLE 3.1. *Reliability of Coding (based on 12 interview sessions)*

	Per cent agreement	
	Range	*Mean*
Selection of elements for coding	88.1– 97.4	93.1
Differentiation into categories of values, beliefs, influences	88.4– 97.6	94.1
Levels within categories:		
I	84.2–100	90.6
II	82.2– 95.4	87.0
III	75.0– 97.2	88.9
IV	60.0–100	81.4

We then tested the reliability of codings within the general categories on four levels, each level progressively more specific. As might be expected, the mean percentage of agreement decreases as the categories become more specific but this decrease is not pronounced until Level IV, which we did not use in any of the statistical analyses, there being relatively few codings at this level. When we finished the initial coding, there were a number of elements under values, beliefs, and behavior of the child which had been assigned to miscellaneous categories. The outline was revised and expanded to appropriately redistribute these elements.

CODINGS

Number of codings. We obtained nearly 22,000 codings, 55.8 per cent contributed by mothers, 44.2 per cent contributed by fathers. These percentages are almost identical to the percentages

* Formula for determining reliability is as follows:

$$\frac{2 \times \text{number of agreements}}{\text{total number identified by M plus total by B}}.$$

of interview pages contributed by mothers (55.9) and by fathers (44.1). Thus, the mean number of codings per interview page is the same for mothers and fathers, 2.5. This fact assured us that the material we had elicited from fathers was as pertinent in content as that elicited from mothers.

The number of codings obtained from each of the 78 interview series varied. For mothers the range is from 120 to 615 (mean, 311.2). The low contributor was a 39-year-old college-educated woman, who was quiet, shy, and somewhat withdrawn. Her home, on a small dairy farm, reflected her artistic interests. Her interviews had to be concentrated into one day because of the distance the interviewer had to travel. The high contributor, a woman of Japanese descent, was 34 years old and a graduate in public-health nursing from a state university. She was relaxed, assured, and cooperative, talking rapidly and fluently for eight sessions. The mother whose number of codings stands nearest the mean (314) was a woman nearly 35, a banker's daughter from a small midwestern town. A plain woman with simple ideas, she scheduled her family's life quite rigidly in order to be able to contribute to the family budget by part-time teaching. She was serious, earnest, and cooperative. All three of these mothers were interviewed by the same person.

The number of codings for the fathers ranges from 80 to 539 (mean, 246.9). A 48-year-old grocery clerk with an eighth-grade education has the least number of codings. He carried a heavy work schedule, both day and night, which precluded much contact with his family and limited the number of interviews. He had little to say in the two interviews because he literally had only brief and sporadic relations with his children. The high contributor among the fathers was a professor, a young man of 32. Although he was serious and tended to be formal, he talked readily for eight sessions. The father whose codings (247) are nearest the mean was also 32 years old, a businessman who worked for his father. He was reserved and often seemed ill at ease in the unusual role of talking about himself and his children. He never went far or deeply into any topic, although he continued for five sessions. The last two men had the same interviewer.

Average coding per page. We used the average coding per

page to evaluate the pertinence of the material obtained from the parents. Although the mean coding per transcript page is 2.5 for both mothers and fathers, the individual parents varied widely in relevance of material. Among mothers, the lowest average coding per page (1.58) is from a mother who came for five sessions and contributed 134 pages, seven more than the mean. She was a 30-year-old high school graduate, had been married 11 years, and had three daughters and a son, whose ages ranged from seven months to eight years. The family was lower-middle class, the mother downward mobile. She and her husband were both deeply religious, and spent much time in Protestant church activities. Perhaps the key to her low contribution lies in her personality. She was shy and seemed quite conscious of a speech difficulty which she tried to cover up by certain mannerisms. She evidenced a real desire to cooperate and was quite frustrated when her speech difficulties interfered.

The mother with the highest average coding per transcript page (3.53) was the one with the least number of pages. The mother nearest the mean (2.43 codings per page) was a woman of Japanese descent, who was 35 years old, had been married 10 years, and had a girl almost seven and a baby on the way. She had had one year of college, in home economics. Her family was near the lower end of Class IV in social position. She came for six interviews and contributed 178 transcript pages, 51 above the average. She had difficulty talking, a difficulty that was probably due more to shyness and a desire to make a good impression than to educational background.

The fathers' average coding per page ranges from 1.78 to 3.36. The father with the lowest average coding per page has the smallest number of pages, as well as the least number of codings, so that the content of his interviews does not compensate for its shortness, as it does for the mother with the least number of pages. The highest average coding per page is from a man of 32 with an engineering degree, a Mormon who looked to his church for guidance in family affairs. He had five children, whose ages ranged from nine months to eight years. In three interviews he contributed 99 pages, which is slightly below the average, but they are rich in content, perhaps because of his obviously high intelligence, his conscious guiding of his life by principles, and his desire to be cooperative and thoughtful.

The father nearest the mean (2.47 codings per page) was one of the youngest fathers, a high school graduate who was high in Class IV social position. There were three young children in the family, two boys and a baby girl. The four sessions with him yielded 116 pages, which is 16 above the average.

Percentage scores. Because of the variability in the number of interview transcript pages and the additional variability in the average codings per page, we have used percentage scores for some of our analyses. The number of tallies in each category under values, beliefs, and other influences for a given respondent is expressed as a percentage of his total codings. For example, the total number of codings for Mo 1 is 377; she has 5 codings for moral values, which, divided by 377, gives her a percentage score of 1.33 in moral values. The score thus obtained is an intensity score, indicating the degree of emphasis a parent placed on a given category in relation to his total contribution. Where mean percentage scores are given for mothers or fathers as a group, they are based on all 39 mothers or 39 fathers rather than on the number reporting a particular item. Such percentage scores allowed us to compare mothers and fathers, even though mothers in general had more sessions and more pages of interviews than fathers, and also allowed us to compare one father with another or one mother with another in spite of the differences in the amount or quality of material they gave us.

Distribution of codings. A general analysis of the codings into the main categories, as shown in Table 3.2, gives an overall picture of the causes of parental behavior ascribed by the respondents in this study. Fathers are more likely to attribute their behavior to their values or beliefs, whereas mothers are more likely to regard other sources of influence, primarily settings or communication sources, as causes of their behavior. To determine the difference scores between mothers and fathers, we paired each mother and father by family and based the calculations on the percentage scores to obviate differences in gross amount of content. All of the differences shown in Table 3.2 between the emphasis given by mothers and that given by fathers

TABLE 3.2. *Distribution of Codings of Values, Beliefs, and Other Influences*

Categories	*Mothers*		*Fathers*		*All*		*Percentage score difference*[a]	
	No.	*%*	*No.*	*%*	*No.*	*%*	t	p
Values	1,926	15.9	2,098	21.8	4,024	18.5	4.28	$<.001$
Beliefs	2,513	20.7	2,459	25.5	4,972	22.8	4.61	$<.001$
Other influences:								
Family members	3,596	29.6	2,707	28.1	6,303	29.0	2.01	$<.10$
Behavior settings	551	4.6	327	3.4	878	4.0	3.49	$<.01$
Previous experiences	777	6.4	656	6.8	1,433	6.6	—	n.s.
Communication sources	2,773	22.8	1,383	14.4	4,156	19.1	5.46	$<.001$
Σ Values and beliefs	4,439	36.6	4,557	47.3	8,996	41.3	6.47	$<.001$
Σ Other influences	7,697	63.4	5,073	52.7	12,770	58.7	6.47	$<.001$
Total	12,136	100.0	9,630	100.0	21,766	100.0	—	—

[a] Difference between mothers and fathers paired by family.

(except for previous experiences, and perhaps intrafamily influences) could be expected in other samples, as the high degree of statistical significance shows.*

The chapters to follow will present the findings of the study on how values, beliefs, intrafamily influences, behavior settings, previous experiences, and communication sources modify the behavior of parents with their children.

* In Table 3.2 and all tables to follow, a p of $<.001$ indicates that the difference is so large that only once in a thousand samples would we expect to obtain it by chance alone; $<.01$ indicates only once in a hundred; $<.05$, five times in a hundred, and so forth. Thus, the smaller the numerical value of p the more confidence we may have that an observed difference is a significant one and not a chance result.

IV
Values for Parenthood

We were interested in finding what values actually enter into a parent's child-rearing practices rather than what values a parent might subscribe to verbally. Much of what a parent does stems from the values he has acquired from living in a particular culture, values that determine what he considers worthwhile, what he seeks for in himself or in his children. In a sense, a parent's values epitomize his identity, what he is, and what he strives for. Practices of parents are integrally related to values, but values are by no means always overtly expressed in every parent-child interaction (Whiting and Child, 1953, p. 29).

Values usually become a regulating force that helps a parent perform his role according to the norms of society (Ackerman, 1958, chap. 21; Brim, 1959, pp. 64–67). In a relatively static, homogeneous culture, a parent's behavior is habitualized, and closely follows that of other parents in the group. In such a culture, values are deeply ingrained and unconsciously accepted as the only right ones. In the United States, however, with its heritage from many different cultures, its geographical and social mobility, and its lack of close ties between new and parent families, mothers and fathers are likely to choose their values consciously and assess them critically. Today in our country, parents discuss their hopes and plans for their children with each other, with other parents, and with relatives. To some degree they feel free to choose what they consider to be the best, the most worthwhile, or the most appropriate goals.

For this reason, we had relatively little difficulty in eliciting from the parents what their values were in relation to their practices. Most of them seemed to know what they were after—that fighting is bad, that children should learn to take responsibility, that family solidarity is good, or that parents should give their children a feeling of security. Only a few parents had to resort occasionally to such ambiguous phrases as "It is right," "It is good for him," or "It will make him grow." Most of them had rather specific goals and standards in mind, or at least could tease them out after a few promptings.

Sometimes a parent seemed to hold conflicting values. For example, Fa 1 placed a high value on intellectual pursuits and individual creativity. Although he reluctantly conceded that good social relations are also important in our present culture, he had difficulty accepting this goal for his children, because he saw that pursuit of good social relations could interfere with the goals of intellectual and artistic creativity. Sometimes a parent was in the process of changing values. Thus, under the pressure of her adolescent son's need for more freedom, Mo 1 was having a hard time giving up her goal of a unified, close family doing things together.

Because of our special interest in the education of parents, we have separated those values relating specifically to the parental role—i.e., what a mother or father thinks he should do as a parent, what he considers makes a "good" parent—from the more general or basic values for himself or his children that guide parental behavior. In this chapter we shall discuss the values for parenthood mentioned by the parents as influences on their behavior. In Chapter V, basic values will be discussed.

Categories of Values for Parenthood

Over one-fourth (27.7 per cent) of all values discussed by parents are related to the role of father or mother. The percentage scores on codings of these values for mothers ranged from .41 to 8.86 (mean, 4.24), for fathers from 1.15 to 11.25 (mean, 6.50).*

* Percentage scores are $\frac{N}{\text{Total tallies}}$. See p. 27.

TABLE 4.1. *Values for Parenthood*

Values	*Per cent reporting*		*Number of codings*		*Mean percentage score*[a]		*Percentage score differences*[b]	
	Mo	*Fa*	*Mo*	*Fa*	*Mo*	*Fa*	*t*	*p*
Parents should provide for:								
Education	92	95	137	207	1.19	2.15	4.38	<.001
Emotional security	95	90	135	167	1.23	1.76	2.43	<.02
Control	90	82	115	123	1.00	1.25	—	n.s.
Nurturance	41	46	21	33	.15	.33	1.97	<.10
Using outside resources	41	41	25	28	.22	.26	—	n.s.
Economic support	26	28	14	18	.12	.23	—	n.s.
Good rearing	44	58	31	43	.26	.44	—	n.s.
Learning about child-rearing	13	18	9	8	.07	.07	—	n.s.
Σ Values for parenthood	100	100	487	627	4.24	6.50	4.64	<.001

[a] Based on all 39 mothers or 39 fathers.

[b] We do not report the value of *t* for those differences that preliminary analyses by the modified *t* test (Lord, 1947) indicated would not have a statistical significance of .10 or beyond. This procedure is followed for all succeeding tables in this study.

The values for parenthood are divided into eight categories: to educate, to provide emotional security, to control, to nurture, to use community resources, to provide economic support, to rear well, and to learn about child-rearing (see Table 4.1). Of these eight categories, the first three are the ones that parents are most conscious of, and that seem to predominate in guiding their behavior. These three values (to educate, to provide emotional security, and to control) account for 79 per cent of the responses in this area.

To educate. Most mothers and fathers in our culture feel that it is the parent's responsibility to educate his children. The respondents state this responsibility in such terms as: to teach, to train, to instill, to give information; to permit a child to learn, not to push him unduly, to help him unfold; to motivate, challenge, stimulate, or encourage him to learn; to help, to guide, to counsel, to lead; and to be an example for learning. Only five parents fail to mention their role as educators. Fathers emphasize it more than any other aspect of their job as parents; a third of their parenthood value codings are in this area. Mothers emphasize it second only to providing emotional security for children.

Parents take seriously both the job of motivating and the job of teaching their children. No doubt this seriousness reflects mainly the need to socialize children to behave in ways the parent approves of, but it probably also reflects the high value most Americans place on learning. In spite of the fact that the egghead is often held up to ridicule by politicians, parents strive to educate their children. This is well exemplified by the answer of Fa 16 when he was asked what part of his role as a parent he enjoyed most:

> Teaching them things. This is the thing I enjoy most. Teaching them ideas, teaching them how to use tools, how to build things.... If the parents don't do this job of teaching—teaching certain values and teaching certain habits—then the school doesn't have much chance.... The greatest thing I can do for my own children is to give them this love and feeling for learning.

To provide emotional security. In this category we include such values as: giving love and affection; offering understanding and sympathy; paying attention to or taking an interest in the child; being just or fair; freeing the child emotionally; and supporting and encouraging. Almost all the parents mentioned being influenced by their desire to provide emotional security for their children. Slightly more than a fourth of all values for parenthood are in this category. Mothers stress this value more than any other parental-role value. Fathers stress it even more than mothers, although it is second to their value for education. One mother discussed in detail her ideas on the importance of giving her young baby affection:

> I think a child can do with all the affection a parent has to spare. ... I know how pleased I am when I am the recipient of affection.... It comes from the way I was brought up. I could always count, no matter how bad I was, I could count on my parents' affection, never scared of losing that. I think that all the love that you can give a child is the best thing in the world. I've read that almost everywhere I read anything: that children do so poorly when they don't have love, that it's a very necessary thing even to their physical well-being ... it's very vital to the emotional and the physical health of the being that a parent should give him love.

To control children. In analyzing the values for parenthood we had to distinguish between beliefs regarding the kind of control that brings the best or the desired results, and values for control per se. There are parents who value control as an end in itself, just as there are those who value more freedom or minimum control in parent-child relations. When a parent has strong values regarding control, his beliefs about what control accomplishes may be rationalizations of the value, rather than the basis for the formation of the value.

It is value judgments about control that are categorized here. They include goals for forcing, steering or requiring; for inhibiting, preventing, restricting; for setting standards or limits; for not spoiling or indulging; for being permissive and not forcing. Such values are third in emphasis for both mothers and fathers.

The child's immaturity, and the hazards in our culture, call for control of adult over child. Control is also desired by parents who wish to protect their adult activities and interests from constant intrusion. In addition, it is important for some mothers and fathers to feel in control of their children because of their own concept of the parent role, or because of their own personal need for dominance. Although parents differ in the degree of control they want, and in the relative importance they place on controlling, only four mothers and seven fathers failed to mention its influence on their role as parents (see Table 4.1).

Most mothers (87 per cent) and most fathers (72 per cent) emphasize the coercive role of parents. Fewer parents (36 per cent of mothers, 46 per cent of fathers) emphasize the permissive role of parents but fathers' emphasis is significantly higher ($t = 2.39$; $p < .05$). Some parents point out that they value being coercive at some times and noncoercive at other times. Fa 1 said:

> I think parents have a responsibility to be strict with their children when it comes to something that involves a child's safety. If we were living in the city and had children where they could run off the sidewalk into the street, I think it would be important to deal extremely strictly. But on the other hand, telling them to go and do their practicing or to "go change your shirt" or to go to bed or something like this—these things can be the subject of some banter between us.

To provide nurturance. Statements referring to the parent's responsibility for providing nurturance for children include such values as feeding the child, seeing that he gets adequate sleep and rest, protecting him, watching out for his health, preventing him from becoming ill, nursing him when sick, providing for his activities and play, and making him comfortable. Less than half of the parents mention this aspect of their role, and they give relatively slight emphasis to it. One wonders why the care of children, which consumes so much of mothers' time, is not mentioned more. Perhaps the reason is that such roles are taken for granted by most parents; being so unequivocally necessary, they do not appear to parents to involve a choice of behavior.

Certain factors in a parent's life may make him more conscious of the importance of his nurturing role. These include feeling that he was deprived of nurturance during his own childhood, having a first baby, and being in a profession related to the care of children. The father who made the highest score on these values (over twice that of any other father, and four times that of any mother) was an unemployed Negro janitor who had grown up in a deprived home, and who, like his own father, found it hard to provide for his children. From inspection of the interviews and data sheets on respondents with high scores in this area, we find three fathers with similarly deprived childhood homes; a woman, of Mexican background from a deprived childhood home, whose husband was unemployed; three young mothers with their first babies; and one mother and one father trained in pediatrics and health education. These findings suggest related influences on values that might be investigated in a larger sample.

To use outside resources. Parents have various opinions on whether they should use as aids in bringing up their children such facilities as baby-sitters or caretakers, music and dancing teachers, swimming instructors, remedial reading clinics, libraries, or organizations such as the Boy Scouts. About a fourth of each parent group mention, but do not stress, such values.

To provide economic support. Under a parent's responsibility to support his children by providing money and material things, we also categorized values placed on income and material objects as means to social status and prestige. There are relatively few references to the economic aspects of the parental role by either mothers or fathers. Fathers' most time-consuming role, that of breadwinner, is, like mothers' nurturant role, almost completely ignored, a fact that is difficult to explain unless one assumes that parents do not perceive it as being a matter of choice behavior.

The factors that bring this value to the forefront are not clear. No single variable describes all five of the mothers who have the highest scores. The mother with the highest score was a younger woman who had four children and was among the lowest in social position. There is a strong tendency for younger mothers to emphasize economic values (see Table 4.2). However, there are mothers in other families, just as large and just as poor, who do not seem much influenced by economic values in their day-to-day life with their children, at least not according to their reports to us.

In one family both mother and father score among the highest five on economic values for parenthood. Both parents had come from low-income minority groups, but had successfully moved up the social scale; both worked in order to improve their status and insure financial security for their one baby. The unemployed Negro janitor also highly valued providing for his family's economic needs, as he did providing care and nurturance, but his wife has the lowest score in this area. The personality or other factors that determine whether values for economic support influence parent behavior should be investigated in later studies, with a larger sample and perhaps other methods.

Other parent-role values. Under the general value for rearing well we include statements such as "to rear properly," or "to raise the best you can." Over a third of the parents express their goals for parenthood in such general terms (about 6.5 per cent of the codings in values for parenthood). One father stated his goal in the following way: "A parent's responsibility means that we brought them into the world—it was our idea, not theirs—and we are responsible to bring them up right. In other words, we should do the best we can to raise them so that they can make their way through life." Finally, a few mothers and fathers think that parents should learn about the job they have to do as parents.

Relation of Values for Parenthood to Demographic Characteristics

Values for parenthood as a whole and nine specific values were correlated with seven demographic characteristics of the parents. (The category of learning about child-rearing is omitted in the

TABLE 4.2. *Correlations between Values for Parenthood and Demographic Characteristics*

Values	*Age of parents*	*Number of children*	*Age of oldest child*	*Consistency in religion*	*Education level*	*Social position*	*Social mobility*
MOTHERS							
Parents should provide for:							
Education	.03	.19	.22	.20	–.15	.23	–.16
Emotional security	–.42[d]	.18	.13	.14	–.43[d]	–.33[b]	–.17
Authoritarian control	–.28[a]	.38[c]	.10	.04	–.16	–.36[b]	.02
Permissive control	.07	.15	–.05	–.17	–.15	.07	.01
Control	–.25	.40[c]	.08	.08	–.19	–.32[b]	.02
Nurturance	.00	–.18	–.28[a]	–.16	.00	–.20	–.03
Use of resources	.14	–.04	–.11	.19	.26	–.13	.09
Economic support	–.53[e]	–.11	–.14	.02	–.35[b]	–.17	.17
Good rearing	.08	–.13	.09	.23	–.18	–.27[a]	.07
Σ Values for parenthood	.15	.27[a]	.14	–.23	–.40[c]	–.27[a]	–.07
FATHERS							
Parents should provide for:							
Education	–.12	.14	.10	.07	.10	.03	.14
Emotional security	.24	–.04	.18	.15	–.11	–.05	.03
Authoritarian control	.44[d]	–.15	.32[b]	.21	–.15	–.07	.08
Permissive control	.04	–.11	.17	–.10	.04	.05	.09
Control	.42[d]	–.19	.38[c]	.14	–.11	–.04	.12
Nurturance	–.14	–.03	–.23	.10	.03	–.15	–.12
Use of resources	.00	–.07	.10	–.09	.14	.10	.08
Economic support	–.16	–.04	.29[a]	.20	–.07	–.21	.12
Good rearing	.17	–.19	.18	.24	–.21	–.05	.20
Σ Values for parenthood	.20	–.09	.22	.23	–.08	–.08	.16

[a] $p < .10$; [b] $p < .05$; [c] $p < .02$; [d] $p < .01$; [e] $p < .001$.

correlations because the percentage of parents discussing it was too small.) The correlations are given separately for mothers and for fathers in Table 4.2. In Table 4.3 we show the significance of these correlations. The significance of each correlation has been tested by the conventional *t* test. Coefficients that are significant beyond the .10 level (for a two-tailed test) are indicated by superscripts.

When a large number of correlation coefficients are computed from a given set of data, some will be "significant" simply because of the operation of chance factors. For example, when we say that a coefficient is "significant at the .05 level," we are reporting that, if there were only chance variations for it to reflect, so large a value would arise, in the long run, no more than five

TABLE 4.3. *Significance of Correlations between Values for Parenthood and Demographic Characteristics*

Level of significance	No. expected by chance (70 r's)	No. observed Mo (70 r's)	No. observed Fa (70 r's)
<.001	.07	1	0
.001 to .01	.63	2	2
.01 to .02	.70	3	1
.02 to .05	2.10	4	1
.05 to .10	3.50	5	1

times in one hundred samples of the size studied. Clearly, if we should compute one hundred correlation coefficients, an average of five of them will be "significant at the .05 level" simply because of the operations of chance. Although we have no way of determining whether a given significant coefficient represents a real association in the population or simply the luck of the draw, we are able to compare the number of significant correlation coefficients we observed with the number that might be expected because of chance alone. This is done in Table 4.3. For the mothers and fathers separately, 70 coefficients were computed to show the relation between their values for parenthood and their demographic characteristics. When 70 coefficients are computed, by chance 2.1 of these will be significant at the .02 to .05 level, 3.5 will be significant at the .05 to .10 level, etc. These chance expectations are given in Table 4.3, and they are compared with the observed number of significant correlations, as reported in Table 4.2.

From Table 4.3 it appears that for mothers the number of correlations at each level of significance is greater than chance expectancy. For fathers only correlations at a level of significance of .01 to .02, and of .001 to .01 are greater than chance expectancy; therefore, only those which reach a statistical significance of .02 deserve detailed discussion.*

The highest correlations for mothers are with the mother's age and educational level, and with the number of children; for fathers with the father's age and the age of his oldest child.

* The method described for evaluation of the significance of correlations is used throughout this study.

In general, values for parenthood are stressed by the less educated mothers, and perhaps by those with lower social positions and larger families as well. Providing emotional security and economic support are strongly emphasized by younger and less-educated mothers. The parent's role in controlling children, especially in authoritarian ways, is stressed by mothers with lower social positions and larger families, and by older fathers with older firstborn children. The value for educating children, which is emphasized so strongly by both parent groups, shows no statistically significant relation with any of these seven variables for either mothers or fathers. It seems to be a value that spreads across demographic groups.

Differences between Mothers and Fathers

Fathers emphasize the influence of their values for parenthood on their behavior with their children more than mothers. This is true not only for parenthood values as a whole but also for all but one of the specific values. The differences in emphasis are statistically significant for the values as a whole ($p < .001$) and for three specific values: for education ($p < .001$), for providing emotional security ($p < .02$), and for providing nurturance ($p < .10$). Notice that the order of magnitude of these probabilities follows the order of emphasis that fathers gave to these values (see Table 4.2). The difference in emphasis on the specific value to control children is in favor of fathers but does not reach statistical significance; however, the emphasis on permissive control is greater for fathers and is statistically significant ($t = 2.39$, $p < .05$). It is the older fathers and the younger mothers who tend to stress authoritarian control.

The contrast between the emphasis given by fathers compared with mothers is well illustrated by Case 4. The percentage score on values for parenthood is four times larger for the father than for the mother (10.1 versus 2.6), the husband being third from highest among fathers and the wife sixth from lowest among mothers. The discrepancy in favor of the father holds for six of the seven specific values for parenthood, neither parent mentioning the value to provide economic support. The wife also has a zero score in values to nurture, to control, and to rear well. Both parents held college degrees. The father was employed in technical research, and the mother had worked in business several years before marriage. Each came from an old California family and emulated to some extent the methods of child-rearing used by their parents, the husband those of his own understanding and adjustable father, the wife those of her somewhat strict and formal mother.

Summary and Comments

Parents are influenced by many "shoulds" and "oughts," concerning their parental role. Over a thousand statements by them are grouped under eight general headings. Almost all the parents emphasize the influence of their job of socializing their children —teaching them and helping them to learn—and of their desire to provide an atmosphere conducive to the development of emotional security. Almost as many parents stress their role in controlling their children, though they differ in the kind of control they think should be exercised.*

Although these three values for parenthood are stressed far more than any others, some parents discuss other values: nurturing their children; using resources outside the home such as libraries or recreation centers; providing the money and things that a family needs; and generally giving their children a "good" rearing. A few parents also felt that they should learn about child-rearing.

The age of the mother, her education, the social position of the family determined by the husband, and the number of children in the family—all were related in some degree to the influence of values for parenthood on mothers. Only the maturity of fathers is related to values for parenthood, older men and those with older first-born children emphasizing control.

Fathers discuss the influence of values for parenthood significantly more than mothers, especially values for education, for providing emotional security, for controlling permissively, and for providing nurturance. One can only speculate why fathers give more weight than mothers to the influence of such parent-

* See Chapters VI and VII for discussion of beliefs about control of children.

role values. It may be that fathers are more self-conscious about their role than mothers, because their function has been expanding, and the importance of fathers given more attention in recent years. Mothers may take their roles more for granted. It could be that fathers talked relatively more about values for parenthood because they are more familiar with generalizations, and less familiar with more specific day-to-day situations with children. We shall find out more about this in Chapter VIII.

V

Basic Values for Child-rearing

Of all the values reported by parents, 2,910 (or 72.3 per cent of the total) refer to a wide range of life's issues directly related to the way a parent behaves with his children. These values, which we have labeled basic values, include: the qualities parents try to develop in their children (generosity, creativity); the welfare they seek for their children (health, safety); the authority relationships they approve of (obedience, religion); the "good" things in life they want for their children (job, travel); the type of atmosphere they try to establish in the family (harmony, order). Value statements are concerned with what is good or bad, desirable or undesirable, important or unimportant; they offer guidelines by providing bases for determining the worth or acceptability of various kinds of behavior.

In this study we analyzed only those values that were directly related to parental practices or beliefs. Our analysis therefore does not consider all the values of these parents, but only those that seem most clearly related to their behavior as parents. It is particularly important to keep this limitation in mind when considering the emphasis parents place on various kinds of values. In spite of the specificity of the research, however, we believe there is ample evidence that the values reported are basic in the sense that each value is an integral part of the personality of the respondent, and has meaning for him in terms of his self-identity.

We systematized the almost 3,000 coded basic values into 11 categories: moral, family, egoistic, interpersonal, emotional security, education, orderly living, biological, play, economic, and finally a category for general values. In organizing these catego-

TABLE 5.1. *Categories of Basic Values*

Values	*Per cent reporting*		*Number of codings*		*Mean percentage score*		*Percentage score difference*	
	Mo	*Fa*	*Mo*	*Fa*	*Mo*	*Fa*	*t*	*p*
Moral								
Obedience	74	67	72	42	.58	.44		
(Obedience, negative)	5	10	2	6	.03	.06		
Religion	59	56	63	74	.52	.84		
(Religion, negative)	8	13	4	10	.06	.11		
Responsibility	56	59	42	72	.36	.75		
Morality	59	59	48	45	.40	.49		
Justice	44	44	26	46	.23	.41		
Citizenship	15	13	9	7	.10	.06		
Σ Moral values	100	97	266	302	2.28	3.16	2.85	<.01
Family								
Unity	79	67	71	64	.61	.65		
Love	59	41	45	43	.41	.36		
Cooperation	49	41	28	25	.24	.24		
Harmony	51	31	35	16	.31	.20		
Democracy	33	36	19	25	.20	.25		
Marriage	31	28	21	14	.18	.13		
Location	10	15	7	11	.05	.12		
Σ Family values	97	85	226	198	2.00	1.95	—	n.s.
Egoistic								
Independence	62	69	73	81	.65	.81		
Aggression	3	15	2	8	.02	.08		
(Aggression, negative)	41	41	23	26	.23	.26		
Achievement	31	38	17	25	.12	.27		
Intelligence	33	23	19	17	.17	.17		
Practicality	33	33	23	20	.16	.23		
Self-respect	28	36	15	25	.13	.25		
Enthusiasm	21	21	15	13	.08	.11		
Determination	10	15	4	6	.03	.08		
Appearance[a]	23	5	10	2	.08	.03		
Modesty	3	5	1	3	.00	.03		
Σ Egoistic values	92	100	192	224	1.59	2.29	1.99	<.05
Interpersonal								
Getting along	72	49	61	40	.49	.45		
Friends	41	13	20	10	.17	.11		
Affection	5	3	2	3	.02	.01		
Generosity	33	33	15	19	.12	.25		
Tolerance	23	23	19	16	.16	.15		
Conformity	21	21	16	10	.10	.08		
(Conformity, negative)	15	15	6	14	.06	.13		
Nurturance	10	10	5	5	.04	.04		
Recognition	5	13	2	8	.01	.08		
Σ Interpersonal values	87	74	146	125	1.17	1.30	—	n.s.

[a] Not included in totals.

TABLE 5.1 *(cont.)*.

Values	*Per cent reporting* Mo	Fa	*Number of codings* Mo	Fa	*Mean percent-age score* Mo	Fa	*Percentage score difference* t	p
Emotional security								
Freedom from anxiety	64	51	57	32	.46	.27		
Happiness	38	46	50	35	.34	.36		
Mental health	38	46	28	27	.19	.24		
Privacy	13	13	8	7	.05	.08		
Σ Emotional security values	77	85	143	101	1.04	.95	—	n.s.
Educational								
Knowledge	51	74	35	58	.26	.66		
Education in general	38	54	23	36	.17	.38		
Level of education	49	38	28	28	.26	.29		
Type of education	8	18	4	8	.05	.08		
Σ Educational values	77	85	90	130	.74	1.41	3.86	<.001
Orderly living								
Manners	72	69	61	55	.56	.59		
Orderliness	33	54	28	28	.24	.35		
Carefulness	21	21	10	8	.08	.09		
Punctuality	15	31	6	17	.05	.17		
Σ Orderly living values	82	87	105	108	.94	1.19	1.68	<.10
Biological								
Safety	46	62	28	39	.22	.42		
Health and sex	28	39	19	28	.14	.30		
Physical activity	23	36	16	26	.11	.28		
Food	31	33	13	19	.13	.17		
Rest	18	23	11	11	.07	.15		
Σ Biological values	74	87	87	123	.67	1.33	4.27	<.001
Play								
Enjoyment, humor	64	46	47	36	.39	.35		
Interesting life, pets	33	36	18	28	.17	.23		
Creativity	28	26	23	18	.18	.15		
Σ Play values	70	69	88	82	.74	.73	—	n.s.
Economic								
Property	51	49	39	27	.33	.30		
Money	31	49	15	25	.15	.26		
Work	31	18	22	14	.16	.14		
Σ Economic values	82	72	76	66	.64	.70	—	n.s.
General	36	28	20	12	.14	.15	—	n.s.
Σ Basic values	100	100	1,439	1,471	11.95	15.16	4.28	<.001

ries we were greatly helped by the work of White (1951). Within the 10 major categories (omitting general values) are 55 subcategories of which four have some negative tallies (obedience, religion, nonaggression, and conformity). (See Table 5.1.)

The three most important of the 10 major categories (judging only by the magnitude of the percentage scores) are moral, family, and egoistic values. Both mothers and fathers stress moral values more than any other category; second and third place order are reversed for mothers and fathers, mothers putting greater emphasis on family values, and fathers, on egoistic values.

Moral Values

The 568 moral values constitute 19.5 per cent of the basic values. In general, fathers emphasize these values more than mothers. Of the six subcategories under moral values, mothers stress obedience and religion, but fathers as a whole stress religion and responsibility. Half of the percentage scores in moral values for both mothers and fathers are in their first two areas (see Table 5.1).

Obedience. Obedience includes respect for elders and other authority figures, and values on the quality of authority relations. Obedience as a value should be distinguished from obedience as a means to other ends, which is an instrumental belief and will be discussed in Chapter VI. For example, Fa 1 was strongly against obedience as an end in itself, but said, when asked how strict parents should be in demanding obedience, "Well, when it comes to something that . . . importantly involves a child's safety, I think very strict obedience is required."

We found obedience to be in first place among mothers' moral values, but only in fourth place among fathers'. The difference between mothers and fathers is evidenced in the percentage of parents reporting, the number of codings, and the mean percentage scores.

The mother with the highest percentage score on obedience (2.06) was a college-educated Negro schoolteacher. Like many of the mothers who emphasize obedience, she was a younger mother in the lower-middle class (see Appendix Table B.8). She impressed the interviewer as a quite "teacherish" person, always trying to do and say the approved thing. (She also had a rather high score in morality values.) She emphasized obedience values five times in her interviews. She said, "And that's the type of child that I like, the child that will do what he's told to do. . . . I think obedience from children to their parents is one of the necessary things, and I think it is something that should be enforced upon that child—that I am your parent and you have to obey me."

The father with the highest percentage score for obedience (1.85) was also below the mean in age (see Appendix Table B.9). There were five boys in his family. This father was a professional man with strong religious convictions, a fact reflected in his high percentage scores on three of the six categories under moral values. In connection with obedience, he said, "We, both my wife and I, feel very keenly about this particular point—that our children should, without reservation, obey."

Ten per cent of fathers and five per cent of mothers were definitely against obedience as an end in itself. Fa 24, who had three children and was below his parents in social position, said, "I don't go for the idea of blind obedience, or unknowing obedience. In other words, the kind that is demanded in a dictatorship way."

Religion. Religion includes values placed on church, on Christianity, and on other religious philosophy or tenets. Religious values show the highest mean percentage score of fathers, and the second highest of mothers. Not as many parents mention these values as discuss obedience, but those that do generally lay greater emphasis on them. It is perhaps surprising that the score on family consistency in religion shows virtually no relationship with the values for religion held by either mothers or fathers (see Appendix Tables B.8 and B.9). A few parents were influenced in their child-rearing by negative attitudes toward religion.

The highest mean percentage score on religious values (4.71) is made by Fa 8, a young man who had five daughters and had recently been converted to an evangelical church. He had grown up in a family of eight children; his father had been an alcoholic and a poor provider. He said:

> A fellow I met worked for the same company; he was a Christian, and he used to talk to me about these things, and gradually I could just see where it was really something to it. I just took the Bible at what it said, that . . . all have sinned and come short of the glory of God, and we are all like sheep that have gone astray. I just realized that I was one of them, and I repented, asked the Lord forgiveness for the things that I'd done, and ever since then I've never been the same, it's changed my whole life. . . . Before I became a Christian, I

didn't think much about raising the children and what would happen when they grow up, and now I do, and I try to raise them as I believe the Bible says to raise them.

Responsibility. Responsibility includes values not only for responsibility, but for truthfulness, honesty, and reliability. They are second among the moral values for fathers, but fourth for mothers. Six fathers have percentage scores greater than the highest score of a mother.

One of the highest scores on values for responsibility and honesty (2.61) is made by the father who has the highest score on religious values. He had five daughters, the oldest eight years old, and he had recently taken his adolescent niece to live with them. Her behavior impressed upon him the value of honesty. In talking about his five daughters, he said:

> I think one thing, if you can get them to tell the truth all the time, that always helps, whether they've done something bad or what. I think you should go maybe even to extremes to get them to be truthful. . . . Like my niece there, how much trouble we have with her. You can't believe when she says she's going to come home or if she's going somewhere, you can't believe what she says, and this thing has never been instilled in her—to tell the truth. . . . She was never taught that she should come home at a certain time. She learned to steal, and what she wanted she'd take. I know it's helped me to realize what a tremendous responsibility I have to my children that they don't turn out that way.

The highest scores among mothers are made by a mother with four boys, another with five, the oldest boy in each family being nine, and a mother with three preschool boys. The fact that all three had boys only may be a factor, but there are two other mothers with boys only who had low scores on responsibility. Still, this might be worth following up in studies of values for honesty with a larger sample.

Morality. Morality includes values relating to conscience and guilt, to right and wrong, to good and bad in general, and is in third place for both mothers and fathers.

The highest percentage score (2.70) is made by a mother who, although relatively high in values for responsibility and justice, emphasizes morality as her strongest value in the moral category. She said:

I feel that children four-and-a-half should have a fine sense of right and wrong in this sense; they should know that taking something isn't right. . . . I think it seems a superficial atmosphere to always distract three- or four-year-old children and never try to teach them the difference between something that is right because it's right, or wrong because it's wrong. . . . I think that the sooner people can have the opportunity for choice and then choose the better way, whether from teaching or from experience, this is a big step forward, with children, with anybody.

Justice. Justice includes values for fair-mindedness, equality, social conscience, and rights of the individual. Mothers seldom mention such values whereas fathers stress them about as much as they do values for obedience.

One father with an unusually high score on values for justice (3.48) also has a high score in moral values as a whole, distributed among morality, responsibility, religion, and justice. Here was a man with a self-conscious philosophy of life, which he termed democratic, and which included values relating to those in the category of justice, especially liberalism, worth of the individual, and social conscience. Over and over again in practical situations with his children, particularly his eight-and-a-half-year-old son, he based his judgments and his teachings on values relating to the worth of individuals and fair-mindedness.

Citizenship. Citizenship includes values placed on patriotism, and on unity with groups beyond the family. It is surprising to find that both mothers and fathers have low mean scores on values for citizenship, only a few parents mentioning values in this category at all. The only father who stressed citizenship values (score .84) was self-conscious about his role in the government service. He felt that his occupation had influenced some of the things he did with his children. He said:

I think for one thing, my work has made me realize that it's important for me to recognize one's stake in society, in one's government, and how important it is for children to understand it, when they grow up. The importance of voting, taking an interest in large concepts that don't appear to bear directly on them but actually have a very profound influence on them, and make them understand that they, contrary to popular notion, exert a lot of influence on plans and policies of politicians and statesmen. . . . I think it's important to develop a social conscience.

Family Values

Under family values we include not only values for marriage and children but also values for the quality of family life. It seemed clear from the interviews that, in the material coded here, emphasis was placed on the quality of family life rather than on the value of a certain quality in general. For example, some parents value harmony in the home without necessarily valuing harmony in social relations in general. Among the seven subcategories of family values, mothers and fathers agree on emphasizing unity first and happy home second, as shown in Table 5.1.

Family unity. Family unity includes values placed on interdependence, cohesiveness, and loyalty within the family. Both groups of parents talked on the average more about their desire for unity and closeness among family members than about any other goal relating to the family. Mo 12, a lower-middle-class mother with four boys, has the highest score in values for family unity as well as honesty. Discussing the time when her eight-year-old boy stole a compass from her, she said, "We told him that it wasn't a very decent thing to do in the family; I mean, it wasn't the right thing to do anywhere but particularly not in a family, because I think they know that we try to make it a family that's bound together."

Love. Love includes values for affection and for happiness in the home. One could assume that all parents want a happy home with affection between members of the family, but only slightly more than half of the mothers and slightly less than half of the fathers discuss this value as influencing their behavior with their children. The three highest scores among fathers are made by men of higher social position, two of whom had preschool first-borns. One of these men (score 1.85) was very religious, with a high score in moral values (especially for obedience and religion). He said, "We love our children and we want them to know it, because the church teaches that, because my parents were loving toward me, and because we feel we should do it. . . . And I want them to feel kindly toward me and toward my wife."

Cooperation in the home. On the whole, neither group of

parents stress strongly the values of housekeeping, or chores for children. Although parents may require their children to help around the house, this is not necessarily a value in itself, but rather a means to other values, such as democratic family living or learning responsibility, as will be discussed in Chapter VI. A mother of three children living on a farm, who is next to highest in family values, emphasized cooperation in family life. She said:

> I think this is most, most important, both my husband and I do, that they learn to take a share in the family's work. It's not just to spare me because mother is tired at night, because we all have years and years of that before they are able to help, but we think it's important for them to do some of the work.

Family harmony. Family harmony includes values placed by parents on not arguing before children, on children not quarreling, and on the performance of appropriate roles by each family member. Some parents, about half of mothers and a third of fathers, place high value on having harmony in the home. Mo 12, mother of four boys, is among the highest 10 per cent in score on family harmony (1.09), in line with a correlation of .33 ($p < .05$) between family size and value for harmony (Appendix Table B.8). She said:

> I think you should try to get along with each other. . . . Where the trouble comes is if parents are constantly fighting with each other. I think it causes a lot of turmoil. In the family where children see that the parents care for each other and treat each other with respect . . . I think that in the long run it will pay off.

Democracy. Democracy includes values placed on having a generally democratic atmosphere in the home and on permitting children to have a voice in family affairs. Such values are mentioned by a third of the parents and emphasized strongly by some. The father with the highest score of any parent (1.57) had been brought up in a highly authoritarian immigrant family, but had moved up the social scale. He definitely wanted to have a different kind of family life for his own two children. In discussing the changes that have taken place since he was a youngster, he said:

It is the fact that the children have a larger place in the family life, that they are listened to, and they are actually a part of the family. Before . . . the child was treated as a child, and that was it; . . . but now the child is a part of the family, and they are allowed more of a hand in all of the activities; there seems to be more family life now. . . . They have more to say around the house. . . . There is so much more of an accent on fun, enjoying life, and being together, . . . and it comes from the fact that they have more of a place in the family.

Marriage and children. Marriage and children were of course values for all the parents in this study, but less than one-third of mothers and fathers mention these values as influencing their behavior with their children. The mother of a five-year-old daughter has the highest score. She said, "I feel a family is not complete without children. My daughter knows I adore children. She already says she wants to be a mommy. . . . She has a general idea of motherhood as a very natural, normal, wonderful thing. This is something else I want my daughter to be, a very happy mother."

Location. Location includes values placed on living in country, city, or suburbs. The two farmers value highly country living. Both parents in one family emphasize the advantages of suburban living with space for their three children's play. The mother said, "I think about 80 per cent of our reason for getting this particular house was the lot. We will have a little over an acre and a little orchard in the back, and four live oaks on the property so the boys and girls can have lots and lots of room for tree houses and all kinds of fun."

Egoistic Values

The values relating to personal qualities of an individual are second in emphasis for fathers and third for mothers, all of the fathers and most of the mothers discussing such values. It is evident that fathers value highly the kind of qualities we included in this category, especially those fathers high in upward social mobility ($r = .48$, $p < .01$). The ten subcategories of egoistic values are shown in Table 5.1.

Independence. Independence includes values placed on self-reliance and on individual freedom. It is the personal characteristic valued most highly by both fathers and mothers, representing 37 per cent of all egoistic value codings. The mother who has by far the highest percentage score (3.83) is the farmer's wife who is also high in family values (especially happiness, democracy, and cooperation in the home). Fa 1 expressed his value for intellectual independence in this way:

> Somehow I feel that the more opportunity you give a person to develop his own initiative, his own sense of freedom, his own way of going about doing things, the better chance he may have of being a freer adult, more able to make his own decisions and look at the world, rather than be dependent upon accepting the mere surface truisms and dogma of the world. . . . But the main thing is that I don't want them to grow up with the idea of just accepting everything that is handed to them, as a sort of an authoritarian kind of way. What I would like is for them to grow to be as independent as possible.

Aggression. Very few parents (though apparently more fathers than mothers) wish their children to express aggression, and they stipulate that it should be only under certain conditions or with certain qualifications. One psychologically sophisticated father recognized the therapeutic value of expressing hostility. It is the aggression of sons that is most often approved. A dairy farmer of Portuguese background and with some high school education seemed to recognize ego strength when he said, "As far as the temper, I like for a boy to have a temper, so he can get things done. If you haven't got a temper, and just lay back and let a guy ride you, why you'll never accomplish anything."

One father, a skilled workman, felt strongly that his eleven-year-old boy should learn to fight even though the boy did not like to fight:

> My son doesn't like to fight. He'd rather walk away. But for about eight months this older boy in the neighborhood would get two or three of his buddies and then they'd beat up [So 11.0]. Finally, one day they were out in my own front yard, and the big ones started picking on [So 11.0]. So I went out there and I told him right then and there that we were going to get this thing settled. I told him, "I want you to go ahead and fight this boy. I expect you to give him a beating. Once you get this thing settled, you'll be good friends."

In direct contrast, a father of Hawaiian-Philippine background who taught school said, "I'm not going to encourage him to fight other youngsters to solve problems, but to think it out and see if there is another way to handle these problems, instead of violence, you see. Maybe by talking these things out."

The relatively slight emphasis on aggressive behavior as an approved characteristic of boys by the fathers in this study differs from the attitude of fathers returning home after the war who feared that their boys were not masculine because they did not like to fight (Stolz *et al.,* 1954, pp. 65–66).

In contrast to their relative unconcern with aggressive values, parents of both sexes express values for nonaggression. Mothers give this value second place and fathers give it third place among egoistic values.

Achievement and intelligence. The goal of achievement, of success, and of superiority, either in relation to others or in relation to one's own standards, appears to be more important to fathers, who give it second place among egoistic values, than to mothers. On the other hand, the value for intelligence is discussed by more mothers than fathers. It is the use of intelligence and the value of intellectual activities, rather than the possession of either normal or high mental abilities, which is stressed most. The three parents who give greatest emphasis to intelligence values are the dairy farmer's wife (score 1.67), an elementary school teacher who had been socially upward mobile (score 2.35), and a music teacher in junior high school (score 1.52). All were college graduates, but there were other college graduates who did not even mention this value.

In values for success and achievement, five fathers have scores higher than any mother. The father who has the highest score (1.31) emphasizes the value of achievement in relation to one's own previous performance, rather than competitive achievement, of which he did not approve. He said:

> We are urgently anxious to have [So 11.9] get on and do a good job so that he will be able to go on to do what he is capable of doing in the way of going to a college of one kind or another. . . . I am really anxious that our children have the greatest encouragement, the greatest freedom, the greatest opportunity to generate a sense of ability to do things, and learn to feel some sense of accomplishment from doing things, and learn to rely upon themselves for creativity of some kind.

Practicality. The value of being practical and realistic is emphasized by a third of the group, the two highest scores being made by a dairy farmer (2.50) and a high school counselor (1.16), each of whom lays stress on the value of being realistic. A Negro technician expressed this value well: "They must learn sooner or later that they can't have everything they want, and I think now is as good a time as any to start teaching them."

Self-respect. Self-respect and confidence in self as values are given about the same emphasis as practicality among the parents as a whole, but fathers have a mean score about twice that for mothers. The two highest scores are made by the parents in a farming family. The father emphasized the importance of letting his almost-twelve-year-old son work out problems for himself. Discussing the way his son handled the problem of a broken fence in the cow pasture, he said:

> And then I tell him that's exactly what I would have done; it makes him feel proud. And then the next time he's not as scared to make a decision. He's not scared to make a mistake. You don't want a kid to be afraid to make a mistake, or live in fear that he's going to do something wrong so his father is going to scold him. A kid won't be worth anything.

Enthusiasm. Relatively few parents discuss the value of enthusiasm, drive, or interest, as a valued characteristic in their children. This seems surprising since zest is such an important concomitant of many other values such as learning, morality, or social relations. The only parent who gave any real importance to this value was Fa 6 (described in Chapter II), who spoke of it in several connections—this time he mentioned it in relation to school. He said:

> There is one thing that I admire in anyone, is a little bit of enthusiasm, and when either child is bubbling over with something I always make sure that I encourage them. It's a very nice asset to have to be vitally interested in something, and they are interested in school which is a wonderful thing.... Any time they do mention school I always make sure that I encourage everything that they have to say.

Determination. Only a few parents emphasize the characteristic of determination or tenacity, most of them being influenced relatively little by their desire to build into their children such personal qualities.

Appearance. Only a few parents, mostly mothers, intimate that they are anxious to have their children dressed well or look nice. Of the parents who mention this value, three mothers were Class II in social position, three parents were Class III, and five were Class IV (three of them very near the bottom of this class, the lowest in our study). All of these parents had gained upward social mobility except two mothers. The lower social class and the upward social mobility may be factors that make the value of appearance more explicitly evident to these parents. However, there are other lower-class parents, and upward-mobile parents, who do not discuss this value. We had too few responses to test these suggestions statistically. A Jewish woman who had moved upward in social position said, "I want them [three children] to look good, their clothes and so on. Of course, in my case, with my parents, it was so different because they had six children and it was difficult to do the things for them that we can do for ours. I'm conscious of that."

Modesty. The personal quality of placing a moderate estimate on one's merits, of not bragging, or of not being boastful, is given little consideration. Perhaps the ignoring of modesty as a value is a reflection of our culture. Even those few who mention this value do not place much emphasis on it.

Interpersonal Values

Values relating primarily to relations with other people are fourth among basic values in emphasis by mothers, and sixth in emphasis by fathers. The eight subcategories of interpersonal values are shown in Table 5.1.

Getting along with people. By far the greatest emphasis among interpersonal values (about 35 per cent) is given to getting along with people, having a pleasant personality, or being easygoing. If one adds to this the values for friends and for affection outside the family, which are closely related in their meaning, mothers have 58.1 per cent and fathers 43.9 per cent of their interpersonal values in the general area of good relations with people one comes in contact with. The mother with the highest score (2.10) is a young woman with three children. In speaking of her six-year-old son she said:

> The other children he don't care for, but I wish he wouldn't be that way, I'd like for him to be with other kids and like them. . . . I think it's pretty important to get in with other children. He has one particular friend, and oh, I don't know, I'd like for him to play with several other children, instead of having one particular friend. . . . Gee, I don't know how to put it—Gee, I really don't know. Well I think it's very important though to have many friends.

This mother had talked often in her interview about getting along with her neighbors, but she had had a good deal of trouble with them, and one had reported her to the police for beating her children. It seemed to us that this mother had genuine yearnings for friendly relations with people, which were defeated by her aggressive impulses, and that she projected on to her six-year-old son her own desires and her own self-criticisms.

Generosity and nurturance. Generosity and nurturance include values for giving and sharing and for caring for others. Although a third of the parents mention values related to generosity, they are given relatively little emphasis, and the value of nurturance is mentioned by only a tenth of the parents. It is worth noting that the eight parents highest in values for generosity all had more than one child; in social position, three were Class IV, and three the lowest in Class III.

The father who stresses the value generosity more than any other parent did not discuss the value of nurturance at all. He was a grocery clerk of elementary education, with four girls five to eleven years old. He saw little of his children because he held two jobs, but he strongly believed in sharing. He said:

> They all share alike. If you bring home one piece of candy, then they will take and divide it in four pieces and give each of 'em a piece. . . . I think sharing's very important. It shows 'em about sharing with one another, and that they should also do the same thing outside with their little friends . . . and I think by sharing with others that way, which they do at home—it makes them feel that they're not a group by themselves in respect of just looking out for themselves.

Tolerance. Tolerance includes values for understanding and consideration for people who look or act different. Relatively few parents discuss these values, but those who do seem to feel quite strongly about their importance. The mother giving greatest emphasis to tolerance (score 2.24) was a woman of high school education who had grown up in a small Southwest town. She said:

> No one was *allowed* in our town except white people. There was very much of a definite line drawn between the Protestants and the Catholics in our town. We had a very strong Catholic Church that would not let their children go to even weddings in ours, and you know, vice versa. And I didn't go along with that, I am afraid. That was one thing I don't like about a small town, . . . so I am trying to teach my children to accept everyone as they are. . . . I hope I get it across to them. . . . I have met some very intelligent Negro people; I have met some very intelligent Chinese and Japanese; and it has been something that I have to actually consciously work on, not to feel different, when I am meeting them, and my husband doesn't because he wasn't brought up with any of that prejudice at all in his makeup. . . . So I really think I am doing all right in this idea, never to let my children think they are better than any other race, creed, or color, as they put it.

Conformity. Conformity includes both values for conformity and values against conformity. We do not include values regarding *manners* here; they are categorized under values for orderly living, to be discussed later. If manners were included, the mean percentage scores for conformity would be the largest under interpersonal values.

One mother stands out for her relatively high score on conformity (1.15). A woman of Oriental descent and the mother of a seven-year-old daughter, she discussed conformity in three out of six interviews, being especially concerned that her little girl should do as other children do. She said:

> In kindergarten she wasn't dressed like the other girls, she told me, and that was awfully sad for her. . . . So I said, "Fine, we'll dress you as they are." I didn't want her to feel that she was really different. . . . I don't like children eating out on the street at all, but when the rest of them are eating out on the curb, well my daughter can have an orange and eat out there, too, because I feel that's part of children and if the other kids are out there with an orange, I'll let her have an orange, but her peelings are not to be thrown in the street.

Recognition. Recognition includes values relating to recognition, appreciation, or attention from others and are scarcely mentioned. One father said what other parents may perhaps feel, but do not always keep in mind when they deal with their children:

"I know I feel good when people recognize what I have done, and I suppose I want to pass this feeling on to my boys. I want them to feel it. Feel that they're important, and feel that they're appreciated."

Values for Emotional Security

In discussing values related to emotional security, the parents tend to emphasize their role in providing emotional security, rather than the values of emotional security per se. Mothers give "to provide emotional security" first place in values for parental role (mean percentage score, 1.23; see Table 4.1, p. 31), while among the 10 basic values, emotional security is given fifth place (mean, 1.04). The discrepancy in mean scores is even greater for fathers who give "to provide emotional security" second place in values for parental role (mean, 1.76), and eighth place in basic values (mean, .95). The values for emotional security are divided into four subcategories, as shown in Table 5.1.

Happiness. About a third of the values under emotional security indicate the desire of parents that their children be happy or get satisfaction out of life. A high school graduate who had been a waitress has the highest score among mothers (1.55). She said of her first baby, a boy:

> I don't want him to be like me. Because I am too sensitive, I want him to be a happy-go-lucky—not happy-go-lucky—just happy, I guess. . . . I always worry about what people think of me because when I was little I didn't have very many friends, and my mother always told me if I wasn't a good girl nobody would like me. So, I have never forgotten that, and it in time leads to difficulties. . . . I would like him to be happy—enjoy life. . . . I am hoping he will be a lot happier than a lot of little kids that I know. I don't want him to be afraid of us.

Of the four families with a first baby, three mothers and three fathers mention happiness for their child as an important goal. There are eight other families who had infants as well as older children. In the twelve families with infants, six mothers and five fathers mention the value of happiness. The relation between emphasis on the value of happiness and the age and number of children should be checked in future studies.

Freedom from anxiety. In a sense this value is the negative expression of the value of happiness and it is worth noting that fathers, as a group, appear to put slightly more emphasis on positive happiness, and mothers put more emphasis on the negative absence of anxiety. In one family, the mother has the highest score (1.39) and the father has the second highest score (.89) among fathers. These parents gave evidence of somewhat high anxiety about their conflicting religious beliefs, about the father's occupational work, and about the extreme emotional behavior of their five-year-old daughter. The father, who had been afraid of his own mother and "in awe" of his father, said:

> Mother used to just beat the daylights out of us when we misbehaved and I don't believe in that. I don't believe that's the way to achieve what you want, although it sure put the fear of God in you, I'll admit that. . . . I was always afraid of mother. Always afraid of her you see, and I don't think a child ought to be afraid of his parents. . . . I don't want my children to feel that way toward me.

The mother reported that she had been afraid of her father, an officer in the Armed Services who assumed the task of punishing when he came home. She added:

> I can remember hearing Daddy come home and a murmur of voices downstairs. And Daddy would walk up the stairs, I could hear his spurs jingle as he came. He usually paddled me very hard. . . . But that is one thing my children are never told, to wait until their father gets home, because that isn't fair to him. And I think that it makes the children a little afraid of him.

Mental health. Mental health includes general values such as adjustment, mental health, or simply emotional security. The family that stands highest in this subcategory had one baby boy. The mother (score .86) was concerned about the regime in the hospital and its effect on her baby. She said:

> I was sure that I was running into trouble the first day in the hospital by letting him be in there by himself. I was sure that would have a terrible psychological effect on him when he was fifteen or twenty. It was quite a worry. You lie awake nights about this thing because you want to do your best in raising him—to make him at least a well-adjusted individual. . . . The doctors, I feel, know a great deal about children, but their main concern is just their physical progress, just their physical well-being. I don't think that's half as important as their emotional well-being.

Thirteen per cent of both parents mention the importance of some privacy for their children, usually because they value a little privacy now and then in their own lives. In one family both mother and father enjoyed privacy at times; the father said:

> They're all individualists; everybody does what they want to do, and we encourage this, but at the same time there are certain family things that we do together, and things that we expect of them. We try to put them apart, or have them so they can have a period by themselves because we both, my wife and I, enjoy this. We think that children do too.

Values for Education

It will be remembered that among values for the parental role, values for educating, teaching, or guiding one's children are those most emphasized by fathers, and, second only to "providing emotional security," by mothers (see Table 4.1, p. 31). Among the basic values, fathers again emphasize education, giving it fourth place, while mothers place it low in their hierarchy of values. A high proportion of the parents mention this value as influential in their behavior with their children. There are four subcategories under education, as shown in Table 5.1.

Knowledge. Knowledge considered valuable for children covers a wide range including civic affairs, government, music, stock market, typing, manual work, mathematics. The main emphasis, however, is on the value of reading and speech, and on knowledge pertaining to sex. Fathers place relatively high value on knowledge or the content of education. One father with an above-average score (1.49) spoke of his desire to have his children learn Spanish (the father was of Spanish origin), learn to type (as his father had insisted he learn), and become acquainted with how the stock market works (the father was a certified accountant). This father was taking steps to see that each of these goals was accomplished.

It seems that the knowledge that each parent wants for his child is occasioned by the parent's own personal experience, and, as with the father mentioned above, is idiosyncratic to each parent; it is not based on any general philosophy concerning the place of knowledge in our culture. Oddly enough, these parents do not follow the present trend of the press and some educators in extolling the values of science in the modern world. By and large, a parent wants his children to have the advantage of learning what has proved useful to him in his own life or, in a few cases, of learning what he wishes he had learned.

Education in general. Over half of the fathers, and a third of the mothers discuss the importance of education in general for their children, and about the value of a "good" education. The parents who stressed the value of education in general most were below the mean age of parents, and had two preschool children. The father, a businessman and son of a distinguished scientist, was steadily increasing in financial success. He had married a woman who had attended many schools but completed only one year at college. The father said:

> I'd like my children to have a proper education . . . . I think I would enjoy traveling and taking the children along. I think that would be a nice part of anybody's education, a chance to get around. I'd like my boy to get a good education and grow up to be a successful whatever he is, businessman or doctor or what have you. I'd like that very much.

His wife was much more vague about this, as she was about most matters pertaining to parenthood. She said, "We'd like to give them a good life, and education of course, and certain standards —I don't know that I've thought about it too much."

Level of education. Level of education includes values for a college education and training for a profession or business. Some parents are concerned about the level of education they wish their children to reach. Several parents want their children to have more education than they themselves had. A research engineer emphasized (score 1.52) his desire for a college education for all his children and professional training for his boys. He discussed this seven different times in three of the six interviews. Here is the way he explained his goals in this area:

> I think both my wife and I would strongly like our children to do the utmost up to their limit of intellectual capacity—go on to college and carry on as far as they can. And the boys probably go into some kind of professional career—into biology or engineering or physics or something of the kind, or we would also be perfectly happy if they decided

they wanted to go into the fine arts of one kind or another. The main idea is that we want them to have as much intellectual development as they're capable of, because we think it will give them a great satisfaction out of life.

Another father, a mechanic, set much more modest goals for his four sons:

I think it is important that the boys learn to work with their hands. I really do. Of course, I think it's important that they learn to use their heads first. I think that would be the first thing I'd want them to do—I'd want them to get an education. . . . I want them to do better than what I'm doing I guess. I want them to have a better education than what I've got. And I think that's why I put that ahead of everything else. I believe that's the most important.

His wife (score 1.19) was much more insistent that the boys should have the opportunity to go to college if they wanted to. She discussed at length the financial difficulties involved in sending four boys through college, and the various ways that these difficulties might be overcome, including getting a job at a college that provides free tuition for children of employees.

Kind of education. A few parents have specific ideas about the kind of school they want their children to attend, or the teaching methods they prefer, or the kind of teacher they want their children to have. One couple emphasized the values of parochial education for their child, while another mother, whose six-year-old son was not doing well in public school, felt he would have done much better if she could have only enrolled him in a Catholic school. A father with an elementary school education was confused about whether schools should follow the interests of children, or teach them the facts of mathematics and history. In general he felt that it is better to make school interesting and enjoyable to children.

VALUES RELATED TO ORDERLY LIVING

We group under orderly living, values that relate to the desire of parents to have their children behave in such a way that the home will run smoothly, the parents will be comfortable, and their possessions will not be harmed (Sears *et al.*, 1957, chapter

8). We have four subdivisions under this category of values (see Table 5.1).

It is a question whether obedience should be included here or under moral values. Certainly, for most parents, obedience of children is a goal that is related to living in peace and comfort (for the parents), but it also has a relation to moral values in its emphasis on authority and respect for elders and authority figures. We follow White (1951) in grouping it under moral values. Another subcategory that might be included here is cooperation in the home, but the emphasis that parents placed on participation and cooperation in family life indicates to us that they were more concerned with values relating to family than to values of orderly living, though their discussions certainly related to both.

The values under orderly living are goals that are involved in the socialization of children. Over four-fifths of the parents mention them. It is surprising, therefore, to find that the rank order of mean percentage scores (and, therefore, the relative emphasis given them by parents) is so low: sixth for mothers, seventh for fathers. It is quite possible that these values for orderly living really are low in the hierarchy of values for parents, even though they consume a great deal of time. In a sense, these may be minor values, but for their own peace of mind, parents feel forced to give them attention.

Manners. Manners are given the greatest emphasis among values for orderly living by both parents. All the manners mentioned by these parents would make a formidable list indeed. Many of the parents say it is difficult to reach their goals, but they persevere nonetheless. Here is a partial list of these goals taken from the interviews of mothers 1 through 17:

Behavior at Meal Times

Skill in eating. Do not eat with fingers. Use spoon, fork, knife correctly. Do not eat from bowls. Use napkins. Keep napkin in lap. Do not spill things on floor, table. Do not be messy with food. Do not put too much in mouth. Do not eat noisily or gobbly. Keep mouth closed when eating. Do not laugh with food in mouth.

Food. Eat what is put in front of you. Have clean plate, eat everything on plate.

Posture. Keep elbows off table. Sit properly, legs under table.

Time. Do not dawdle. Take time to eat, do not gulp.

Conversation. Do not talk with mouth full. Take turns talking, no interrupting. Do not discuss unpleasant subjects.

Other mealtime behavior. Do not scuffle feet. Do not play with other children. Do not horse around. Do not kick under table. Do not quarrel. Do not leave table in restaurant. Do not grab.

Behavior in Social Situations with Adults

Speak to adult guest. "Be seldom seen and seldom heard" in adult company. Do not interrupt adult conversations. Act like adults in adult world outside home. Be quiet when adults are around. Say "thank you," "excuse me," "please."

Behavior with Parents

Be polite in speaking to parents. Do not talk back to parents. Do not be rude to parents. Do not interrupt.

The mother who has the highest score (2.24) was a high school graduate. She mentioned manners at least once in every interview. She had grown up in a small midwestern town, and was married to a successful manager of a hardware store. She was a conscientious mother, concerned with table manners, manners in church, manners when there were guests. She said:

> Social manners are very definitely important, I think, to say thank you, not to ask for seconds, not to grab, or things like that. . . . We are trying to teach our children to eat—well, shall we use the old-fashioned word "graciously"—to teach them so that when they are out they will know what to do. I hope we are getting it across—of course that is a long drawn-out process. . . . We don't believe in children taking over when we have guests; if they want to be with the guests, it's fine, if they behave themselves and sit and act like little ladies and gentlemen. Otherwise they are sent to their rooms to stay.

All except one of the four fathers with the highest scores on values for manners had large families (four, five, and seven children, respectively). One father had two children and therefore is an exception to the general trend, as is his wife. For this pair, manners are important because everyone they know has them. They are only comfortable living with people who know the "proper" thing to do and do it. The mother (score .86) emphasized through gestures and a tense voice how important manners are to her. She said:

When I was a child, children did not call their parents names, and they didn't talk back to them, and they weren't rude to their parents. And that was just something we never had a chance to be. . . . Well, I still feel that. I just can't bear children who are rude to adults. I think they should have a chance to explain what they've done and give their ideas, but I think they should do it nicely, and I don't think they should talk back when you tell them something.

Later, when she was describing an episode in the family, the interviewer asked her, "What is it you are striving for in terms of what you have called manners?" She replied:

I would merely strive to have them be acceptable and be pleasant so that they won't be obnoxious. I don't like obnoxious children; I don't think anyone does, . . . and I would say that that would carry through every field—in table manners—because if they eat noisily and gobbly, they're unpleasant to have around, and I think they have to learn to behave so that they are pleasant to have around.

Her husband was more relaxed about such matters, but emphasized them nonetheless (score 1.50). He mentioned table manners, not making too much noise, acceptable public behavior, politeness, and proper language.

Orderliness. We group under this category values not only for orderliness but for neatness and cleanliness as well, since there are so few mentions of the last two. Such goals, if carried to the extreme, have been said to identify "the compulsion neurotic who struggles, by means of those character traits, against his instinctual demands for dirt and disorder" (Fenichel, 1945, p. 151). The parents in this study have relatively low scores in this category.

Mo 19, who has one of the two highest scores in values for orderliness (1.63), is below the mean of mothers in education and social position but above the mean in age. She has three children. This mother not only is relatively high in values for orderliness, but shows other tendencies related to the syndrome of the compulsive neurotic in her attitude toward sex, particularly in her emphasis on the importance of girls not playing with boys. She is a woman who struggled to keep her family together after her husband returned from the war, and who went to work when her children were of school age to help pay for their home. She patterned her own life as a parent closely on that of her own mother, who, by her ideals and her strict control, had been able to rear her girls in a lumber camp to be respectable young women.* Mo 19, tried to build strong controls around her children by means of schedules and penalties, so that they, too, would grow up to be good, in spite of the fact that their mother worked away from home all day, and in spite of the run-down neighborhood in which they lived. She was strict about where they could go, with whom they could play, the chores they must do. But more than anything else she stressed the importance to her of cleanliness and order. She said:

> One of the most important things I like to do as a mother is to have clean clothes on the children every morning. I've seen so much of children that haven't had it, and that to me is one of the most important things.... They're all very sensitive about being clean and what they want to wear, and [So 11.0] never thinks of wearing the same shirt twice. It's just something I've always started with them and they've always been that way.

When asked in what areas she thought she was most strict, she replied:

> Oh, cleanliness for one thing. That's one thing where I have an awful hard time. I don't know why boys think their ears don't belong to them and their neck.... And picking up after themselves, that's one thing. I don't mind housework and I don't mind cooking and doing the dishes and doing washing and ironing and general cleaning—but, boy, I can't stand to go around from one room to the other, and pick up after people. I just can't see it—that's one thing I really get after them.... They can play with whatever they want in the front room in the evening when we're there, but when they go to bed, then they have to take it all back where they got it.

All the mothers with highest scores in orderliness and cleanliness are women who had had hard times, who were in Class IV in social position, and who had little hope of social mobility, but a strong drive to hold on to what they had. The two fathers who have highest scores in orderliness are not of this lower group in social position, and had relatively small families. Both were successful businessmen, somewhat rigid and aloof from their chil-

* See further discussions of the relation of Mo 19 to her own mother in Chapter X.

dren. It seemed to the interviewers that each of these men had some conflict in the area of sex, which was evidenced by undue concern about sex in one case, and evasion of the topic in the other.

Carefulness. Carefulness includes values for respecting things, and not injuring furniture or buildings. The value for things, which is so much a part of American culture and which is so much exploited by Madison Avenue, is not stressed much by this group of parents (this will be discussed under economic values) and the care of things is also little stressed. There are parents who mention the importance of respect for nice things, of not jumping on or climbing on furniture, of not marring walls, and of taking care of possessions, but such parents are in the minority. Even those who discuss such values do not stress their importance. In fact, one could conclude that this value is relatively unimportant to these fathers and mothers.

Punctuality. A few parents, decidedly more fathers than mothers, discuss the value of punctuality. Two fathers have relatively high scores in this value; both were engineers, each with four children, the two men with the highest scores in social mobility. Fa 5 was strict about his children being on time, and severely punishing if they were not. When the interviewer asked him, "Now why do you feel this is so important—to be on time?", he replied:

> Well, first it imposes a handicap on my wife if they don't eat on time, and they all string out. Secondly, I think it's a matter of discipline for an orderly household for everyone to come and eat on time. From the standpoint of learning this now as part of their future life, when they go to school or whether they go in the army or somewhere else, they're going to have to do this anyhow, and in most organizations you have to be on time—not only eating, but at other functions, going to school on time, going to class, or meeting an appointment, anything like that, and it's just as easy to do the thing properly. It's better to do the thing properly than to get in the habit of letting the thing string out.

Biological Values

The values that we call biological because they include values related to basic needs of the organism for physical well-being and survival are mentioned more by fathers than by mothers. There are six subcategories in biological values. Since only three mothers and one father mention sex, we have combined it with health in Table 5.1.

Safety. Within biological values, safety is mentioned by more parents than any other subcategory, though the mean percentage scores are relatively low. Fathers give greater emphasis to safety values than mothers ($t = 2.22$, $p < .05$). A mechanic with a high school education, the father of four boys, made a high score on safety (2.42), higher than any other parent. In discussing the strict restrictions he placed on his boys when they were young, he said:

> I was always afraid that they weren't old enough to realize the fact that they shouldn't cross the street. . . . I taught the oldest one, I think we taught him as soon as he was old enough to walk out on the sidewalk, not to go out in the street. In fact when they were so small that they'd even wander off the curb, why we'd just slug them until they couldn't stand.

Before that he had said:

> They run down the hallway, they run into the kitchen or they're running just for the kick of running in the house, I guess. . . . You can yell and scream but it doesn't seem to stop them; they're not aware of how dangerous it really is . . . that's one of the things I have to crack them for.

Health. Health includes values for immunity from disease, long life, adequate development. These values are probably important to most parents and influence their behavior with their children, but only a few mothers and fathers mention them, and the mean percentage scores are extremely low. Some of the parents who mention health as a value are parents of a child who has had a serious illness, which has influenced their behavior as parents. Very few parents discuss sex activity or sex regulation as a value. Even the seven families with adolescent children did not do so. Areas related to sex are discussed more in relation to beliefs, as will be seen in Chapter VI.

Physical activity. This category includes values for sports, athletics, and motor development in general. Twenty-three per cent of mothers and 36 per cent of fathers mention some form of physical activity or motor development as a goal for their children. The two fathers with highest scores (1.88 and 1.49) are interested in sports for their sons. The mother with the highest score (1.05) is interested in motor development and physical activities for her young children.

Food. Food includes values for adequate or tasty food, for a well-balanced diet and for good nutrition. About a third of the parents mention these values, but again the mean percentage scores are low. A mother who had been in a hospital training section of one of the Services had the highest score (1.44). She said what many other mothers probably feel. "I think a good diet—a well-balanced diet—is very important. In fact our children are very healthy, and I like to feel that it does have something to do with the fact that I get good nourishing food down them."

The man with the highest score among fathers (1.18), was much more emotional about his value for food: "To me eating is the most important thing in the world; I sound like a glutton but I never overeat, but I feel like it is almost a sin to miss a meal, and sometimes I blow my top if at three or four o'clock I find out that the kids haven't had lunch .... I don't feel you ever make up for a lost meal."

Rest. Rest includes values for rest and for sleep. Such values are discussed by only a few parents, and are given little emphasis. One father (score 2.16) far exceeded any other parent in emphasis on sleep:

> We have always felt—and we think it's paid off—that the proper rest for the kids is an asset for them. . . . We tried not to have them out anywhere when they were so darned tired . . . We get on our way home, or to some place where they can rest, because we feel it's too hard on the kids to get them overly tired. . . . We've always said eight o'clock is bedtime, and so they get to bed between 8:00 and 8:30; and on a school night, we feel like we're doing a good job and they're getting their sleep and their rest, and we feel it's important. I think this idea has come from, oh, the doctors, many sources, about a child having sufficient rest because they certainly do expend an awful lot of energy.

Play Values

The joys of living receive relatively scant attention from this group of parents. Their values for their children are, for the most part, the more sober values: moral, educational, egoistic, and family. The mean percentage score both for mothers and for fathers is relatively small, placing play low in their hierarchy of values. However, over two-thirds of the mothers and fathers did talk about play values, and there are a few parents who emphasize these values and give them precedence over more "serious" goals. There are five subdivisions under play values, but since only 15 per cent of the parents mention the value of pets, and only one mother mentions humor (including values for laughter and joking) we have combined humor with enjoyment, and pets with interesting life in Table 5.1.

Enjoyment. Enjoyment includes values for fun and good times. They are the values most frequently mentioned among play values. Two fathers, one high and one lower-middle in social position, particularly emphasize enjoyment values. Fa 4 (score 2.62), who was high in Class II in social position, talked about these values seven different times in his four interviews, and often used fun as a yardstick for deciding what to do with his children or what to let them do. He said, "I think that a good father helps to develop a sense of fun, teaches them how to enjoy themselves, how to have fun . . . I mean, just how to relax and enjoy themselves."

As has been pointed out, the parents seem decidedly lacking in appreciation of the value of humor and laughter. However, it is quite possible that some of the parents who discussed fun and good times might also have defined these values as including humor and laughter, if there had been sufficient probing.

Interesting life. This subcategory includes values for new and varied experiences, for travel, and for other enriching activities. Some parents had some of these experiences in their own childhood and valued them; others had not but hoped that their children might have what had been denied them. The father with the second highest score (1.57), was a sophisticated man, one who yearned to give his children a rich life filled with varied experiences on a broad scale. He discussed this value in relation to tasting a wide variety of foods, of understanding various systems of government, of understanding many different methods of worshiping God, of appreciating a variety of kinds of music and literature.

For some parents pets are primarily a means to other ends

such as reducing fear of animals, or learning how to care for them; such elements of discussion are appropriately coded under instrumental beliefs in Chapter VI. But 8 per cent of the parents valued pets for their children just because pets are good to have.

Creativity. Creativity includes values not only for creativity but for self-expression as well. Over a fourth of the parents discuss these values, but the percentage scores are not high. Several of the parents who have the highest scores were themselves creative people: an artist (1.27), an amateur musician (1.60), and a research scientist with musical interests (.65).

Economic Values

Although economic values are next to the lowest in mean percentage scores of basic values, for both mothers and fathers, a large proportion of parents discuss these values. Among fathers there is a strong relation between emphasis on economic values and lower social position as will be discussed later in this Chapter. Economic values have three subcategories (see Table 5.1).

Property. Property includes values for material possessions and things. Among economic values, property is mentioned most. About half of the parents discuss property values, mothers and fathers giving them about equal emphasis. In addition, parents emphasize the importance of having things of one's own, especially a room of one's own, or some particular area—a shelf in a hall closet, a bookcase, or a dresser drawer—that is one's own place. One father, with a social position low in Class III, said, "I see children outside climbing over everybody's car, up on the front lawn with their bikes and roller skates. . . . I don't permit that . . . . I don't want that to happen to *my* property, and I want my children to have respect for other people's property."

Three fathers—all of them avid gardeners—were especially emphatic about their gardens. Fa 6 was particularly proud of the landscaping he had done in the yard. His wife said:

> My husband is most strict about the yard. He's always hollering at them if they get gravel on the cement. . . . he doesn't like children playing in the yard, and, like if there are pogo sticks, he doesn't want them in our patio, or he won't let them ride their bikes there. I guess the yard—that's his. He's kinda fussy with his yard.

A few parents (21 per cent of mothers, 13 per cent of fathers) express negative attitudes toward materialistic values. One of the statements of nonmaterialistic values was made by Fa 1 when he explained why he and his wife had become less strict with their fourth child than with their first. He said, "We've grown to recognize that some of the things we used to think very important in life—material possessions—were not really very important, but that the children are a good deal more important than these things."

Money. Money includes values for income and thrift. More fathers mention these values than mothers, and their mean percentage score is slightly higher than that of mothers. The nine mothers and fathers who have the highest scores are distributed among all classes in social position, but there is a much higher percentage from Class IV than there is in the total percentage of parents in this social position (56 per cent vs. 28 per cent). This tendency for some lower-class parents to be exceedingly conscious of money values agrees with the more general finding that for fathers economic values as a whole are significantly related to lower social position ($r = .43$, $p < .01$).

The father who has the third highest score (1.17) emphasized thrift: taking care of shoes and clothes because they cost money, not wasting food, saving for a college education. He was the youngest man in the group, an unemployed Negro janitor with five children. The mother with the highest score (1.27) emphasized the value of money because both she and her husband had grown up in homes patterned after the "old country" where a child's earnings belong to his father. She said:

> Well, my folks were from the old country, and we went out and we picked prunes and my father farmed, and we didn't get any salary at all, and it was a rare day we got a nickel for soda pop or something, even until the day I was married. . . . And we thought that was the way it was supposed to be. . . . My husband had the same background as myself. We worked and we didn't get anything, you know—no salary. Well, we didn't think that was the right way. We'd like to help our boy to get more out of life—to learn the right way, how to earn money, and how to save it, and that you have to save in order to get something.

Work. Work includes values for an occupation and for jobs. Few parents talked about the values of work. Here again, parents of lower social position have a larger proportion of the highest scores in work values (six out of eight in the lower part of Class III or in Class IV). The man who has the highest score (1.17) is the same unemployed Negro who emphasized thrift. He said:

> I started out when I was about ten or eleven years old. I used to shine shoes, deliver papers. . . . And myself, I just don't feel right unless I'm working, see, so I think it's very important if a kid learns some kind of habit of working while he is young; then when he grows older, it won't be a problem to him.

Hierarchy in Basic Values

There are 55 subcategories under the ten major divisions of basic values in Table 5.1. Ignoring the divisions we had superimposed upon the subcategories, we rearranged them from one to 55, according to the order of magnitude of the mean percentage scores (see Appendix Tables B.1 and B.2).

For mothers, values for independence have the highest score, and values for modesty the lowest; for fathers, values for religion have the highest score, while values for affection outside of the family are in last place.

If we look at the basic values receiving the highest mean percentage scores in Appendix Tables B.1 and B.2, we find among the top 20 per cent (eleven subcategories), that mothers and fathers agree on eight: independence, family unity, obedience, manners, religion, getting along with others, responsibility, and morality. However, the order of magnitude of scores of each of these eight values differs for the two groups of parents. Fathers' scores are higher than mothers' for six of the eight values and significantly higher for two—religion and responsibility. Mothers' scores are significantly higher for obedience (Table 5.2).

To the eight values stressed by both parent groups, mothers add freedom from anxiety, family love, and enjoyment. For these, the scores of mothers are higher than those of fathers, the difference for freedom from anxiety reaching statistical significance. Fathers add knowledge, safety, and justice. The differences between scores for mothers and fathers on these categories are all in favor of fathers, and statistically significant.

Of the eight values both mothers and fathers place in the top

TABLE 5.2. *Highest Ranking Basic Values (by mean percentage score)*

	Rank order		Percentage score difference	
	Mo	*Fa*	*t*	*p*
Independence	1	2	—	n.s.
Family unity	2	5	—	n.s.
Obedience	3	9	1.78	<.10*
Manners	4	6	—	n.s.
Religion	5	1	1.86	<.10
Getting along	6	8	—	n.s.
Freedom from anxiety	7	—	2.55	<.02*
Family love	8	—	—	n.s.
Morality	9	7	—	n.s.
Enjoyment	10	—	—	n.s.
Responsibility	11	3	2.63	<.02
Knowledge	—	4	3.82	<.001
Safety	—	10	2.22	<.05
Justice	—	11	1.79	<.10
Additional values, over 50 per cent of either parent group reporting:				
Property	12	17	—	n.s.
Family harmony	14	32	—	n.s.
Orderliness	17	15	—	n.s.
Education in general	26	12	2.69	<.02

* Mothers' score higher.

20 per cent, four fall into four of the major categories: egoistic (independence), family (family unity), orderly living (manners), and interpersonal (getting along with people), and four belong in one major category—moral values (religion, obedience, responsibility, morality). This emphasis on moral values is not surprising, since this category is the one most stressed by both mothers and fathers. Of all 11 values stressed most by mothers, none fall into the biological, educational, or economic categories. None of the fathers' top 11 values fall into the economic, emotional security, or play categories. Here again is evidence of the fact that the mothers are not as conscious of their biological goals, or the fathers of their economic goals, as one would expect from their role performances.

Of the 20 per cent of values ranked lowest in Appendix Tables B.1 and B.2, mothers and fathers agree on nine: modesty, recognition, affection outside the family, aggression, sex, determination, privacy, nurturance, and obedience (negative). To this list, mothers add family location and type of education, and fathers add appearance and citizenship. In general, the parents emphasize the interpersonal-values subcategories less than those belonging to any other general category. No economic or play-values subcategory appears among the 11 lowest-ranked values. Fathers, in addition, have no family values in the lowest eleven.

Interrelations of Basic Values

We were interested in finding out how the values that are ranked high by both mothers and fathers are related. We wanted to know, for example, whether the mothers who stress obedience as a desired goal also emphasize other rigid socialization goals such as manners, orderliness, and morality, or whether the fathers who emphasize religious goals also stress other moral values such as morality, justice, and responsibility.

As a first step in answering such questions, we intercorrelated 18 values, adding to the 14 value subcategories in the upper 20 per cent of values of mothers or fathers, four others reported by 50 per cent or more of either parent group. These are: property, family harmony, orderliness, and education in general (see Table 5.2). The 153 correlations of these 18 value categories for each parent group are in Appendix Table B.3. On the whole, the correlations are of relatively low order, 19 for mothers, and 17 for fathers being statistically significant at the level of .10 or beyond. Only 22 correlations reach a statistical significance greater than would be expected by chance, nine at the level of $<.10$, two at the level of $<.02$, nine at the level of $<.01$, and two at the level of $<.001$ (see Appendix Table B.4).

Next, to find out how these intercorrelations clustered, we used factor analysis, which allowed us to estimate the number of "common factors" that are required to explain the intercorrelations between the 18 value variables. In spite of the fact that 39 cases are too few to give us much faith in a factor analysis, and that the intercorrelations are relatively low, we hoped to find some patterns that would provide suggestions for future research on the influence of values on parental behavior.

We isolated eight common factors for mothers that account for 76.64 per cent of the total variance in the 18 values, and another eight for fathers that account for 73.39 per cent of the variance (see Appendix Tables B.5, B.6).* We can best describe each factor by listing the value categories that have a loading of .33 or more. This figure, taken arbitrarily, indicates that 11 per cent of the variance in the value is contributed by the underlying factor. In listing the value categories that contribute to each factor, we give the loading of the factor on each value category in parentheses. The factors are listed in the order of their importance in accounting for the common variance among the 18 values; i.e., Factor 1 accounts for more of the common variance than any other, Factor 8 for less than any other.

Patterns for mothers. The eight factors for mothers and the contributing values in order of weighting are given below.

Mo Factor 1. Homemaking goals.
a. Mothers value family unity (.80).
b. They want their children to be orderly (.70).
c. They desire family harmony (.61).
d. They want their children to take responsibility (.54).

We labeled this factor Homemaking goals because it seems to identify the women who want a close-knit family group made up of parents who carry out their "appropriate" roles without bickering, and of children who have learned the kind of behavior that contributes to a smoothly run and orderly family life. This interpretation is somewhat supported by the fact that manners (loading, .28) just missed inclusion in this factor.

Mo Factor 2. Social-prestige goals.
a. Mothers value getting along with people (.83).
b. They value property (.69).
c. They stress the importance of good manners (.66).

This factor seems to represent the goals of mothers who have social aspirations, and who want their children to have pleasant, easy-going personalities, to behave properly, and to have the material things that win recognition in our society.

Mo Factor 3. Humanistic goals.
a. Mothers stress morality values (.83).
b. They value justice (.68).
c. They are not influenced by values for safety (—.50).
d. They are not influenced by religious values (—.43).

* The method used is the principal component method of factor analysis. The final matrix was obtained from the original solution by varimax rotation.

In designating Factor 3 as Humanistic, we were influenced by the fact that this factor seems to select mothers concerned with inner direction for broad social ends. Such mothers do not place importance on whether their children go to church, obey church tenets, develop a "Christian character," or prepare for the life hereafter, and they do not restrict their children under the guise of safety values.

Mo Factor 4. Security-independence goals.
  a. Mothers want their children to be independent (.90).
  b. They also stress the importance of family love (.81).

This factor was somewhat more difficult to label than the first three factors. The mothers who are high in this factor seem to be women who want their children to have the emotional support of an affectionate, happy home that will insure the development of self-reliance. These are not women who push their children into standing on their own two feet; rather, they are women who give children the basic security that leads to independent action. These mothers also tend to stress manners; the value just misses inclusion in the factor (loading, .32).

Mo Factor 5. Austerity goals.
  a. Mothers value knowledge (.79).
  b. They stress religious values (.68).
  c. They want their children to be responsible (.64).

Factor 5 was also difficult to label; in this group we have women whose values are somewhat like those held by New England women in the early nineteenth century. (An analysis of the writings of Mary Lyon, founder of Mount Holyoke Female Seminary in 1836, would probably yield high scores on values for education, religion, and individual responsibility.) These mothers are upright women, austere in their desires for "goodness." Perhaps because of their concern with broad human goals, they tend not to be concerned with inculcating manners (loading, —.30).

Mo Factor 6. Prudence.
  a. Mothers value safety for their children (.55).
  b. They value property (.35).
  c. They are not influenced by values for enjoyment (—.82).

The mothers identified by Factor 6 are going to "play it safe." They want to be sure their children do not play in the creek bed, take chances with fire, play where there is traffic. They protect furniture and other things that are important to them. They are alert to the dangers in our mechanized culture, and life for their children is highly restricted because of this. This interpretation was strengthened by the fact that obedience (loading, .30) just missed inclusion. The values for safety seem to push aside those for good times, perhaps because of the hazards involved. These mothers are cautious, and are therefore "killjoys," but withal they tend to be warm and affectionate; family love (loading, .32) also just missed inclusion.

Mo Factor 7. Socialization goals.

a. Mothers value obedience (.75).
b. They are sure of the importance of education in general (.75).

We labeled this factor Socialization because it seems to emphasize the importance of adults. It says that doing what a parent requires, and learning what the school teaches, are parallel roads that lead to acceptance in society. Mothers high in this factor may also want to be "good mothers" who do not bicker with their spouses; the value for family harmony (loading, .31) just missed inclusion.

Mo Factor 8. Anxiety-protection goals.

a. Mothers want their children to be free from anxiety (.78).
b. They value justice (.48).
c. They desire family harmony (.37).
d. They value safety (.33).

The eighth factor was labeled Anxiety-protection because it seems to identify mothers who do not want their children to be afraid, have conflicts, or be emotionally upset. The values for fair-mindedness, "good" parents, and safety are apparently means for achieving an emotionally relaxed and complacent atmosphere, where life is pleasant and protected. One might assume that these mothers tend to be somewhat anxious.

Patterns for fathers. The eight factors for fathers differ from those for mothers, though there do seem to be some relations between them, which we will discuss. The factors for fathers and their contributing values are as follows:

Fa Factor 1. Puritan goals.
a. Fathers value justice (.81).
b. They emphasize religious values (.67).
c. They value property (.66).
d. They want their children to be independent (.38).

These values seem to reflect the Puritan influence in American life. The constellation identifies an "upright" man with a strong social conscience, backed by religious convictions. Such men are practical, respect material goods, and recognize the worth of independence as a character trait. The pattern in Factor 5 for mothers, labeled Austerity (knowledge, religion, responsibility), seems to point to a complementary constellation among mothers.

Fa Factor 2. Controlling goals.
a. Fathers value manners (.83).
b. They value obedience (.82).
c. They value family love (.38).
d. They want their children to be orderly (.38).

The constellation of values in Factor 2 identifies men who are rigid, who want their children to be socialized and to fit into a culture that is comfortable for adults. They want to control their children, but within a framework of family love. In fact, one might surmise that love and happiness can exist in the home only if children "toe the mark." This is the only factor for fathers in which the value for obedience appears. Mothers, too, have only one factor that includes obedience: Factor 7, made up equally of obedience and education in general, with family love almost strong enough for inclusion. One senses a difference here between patterns: fathers emphasize control for the peace of adults, but mothers emphasize it for the learning of children.

Fa Factor 3. Family-life goals.
a. Fathers value family unity (.92).
b. They desire family harmony (.57).
c. They want their children to be responsible (.50).
d. They value family love (.38).

The pattern that emerges here is very similar to one found for mothers (Homemaking goals, Factor 1). But there are two very important differences: the factor for mothers has a strong component of desire for "orderly" children (loading, .70), while the factor for fathers includes family love. It seems to us that the fathers who have these family values must have more warmth in their personalities, and that the mothers must be more demanding and organizing.

Fa Factor 4. Inner-direction goals.

a. Fathers stress morality (.81).
b. They value knowledge (.50).
c. They are not influenced by desires that their children be free from anxiety (—.65).

In this pattern fathers seem influenced by desires to have their children know right from wrong, develop a conscience, and learn specific facts. The fathers seem to imply that such goals will give a child more strength than the security which comes from being free from anxiety. This factor relates morality values to values for knowledge, whereas in the mothers' values (Humanistic goals, Factor 3) we find morality related to justice, another value in the moral category; that is, mothers emphasize the humanistic rather than the individualistic aspects of morality.

Fa Factor 5. Freedom goals.

a. Fathers want enjoyment for their children (.82).
b. They value independence (.38).
c. They strive to have their children free from anxiety (.34).
d. They are not influenced by values for orderliness (—.68).

We have called Factor 5 Freedom goals because the pattern stresses freedom of the spirit: joyousness and independence unhampered by fear, emotional conflict, or the necessity of keeping neat and clean. These fathers are the antithesis of the controlling fathers described by Factor 2. There is no comparable pattern for mothers; enjoyment enters into just one factor and then only negatively (Prudence, Factor 6). Freedom from anxiety is found in only one factor for mothers, Factor 8, Protection. It seems that fathers see freedom from anxiety as part of liberation and fun, whereas mothers see it as related to shielding and protecting.

Fa Factor 6. Bureaucracy goals.

a. Fathers want their children to get along with other people (.87).
b. They want them to be responsible (.65).
c. They value orderliness (.42).
d. They are not influenced by values for family love (−.35).

Whereas mothers relate the value of getting along with people to property and manners in Factor 2, Social-prestige goals, fathers seem to relate social ability to abilities, such as responsibility and orderliness, that are valued in their occupational lives. That this factor has a negative loading for family love would tend to support the interpretation that it relates to fathers' work roles. We labeled it Bureaucracy goals because it is a constellation of certain characteristics that Miller and Swanson (1958) delineate as useful in a bureaucratic, as contrasted with an entrepreneurial, industrial society.

Fa Factor 7. Education goals.

a. Fathers stress the importance of education in general (.86).
b. They want their children to acquire knowledge (.53).
c. They value family love (.38).

This factor primarily stresses the value of education, but it also suggests that the fathers who stress education values for their children have warm family relationships. No pattern for mothers gives such clear-cut prominence to education, although the value for knowledge is the primary element in Austerity goals (Factor 5), and education is of equal importance with obedience in Socialization goals (Factor 7).

Fa Factor 8. Protection goals.

a. Fathers are concerned with safety (.72).
b. They want family harmony (.59).

We labeled Factor 8 Protection because safety is such an important component. This is the only factor for fathers in which safety appears. If we compare this with Factor 6 for mothers, labeled Prudence, we can see that for mothers safety is combined with a strong negative weighting of enjoyment; but for fathers the index for safety is higher, and it is combined with values for being a "good" parent in a harmonious home. Safety also appears in Factor 8 for mothers combined with values that indicate anxiety on the mother's part. There is no comparable factor for fathers.

Relation of Basic Values to Demographic Characteristics

Seven of the demographic characteristics of parents reported in Chapter III were correlated with parents' percentage scores on the 10 major categories of basic values (see Appendix Table B.7) and with the 18 most-emphasized subcategories (see Appendix Tables B.8 and B.9). In the correlations with the 10 major categories (Appendix Table B.7), the numbers at the significance level of $<.10$, and for fathers, those at $<.05$, are less than would be expected by chance. In the correlations with the 18 subcategories (Appendix Tables B.8 and B.9), the number at the significance level $<.05$ is less than would be expected by chance (see Appendix Table B.10). If therefore we conservatively limit our discusion to those correlations at the significance level of .02 or beyond, we find that in general the demographic characteristics are related to value emphasis more for fathers than for mothers. Table 5.3 gives a convenient summary of the more highly significant correlations between demographic characteristics and value categories.

Mothers and fathers with larger families emphasize values for orderly living (including the subcategory of orderliness for both parents, and manners for fathers). These values are also emphasized by mothers of lower social position and lower educational level. No other value category seems so closely related to demographic characteristics of both mothers and fathers.

Moral values are emphasized by more mature fathers (those with more children and older firstborns), and the subcategory of responsibility shows a similar trend toward mature fathers (older with older children). The younger mothers are guided by values for obedience, and mothers with an inconsistent religious background stress justice.

Safety is the only other value category related to more than one demographic variable. Fathers of lower educational level, of lower social position, and with larger families emphasize this

TABLE 5.3. *Summary of Correlations between Basic Values and Demographic Characteristics (significance of .02 or beyond)*

Values	Age of parent		Number of children		Age of oldest child		Consistency in religion		Education level		Social position		Social mobility	
	Mo	Fa	Mo	Fa	Mo	Fa	Mo	Fa	Mo	Fa	Mo	Fa	Mo	Fa
Orderly living	—	—	.39	.50	—	—	—	—	–.44	—	–.37	—	—	—
Orderliness	–.37	—	.41	.41	—	—	—	—	–.41	—	–.58	—	—	—
Manners	—	—	—	.50	—	—	—	—	—	—	—	—	—	—
Moral	—	—	—	.37	—	.39	—	—	—	—	—	—	—	—
Responsibility	—	.43	—	—	—	.49	—	—	—	—	—	—	—	—
Morality	—	—	—	—	—	.39	—	—	—	—	—	—	—	—
Obedience	–.40	—	—	—	—	—	—	—	—	—	—	—	—	—
Justice	—	—	—	—	—	—	–.41	—	—	—	—	—	—	—
Egoistic	—	—	—	—	—	—	—	—	—	—	—	—	—	.48
Educational:														
Education in general	—	—	—	—	—	–.40	—	—	—	—	—	—	—	—
Knowledge	—	—	—	—	.37	—	—	—	—	—	—	—	—	—
Biological:														
Safety	—	—	—	.39	—	—	—	—	—	–.43	—	–.42	—	—
Economic	—	—	—	—	—	—	—	—	—	—	—	–.43	—	—
Play	—	—	—	—	—	—	—	—	—	—	—	.38	—	—

NOTE: For $r = .37, p < .02$; $r = .41, p < .01$; $r = .51, p < .001$.
Data are from Appendix Tables B.7, B.8, and B.9.

value. Egoistic values are stressed by the more upward-mobile fathers.

We find an interesting contrast with respect to the influence of educational values. Fathers with younger children (and perhaps those who are themselves younger, and those with fewer children) stress the importance of education in general, whereas mothers with older children stress the gaining of knowledge. Finally in another contrast economic goals are stressed by fathers of lower social position, whereas play goals are stressed by fathers of higher social position.

Differences between Mothers and Fathers

The differences in percentage scores of matched mothers and fathers for the 11 general categories of basic values are given in Table 5.1, those for the 18 subcategories most emphasized by parents are given in Table 5.2. The number of scores observed at each level of significance is on the whole greater than the number expected by chance (see Appendix Table B.11).

As with values for parenthood, fathers stress basic values more than mothers, and the difference between their mean percentage scores for the category as a whole is highly significant ($p < .001$). However, this overall difference does not hold for all 10 major categories (omitting general values) or for all 18 most emphasized subcategories, either in the direction or in the magnitude of the difference scores.

Fathers exceed mothers in seven of the 10 major categories of basic values, five of these differences being significant at the level of .10 or beyond. Of the 18 subcategories, fathers exceed mothers in 11, six of the difference scores reaching a significance of .10 or beyond. Mothers significantly exceed fathers in two subcategories.

The most highly significant differences between mothers and fathers are in values for education (including the subcategories of knowledge and education in general) and in biological values (including the subcategory of safety), in each case fathers giving greater emphasis than mothers. The next most highly significant differences are found in moral values (including responsibility, religion, and justice), in which fathers exceed mothers. Fathers also stress egoistic values (though not independence) and values for orderly living (though not the subcategories of manners or orderliness) significantly more than mothers. Mothers stress only two subcategories significantly more than fathers: freedom from anxiety and, to a lesser degree, obedience.

Summary and Comments

The material presented in this chapter and in Chapter IV is convincing evidence that the parents we interviewed had values or goals that influenced their behavior to some extent.

There are 2,900 codings of values which, although not specifically concerned with parental roles, cover a wide range of what is considered worthwhile in life and influence the behavior of the parents toward their children. We labeled these basic values. The basic values were classified into ten categories (plus one of general values). In the order of emphasis by parents, they are: moral, family, egoistic, interpersonal, emotional security, educational, orderly living, biological, play, economic.

Within the 10 major categories of basic values, 55 subcategories were identified. Of the 20 per cent of subcategories mentioned most by parents, mothers and fathers agree on eight: independence, family unity, manners, getting along with people, obedience, religion, responsibility, and morality. To these, mothers add freedom from anxiety, family love, and enjoyment; fathers add knowledge, safety, and justice.

A factor analysis of 18 of the subcategories (selected on the basis of highest scores) isolated eight factors for mothers and eight different factors for fathers. The value for a close-knit, unified family is emphasized by a large percentage of mothers, and by two-thirds of the fathers. This value is the most heavily weighted in Factor 1 for mothers, Homemaking goals, and in Factor 3 for fathers, Family-life goals. One might expect that mothers would place a high value on having a close-knit family, because the family is the power structure of the mother, and when the ties between family members are loosened, the prestige and dominance of the mother diminishes. But why is it that a large proportion of fathers stress this value, too? Is it the influence of the wife on the husband? Have communication sources been emphasizing the importance of family cohesiveness? Or are the stresses of an increasingly complex society making men value more than ever the close supporting relations of family life?

A desire to have their children learn to be independent is also a strong motivating force for these parents. They want their children to think independently, to stand on their own two feet, and even to be rugged individualists. Such goals might seem to conflict with the goal of family unity, which can be seen as a desire to build dependence rather than independence in children. But for these mothers the goal of independence is strongly related to family love, as Factor 4, Security-independence goals, shows. Sears *et al.* (1957) found that mothers' rejection of dependency needs and their desire for independence in children were related to strictness in control, and to a personality characterized by coldness and lack of affection. However, our findings lead us to suggest that there are mothers who are warm and affectionate, who can accept the dependency needs of their children, and who can at the same time want them gradually to learn to think for themselves and stand on their own two feet.

Fathers' value for independence is related to two factors. In Factor 1, Puritan goals, independence is related to values for justice, religion, and property. We described fathers high in this factor as upright, practical men who respect material possessions and value independence as a character trait. But independence is also found in Factor 5, where it is related to enjoyment and freedom from anxiety and opposed to orderliness. Fathers identified by this factor seem to value freedom of the spirit, freedom to enjoy life without being restricted by the demands of orderly living.

Obedience is a strong goal. It was stressed by younger parents, and emphasized slightly more by mothers than by fathers. It is most highly related to education for mothers (Factor 7), indicating that mothers may see obedience as a goal related to the socialization process. For fathers, it is a strong constituent in Factor 2, Controlling goals, where it is related to manners and orderliness, indicating its relation to orderly living rather than morality values.

There are several categories that were surprisingly low in the hierarchy of values—citizenship, for one. Only a few parents said that they wanted their children to become good citizens. This lack of emphasis may be due more to the fact that values related to citizenship do not usually enter into the practices of parents with their children, rather than to the fact that these men and women had no values in this area. One might easily hypothesize that teachers would emphasize citizenship values much more. It might also be assumed that parents who belong to certain conservative "patriotic" organizations might emphasize this value more; however, we had no parent of this kind in the sample. Another goal that is mentioned infrequently is the egoistic value of determination or tenacity, a characteristic that one might expect to find much admired in a striving, individualistic culture. Perhaps Miller and Swanson (1958) are right in their belief that the individualistic economy of the late nineteenth and early twentieth century is giving way to a bureaucratic society in which competitive characteristics are less highly valued.

The value of appearance was eighteenth from the lowest in emphasis for mothers, and the next to lowest in emphasis for fathers. One is tempted to say that parents are perhaps more influenced by this value than they realize—that appearance is so strong a value in middle-class culture that it is taken for granted. There is a hint that the parents who mention the importance of having their children look nice and be neatly dressed are the upward-mobile ones in social position, but the codings were too few to test the relation statistically.

Finally, mothers do not stress biological values, and fathers do not stress economic values to the degree that one might expect from their role performances. Possibly such goals are so much a part of routine life that parents are less conscious of them than goals that they take less for granted.

There is some evidence that parents change their values as they become more mature. One sees a shift in the goals that guide them as their children increase in number and age, and to a lesser extent as they themselves get older. The relations are not equally strong for mothers and fathers, but there are some similarities in the general directions of the change. When families are small and firstborns are young, there appears to be a tendency for parents to stress biological goals, and goals for providing emotional security. As families mature, parents place less emphasis on values concerned with nurturant goals (with the exception of fathers' concern for safety), and begin to stress values that make life more comfortable for themselves, such as orderliness and manners, and perhaps other values grouped under orderly living.

There are indications that the cultural background of a parent may influence some of his values. Values for orderly living, which are highly weighted by mothers' desires to have their children learn manners and be clean and neat, are particularly important to the mothers who are less well-educated or of lower social position. The men who had moved upward in social position have strong egoistic values, especially the much-emphasized value for independence, as well as values for achievement and practicality, all virtues that may have been useful to the fathers in their climb up the social ladder.

Fathers of lower social position emphasize economic values, and mothers stress values for orderly living, facts that seem to indicate that these parents value the middle-class virtues of our culture: behaving properly, having the money for a proper setting of material possessions. That parents in relatively low social positions stress these values perhaps indicates their desire for better status. Fathers of higher social position, who are in better economic condition, are free to express their desires for fun and enjoyment, and for an interesting life of travel and new experiences, and to value creativity in their children—all values that we subsumed under play.

It is surprising that the score on consistency in religion shows virtually no relationship to values for religion for either parent group. Basic values related to education spread across demographic groups, just as the parent-role value to educate children (Chapter IV) was not emphasized by any group of parents.

The values reported are not the same for fathers and mothers in the same family. Fathers are relatively more conscious of values, and discussed them more. This is true not only for values as a whole, but also for values for parental role, for basic values, and for many of the subcategories under these divisions. In Chapter XII, we will discuss some possible explanations of the fathers' greater emphasis on values.

VI

Instrumental Beliefs

The parents in this study were influenced not only by their values, what they felt to be good or bad, but also by their beliefs, what they felt to be true or false. A parental practice always involves, either implicitly or explicitly, some belief. A father sends his child to Sunday school every week because he believes religion will give the child security. A mother spanks her two-year-old for turning on the gas burners because she believes that spanking will break the habit. A father does not use authoritarian control because he believes it is brutal (Whiting and Child, 1953, p 29).

Nearly five thousand beliefs (4,972) were coded from the parent interviews, about half from mothers and half from fathers, as shown in Table 3.2 (p. 28). The percentage scores show that fathers emphasize beliefs as influences on their behavior with their children much more than mothers. The relationship between educational level and emphasis on beliefs is strikingly different for mothers and fathers: beliefs are stressed by the more highly educated mothers $p < .05$) and by the less highly educated fathers ($p < .01$), as well as by fathers of lower social position ($p < .001$).*

Beliefs that influence the practices of parents are of two kinds —descriptive and instrumental. A descriptive belief assigns an attribute to a person or an event. Children like to play; learning now is for the future; permissive control lets children run wild—

* The correlation between education and social position of fathers is .86 (see Table 2.1, p. 17).

these beliefs describe what the parent believes a child, learning, or permissive control to be. We will discuss descriptive beliefs in Chapter VII.

An instrumental belief asserts that a relation exists between an act and a value. Such beliefs concern the ways in which parents believe they can attain the values described in the last chapter. Consider this statement by a parent: "Going to nursery school makes children more independent." Here, *independence* is the value, and *going to nursery school* is the instrumental act by which the parent believes the value can be attained. Such instrumental beliefs comprise about a third of the beliefs of both mothers and fathers.

Altogether, 1,678 instrumental beliefs were coded from the interviews, 887 from mothers' and 791 from fathers' interviews. This seems like a sizeable sample of material for analysis. However, the beliefs and the instrumental acts within the beliefs are widely disparate. The beliefs extend over the 11 general categories of values, and over 38 of the 55 subcategories, with the result that the number of beliefs in some specific categories is so small that we were not able to compare differences between mothers and fathers as consistently as we did for values, or make meaningful analyses of the relation of some specific beliefs to demographic variables. Even though the wide variation in instrumental beliefs limits the analysis, the findings may still be useful as a guide for more circumscribed and intensive research in the future. We shall first discuss beliefs in relation to the specific values with which they are concerned. Later we shall summarize the variety of instrumental acts found in these beliefs.

The 11 categories of instrumental beliefs in Table 6.1 parallel the 11 major categories of basic values discussed in Chapter V. Both mothers and fathers report the largest numbers of instrumental beliefs in relation to biological, moral, and emotional-security values, in that order. The emphasis differs to some extent from the emphasis parents give to basic values. In basic values, parents have their highest scores in moral values, but biological values are given relatively slight emphasis (ninth for mothers; fifth for fathers), as are values for emotional security (fifth for mothers; eighth for fathers (see Table 5.1, pp. 42–43).

TABLE 6.1. *Analysis of Instrumental Beliefs by Value Category*

Beliefs about achievement of:	*Per cent reporting*		*Number of codings*		*Mean percentage score*		*Percentage score difference*	
	Mo	*Fa*	*Mo*	*Fa*	*Mo*	*Fa*	*t*	*p*
Biological values								
Nutrition	85	82	204	203	1.98	2.27		
Health	64	49	37	33	.34	.36		
Regulation of sexual behavior	46	41	84	67	.66	.72		
Safety	31	15	14	8	.10	.07		
Σ Beliefs, biological values	95	100	399	311	3.08	3.42	—	n.s.
Moral values								
Obedience	79	68	68	51	.60	.62		
Morality	64	67	52	67	.42	.79		
Responsibility	21	23	11	11	.10	.12		
Religion	5	10	2	5	.02	.06		
Citizenship	3	8	1	4	.01	.03		
Justice	8	3	3	1	.02	.01		
Σ Beliefs, moral values	97	90	137	139	1.17	1.63	2.07	<.05
Emotional-security values								
Security, mental health	72	51	65	52	.54	.47		
Insecurity, problems	56	33	53	28	.47	.25		
Happiness	31	28	21	14	.18	.14		
Unhappiness	8	8	3	3	.02	.02		
Σ Beliefs, emotional-security values	82	64	142	97	1.21	.88	1.72	<.10
Egoistic values								
Independence	49	44	31	29	.25	.31		
Self-confidence	18	18	10	12	.09	.13		
Aggression	13	8	5	4	.05	.04		
Nonaggression	26	23	10	15	.08	.15		
Achievement	8	15	3	7	.02	.07		
Intelligence	5	3	8	3	.02	.03		
Σ Beliefs, egoistic values	69	74	61	70	.51	.73	1.79	<.10
Family values								
Harmony	49	8	41	4	.41	.03		
Unity	33	15	15	8	.14	.10		
Love	26	21	14	10	.11	.10		
Cooperation	13	8	5	3	.07	.06		
Democracy	10	15	4	8	.04	.06		
Σ Beliefs, family values	79	49	79	33	.77	.35	2.65	<.02
Interpersonal values								
Getting along	36	28	26	14	.20	.16		
Tolerance	15	15	6	7	.05	.08		
Generosity	8	13	3	5	.02	.06		
Friends	8	8	3	3	.03	.03		
Σ Beliefs, interpersonal values	51	41	38	30	.30	.33	—	n.s.
Σ Beliefs, educational values	36	49	24	33	.22	.35	—	n.s.

TABLE 6.1 (*cont.*).

Beliefs about achievement of:	*Per cent reporting*		*Number of codings*		*Mean percentage score*		*Percentage score difference*	
	Mo	*Fa*	*Mo*	*Fa*	*Mo*	*Fa*	*t*	*p*
Orderly-living values								
Manners	23	8	16	3	.10	.03		
Orderliness	8	3	5	1	.05	.01		
Carefulness	3	13	1	5	.01	.05		
Punctuality	3	8	1	3	.02	.04		
Σ Beliefs, orderly-living values	33	31	23	12	.18	.13	—	n.s.
Play values								
Enjoyment	21	26	13	12	.10	.11		
New experiences	3	8	1	4	.01	.02		
Creativity	5	3	3	1	.02	.01		
Σ Beliefs, play values	28	31	17	17	.13	.14	—	n.s.
Economic values								
Work	10	13	4	7	.03	.08		
Money	3	13	1	5	.01	.06		
Property	8	10	3	4	.02	.05		
Σ Beliefs, economic values	18	31	7	16	.06	.19	2.07	<.05
General values	31	51	20	33	.15	.34	2.44	<.02
Σ Instrumental beliefs	100	100	887	791	7.78	8.49	—	n.s.

BELIEFS RELATING TO BIOLOGICAL VALUES

Although only 74 per cent of the mothers and 87 per cent of the fathers discuss biological values, practically all the parents discuss beliefs about how to attain such values, and 38 per cent of mothers' instrumental beliefs and 39 per cent of fathers' are in this category. The largest category of beliefs for both parent groups is concerned with four biological values: nutrition, health, regulation of sexual behavior, and safety (Table 6.1).

Nutrition. Both mothers and fathers stress beliefs relating to food and nutrition more than they stress beliefs in any other biological category. This emphasis on beliefs may have been caused by our selection of the evening meal as a behavior setting to discuss with all parents, though this fact did not seem to lead to undue emphasis on nutrition or food as a value. The beliefs about nutrition are grouped into two sections: those concerning the nutritional values of different foods, and those concerning conditions that affect the proper eating of food (see Appendix Table C.1).

These parents have absorbed in one way or another a great deal of the lore of nutritionists and doctors about nutrition. They believe that fruits, vegetables, meat, and milk are essential ingredients of an adequate diet. They also mention the importance of vitamins, pure (nonsynthetic) food, a well-balanced diet, and well-prepared meals. Over one-third of the parents (more mothers than fathers) believe that their children should eat a variety of foods for adequate nutrition. The parents also mention some foods they believe harm children, such as sweets (candy, cookies, cake, ice cream), stimulants (coffee, tea, soft drinks), and a few odd items (peanut butter, chocolate, rice, bread, tomato soup, raisins, hot food, and highly seasoned foods).

Parents believe that a child will eat well if he has an appetite; and that an appetite is assured if he does not eat between meals, eats on schedule, and receives no dessert until he has eaten the main course. More fathers than mothers mention that a relaxed atmosphere during meals (including no television and little talking) also helps. Some parents believe that eating together as a family, and breast-feeding and demand-feeding of infants, also contribute to adequate nutrition.

Health. Over half the parents mention beliefs about the development of healthy children. Some believe that health depends on adequate nutrition, a few think that a happy family life makes healthy children. Inheritance, cleanliness, fresh air, adequate elimination, rooming-in, breast-feeding, and demand-feeding all are mentioned once. In addition, 28 per cent of mothers, and 13 per cent of fathers report being influenced by beliefs that illness can be prevented by such things as warm clothing, emotional well-being, vitamins, and parental supervision.

Regulation of sexual behavior. Less than half of the parents discuss beliefs about socializing the sexual impulses of children. The general topic of sex education is discussed most, but a few parents, especially those with adolescent children, discuss beliefs about masturbation and sex experimentation (see Appendix Table C.2).

There is great diversity in beliefs about sex education. Some parents believe that sex education to be effective must be begun early in a child's life; others believe that adolescence is the time. Some believe in no differences in the sex education of boys and girls; others in teaching girls earlier than boys, or in giving them more information. And parents mention different beliefs concerning the best way to teach about sex; some mention group instruction; some, books; some, observation of farm animals or pets.

Most of the parents who discuss sex educations believe that an open, above-board, and matter-of-fact parental attitude is desirable. However, they differ on who is the best person to give the child such education. All who discuss this, except one father, believe that parents are responsible for educating their children about sex; but some believe that best results come when the father educates the boy, and the mother, the girl; others believe that the mother is best for both boy and girl. A few (13 per cent) believe that someone other than the parent should give sex education: a teacher, minister, or priest.

The parents who discuss masturbation are equally divided between those who think it a normal phenomenon and part of growing up, and those who think it abnormal, bad, or caused by other problems. A few parents who mention their beliefs about how to control masturbation suggest such commonly held prescriptions as diverting activity, not permitting the child to lie in bed, and discussing the problem with him. The few mothers who discuss sex experimentation believe that it is caused by boys and girls playing together, or sometimes by an older boy taking care of a little girl, and that it can be controlled by separating boys and girls in play, by an increase in physical activity, or by threats of punishment. Some parents believe that feminine activities or over-protective mothers interfere with the normal heterosexual development of adolescent boys.

Safety. Obedience is the way to insure safety, according to 26 per cent of the mothers and 15 per cent of the fathers. A few mothers of young babies believe the responsibility for safety lies with parents; for example, keeping dangerous objects away from babies.

Beliefs Relating to Moral Values

Just as fathers discuss moral values significantly more than mothers, they also tend to discuss beliefs about attaining moral values significantly more. Among the various subcategories, fathers emphasize most beliefs about instilling "good" behavior in their children (morality); mothers emphasize most beliefs about gaining obedience (see Table 6.1).

Obedience. In general, beliefs about how to obtain obedience are emphasized more than beliefs about any other category under moral values. Among the 55 subcategories of values, obedience is emphasized third (more than any other moral value) by mothers, and ninth by fathers. Sixty-nine per cent of the mothers and 56 per cent of the fathers believe that parental control is the principal factor in securing obedience. Some believe that strict control (directing, forbidding, punishing) will promote obedience; others emphasize such methods of control as following through on demands, explaining, helping children to understand, avoiding issues, making indirect requests.

Except for one mother and one father (not in the same family), all parents believe that children obey their fathers better than their mothers. They give several reasons for this: children do not see their fathers as much; the father is more strict; the father can spank harder; the father is a man and therefore to be obeyed. In two families the mother and father disagree about which parent is more effective in obtaining obedience from children. Contrast these two excerpts from the interviews of Mo 7 and Fa 7. The mother said:

> My husband isn't home a lot, and when he is home, he doesn't seem to have as much control over them as I do. For example, if we have company, I really have to get after them. If we want them to behave in the daytime when we have to take them out, I'm the one who winds up taking them in the other room and saying, "Now, you behave or else." I don't know why, I think it's because he's just not home too much, and when he is, he doesn't like to.

The father in the same family said:

> I think the children obey me quicker. I can spank harder. And perhaps, the fact that my wife does a larger amount of the scolding than I do, since she is with them more of the time.

Other beliefs about obedience concern the influence of the child's maturity, of a strong conscience, and of assigned responsibilities.

Morality. Beliefs about attaining morality center around ways to make children "good." Some parents believe that giving their children emotional security and religious values, and instilling respect for others, will make them good. Another group of beliefs about obtaining "good" behavior, discussed by 21 per cent of mothers and 33 per cent of fathers, emphasizes the importance of experiences with children's peers: friends and associates, children in the neighborhood, in organized play groups, and in church groups. A few parents believe forces within the child—fatigue, needing to prove himself, feeling secure—influence his behavior.

Most of all, however, the parents (36 per cent of mothers; 41 per cent of fathers) stress beliefs that it is the parent himself who determines a child's "good" behavior—either by his interest, example, or strict discipline. A few parents (21 per cent mothers; 15 per cent fathers) believe that parents are responsible for bad behavior, too, and place the blame on either strict or too lenient control.

Responsibility and honesty. Fathers are greatly influenced by their values for responsibility or honesty (their third most emphasized value), but relatively few parents report beliefs in this category. Some believe that having chores to do at home or caring for pets builds responsibility in children, and that children are made more honest by having to admit wrongdoing, as well as by observing honesty in their parents. A few parents believe that obedience is a necessity for such moral characteristics as responsibility or honesty, but only one couple strongly emphasizes this. The mother said:

> I believed that if they learned obedience then [when young], they were more dependable. . . . I think that if you train them to be obedient they are more dependable. I mean that's just my feeling that they are. . . . We have the children help in the house for the training. . . . I think they need this responsibility and the training they get. . . . I feel they need to learn to do a job well, but I feel that they need to learn the responsibility of helping others.

Other values. Beliefs about the attainment of three other moral values, religion, citizenship, and respect for others (a subcategory of justice) are mentioned by a few parents. Although religious values have relatively high intensity scores for both fathers and mothers, only a few parents discuss beliefs about how to obtain these goals. The importance of parental example and of obedience in inculcating Christian character, and the ineffectiveness of forcing a child to go to Sunday school, are mentioned. Only a few parents mention beliefs related to citizenship. Breadth of interest, knowledge, education, tolerance, and emotional control are believed to help make children good citizens. Respect for parents or others is the only belief about obtaining justice that is discussed. The parents believe that requiring obedience or good manners increases respect for people, and that if a child learns respect for his parents, he will have respect for others.

Beliefs Relating to Emotional Security

A relatively high proportion of parents express beliefs about obtaining emotional security for their children. Mothers emphasize these beliefs second only to beliefs about realizing biological goals: for fathers these beliefs are third in emphasis (see Table 6.1).

The instrumental beliefs in this area were difficult to assign to specific subcategories because parents do not discriminate very clearly between the various aspects of emotional security. For example, Fa 27 believes that requiring strict obedience, tempered by kindness and love, leads to many desirable qualities in children—happiness, sense of security, adjustment, and lack of conflicts—and that without this kind of control children flounder and become confused, insecure, and guilty. Some parents use the terms happy, emotionally secure, well-adjusted, and in good mental health interchangeably to mean the general emotional well-being of the child. One example of the vagueness of concepts in this area is the following excerpt from an interview with a new father, who had just stated that he thought "rooming-in" (having the newborn baby and the mother in the same hospital room) would be good for the baby.

Interviewer: In what way do you think rooming-in might be good for the baby?

Fa 25: Oh, we don't know. We just think it might be. Sort of like—the idea that, you know, if the baby nurses rather than is bottle fed, it has a little more warmth. Now, what this warmth will accomplish, we have no idea. You don't know why they are necessarily good, but you have a feeling at least you haven't left a stone unturned, so maybe you've wasted your effort, but—you're afraid if you hadn't done it, you might have done something wrong. It's more a matter of that.

Similarly, statements referring to problems, trouble, upsets, maladjustments, insecurity, nervous tension, conflicts, complexes, and even hysteria all seem to refer nonspecifically to what one mother described as "a terrible psychological effect."

We divided the 239 beliefs about the attainment of emotional security into four categories, security, insecurity, happiness, and unhappiness. More parents emphasize positive beliefs about security or happiness than emphasize the corresponding negative beliefs. (The contrasting mean percentage scores for mothers are .72 and .49; for fathers they are .61 and .27.)

The beliefs about ways to attain emotional security in children are reported in Table 6.2. In order to bring these scattered beliefs into some order, we restated the negative beliefs in positive form; e.g., the belief that bottled-up emotions make a child maladjusted was grouped under beliefs that freedom to express emotions helps a child become emotionally secure.

Over two-thirds of the beliefs about developing emotional se-

TABLE 6.2. *Beliefs about Ways to Attain Emotional Security*

	Per cent reporting		*Number of codings*		*Mean percentage score*	
	Mo	*Fa*	*Mo*	*Fa*	*Mo*	*Fa*
Control of parents	64	51	60	37	.51	.35
Strict discipline, authoritarian	21	13	11	7	.09	.06
Limits, schedules	18	23	8	12	.06	.12
Adjusted to needs	36	28	19	12	.16	.13
Freedom for emotional expression	46	8	22	6	.20	.04
Expression of parental love	28	26	15	19	.12	.15
Unified family	31	10	13	5	.11	.06
Other parental practices	13	5	8	4	.07	.03
Adjustment of parents	10	5	5	2	.05	.02
Behavior of child	44	13	28	13	.24	.11
Other beliefs	26	28	13	17	.11	.16
Σ Beliefs, emotional security values	82	64	142	97	1.21	.88

curity in children (71 per cent of mothers' total, 69 per cent of fathers' total) emphasize the role of parents in providing the appropriate conditions. Fa 17 expressed his feeling of responsibility for the insecurity of his oldest daughter, who was six years old, in this way:

Of course this is all conjecture on our part, but we hold ourselves, my wife and I, responsible for the oldest girl's feeling of insecurity, because when she was first born we moved quite a bit, and to the extent it affected her personality, we don't know, but she is a different temperament than the youngest girl. She is very sensitive—very affectionate, but very stubborn. The first year of her life—I guess by Dr. Spock that is the time when the child is most susceptible to changes, or it is the time when they should remain in one place—well, we moved. I was in the Service when she was born, then we moved to another town, then to our present home; but the job I had, I used to travel to nine western states, and occasionally I'd take my wife and our one girl . . . for a couple of weeks in motels. Once for about six weeks, my wife visited her folks in a distant state; . . . so all of those things, we feel, might have had an effect on her. . . . I know I was insecure in my job; we wanted a house and we felt probably insecure about not having a house; we were hundreds of miles from both my folks and her folks, so we definitely weren't the best parents in the world for the first one.

Parents emphasize different beliefs about what they should do to insure emotional security for their children. By far the greatest emphasis is on beliefs that the control parents exercise affects the child's happiness and security, although parents disagree about what kind of control works best, some favoring strict discipline, others favoring more lenient control. A few mothers believe that the father's being the head of the family gives children the security they need. One mother with her first child, an eight-month-old baby girl, states emphatically that children need an authority figure for emotional security:

I don't think children like to feel that they rule the roost. Not really. I think that their big bid is for security. They want to feel that you know best. . . . You're not doing them any favors by . . . letting them have their own way, like free expression, or permissiveness, as they call it, I think that's wrong. . . . It stands to reason that a child can't be enamored of something it doesn't trust and look up to. I cannot feel secure that way. We all have a need to feel secure in something, either in religion or government or parents, when we're young. They all have to believe in someone and think that person knows right: God knows what's best for us; or the President, he's doing the right thing; or the King and Queen, well, they're in charge of us all. Everybody, I think, needs something like that, whether they admit it or not. And I think a child needs to have somebody to look up to.

A small number of parents believe that lenient control is the key to emotional adjustment. However, they do not believe in abrogating their control, but rather in adjusting their requirements to the needs of children. They are also critical of rigid schedules, overly high standards, strict discipline, and aggressive techniques. Some mothers, and a few fathers, believe that if children are allowed to express their emotions when angry they will be better adjusted, or, conversely, if these emotions are not expressed, they will become "bottled up" and cause trouble later.

Over a fourth of the parents mention the importance of expressing affection for a child and of assuring him of love and acceptance, sometimes stating the belief in a negative form: not giving a child love and attention makes him suffer, or withdrawing love leads to an inferiority complex. It is primarily mothers who believe that a unified, harmonious family is the foundation for emotional security, and that separation from parents, or arguments between husband and wife, lead to rebellion and insecurity. Other beliefs connecting mental health with such parental practices as breast-feeding, rooming-in, demand-feeding, and consistent behavior are discussed rarely. A very few parents believe that the emotional problems of parents affect the adjustment of children. The quotation from one father on page 98 illustrates such beliefs well.

Some parents believe that certain kinds of child behavior lead to emotional security. Indirectly, of course, these parents are pointing to parental practices that help the child to acquire such behavior. They emphasize beliefs that obedience, independence, or contacts with peers lead to emotional well-being. A few believe that table manners, liking a variety of foods, and easy relations with the opposite sex provide bases for security in social life. Some parents believe that church, school, or television, as well as general standards and conditions of living, can influence emotional well-being. One father said:

> I really want them [his four sons] to go to church, ... because I want them to develop a sense of security. I know a lot of other people that do go to church regularly—they got that certain look—and you know they've got that sense of security about them; that no matter whatever did happen to them they would come through it with shining colors; that it seems like nothing would faze them.

We have brought together in Appendix Table C.3 beliefs about parental practices leading to emotional security that may be labeled child-oriented or adult-oriented. Both mothers and fathers emphasize beliefs incorporating child-oriented practices much more than beliefs incorporating adult-oriented practices. Of the mothers' 142 beliefs related to emotional security, 54 per cent concern child-oriented techniques and only 13 per cent, adult-oriented techniques. Of the fathers' 97 beliefs related to emotional security, 47 per cent concern child-oriented techniques, and 20 per cent adult-oriented techniques.

Beliefs Relating to Egoistic Values

Beliefs relating to egoistic values are discussed by over two-thirds of the parents (see Table 6.1). Fathers appear to emphasize beliefs in this area more than mothers ($p < .10$), but this difference is not as statistically significant as the difference for egoistic values ($p < .05$).

Independence. Independence is high in the hierarchy of values for both mothers and fathers, and more parents have beliefs about the acquisition of independence than about the acquisition of any other personal characteristic. Over one-third of the parents believe that independence and self-reliance are best attained by giving the child freedom: freedom to make choices, freedom to be away from parents, encouragement to find his own answers, or, in general, freedom through lenient parental control. One mother said:

> I don't like to be forced into doing things myself. I was always told what to do and what I couldn't do. As far as my parents were concerned I didn't have a mind of my own. And I don't believe that's true. I would rather let my baby do things for himself if he wants to.

Other beliefs about parental practices that encourage independence in children are: not helping the child, not going to him when he cries, or not requiring household chores. A few fathers believe that school or college trains for independence; and a few parents believe that independence comes with growing up. One mother said of her adolescent son:

> I'm sure independence is one of the criteria for growing up. You just get more and more independent, and this is, I think, why the role of being a parent at this particular time is so difficult. You have to be very careful to walk the straight and narrow between permissiveness and too tight control.

Self-confidence. Only a few parents mention beliefs about how to develop self-confidence. They believe that parental support influences the child's confidence in himself. A few fathers believe that parents who engage in such practices as shaming, talking about a child's faults, or using strict discipline hinder the development of self-confidence in the child. The usefulness of social contacts, table manners, and independence are mentioned. One father, who has an adolescent son, believes that the physical changes which take place during adolescence interfere with the development of a boy's self-confidence.

Aggression. Only a few parents mention beliefs related to aggression. They believe that physical punishment by parents increases aggressive behavior in children. Two fathers believe strongly that certain television programs make children more aggressive. There are, however, over twice as many beliefs related to stopping aggression. Some parents (16 per cent) believe that the way to handle a child's aggression is to use retaliatory aggression: if a child bites you, bite him back; if he hits you, slap him. Other beliefs concern the usefulness of strict parental control, attendance at nursery school, supervised play activities, or the ameliorating effect of experience and maturity.

Achievement and intelligence. The few beliefs related to achievement and intelligence are discussed mostly by fathers. They believe that education, motivation, emotional support from parents, or shaming a child for poor work can increase achievement, and that the interest shown by a parent and the child's rate of development influence his level of intelligence.

Beliefs Relating to Family Values

As reported in Chapter V, family values were given high priority. Beliefs about attaining these values are discussed by 79 per cent of the mothers, and by 49 per cent of the fathers. The percentage scores show a significant difference in favor of mothers ($p < .02$) (see Table 6.1).

Harmony. Decidedly more mothers than fathers stress beliefs about the ways to create harmony in the family ($t = 3.65$, $p < .001$). Mothers (36 per cent) believe that the mother's place is in the home if all is to go well. Even the one working mother emphasizes this, and was planning for the day when she need no longer have a job. Only one father expresses the same belief. There are a few beliefs that outside interests, a college education, and religion make better mothers. The two mothers highest and lowest in social position believe that requiring obedience reduces quarreling and bickering, whereas four other mothers believe that things will go more smoothly in the home if a mother remembers her own childhood, and tries to put herself in the child's place. There are also a few beliefs about the fathers' part in creating a harmonious home. Mothers mention various aspects of his role as economic provider and various ways in which he can help with the children or the housework. A few fathers believe that family life is smoother when the father helps with the children.

Family unity. Many of these families wanted to have a close-knit family group, mothers ranking family unity second, and fathers ranking it fifth, among the 55 values (see Appendix Tables B.1 and B.2). However, relatively few parents are influenced by clear ideas about how these goals might be accomplished. The most emphasized belief is that showing affection, having close contact, and not ostracizing makes a child feel close to his parents. Other beliefs concern sharing activities with the child, teaching him obedience, and going places as a family.

Family love. Almost twice as many parents discuss the value of family love and happiness as report beliefs about how such goals may be reached. Fathers stress the relation between freedom for the child or parent and a happy, loving family life. Mothers more often stress the personality of the parents, stating that happy, loving, or nonbickering parents promote affection and happiness in the family. Two mothers believe from personal experience that excessive drinking can bring unhappiness to the family. Other more positive beliefs about how to obtain a happy family life include: not neglecting children, requiring obedience from them, or sharing family responsibilities.

Cooperation. In discussing values parents do not place much emphasis on children doing chores around the house as an end in itself; rather, they see doing chores as a means to other ends. This may explain why there are so few beliefs about ways to get children to cooperate in the chores that go along with everyday life in the family. Those that are mentioned include: teaching a child to share in work early in life, rotating his chores, not giving him too much to do, and limiting the amount of television.

Democracy. Although a third of the parents want a democratic atmosphere in family life, few express specific beliefs about how to achieve this value. Those who do mention beliefs are extremely limited in their concepts. All the fathers, and all but one mother, place greatest emphasis on the belief that sharing work responsibilities leads to democracy in the home. Other beliefs include giving regular allowances and exercising lenient control over children.

Beliefs Relating to Interpersonal Values

Beliefs are reported for only four of the eight subcategories of interpersonal values, and most of these are related to *getting along with people* (see Table 6.1).

Getting along with people. We also include the few beliefs about making friends here. Some mothers (33 per cent) and a few fathers (10 per cent) believe strongly that controlled children (that is, children who are obedient, mannerly, and have learned to share) get along better with other people. Some parents believe that going to school, getting a college education, attending Sunday school, or being religious will help a child make friends and develop better social relationships. There are a few beliefs that having an unpleasant personal appearance, or parents who are "real strict," makes it hard for children to get along with others. One father, a counselor in a junior high school, believes that a child who has a parent teaching in the same school he attends has a hard time being accepted by the other children.

Tolerance. About one-fourth of the parents want their children to be tolerant of other people; a smaller percentage of parents report beliefs about how tolerance can be acquired, but the beliefs that are expressed are usually expressed strongly. Most thought that experiences with different kinds of people, having a large number of acquaintances, or knowing people of different religions help develop tolerance. According to a few mothers and fathers, a child will learn to be tolerant if parents do not make an issue of racial differences, are tolerant themselves, or punish a child for intolerance.

Generosity. The few beliefs elicited about ways to develop generosity in children focus on the behavior of parents: if children are asked nicely for things, they will share them; if appreciation is shown to them, they will enjoy sharing. A few parents believe that being with other children helps a child learn generosity. One father told about his children going to Sunday school for the first time:

> They loved it because they weren't old enough to go to school then —and it was terrific—a preparation before going to school for them. I think it really made a difference—as far as them learning to share things with other children, and getting along with other children, prior to going to kindergarten in a regular public school.

Beliefs Relating to Other Values

Education. All the beliefs about education concern either the ways in which children gain knowledge or the factors that interfere with their gaining an adequate education. Most of the parents reporting (21 per cent of mothers; 33 per cent of fathers) believe that both the parent's ability and his interest in his child's education affect how well the child does in school. Some parents (more fathers than mothers) think that children learn from television, but about the same number believe that television interferes with studies. Other beliefs about gaining an adequate education include: regular attendance at school, going away to school, and belonging to Boy Scouts. Parents disagree about the relative merits of public and parochial schools, some believing that Catholic schools teach reading better and have stronger discipline, others believing that public schools are better because the teachers know more. Fathers emphasize the belief that a boy is likely to study harder if he has to work for his college education, but mothers think that working makes it difficult to get the most out of college.

Orderly living. Although over four-fifths of the parents report values for various aspects of orderly living, only about one-third discuss beliefs about how such values may be attained. Most of these beliefs are in the subcategory of manners (see Table 6.1). Of the beliefs concerned with an orderly and comfortable family life, the usefulness of parental example is mentioned most often. Beliefs about how to instill *manners* (discussed by 23 per cent of mothers and 8 per cent of fathers) emphasize the usefulness of parental example and early training. Beliefs about *orderliness* center around parental example and the assignment of regular chores. One mother believes that rules make children *careful,* but five fathers believe that children are more likely to be careful of possessions if they do not have too many, or if they have to work for them. Parents believe that *punctuality* is the result of keeping children to schedules and letting them suffer the consequences of tardiness.

Play. Although over two-thirds of the parents report that their parental behavior is influenced by play values, less than half this number discuss beliefs about how goals such as *enjoyment, new experiences,* and *creativity* might be attained for their children (see Table 6.1).

Twenty-one per cent of mothers and 26 per cent of fathers discuss beliefs about how to get fun and enjoyment out of life. They emphasize most that a variety of experiences (including television programs) increases one's enjoyment of life. About equally emphasized are beliefs that freedom and physical activity (including sports) provide enjoyment. A few parents believe that the well-socialized (i.e., obedient, educated) child enjoys life more. Achievement as a means to enjoyment is also mentioned. The few beliefs about attaining new and varied experiences mention television and education as sources. The few parents who mention beliefs about creativity state that self-expression leads to creativity, and that rigidity or social activities interfere with it.

Economic. There are fewer instrumental beliefs relating to economic values than to any other group of values, even though most of the mothers and fathers report values in this area. Fathers emphasize economic beliefs significantly more than mothers (see Table 6.1). Most of the beliefs about obtaining economic values have to do with *getting a job*; for example, parents believe that doing chores when young, going to college, or having influential parents helps a young person get a good job. A few parents believe that children value *money* if they have to work for it; others believe that giving children an allowance helps them understand the value of money. Some parents believe that you can teach children to respect *property* by making them responsible for taking care of things, or by punishing them when they do not show such respect. One father believes that emphasizing money gives children materialistic values, of which he heartily disapproves.

Most Emphasized Instrumental Beliefs

In Table 6.3 we list the nine categories (20 per cent) of instrumental beliefs most emphasized by mothers and fathers respec-

TABLE 6.3. *The Most Emphasized Instrumental Beliefs (highest 20 per cent in mean percentage scores)*

	Rank order		*Mean percentage score*		*Per cent reporting*	
Beliefs about the attainment of:	*Mo*	*Fa*	*Mo*	*Fa*	*Mo*	*Fa*
Nutrition (biological values)	1	1	1.98	2.27	85	82
Sex regulation (biological values)	2	3	.66	.72	46	38
Mental health (emotional-security values)	3	5	.65	.52	72	51
Obedience (moral values)	4	4	.60	.62	79	68
Emotional problems (emotional-security values)	5	9	.53	.28	56	33
Morality (moral values)	6	2	.42	.79	64	67
Health (biological values)	8	6	.34	.36	64	49
Independence (egoistic values)	9	8	.25	.31	49	44
Family harmony (family values)	7	—	.41	.03	49	8
Knowledge (education values)	—	7	.22	.35	36	49

NOTE: Obedience, morality, and independence are among the 20 per cent of values most emphasized by mothers and fathers. Emotional problems are the negative value for freedom from anxiety, which is one of the 20 per cent of values most emphasized by mothers; knowledge is among the highest 20 per cent for fathers.

tively. Eight of these categories are ranked high by both mothers and fathers, though only two—beliefs related to nutrition and beliefs related to obedience—have the same rank order. Beliefs about attaining family harmony ranked high only for mothers; beliefs about knowledge ranked high only for fathers.

Instrumental Acts in Beliefs

The foregoing discussion of instrumental beliefs focused on parental beliefs in terms of the particular goals, or values, they were concerned with. Now we shall consider these same beliefs from the standpoint of the particular instrumental act that was thought to lead to those goals. The parents reported 18 instrumental acts leading to more than one goal, and 58 leading to only one goal.

We used three measures to determine the importance of a value: the percentage of parents mentioning the value, the number of codings, and the mean percentage score for each parent group. To indicate the importance of an instrumental act, we used two additional criteria: the number of values to which a particular instrumental act is believed to lead, and the degree of emphasis given to these values. It seems reasonable to suppose that the acts parents believe lead to multiple goals, particularly goals given high priority, will in all likelihood be the ones that are most often performed by parents or approved of for their children.

The 18 instrumental acts believed to lead to more than one goal are shown in Table 6.4. The miscellaneous categories include those instrumental acts, each of which was mentioned as leading to only one value. The instrumental acts are organized into three general categories: acts of parents, acts of other socializing agents, and acts of children. Within each general category the order is determined by the number of values to which the act is related.

Acts of parents. All indicators point to the fact that parents believe that *parental control* is the most effective way to attain the values they want for their children. Parental control is believed to lead to 20 specific goals, the largest number ascribed to any instrumental act. We divided parental control into two general

TABLE 6.4. *Instrumental Acts in Beliefs Related to Values*

Instrumental acts	*Number of values obtained*			*Per cent reporting*		*Number of codings*		*Mean percentage score*		*Percentage score difference*	
	Total	*Mo*	*Fa*	*Mo*	*Fa*	*Mo*	*Fa*	*Mo*	*Fa*	*t*	*p*
Acts of parents	35	30	32	100	100	600	498	5.39	5.34	—	n.s.
Control	20	17	14	95	95	168	119	1.47	1.24	—	n.s.
Love, interest	10	8	10	82	62	68	50	.61	.52	—	n.s.
Teaching methods	10	7	8	69	67	73	82	.57	.89	1.70	<.10
Example	6	5	6	31	36	23	22	.17	.26	—	n.s.
Feeding techniques	5	4	4	90	85	184	185	1.81	1.97	—	n.s.
Miscellaneous	13	10	9	82	62	84	40	.76	.46		
Acts of other socializing agents	24	21	20	80	90	89	132	.76	1.40	3.33	<.01
Peer groups	13	11	8	54	51	31	32	.27	.33	—	n.s.
School, education	11	8	10	23	33	14	23	.10	.22	2.43	<.02
Church, religious groups	9	7	7	31	49	23	30	.20	.35	—	n.s.
Television	8	6	7	31	46	14	28	.14	.32	2.35	<.05
Neighborhood	1	1	1	15	36	7	19	.05	.18	2.75	<.01
Acts of children	30	24	27	95	92	198	161	1.63	1.75	—	n.s.
Obedience	11	9	6	56	39	43	31	.35	.27	—	n.s.
Responsibility	11	8	10	28	31	14	23	.13	.27	—	n.s.
Experience, development	8	6	8	44	44	27	23	.23	.29	—	n.s.
Manners	4	3	3	18	10	9	5	.06	.05	—	n.s.
Physical activity	3	3	3	28	13	13	5	.11	.05	—	n.s.
Emotional security	3	2	2	18	5	7	2	.04	.02	—	n.s.
Self-control	3	1	3	15	10	6	5	.06	.05	—	n.s.
Independence	2	2	2	44	23	26	10	.21	.11	—	n.s.
Miscellaneous	14	7	11	67	74	53	57	.44	.64		
Σ Instrumental acts	39	39	39	100	100	887	791	7.78	8.49		

levels: child-oriented and adult-oriented (see Appendix Table C.4), although we realize in so doing we have obscured the nuances of control parents discussed. *Child-oriented parental control* includes not forcing, giving freedom of expression to the child, adjusting standards to needs or ability of child, and being lenient. Control of this order is believed to lead to 14 specific values, eight of which are among the highest 20 per cent stressed by parents. Parents give greatest emphasis to beliefs that such control creates emotional security, independence, and obedience in children. Four family values and three moral values are believed to be related to child-oriented parental control.

Parental control labeled *adult-oriented,* that is, more oriented toward the needs of parents, includes strictness, punishing, shaming, rules, and schedules, and is believed to lead to ten goals, all but three of which are values not greatly stressed by parents. Most emphasized are beliefs that adult-oriented control makes children obedient and gives them emotional security. A few parents believe that this kind of control makes children nonaggressive, and a very few that it makes them aggressive.

It is clear that parents differ in beliefs about the kind of control to use with children to attain obedience and emotional security, because both kinds of control are thought to lead to these values. The difference in approach to goals is striking in the following two excerpts:

Child-oriented control: I think it is better for me as a parent to suffer a little discomfort or criticism by the child, . . . not restricting or restraining him . . . . It will make for a healthier—emotionally healthier—child.

Adult-oriented control: You should discipline your children, it gives them a sense of security. . . . When children are not furnished positive leadership they flounder, and they're confused and insecure.

Both mothers and fathers emphasize adult-oriented control more in relation to obedience, and child-oriented control more in relation to emotional security. The only difference that reaches statistical significance is the mothers' greater emphasis on beliefs that child-oriented control brings emotional security to children ($t = 2.84$; $p < .01$). In a third of the families, both the mother and the father believe that child-oriented control helps to make children emotionally secure.

If we consider the beliefs of individual parents, rather than the beliefs of either mothers or fathers as a group, we can determine the number of parents who stress only one type of control in all beliefs, and the number who stress one or the other type, as it is deemed appropriate to the situation. We find that by far the largest number of parents (67 per cent of mothers; 40 per cent of fathers) discuss both child-oriented and adult-oriented control, believing that each is effective in relation to different goals. The number of parents who emphasize only one kind of control in their instrumental beliefs are much smaller: 18 per cent of mothers and 28 per cent of fathers mention only child-oriented control, and 10 per cent of mothers and 18 per cent of fathers mention only adult-oriented control.

Next, we considered the situation within the families to determine to what extent the husband and wife in each family believe in the same kind of control in reference to obtaining their goals. In nearly half of the families (46 per cent), the parents generally seem to agree about control: in one family, both parents mention only adult-oriented control; in two families, both stress child-oriented control; and in 15 families, both father and mother are flexible, believing that child-oriented control is useful for some goals, adult-oriented control for others. The rest of the couples who report instrumental beliefs concerning control do not agree. There are six general patterns of disagreement between husband and wife:

Mo	*Fa*	*Families*
child-oriented	adult-oriented	2
child-oriented	child and adult	2
adult-oriented	child-oriented	1
adult-oriented	child and adult	1
child and adult	child-oriented	7
child and adult	adult-oriented	5

As we can see, there are only three families in which the father and mother believe in completely different control methods. In the rest of the families, one parent believes that either kind of control can be useful, depending on the objective. Thirty-one per cent of the mothers and eight per cent of the fathers show this kind of flexibility, in contrast to their more restricted spouses.

No other instrumental act is believed as useful as parental control. *Parental love and interest,* though mentioned by 82 per cent of the mothers and 62 per cent of the fathers, is not stressed half as much as parental control (see Table 6.4). Parents believe that a parent's affection for his children, or his interest in them, leads to ten different values, five of which are among those most stressed by parents (see Appendix Table C.5). Parents place most emphasis on beliefs that parental affection or interest helps children feel emotionally secure. Next in emphasis, though decidedly less, are beliefs that parental love helps children learn, helps unify the family, and helps obtain good behavior from children.

Mothers and fathers believe that various *teaching methods* are useful in helping children learn desirable behavior. Eight specific goals, three of which are among those most emphasized, are believed to be influenced by parental teaching methods (see Appendix Table C.6). Among these, the methods used in teaching sex education and control of sexual impulses are most stressed. Beginning to teach a child when he is young is believed important for insuring good behavior, obedience, cooperation in the family, manners, and regulation of sexual behavior. The following excerpts illustrate these beliefs:

> Another thing I believe is when the kids is young is to teach them table manners.
>
> I think that children should obey their parents . . . and I think the sooner they learn that lesson, the better off they are.
>
> I think that you have to start [teaching them] real young so a child knows what's right and what's wrong.

Only fathers express beliefs about the usefulness of giving children allowances for a more democratic family life and an appreciation of money values.

About a third of the parents emphasize *parental example* as an important influence on children's behavior. Parental example is believed important for six values: morality, responsibility, religion, tolerance, orderliness, and manners, all of which, except for tolerance, are among the highest 20 per cent of values. The following statements illustrate some of the goals parents believe are affected by parental example:

> It is important for the family to eat together because I think the children learn manners by observation. . . . They watch and they make note of the way you eat.
>
> Children pick up more than we hope they will from the things that parents do and the way that they treat each other—they can't simply act any way they wish to, if they want their children to act in a certain way.
>
> If I expect the children to be honest, I have to be honest, too, even when it hurts.
>
> I feel that my going to church on Sunday gives the children the idea that going to church is a normal part of a person's routine.

Mothers and fathers believe that *feeding techniques* affect five different values: nutrition, health, physical activity, emotional security, and family unity. The greatest emphasis is on beliefs concerning the effect of various kinds of food on nutrition and health. Parents of first babies believe that breast-feeding and demand-feeding aid nutrition, insure health, and provide emotional security (see Appendix Table C.7).

Each of the instrumental acts that we have been discussing is mentioned in connection with more than one value. In addition to these, mothers and fathers report 27 parental practices, each of which relates to the attainment of only one value. (These are grouped under *miscellaneous values* in Table 6.4.) In all, 13 different values, six of which are among the highest 20 per cent of values, are mentioned in connection with these 27 practices (see Appendix Table C.8).

Acts of other socializing agents. Parents believe that other socializing agents also affect the behavior of their children. These other agents include: peer groups, school and education, church and religious groups, television, and the neighborhood. Each of these is related to more than one value. Fathers consistently stress such beliefs more than mothers, and these differences reach a statistical significance of .05 or beyond for school, television, neighborhood, and the general category of "other socializing agents" (see Table 6.4).

We include under *peer groups* all interpersonal experiences involving playmates, neighborhood groups, organized play groups, and school groups in which the social rather than the learning experience is emphasized. Membership in church groups, and experiences in Sunday school or religious schools, are analyzed separately, because here the religious experience, rather than the interpersonal social experience, seems to be stressed.

About a third of the parents believe that peer-group experiences are related to the attainment of 13 different values, four of which (morality, getting along with others, family unity, and emotional security) are among the 20 per cent most emphasized by parents. The beliefs are scattered, no specific value to be attained is mentioned by more than 15 per cent of either the mothers or the fathers. The three values most mentioned as being obtained from peer-group experiences are morality, tolerance, and getting along with others. A few parents mention nonaggression, generosity, and friends, in that order of emphasis. In addition, mothers believe that group experiences help children to develop closer ties to the family, to feel more secure, to learn better in school, and to develop appropriate heterosexual relations. A few fathers believe that these social experiences lead to greater self-confidence. There are a few parents who have negative beliefs about peer-group activities, thinking that they interfere with individual creativity.

The following excerpts illustrate some of the values that parents believe come from associating with peer groups:

> Well, I think if they get along with other people, it has to start in childhood ... by having them play with other children—the rough ones, the nice ones, the mean ones, and the sneaky ones—and learn about people.
>
> If a kid is raised socially ... has some relations socially with groups of children, with other races for a given time, he finds out that there is no difference.
>
> There are a lot of social activities such as the Boy Scouts.... It's the youngsters that don't participate in these activities who are the ones that are in trouble, ... such as stealing.

Eleven different values are mentioned in beliefs concerned with *education* or *school* attendance. Four of these values (getting along with others, independence, enjoyment, and freedom from anxiety) are among the highest 20 per cent of values for either mothers or fathers. The beliefs most frequently mentioned are that education helps one secure a job and get along with people, and that it increases independence. Parents also believe that school makes better citizens, provides new experiences, and increases enjoyment. A few mothers think that education increases family harmony, and a few fathers believe that education leads to greater achievement, self-confidence, and generosity. The various values believed to be gained from education are illustrated by the following excerpts:

> I feel a college education is essential today because just about everybody is going; and if they don't have a degree, it'll make it harder to get into the field they are interested in.
>
> My son, I want him to go all the way through college, even if he comes back and handles the dairy. Just think how much better off he is with all that knowledge. He'd be liked that much more, because he could express himself that much better.
>
> I hope that they go to college.... I think that education helps people enjoy life.
>
> That's one reason we sent [Da 6.8] to nursery school, so that she'll really get on to that sharing and playing together.

Beliefs about going to *church* or belonging to *religious groups* are related to eight specific values and values in general; four of the specific values (morality, getting along with others, emotional security, and education) are among the 20 per cent of values most emphasized by parents. The beliefs are scattered; no one value is mentioned by more than 18 per cent of the parents. The most emphasized beliefs are that experiences in church or with religious groups lead to good behavior and emotional security, and generally help children become what their parents would like them to be. A few parents also believe that attendance at church or religious groups helps a child make friends, and increases his ability to get along with others and to share. There are, as we have mentioned, different opinions about whether religious schools provide better or worse education than public schools. A few examples of values believed to be related to church or religious groups are:

> I think children are naturally a little bit selfish, and maybe try to cheat in school and that sort of thing, and I think a religious background keeps this in check a little more.
>
> I want the children to develop their own concept . . . about religion . . . from me talking, and from going to Sunday school . . . because I think religion can bring a psychological aspect such as peace of mind.
>
> We found that the church benefits the children an awful lot. . . . It helps them very well socially.

About a third of the mothers and half the fathers have beliefs about *television,* relating it to eight values, three of which (emotional security, education, and enjoyment) are among the highest 20 per cent of values. However, almost all the mothers' beliefs, and at least half the fathers', are negative; that is, parents believe television interferes with such values as cooperation in home chores, getting an education, and health. A few fathers believe it incites children to aggression. The positive values that a few fathers relate to television are: education, emotional security, new experiences, and enjoyment. Typical positive or negative values believed to come from television are:

> Television affords good entertainment at inexpensive cost . . . especially in the wintertime, when the children can't go outside, they do enjoy watching television.

[So 8.3] is very interested in travel and the educational-type programs that are available on television, and we encourage him. . . . We feel that travel is a broadening experience, and that many of the programs explaining the basic scientific facts are well done, and that he learns from these.

We found out that watching TV at dinner didn't work out very well. . . . Everyone was not eating as they should. . . . They have a tendency to stop and watch to see what's going on.

We don't want him to watch too much TV. . . . We think it isn't good for the eyes.

Acts of children. Parents believe that if a child learns a certain kind of behavior, this can lead to other desirable goals. They mention eight specific behaviors that lead to more than one goal (see Table 6.4), and another 18 that lead to only one goal each (see Appendix Table C.9).

As control is the most emphasized among instrumental acts of parent behavior, so *obedience* is the most emphasized aspect of child behavior. Parents believe that obedience leads to values in general, as well as to ten specific values, all of which are among those most emphasized by parents. By far the greatest emphasis is on beliefs that obedience insures emotional security (33 per cent of mothers; 21 per cent of fathers) and provides for safety (26 per cent of mothers; 15 per cent of fathers). A few parents believe obedience makes a child more responsible, helps him respect and get along better with people, makes him more religious, gives him enjoyment, and insures family love, unity, and harmony. The following excerpts illustrate some of the values parents believe come through obedience:

When it comes to something that involves a child's safety, I think very strict obedience is required.

I think it's important for children to learn obedience. . . . Then they are more dependable.

I believe that we are placed here on earth to learn obedience, . . . and that if we learn these things here, we shall progress so much the faster in the world to come.

I think obedience is important . . . because they have to learn to accommodate to other people.

Beliefs that learning to take *responsibility,* especially through chores and work, leads to other desirable goals are next in emphasis. They are scattered throughout 11 categories, seven of which are among the 20 per cent of values most emphasized by parents. Parents emphasize most that taking responsibility leads to democracy in family life, an increase in orderliness, and a tendency to greater honesty. Mothers mention family love, and fathers mention obedience, citizenship, and independence. Two or three parents refer to economic values, such as thrift, property, and job, and the importance of responsibility in acquiring a college education.

The very fact that children grow up, *develop,* and have a variety of *experiences* along the way is believed to lead to eight values, three of which (independence, enjoyment, and obedience) are among those most emphasized by parents. Parents stress the belief that control of sex impulses comes with increased maturity. Obedience is emphasized more by fathers, and enjoyment more by mothers. Other goals mentioned (by not more than 8 per cent of parents each) are nonaggression, self-confidence (by fathers), independence, intelligence, and health.

Parents believe that if children have *manners* four other goals, fair-mindedness, self-confidence, getting along with others, and emotional security, will follow. Mothers place greatest emphasis on the belief that manners help in interpersonal relations, while fathers believe that adequate manners make a child feel more self-confident.

Parents believe that the greatest value in *physical activity* or sports is the fun and enjoyment children get out of it; however, they stress almost as much their beliefs that physical activity encourages good behavior and deters masturbation and sex experimentation. Among these values, morality is high in the hierarchy for both mothers and fathers and enjoyment for mothers.

Parents believe that *emotional security* helps in the attainment of good behavior, better health, and increased intelligence. They believe that *self-control* makes children better citizens and more tolerant, and helps them get along with others. The child who has learned to be *independent* is believed to be more emotionally secure (by 41 per cent of mothers and 21 per cent of fathers) and more self-confident. Each of the remaining 18 instrumental acts that concern child behavior is believed to lead to only one goal (see Appendix Table C.9).

Relations between Instrumental Beliefs and Demographic Characteristics

We correlated the parents' demographic characteristics with their instrumental beliefs in terms of both the values and the instrumental acts involved. Tables 6.5 and 6.6 give these correlations,* and Table 6.7 shows the relation of the number of observed significant correlations to the number expected by chance. Although 37.1 per cent of the correlations of demographic characteristics with instrumental beliefs, and 26.7 per cent of the correlations of demographic characteristics with the instrumental acts involved, are significant at the .10 level or beyond, the number of correlations for fathers at the .10 level are fewer than would be expected by chance. Therefore, we will conservatively limit our discussion to those correlations of a statistical significance of .05 or beyond.

The descriptive variable which has the most highly significant correlations with mothers' instrumental beliefs is the number of children in the family, while for fathers, social position and education yield the most highly significant correlations.

There are three ways in which the maturity of a parent may be indicated: by his chronological age, by the number of children he has, and by the age of his oldest child. We found that as mothers have more children, they become more influenced by instrumental beliefs, especially those relating to family values and those incorporating adult-oriented control, and that as they grow older they become more aware of the importance of showing their love for their children. Fathers, in contrast, are more influenced by beliefs concerning the expression of love when their families are smaller.

Mothers with a background of religious consistency emphasize beliefs relative to attaining moral, family, and emotional security values. Fathers from similar backgrounds tend to stress the category of instrumental beliefs as a whole.

Fathers of lower social position (and to some extent those with less education) emphasize instrumental beliefs as a whole, beliefs

* Beliefs about economic values are omitted from the correlations because so few parents discussed such beliefs.

TABLE 6.5. *Correlations between Instrumental Beliefs and Demographic Characteristics of Mothers*

	Age of parent	*Number of children*	*Age of oldest child*	*Consistency in religion*	*Education level*	*Social position*	*Social mobility*
Values attained:							
Moral	−.24	.29[a]	.15	.34[b]	−.16	−.28[a]	−.14
Family	−.03	.63[e]	.25	.36[b]	−.26	−.40[c]	−.20
Egoistic	.04	.00	.17	.10	.11	−.05	−.37[c]
Interpersonal	.13	.18	.08	−.03	.00	.09	.18
Orderly living	−.14	−.11	−.11	.02	−.05	−.01	.07
Biological	.02	.17	.19	−.09	.12	.04	−.34[b]
Play	.26	.16	.14	.14	.40[c]	.12	.22
Emotional security	.00	.11	.07	.32[b]	−.06	−.17	−.09
Education	−.25	−.01	−.01	.18	−.12	.16	−.29[a]
Instrumental acts:							
Child-oriented control	−.04	.02	.11	.09	−.16	−.18	−.09
Adult-oriented control	−.09	.46[d]	.01	.17	.01	.00	−.04
Parental love	.41[d]	.30[a]	.06	.30[a]	−.30[a]	−.02	−.32[b]
Parental example	.02	−.04	−.08	.26	.13	.04	.10
Peer groups	.12	−.02	.15	−.12	.07	−.05	.07
Child obedience	.04	.30[a]	.02	.25	.15	−.10	−.13
Σ Instrumental beliefs	−.06	.38[c]	.27[a]	.24	.00	−.13	−.33[b]

[a] $p < .10$; [b] $p < .05$; [c] $p < .02$; [d] $p < .01$; [e] $p < .001$.

in moral, interpersonal, biological, and educational value categories, and beliefs about the usefulness of peer groups for obtaining values. This is in contrast to the correlations of demographic characteristics with the basic value categories; there we found no significant relationship with fathers' educational level, and only two with social position—fathers of lower social position stress economic values; those of higher social position stress play values. Mothers of lower social position emphasize only beliefs related to family values. Those with more education stress beliefs concerned with play values.

Mothers who have not been upward mobile socially tend to emphasize instrumental beliefs, particularly beliefs related to egoistic and biological values. They also tend to stress the importance of parental love as an instrumental act. Fathers who are less highly mobile socially tend to emphasize beliefs related to family values and the usefulness of parental example in obtaining goals for their children.

TABLE 6.6 *Correlations between Instrumental Beliefs and Demographic Characteristics of Fathers*

	Age of parent	*Number of children*	*Age of oldest child*	*Consistency in religion*	*Education level*	*Social position*	*Social mobility*
Values attained:							
Moral	−.18	.25	.10	.15	−.45[d]	−.39[c]	−.19
Family	−.07	−.11	−.25	−.27[a]	.23	.08	−.33[b]
Egoistic	−.04	−.09	.13	.13	−.14	−.23	.10
Interpersonal	.11	−.07	.14	.03	−.18	−.34[b]	−.25
Orderly living	.00	−.27[a]	−.19	.08	.03	.03	.20
Biological	−.02	.17	.04	.24	−.24	−.37[c]	−.03
Play	.25	−.09	.05	−.18	.15	.24	−.15
Emotional security	.10	−.08	−.17	.08	.22	.13	−.13
Education	−.08	−.22	−.06	.08	−.32[b]	−.33[b]	−.06
Instrumental acts:							
Child-oriented control	.06	.03	−.07	.20	.14	.08	.03
Adult-oriented control	−.02	−.19	.04	−.01	−.24	−.15	.10
Parental love	−.09	−.40[c]	−.15	.04	−.19	−.21	−.07
Parental example	−.14	−.19	−.20	−.04	−.11	−.10	−.34[b]
Peer groups	−.21	−.06	.01	−.13	−.35[b]	−.33[b]	−.15
Child obedience	.02	.09	−.05	.02	.26	.20	−.08
Σ Instrumental beliefs	−.05	.07	.02	.32[b]	−.43[d]	−.58[e]	−.25

[a] $p < .10$; [b] $p < .05$; [c] $p < .02$; [d] $p < .01$; [e] $p < .001$.

No instrumental belief category is as highly related to demographic characteristics of parents as orderly living was found to be in the discussion of values (see Table 5.3, p. 82). The belief category most highly related to demographic characteristics concerns family values (for mothers with larger families, of lower social position, or of greater consistency in religion, and perhaps for fathers of lower social mobility). The instrumental act most highly related is parental love (for older mothers, perhaps for

TABLE 6.7. *Significance of Correlations between Instrumental Beliefs and Demographic Characteristics*

	Values in instrumental beliefs			*Instrumental acts*		
	No. expected by chance	*No. observed*		*No. expected by chance*	*No. observed*	
Level of significance	*(70 r's)*	*Mo (70 r's)*	*Fa (70 r's)*	*(42 r's)*	*Mo (42 r's)*	*Fa (42 r's)*
<.001	.07	1	1	.04	0	0
.001 to .01	.63	2	2	.38	2	0
.01 to .02	.70	2	2	.42	0	1
.02 to .05	2.10	5	5	1.26	1	3
.05 to .10	3.50	4	2	2.10	4	0

those with more children, and of less social mobility, and for fathers with fewer children).

Differences between Mothers and Fathers

Mothers and fathers actually differ very little in the emphasis they place on instrumental beliefs. The few differences in Table 6.1 are at relatively low levels of significance, though the number observed at each level of significance exceeds chance expectancy.

Mothers discuss beliefs related to the family more than fathers ($p < .02$), especially beliefs concerned with the attainment of family harmony ($p < .001$). Mothers appear also to show a slight tendency ($p < .10$) to place greater stress on beliefs related to emotional security. Fathers, on the other hand, tend to emphasize more than mothers beliefs relating to moral and economic values (both $p < .05$), and appear to show a slight tendency to stress beliefs related to egoistic values more ($p < .10$).

With these few exceptions, there are no significant differences between mothers and fathers in emphasis on instrumental beliefs. They do not differ significantly in the instrumental acts related to parent or child behavior; but in three of the five categories of beliefs relating to other socializing agents there are significant differences: fathers place greater stress on beliefs that school, television, and neighborhood influence the behavior of their children.

Summary and Comments

All the parents in this study were influenced by beliefs about the ways in which various values or goals might be obtained for their children. However, they differed greatly in the degree to which they seem guided by these beliefs. In addition, there seems to be little relation between a parent's emphasis on a particular value and his emphasis on instrumental beliefs about obtaining that value.

In general, both mothers and fathers gave greatest emphasis to beliefs about how to obtain values in three general categories: biological, emotional security, and moral. Of these three categories, only one, moral, was highly emphasized as a value category.

Within these three categories of instrumental beliefs, the subcategories related to obtaining nutrition, sex regulation, and health (biological values), obedience and morality (moral values), and mental health (emotional security values) elicited the greatest number of mentions from both parent groups.

There were comparatively few beliefs reported concerning two-thirds of the most-stressed value subcategories (for example, family unity, manners, religion, getting along with others, and responsibility). It may be that parents are not sure how to go about achieving such goals for their children. But it is also possible that parents take their beliefs about some of these goals for granted, and therefore do not think of them as influences on their behavior. For example, there was little emphasis on beliefs about how to teach children manners, but parental example was mentioned more often than any other means. For many parents, the influence of parental example may be so much an accepted fact that they failed to mention it. If so, this would help to explain the relatively few mentions of parental example in instrumental beliefs as a whole.

On the other hand, parents sometimes take their goals for granted, and stress beliefs related to a value that has been given little emphasis. Parents' concern with beliefs about health, nutrition, and sex regulation, values that were seldom mentioned, would seem to support this suggestion. One senses as one reads these interviews that parents sometimes have values without having clear-cut beliefs about how to acquire them; on the other hand, that some parents are influenced by instrumental beliefs without being too sure of the ends to which such beliefs may lead.

In general, the parents believe that their own behavior determines how their children will develop. They believe strongly in the efficacy of parental control, but differ about whether child-oriented or adult-oriented control is more effective in securing obedience or in providing emotional security. Mothers as a group believe that child-oriented control leads to emotional security; and both mothers and fathers believe that it helps develop independence in children, whereas adult-oriented control is considered more useful in preventing aggression.

Most of the parents were flexible about methods of control,

believing that each type has its appropriate uses. In about half of the families both parents were in general agreement about types of control, believing in child-oriented or adult-oriented control as they deemed it necessary for a particular goal. In those families in which mother and father stressed different methods of control, mothers were more often flexible, whereas fathers stressed only one kind of control.

The parents placed much less emphasis on the usefulness of letting the child know of the parent's interest in and affection for him, except in connection with emotional security. They also seemed almost unaware of the subtle way in which a parent's behavior becomes a model for the child's, setting the standards and goals toward which he strives.

Just as control was the most stressed instrumental act in parent behavior, so obedience was the most stressed instrumental act in child behavior. Parents also believed that responsibility and manners, as well as other characteristics such as independence and self-control, lead to other desirable behavior in children.

Relatively less emphasis was given to the effect of other socializing agents on children's behavior. Fathers believed in the effectiveness of school, television, and neighborhood more than mothers. Both parent groups seem convinced that such experiences have beneficial effects, but there was no strong consensus on what these effects are, except perhaps for beliefs that peer groups, church, or school help children learn to get along with others, to share, and to make friends.

The fathers who are most influenced by instrumental beliefs (in various categories) were those with less education and of lower social position. The mothers who were most strongly influenced by instrumental beliefs were those who were older or had larger numbers of children.

VII
Descriptive Beliefs

Descriptive beliefs, unlike instrumental beliefs, do not concern the ways and means to achieve ends, and therefore are not specifically related to values. Each person, as he develops, gradually builds descriptive beliefs about the world he lives in. These beliefs help him understand, predict, and in some measure control the forces in his environment, and thus bring some feeling of security into his life. Descriptive beliefs represent facts—facts that enter into many parental practices, either explicitly or implicitly. Children are noisy; a fever is a sign of illness; adolescents strive for independence; praise is constructive; a baby is too young to spank —all of these are descriptive beliefs. The verb *is* and its derivatives often provide a key to the recognition of descriptive beliefs.

The descriptive beliefs of any person include many general convictions (for example, about God, illness, politics, government) that may indirectly affect his behavior with his child, but we have selected for analysis only those descriptive beliefs that parents discuss as directly influencing their behavior with their children.

We coded the 3,294 descriptive beliefs reported into six major categories: characteristics of children; heredity and environment; learning; reward; punishment; and control. The distributions are presented in Table 7.1. The total number of descriptive beliefs is about equally divided between mothers and fathers, but, as the percentage scores show, fathers lay considerably more stress than mothers on the influence of these beliefs. Practically all parents are influenced by beliefs concerning characteristics of children, learning, and parental control, and only a few fail to discuss heredity and environment.

Beliefs about Characteristics of Children

Beliefs about the characteristics of children are divided into three sections: characteristics of children in general; more specific characteristics of children of a certain age or level of development; and characteristics of children affected by individual or sex differences (see Table 7.1).

General characteristics of children. Beliefs in this category refer to what parents think children in general are like. Some parents believe children can't sit still, or that they forget easily, or

Table 7.1. *Descriptive Beliefs*

	Per cent reporting		*Number of Codings*		*Mean percentage score*		*Percentage score difference*	
Beliefs about	*Mo*	*Fa*	*Mo*	*Fa*	*Mo*	*Fa*	*t*	*p*
Characteristics of children								
In general	90	95	199	194	1.65	2.08	1.92	<.10
By age and development	95	97	315	241	2.29	2.72	—	n.s.
Differences in children	92	90	170	113	1.34	1.25	—	n.s.
Individual	72	44	44	29	.40	.29	—	n.s.
Sex	82	79	126	84	.94	.96	—	n.s.
Σ Characteristics of children	97	100	684	548	5.28	6.05	—	n.s.
Heredity and environment								
Heredity (primary)	72	56	76	54	.54	.57	—	n.s.
Environment (primary)	54	56	34	49	.31	.69	2.47	<.02
Interaction	21	26	11	15	.08	.16	2.21	<.05
Σ Heredity and environment	85	85	121	118	.93	1.42	2.12	<.05
Learning								
Ability	31	41	16	21	.13	.28	—	n.s
Readiness	79	87	101	132	.90	1.43	2.30	<.05
Age, maturity	64	79	66	90	.55	1.02	2.75	<.01
Other	38	44	35	42	.35	.41	—	n.s.
Process	92	95	179	201	1.43	2.14	3.04	<.01
Practice	74	77	92	65	.74	.67	—	n.s.
Example	67	82	61	102	.50	1.10	3.84	<.001
Reasoning	13	31	5	21	.03	.25	2.85	<.01
Other	33	23	21	13	.16	.12	—	n.s.
For future	49	38	45	20	.33	.20	—	n.s.
Σ Learning	100	100	341	374	2.79	4.05	3.66	<.001

TABLE 7.1 *(cont.)*.

Beliefs about	*Per cent reporting*		*Number of Codings*		*Mean percent-age score*		*Percentage score difference*	
	Mo	*Fa*	*Mo*	*Fa*	*Mo*	*Fa*	*t*	*p*
Reward								
General (positive)	18	26	10	13	.12	.16	—	n.s.
Psychological (positive)	41	44	22	22	.19	.21	—	n.s.
Material (positive) ...	21	23	10	12	.10	.11	—	n.s.
Σ Positive effects	51	54	42	47	.41	.48	—	n.s.
Σ Negative effects	10	21	5	11	.04	.10	—	n.s.
Σ Reward	56	64	47	58	.45	.58	—	n.s.
Punishment								
Physical (positive)	51	62	36	40	.38	.42	—	n.s.
Physical (negative) ...	41	72	31	61	.28	.64	3.55	<.001
Social (positive)	44	49	25	33	.21	.37	2.06	<.05
Social (negative)	36	13	23	8	.19	.07	2.71	<.01
Verbal (positive)	33	41	17	21	.13	.23	—	n.s.
Verbal (negative)	31	23	17	12	.12	.15	—	n.s.
Deprivation (positive).	41	41	17	27	.15	.37	2.39	<.05
Deprivation (negative).	5	3	2	1	.02	.01	—	n.s.
Restitution (positive) .	5	13	3	6	.02	.09	—	n.s.
In general (positive) ..	13	38	5	21	.05	.29	2.83	<.01
In general (negative) .	10	13	5	7	.03	.05	—	n.s.
In general (qualified) .	46	44	27	34	.24	.35	—	n.s.
Σ Punishment	97	97	208	271	1.82	3.02	4.47	<.001
Positive effects	85	95	103	148	.94	1.77	3.73	<.001
Negative effects	59	77	78	89	.64	.92	1.93	<.10
Control								
Method	87	92	105	138	1.00	1.43	2.17	<.05
Inhibition (positive).	36	56	18	33	.16	.34	2.32	<.05
Inhibition (negative)	21	24	11	14	.09	.13	—	n.s.
Reasoning (positive).	51	59	27	41	.27	.46	1.88	<.10
Consistency (positive)	46	31	26	23	.25	.20	—	n.s.
Insistence (positive).	10	15	5	6	.06	.07	—	n.s.
Insistence (negative).	21	18	9	8	.07	.08	—	n.s.
Other	21	26	9	13	.10	.15	—	n.s.
Level	90	87	81	103	.72	1.03	2.14	<.05
Permissive	23	21	13	13	.11	.15	—	n.s.
Lenient	44	31	19	22	.15	.18	—	n.s.
Firm	36	36	23	21	.21	.22	—	n.s.
Strict	10	31	4	17	.04	.18	2.74	<.01
Authoritarian	46	56	22	30	.21	.30	—	n.s.
Comparing mother and father	64	72	39	58	.37	.68	2.06	<.05
Strictness	39	54	17	28	.16	.31	1.94	<.10
Responsibility	26	28	14	15	.14	.17	—	n.s.
Disagreements	18	28	8	15	.07	.20	1.74	<.10
Σ Control	97	97	225	299	2.09	3.14	3.07	<.01
Σ Descriptive beliefs ...	100	100	1,626	1,668	13.36	18.26	4.69	<.001

that they are selfish, or that they are persons in their own right. We divided such beliefs into eight subcategories (see Appendix Table D.1). Fathers appear to emphasize beliefs about children's general characteristics slightly more than mothers.

The beliefs discussed by 72 per cent of mothers and 64 per cent of fathers, and most emphasized by both mothers and fathers, are those about the *intelligence* or mental functioning of children. However, parents do not agree on the extent of children's ability to think and understand. Some believe that a child is intelligent enough to understand what parents want, others that a child's intelligence is immature and limited. For the most part, these beliefs are specific, in the sense that they are related to a particular situation encountered by the parent. But for some parents, beliefs about intelligence seem to be rationalizations for practices stemming from other sources. Mo 28, for example, who was very high in values for conformity, safety, regulation of sexual behavior, and achievement, laid great emphasis on her belief that children understand what a parent wants and that they know right from wrong. This belief seemed to make her more comfortable when she physically punished her only child, a boy of eighteen months.

On the other hand, other parents who express beliefs about children's mental immaturity seem to gain these beliefs from experience. Mo 29, for example, with two children, was among the highest 20 per cent in values for education, intelligence, and citizenship. Telling about her son's tendency to interrupt when other people are talking at school, she said:

> The teacher said when he interrupts you, he should . . . be made to wait for his turn. . . . At first we started out really making him wait, and then [when we finished] I would tell him "Okay [So 7.5]," and then he would be so furious he'd say, "Well, I don't even remember what it was." So now I try to cut it off as soon as possible and let him talk. . . . I don't think we should wait too long afterward to let him talk because I think children are different from grown-ups. Grown-ups can wait and still hold in their minds what they want to talk about, but I don't think it's the same way with children. It seemed like he would forget or get discouraged.

Some parents (41 per cent of mothers; 31 per cent of fathers) discuss beliefs about children's lack of *impulse control*: they can't sit still long, they can't wait, they can't keep from talking, they are unpredictable. Fa 17, with two girls, six and four, said: "You can't expect a normal child with a healthy body, full of pep [to keep still on a rainy day]. They can't—it's like a sizzling firecracker. They just have to go off."

Thirty-eight per cent of the parents were influenced in rearing their children by what they believe to be the basic or *intrinsic needs* of children, especially dependency needs for succorance, and security needs for protection, structure, and limits.

A third of the mothers, and almost half of the fathers, mention beliefs about *children's relations with their parents,* but these beliefs are given relatively slight emphasis and are widely scattered. Fathers emphasize them more than mothers ($t = 2.45$, $p < .02$). A few parents seem to believe that children feel aggression toward their parents. A few believe that children are closer to their mothers, that they fluctuate in relation to mother and father, or that a child may identify with the feelings of a parent.

Relatively slight emphasis is given to beliefs about children's *interests,* likes, or dislikes, and less than a third of the parents discuss them. There appears to be a tendency for the parents in 19 of the 22 families that have three or more children to discuss these beliefs, and to verify their beliefs about children in general by referring to their own offspring. These parents mention children's interest in stories and in other children, their likes and dislikes in food, and their desire to know more about themselves. Mentions of children's interests are mainly in relation to a specific age or developmental level, as we shall see later.

More fathers than mothers discuss beliefs about sibling relations, and they emphasize them more ($t = 2.13$, $p < .05$). Most of these mothers and fathers believe that there is hostility between siblings as evidenced in friction, teasing, competition and jealousy, but a few parents believe that brothers and sisters have a close unity, or that relations improve with age. One father, discussing his fourteen-year-old son and twelve-year-old daughter said:

> Well, you know they fight us together now. I feel this is very desirable because it brings them a little bit closer. When there is trouble—trouble with us, you know—they stick together. Otherwise,

when there is no trouble with us, they fight each other as before. But their fighting is only teasing. I feel this is a transition period, and before long it will change to a desirable relationship.

Some parents discuss beliefs about *"problem" behavior* in children: children cheat, are selfish, have fears. Fathers appear to emphasize such beliefs slightly more than mothers ($t = 1.76$, $p < .10$). A few parents believe that certain so-called problem behavior, for example, testing limits or throwing tantrums, is normal for children. Thumb-sucking is the problem behavior most discussed, fathers emphasizing it more than mothers ($t = 2.77$, $p < .01$). Parents vary in their beliefs about the causes of thumb-sucking, some stating that it is normal and to be expected, others attributing it to the sucking impulse, not getting enough food, teething, frustration, or insecurity. Parents also have various beliefs about the effects of thumb-sucking: some think it has no particular effect—good or bad—if it stops at an early age; some think it provides emotional security or comfort; and some think it deforms the mouth or has a bad psychological effect.

Age and development of children. Most of the parents are influenced by beliefs about children that are in some way related to chronological age or to a developmental level. At first we separated these beliefs into two groups—those that specifically mentioned a chonological age, and those that mentioned a developmental level—because we wanted to compare the parents who stressed one or the other. Unfortunately, there were too few codings for this kind of comparison, so we had to combine ages and developmental levels, although we realize that the developmental levels are not necessarily synonymous with the chronological ages we assign to them. The beliefs under age and development of children are divided into five categories: infancy, early childhood, late childhood, adolescence, and nonspecific levels (see Appendix Table D.2).

Beliefs about *infancy* tend to be emphasized by mothers and fathers in the five families with first babies; the 12 other families with infants less than two years old did not stress these beliefs as much. Two areas of beliefs about infants are mentioned most: the baby's activities and interests, and his immaturity. Parents are influenced by their beliefs that babies like to mouth and suck, touch and manipulate, explore visually, and be active physically. Although some parents mention the immaturities of babies, a few others—all but one parents of first babies—believe that a baby is mature in certain ways; for example, he makes his wants known; he cries for a reason.

More families (28) had children at the *early childhood* level of development than at any other level; in all there were 39 children from two to five years of age. This is probably why more parents mention beliefs about this level of development than about any other level. However, both mothers and fathers put less emphasis on beliefs about young children than they do on beliefs about adolescence.

The beliefs about young children can be grouped into four categories: lack of impulse control (they cannot wait, push limits, take what they want, are aggressive or stubborn), activity level, maturities, and immaturities. Some parents believe that children of this age are both intellectually immature and dependent. Other parents are influenced by beliefs about the growing maturity of young children: that they know right and wrong, can understand rules and obey them, are easy to keep on schedule, and can walk, feed themselves, talk, and understand speech.

Almost two-thirds of the families (64 per cent) had a total of 44 children between the ages of six and twelve (*late childhood*). However, this period of development is the least emphasized in both mothers' and fathers' descriptive beliefs. The few beliefs that parents mention about this stage of development seem to indicate that it is a relatively relaxed one for parents. They believe this to be "a good age," one in which children are full of energy and show increasing maturity, understanding the demands of parents, knowing right from wrong, and willing to obey. Their immaturities are mainly intellectual, and are evidenced when they attempt to deal with scientific or social questions. The beliefs most emphasized concern the growing independence of children during this period. A few parents believe that the advancing maturity, increasing independence, and physical energy of children lead to such problems as lying, getting into trouble, disobeying, and being boistrous.

Although only 10 per cent of the families had children of an age indicating they might be close to the period of adolescence, beliefs about *adolescence* are stressed more than those about any other level of development. The emphasis on such beliefs is probably somewhat influenced by the fact that an additional 18 per cent of the families had children over ten but below twelve years of age, and some of these, judging from their parents' descriptions, were undoubtedly early developers already in the period of adolescence. Parents discuss, in this order of emphasis, general developmental characteristics of adolescents, their relations with parents, and appropriate adolescent behavior. A few fathers believe that adolescence is just a normal phase in development when changes occur in the child's behavior, but most mothers and fathers believe that adolescence is a time of problems: for example, moodiness, increased sensitivity, and delinquency.

The few parents who discuss beliefs about somatic development during adolescence had either a daughter or son already showing physical changes. These parents believe that certain physical characteristics, mainly increased growth in height and appearance of acne, indicate the onset of adolescent development. Other physical characteristics are also mentioned: the increased width of hips, changes in facial contours, voice change, appearance of facial and body hair, breast development, and onset of menses. Interestingly enough, most of these physical signs of adolescence occur not at the onset of the period but toward the middle (breast development, onset of menses) or even late in the period (voice change, acne, increased facial and bodily hair, change in facial contours).

About a fifth of the parents discuss beliefs concerning adolescents' relations with peers of both sexes. Beliefs emphasize the adolescent's need to belong to a group, to conform to the standards of his peers, and to have friends for emotional support. Parents' beliefs about the adolescent's interest in the opposite sex range from a belief that adolescent boys have no time for girls to a belief that this is the time for girls to "go steady." Most of the parents who express beliefs in this area believe that adolescents are shyly interested in the opposite sex and that they like to socialize in mixed groups. It seems quite evident to us that the parents' beliefs about peer relations were directly influenced by their own children's particular level of adolescent development.

Very few parents (13 per cent of mothers, 8 per cent of fathers) mention beliefs about the interests of adolescents. Again, those that did seem to base their beliefs on the behavior of their own children rather than on more general principles underlying adolescent development. These parents believe that adolescents of both sexes are interested in personal appearance, that boys are concerned with their own strength and with sports, and that both sexes show an increased interest in adult-like recreations (smoking, drinking, driving automobiles) and in general prefer real things to the toys of their childhood.

Some of these parents (21 per cent of mothers, 18 per cent of fathers) were influenced by beliefs about appropriate adolescent behavior. These beliefs touch on such matters as smoking, drinking, swearing, driving, relations with the opposite sex (including "petting" and marriage), and what the parents call "sophisticated" behavior, for example, using lipstick. We grouped these beliefs into three general categories: conservative (e.g., never smoke, or postpone smoking), moderate (e.g., smoking should always be in moderation), and liberal (e.g., the child should be free to make his own decision about smoking as he matures). Although the beliefs of these parents are distributed over all three categories, showing a wide difference of opinion on such matters, there is a heavy weighting toward conservatism: of 88 codings, 51 per cent are in the conservative category, 29 per cent in the moderate, and 20 per cent in the category allowing freedom of choice.

Some parents (22 per cent) discuss beliefs about the changes that take place in the parent-child relationship during adolescence. All except one parent (who believes adolescents want parents to provide some structure or control) believe that these changes take place because of the child's general desire for independence; they noted such specific expressions of independence as questioning parental rules, acting hostile when disciplined, objecting to being with parents, and wanting to do their own shopping and choose their own friends.

A number of parents' beliefs did not refer to a specific age or developmental level, but instead implied that there are certain *stages* children go through. These are included in the general category in Appendix Table D.2. Certain characteristics of the stages are mentioned. First, parents believe that these stages are something a child "goes through"; they do not last, and the child will outgrow them. As one mother said, "They'll grow out of a certain stage and into another one that doesn't last." Second, parents believe that these stages are universal—all children go through them. As one mother said, "They all go through this 'I'm not going to eat' stage." Third, parents imply, if they do not state outright, that there is very little that can be done about such behavior; a parent must just wait (and suffer!) until the stage passes, that is, until the child outgrows it. One mother said, "Parents shouldn't fight behavior problems—you just have to wait until they get past that stage."

Of the 46 specific items of behavior related to stages that are mentioned, 34 (74 per cent) refer to behavior parents disapprove of. A few examples are: not eating, using bad words, talking back, sulking, being independent, masturbating, being belligerent, writing on walls, wetting the bed, and being forgetful. The few stages that do not concern "problem" behavior include such behavior as playing with another child, eating well, competing in sports, wanting to be cuddled, forming ideas and being interested in birthday parties.

Parents, 28 per cent of mothers and 39 per cent of fathers, also express beliefs that include such indefinite terms as "at an early age," "when he is old enough," and "too young," indicating a not-too-specific level of development. (These are also included in the general category, Appendix Table D.2.) For the most part, these beliefs focus on the time when certain behavior may be expected. Examples of such beliefs are: "It isn't good for children to memorize the catechism at an early age"; "Children can learn to eat out when they are old enough"; "A younger child is more interested in playing with his father."

As parents discuss the influence of beliefs about various levels of development of children, they usually stress either the *maturities* or the *immaturities* of a certain age. An analysis of parents' beliefs emphasizing maturity or immaturity of all ages or developmental levels is shown in Table 7.2. Both mothers and fa-

TABLE 7.2. *Emphasis on Beliefs Concerning Maturity or Immaturity of Children at Various Levels of Development*

	Per cent reporting		*Number of codings*		*Mean percentage score*		*Percentage score difference*	
	Mo	*Fa*	*Mo*	*Fa*	*Mo*	*Fa*	*t*	*p*
Maturity	62	67	57	44	.46	.51	—	n.s.
Immaturity	85	80	116	93	1.00	.94	—	n.s.

thers stress immaturity of children much more than maturity (mothers, $t = 3.11$, $p < .01$; fathers, $t = 2.62$, $p < .02$). It seems parents are more influenced by beliefs about what children do not know and cannot do than by beliefs about their emerging abilities and independence.

Individual and sex differences. Most of the parents express beliefs about sex or individual differences between children (see Table 7.1). The greatest emphasis (74 per cent of all such codings) is given to sex differences. Some parents (44 per cent of mothers, 23 per cent of fathers) believe that there are no differences between boys and girls during infancy and childhood, in temperament and personality, in obedience, or in learning. However, two-thirds of the parents believe that there are differences between boys and girls in specific areas of behavior (see Appendix Table D.3). Some parents believe that during childhood and adolescence girls take on feminine roles and boys masculine roles. They believe that boys have stronger drives, are more active physically, and are noisier, dirtier, more aggressive, more jealous, more likely to masturbate, less interested in studying, and more difficult for mothers to understand. Boys are believed to be more obedient and, by some parents, to have more self-control. Girls, on the other hand, are believed to be more mature for their age, more conforming, and more creative, but also more underhanded.

Parents are not as influenced by beliefs about the individuality of children as by beliefs about age and developmental and sex differences. Still, 72 per cent of mothers and 44 per cent of fathers mention such beliefs. They are convinced that there are genuine differences between children in the same family, and that these differences influence their parental behavior. About a third of the mothers (31 per cent) and a few fathers (8 per cent) are particularly concerned with the differences between children in their responses to the demands, requirements, or teaching of parents. One mother said:

I just think some children react differently than others. We're training our little girl to sleep all night without going to the bathroom, and she's pretty good. But with my other child I had to wait a lot longer; . . . even though you try to go about it the same general way and at about the same age, it's a lot different.

Parents emphasize various differences between children: personality, physical development, motor skills, mental development, and ability to learn; in addition, they slightly mention curiosity, eating habits, drives, and behavior problems.

Beliefs about Heredity and Environment

We grouped the 239 beliefs about the effect of heredity or environment upon the child's development into three categories: those implying that heredity is the primary or sole determinant; those implying that environment is the primary or sole determinant; and those implying that development is determined by interaction of the two. (See Table 7.1.) Very few parents express beliefs concerning the interaction of hereditary tendencies with environmental conditions. Most of them believe that the causes of behavior lie either in what the child inherits or in what he experiences in life.

There are some differences between fathers and mothers. Fathers emphasize environmental influences significantly more than mothers, although about as many mothers as fathers discuss such beliefs. Fathers also emphasize the interaction of hereditary and environmental factors significantly more than mothers, though the number of parents discussing interaction is relatively small.

Mo 1, who had four children, was one of the parents who discussed heredity only. She mentions her beliefs about heredity frequently and emphatically, saying at one point:

I was once of the environmental school, but I really think there's a little to be said now for the innate character of the child. [Da 3.3] was born this way [dominating], and [So 7.4] was born the way he is, smiling and happy. [Da 3.3] screamed with colic, the only child who caused trouble. She was nursed and she was wanted. I don't think it was my attitude that did it—that's one school of thought, and I don't believe it. She was that way in the hospital, screaming. She grew up into being a demanding, screaming sort of child.

Other parents discuss beliefs only about environmental influences. One father was impressed with the difference in temperament between his four small boys. He said:

I think it may be due to the attention that the kid gets from the parents. We know that the oldest one, when he was a baby, was really spoiled, him being the first one. We haven't looked into the second one as much as the oldest one. The third one, whenever he cries or anything like that, we just shun it, just let him cry until he gets over it.

About half the parents explained different aspects of behavior or personality of children in different ways, some mentioning heredity or environment, others mentioning heredity or interaction of heredity and environment, some environment and interaction, and so forth (see Appendix Table D.4). Fa 16, for example, discusses the differences among his three preschool boys several times. At one point he discussed the tendency of his oldest boy (So 4.5) to dominate, and the tendency of his second son (So 3.1) to be more affectionate and somewhat slower to take offense. He believed heredity accounted for these differences:

I would say it is just a different combination of genes. . . . As we look at the two of us [husband and wife] and our four parents, he [So 3.1] tends to reflect the temperament of my father. . . . My mother is very nervous and always has been. [So 4.5] tends to reflect my mother. . . . [So. 3.1] just happened to get the genes for a different temperament, a real calm temperament. We can't recall any different ways he was treated.

Later, he contrasted these two boys' responses to the birth of a younger sibling. So 3.1 had shown more jealousy than So 4.5; and when asked how he explained such differences, the father stressed the interaction of heredity and environment:

I'd say that some combination of different heredity and different environment, in the sense that out of their basic selves they select certain things to respond to out of their environment. We tried to keep this as near as possible alike for all of them but they make a different selection of what they respond to.

When he discussed the differences between the behavior of boys and girls before adolescence, he emphasized the influence of environment: "I still think at these early ages that the difference [between boys and girls] is essentially the way they are treated, the kinds of actions that they come to see are expected of them."

We analyzed the records to see what aspects of child development or behavior parents believe to be determined by heredity, by environment, or by an interaction of the two. In general, parents are most concerned about how personality is determined, even though they do not agree about the determinants. The greatest emphasis is placed on beliefs that heredity is the basic influence on a child's personality, not only on personality as a whole, but also specifically on selfishness, hostility, determination, anxiety, sociability, and tendencies to be cheerful and happy. The quotation from Fa 16 on page 135 illustrates such beliefs well. Fa 3, on the other hand, was one of those who favored environment; he said, "The emotional characteristics of the child are probably determined by the child's own environment, his own playmates, school environment, and of course the home environment."

When asked to explain the differences in personality between her four children, Mo 23 stated her belief in the interaction of heredity and environment:

> Very definitely the difference is a question of temperament, what they've been born with, because I think these traits have shown up within a few months after they were born. And I think then, too, the environment, the differences as time goes by in our circumstances, and the differences in their sibling relationships. The effect of grandparents' personalities, too, has made some difference; my father, who had a strong personality, had a strong relationship with [Da 9.8].

Such differences are found for nearly all the aspects of child behavior the parents discussed. There is little unanimity in beliefs about the basic causes of behavior in general, or of such specific behavior characteristics as selfishness, intellectual ability, obedience, sex differences, health, or likeness to parents.

Beliefs about Learning

All the parents had beliefs about learning. The mean percentage scores for both mothers and fathers are the highest of any descriptive-belief category (see Table 7.1). Fathers emphasize beliefs about children's learning significantly more than mothers. We divided beliefs about learning into four general categories: ability to learn; readiness for learning; process of learning; and learning as preparation for the future.

Ability to learn. The parents who discuss whether children learn almost unanimously believe that children can learn or like to learn. Some add qualifications concerning the time necessary for learning, or the reluctance of adolescent boys to learn.

Readiness for learning. Over four-fifths of the parents discuss beliefs about the age or conditions that influence children's readiness for learning. Fathers emphasize these beliefs significantly more than mothers. Parents had specific beliefs about what children are able to learn at different ages or stages of development, especially during infancy and early childhood. Parents (36 per cent) believe that the infant begins to learn discipline, right and wrong, motor skills, and elimination control. Mothers (33 per cent) and fathers (39 per cent) believe that early childhood is the appropriate time for children to learn eating skills, self-care, emotional control, obedience, and complete elimination control.

About a fourth of the fathers, but only a few mothers, discuss beliefs that children in late childhood are ready to learn to get along with other children, to help with chores, to study school subjects, and to learn about the world around them. A few mothers (5 per cent) and fathers (10 per cent) have beliefs about adolescents' learning: that they can learn about science and communism, and how to study independently, and that adolescent girls learn about cooking and housekeeping. Some parents (26 per cent of mothers, 49 per cent of fathers) do not state their beliefs about readiness for learning in terms of ages or stages, but instead emphasize that learning should take place when a child is "ready" or "able" to learn.

Parents also have beliefs about other influences that facilitate or interfere with readiness for learning. The facilitating influences include: the authority of the teacher, the child's trust or confidence in the teacher, and the child's emotional security, self-confidence, independence, and ability to compete with his classmates. Influences interfering with readiness for learning include: fatigue, emotional problems, lack of social adjustment, parental pressure, and parental indulgence.

Process of learning. More emphasis is given to the process of learning than to any other aspect of learning, especially by fathers, who emphasize learning by example or imitation and learning by reasoning or understanding significantly more than mothers. Learning by practice or experience is the most emphasized process by mothers, and learning by example or imitation the most emphasized by fathers. There are also a few scattered beliefs, such as "visual learning is more efficient than auditory learning," or "being told specifically what to do is important." These excerpts illustrate beliefs about how children learn:

> All kids are little monkeys, they like to "ape" adults in just about every respect. This is how they learn.
>
> If you explain, I think they will absorb it more. They'll think it over and it'll just kind of stay with them more, than just telling them.
>
> I'd rather see him feed himself than me feeding him. It will teach him to eat by himself.

Learning for the future. Some mothers and fathers emphasize the importance of learning as a preparation for the future. One mother, who stressed such beliefs more than other parents, said:

> If they learn to obey their parents—they just can't go through life doing what they want to do—if [Da 8.0] learns to do the things I tell her . . . it will be easier for her when she grows up. . . . If they grow up and get in the Army . . . and they're given an order and they don't carry it out right away, it could cost them their life . . . but if they are used to having something told and have learned to do it right away, it's better.

Later she told us that she believed her son's learning about guns in the Scouts was important because "if they ever come across something that would mean their life . . . if they didn't know how to shoot this gun, well, it would certainly come in handy."

Beliefs about Reward

Beliefs about reward are closely related to beliefs about children's learning, but in the discussions of parents, reward is more often related to beliefs about acquiescence and dependability, i.e., the child's doing what he already knows how to do. Such behaviors must also be learned, but the parents tend to perceive them as a function of obedience or responsibility (the child's doing what he has already learned is right) rather than of learning. Parents discuss beliefs about reward in general, and about psychological rewards (love, praise, attention, thanks) and material rewards (gifts, money, privileges) in particular (see Table 7.1). Only a few parents believe that rewards are neither useful nor advisable. Over half of the parents emphasize the usefulness of rewards, especially psychological rewards.

The father with the highest percentage score on beliefs about rewards (2.25) stressed only their positive effects:

> Praise is so effective and ... obviously much more constructive than a critical type of training. ... I learned as a youngster with dogs. ... I'd teach them a lot of tricks, ... and you soon learn that reward is about the only thing that's effective ... because punishment really confuses an animal when you are teaching him. They're just so lost, but when you reward them for doing something, then they learn very rapidly. And so I have that little bit of experience, in addition to discussing situations about [Da 4.1] with my wife, ... to make me believe that rewards are more effective than punishment.

Beliefs about Punishment

Most of the parents said they were influenced by their beliefs about punishment—both punishment in general and specific kinds of punishment such as spanking, sending a child to his room, scolding, keeping him home from a party, or making him pay for a window he has broken. We grouped the kinds of punishment discussed into five categories: physical, social, verbal, deprivation, and restitution (see Table 7.1). Punishment is discussed by more parents and is emphasized more than reward — four times as much by mothers and over five times as much by fathers. The differences between the scores for reward and for punishment are highly significant (mothers, $t = 5.97$, $p < .001$; fathers, $t = 8.57$, $p < .001$). The positive effects of punishment are stressed more than the negative effects, but the difference in emphasis for mothers is slight ($t = 1.77$, $p < .10$), whereas the difference for fathers is highly significant ($t = 4.03$, $p < .001$). Fathers emphasize beliefs about punishment a great deal more than mothers, especially their beliefs in the positive effects of punishment.

Physical punishment. Punishment by whipping, spanking, or slapping the hands, face, or buttocks with hands, belt, strap, or whip is discussed by both mothers and fathers, but both the percentage reporting and the emphasis given are greater for fathers than for mothers. However, the most striking difference between the two groups is the greater number of fathers who strongly disapprove of physical punishment.

The parent who perhaps believes most wholeheartedly in physical punishment (mainly in whipping with a switch or strap) is a mother of Mexican background with seven children between the ages of one and eight. She told her interviewer:

> You have to spank them, once in a while you have to spank them. That's my way of thinking. If you don't spank them, . . . sooner or later they take over. . . . They don't mind you. They're not afraid of you. . . . If you use the belt once in a while, they'll remember that—they'll mind you next time. . . . I think you should whip your children once in a while.

Most of the parents, however, have qualified beliefs about physical punishment. Some believe spanking all right for young children, but not as appropriate for older ones.

> I feel somehow that the type of disciplining is somewhat a function of age. We might spank [Da. 2.5], whereas we might send [So 4.25] to his room . . . or stand him in the corner. I don't feel that we spank [So 4.25] as much as we might spank [Da 2.5] because of the difference in age.

One couple who were generally demanding and punishing believe that physical punishment should always be given with love. The mother said:

> We believe in discipline, with love, let's put it that way. Many times I have to get a little stick or use my hand. I've always felt that a pat on the back couldn't hurt anyone as long as it's low enough

and hard enough at the same time. . . . [So 7.7] is sometimes inclined to be just a little sassy and we just won't stand for it. . . . I just have to swish his mouth out with soap.

Her husband stated their beliefs more clearly:

> After punishment [such as spanking], we believe we should always end up reconciled, with a hug and a kiss, and the situation is over. No matter what the situation is or what the punishment is, we always love them afterward. As a matter of fact we show more love toward them after we have punished them. We don't detract from the severity of the situation, but we want them to know they are not rejected, we still love them very much.

If children understand the reason for physical punishment, and if it is given with adequate explanations of why the parent "has" to inflict it, some parents (more fathers than mothers) think it more effective. A father of four said, "We use a strap on the children. . . . I always make it a point to try to tell them why they are being punished, rather than just assuming they know why they are being punished. . . . Then I'll get a strap and whip him, and in all cases they never seem to hold a grudge about that."

Only one father believes there might be an advantage to spanking a child when angry. Other fathers (21 per cent) and a few mothers (8 per cent) express concern about giving physical punishment in anger, and do not think it particularly effective: "It seems to me that where someone will take a belt at a kid, the child feels they are being beaten, not because they have done something wrong, but because Mommy is mad. And this to me mediates the whole purpose of the deal." Several parents believe that the only reason they spank their children is to let off steam; whether doing so is a good idea or not is a moot question. Fa 16 finds punishing his children particularly distasteful. He told about an episode on a summer evening when he had put his three preschool children to bed before dark:

> I paddled them again for getting out of bed . . . . They probably would have stayed in bed by that time anyway because it was getting dark, but it makes me feel better sometimes. I think that's probably as good a reason as any. . . . I punish more often than not just because I feel I've got to do something myself, make myself feel better. I rarely punish with the idea that this is really going to do them a lot of good. . . . I think punishment in itself is relatively worthless.

Many parents disapprove of physical punishment, believing it has deleterious effects on children. One mother, with an adolescent boy and an almost adolescent girl, believes it is difficult to punish children of this age because "you certainly cannot spank them." Another mother of an infant (her firstborn) does not believe in physical punishment for infants: a baby is "too young to understand force." One father said that he had slapped his first two children when they were younger mainly because he became frustrated, but he added:

> I don't ever use corporal punishment now. I don't seem to be inclined to. Somehow, as the children . . . and I've grown older, I've found no need for it. It doesn't seem to be sensible any more, so the younger ones have not been subjected to this. . . . There just doesn't seem to be any evidence of a need for corporal punishment in the family.

Not many parents completely disapprove of physical punishment. A mother of four girls said:

> I think that some of the older parents had the older ideas, like . . . hitting children with a strap, which I don't believe in; it is not necessary. . . . That is cruel. . . . I think you just make them more nervous, and I think they will grow up with a feeling they hate you. I really do. I think that I would remember it forever.

Social punishment. Social punishment includes three types of punishment: isolating, ostracizing, or ignoring; disapproving or withdrawing love; and shaming, belittling, or humiliating. Fathers emphasize the positive effects of social punishment more; mothers stress its positive and negative effects about equally. Over 80 per cent of the beliefs favoring social punishment concern some form of isolation. About 40 per cent of both mothers and fathers believe that such punishment is useful and effective; only one mother disapproves of it. Fa 16, who strongly disapproves of spanking (though he spanked when angry) believes that social isolation is the best method of punishment for young children, especially for emotional outbursts. The parents tend to believe that as children get older, social isolation is more effective than any other kind of punishment. One family coined the expressions "yard lockup" and "room lockup" to designate social-isolation punishment. The mother said, "It is better than any other kind of punishment for [So 13.9]. It gets him out of my hair, and me out of his hair. And it prevents him from getting into further trouble. Usually after [being isolated from family and/or friends] everything is very peaceful."

Only three parents mention withdrawing love from a child as punishment, and they tend to disapprove of it. Mo 1 was quite straightforward in her belief, though she admitted it was difficult to put into practice. She said:

> Withdrawing love from a child because he hasn't obeyed you is wrong. Sometimes you may have a situation in which the child is always disagreeable and disobedient and . . . not lovable. While we realize that the unlovable needs love, it requires a great deal of effort to consciously go about showing him that you love him. It is one of those situations where your beliefs and your behavior may be different, but that's not an argument for abandoning your beliefs.

Parents are divided over punishing by humiliation or shame: 23 per cent of fathers approve of it; 40 per cent of mothers and 21 per cent of fathers disapprove of it. One couple agreed that it is not an acceptable method of control, the mother saying:

> I don't like to belittle [Da 5.3 and So 11.7], so sometimes we'll let things go until the company has left, and then we'll talk to them, because they are old enough to understand. I don't believe in belittling them at all, especially my boy; I know it would hurt him terribly. I wait until the people go, and then I'll explain things, and I find that works out quite a bit better. . . . If you belittle them, there is a certain amount of pride; they would feel cheap, and I don't like to hurt anyone like that.

Verbal punishment. Beliefs about punishing by scolding, threatening, lecturing, using sarcasm, raising the voice, or yelling are included under verbal punishment. Mothers emphasize the positive and negative effects of such punishment about equally, but fathers emphasize its positive effects more. Four couples agree on the acceptability of verbal methods. One of these couples believes that verbal methods are useful, whereas physical punishment brings unfortunate results. The father talked about the chores he required of his ten-year-old daughter: "We argue her into doing these, for we believe that is the best way. Sometimes we threaten her with loss of privilege [contacts with friends], threaten her with the fact it isn't fair if she doesn't carry her load of things. Sometimes if I get angry, I just bawl her out." Only two couples agree that verbal punishment is not acceptable. One of these mothers, talking about her three sons, said:

> To bawl them out in front of people, that's embarrassing. That's degrading to the morale and that makes for hurt feelings without actually really accomplishing what you wanted to. . . . I don't like to use sarcasm. Lots of times they don't realize it's sarcasm, and you've lost your point right away. . . . If they've made a mistake . . . you correct the mistake. But you don't try to browbeat them . . . that will destroy their confidence in themselves.

The parents, for the most part, believe that verbal punishment is best confined to the privacy of the family. Verbal punishment is often related to social punishment and to threats of more dire punishment: deprivation of privileges, or physical punishment.

Deprivation. Withdrawing privileges from children is considered effective punishment by most of the parents who discuss it. An equal number of mothers and fathers mention it, but fathers emphasize its positive aspects more.

Restitution. A few parents believe that enforced restitution—that is, making children restore something they have broken, or clean up a mess they have made—is a useful form of punishment. A father of four boys said:

> I used to get furious when something was spilled. But my wife's father is one who would beat you to death if you dropped a glass or spilled something. After I saw that a few times, I realized it wasn't so very important, that once something was spilled, why it seems so much nicer if you just make the person that spilled it just clean up the mess.

Punishment in general. Fathers believe in the general usefulness of punishment significantly more than mothers. The greatest emphasis is placed on certain qualifications; for example, punishment should immediately follow the offense and not be delayed, it should be specific to the situation, and it should be adjusted to the age of the child.

Beliefs about Parental Control

In addition to parental values for control and instrumental beliefs about control, there are over five hundred codings for control that we categorized as descriptive beliefs because they describe the type and level of control that parents approve or disapprove of. But, in many instances, these beliefs represent parents' convictions about whether a certain kind of control does or does not lead to a desired outcome. They might therefore have been classified as instrumental beliefs, but we decided to consider them descriptive beliefs because the goal is either omitted or not clearly stated, and the emphasis is on the description of control. In order to clarify the three distinctions, we give three excerpts from one father's interviews:

Parental value: "I still am basically oriented toward the idea that parents should have a permissive attitude toward the rearing of children."

Instrumental belief: "If he [So 8.6] makes a bad decision, I do not stop it. I make certain he knows what is going to come from this. This isn't saying he's not going to make mistakes; certainly he is—but this is how he learns and becomes a bigger and better person—through the freedom to choose among alternatives."

Descriptive belief: "By and large, being permissive is making them aware of the consequences of what they might do, and not to put a dampening effect on their activities, by saying that this is bad and that this is dangerous, and you might get hurt for the rest of your life."

Descriptive beliefs about control are divided into three categories: beliefs about the method of control (inhibition, reasoning), beliefs about the level of control, and beliefs that compare the control of mothers and of fathers (see Table 7.1). Of these three categories, parents give greatest emphasis to beliefs about methods of control (47 per cent of all mothers' descriptive beliefs about control; 46 per cent of fathers'). Fathers emphasize beliefs about control significantly more than mothers, both in general and to a lesser extent in terms of all three categories.

Method of control. Parents describe four methods of control, which we have labeled inhibition, reasoning, consistency, and insistence. There are also a few other methods, including fear and joking, that are mentioned infrequently. Some parents disapprove of each of these methods, except reasoning and being consistent.

Control by *inhibition* may be through rules or by physically keeping a child from doing something. Most of the parents discuss inhibition by rules, which they generally approve of, though a few do not. Fathers believe in rules more than mothers. Most of the rules are specific to a particular situation; for example, limiting the time for eating, preventing injury to adult property, or protecting children in dangerous situations. A father of four daughters said, "I see children outside climbing over everybody's car, up on people's front lawns with their bikes and roller skates—that I can see. I don't believe in having my children run over everybody's lawn, tearing up their lawn, or scratching their cars. I won't allow it." About half as many parents as approve of inhibition consider it inappropriate for certain situations. One mother said she believed that rules are "a challenge to children to see if they can get away with it."

The use of *reasoning* in controlling children is emphasized most by both parent groups, with fathers tending to stress it even more than mothers. One father mentions the problem of protecting his flower garden when his son was playing football with neighbors' children:

> These three boys are approachable [So 8.1 and his two friends], and I can sit down and show them my flowers and tell them what this means to me. I ask them how many hours they think I spend working on them. Ask them about the possibilities of other places to play. I tell them how unhappy it makes me. I think they understand such reasoning.

The next most emphasized method is *being consistent,* with more mothers than fathers discussing it, and no parent believing it a poor method. The *other methods* mentioned—being insistent, making children afraid, and getting children to do things by "kidding them along"—are discussed by relatively few parents. Rather more parents disapprove of being insistent with children than approve of it.

Level of control. The descriptive beliefs about levels of control range from the level labeled "permissive" to that labeled "authoritarian." In between there are three levels: lenient, firm, and strict (see Table 7.1).

Parents who describe *permissive control* as a lack of any discipline, complete freedom for the child, with no limits of any kind, seem to see life as a struggle between parent and child in which the child always wins. These parents see any leniency in parental control as a sign of weakness. Being sweet and gentle, relaxed, easy, or considerate will only spoil children. Such parents believe that permissive control means children run over a parent, will "get away with murder," get their own way, do what they want, or even take out their aggressions on parents.

All the parents who describe permissive control in this way (about a fifth of the parents) disapprove of it strongly. They think they have seen other parents using it, or think it was recommended in books on child-rearing. But these parents were against such methods of control, seeing them as an abrogation of parental responsibilities, as a sign that the parent has let the child win the struggle for supremacy. The following excerpts from two parents illustrate this kind of control:

> Our friends spoiled their child, rotten. He got his way, no matter what he did. He yelled. He got his way. I never see that.

> The one thing I'm worrying about is this modern day trend—following all the books on child rearing—of letting the kid have his own way. I've watched parents who let children get away with everything, and it is difficult on the parent. Spoiling is a problem.

The second level of control we labeled *lenient,* though some parents used the word "permissive" to describe it. This level of control is similar to that included in the child-oriented techniques discussed under instrumental beliefs (Chapter VI). In lenient control, the parent adjusts to the situation at hand. He is flexible in his requirements, taking into account the child's age, abilities, emotional condition (angry, tired, sick), and activities or interests. Such control gives the child as much freedom or independence as possible, with as little interference as possible. None of these parents describes such control as giving complete freedom, but only as much as possible. They determine the limit of this freedom by its effects on the child and on his parents, giving it only as long as the child is behaving himself, does not hurt or annoy others, or does not become destructive. Lenient control emphasizes what the child may do, rather than what he may not do, and tries to avoid problems, especially with young children, by removing the child from the situation. More mothers believe in lenient control than in any other kind, and almost a third of the fathers approve of it as well. Examples from different parents of beliefs about lenient control follow:

> Every situation is different, and you can't follow any rigid rules because the child is different, the situation is different. All you can get is a kind of guide to go by, and you have to be ready to be flexible. You can't just say this is the way it's supposed to be.

> I firmly believe in very little intervention. Let children bring themselves up as long as they are doing things they should, and they are happy and we are happy. I believe in a minimum of intervention and maximum of happiness.

> Everybody should be given as much freedom, independence as possible.... They should make their own decisions and take responsibility as soon as they are able.... There should be as little external discipline as possible.

The third level of control, which we labeled *firm,* definitely switches emphasis from the child to the parent, from flexibility in certain situations to rigidity. Slightly over a third of each parent group describe firm control and indicate their approval of it. Parents describing firm control stress the importance of having specific rules and rigid standards for certain situations; for example, situations in which the parent assumes there is danger (fire, traffic, climbing fences, neighborhood after dark), or situations in which the parent is in a hurry. These parents also believe that there should be special places in the home that are the parents' property (living room, dining room, garden, bathroom). They also believe that they should be firm about anything they consider important. The only adjustments to the child that are mentioned refer to postponing freedom or independence until the child is older, or can think for himself. Some examples of firm control are:

> Safety is the main reason for having obedience—to be strict about climbing fences and things like that.

I don't think children thrive on complete freedom; they go to pieces. I think they should have a certain very definite set of rules. Some things you can give them a choice, but on important things there's no choice. You just do it because we do it in this family.

The fourth level of control described by parents we labeled *strict control.* Few mothers approve of it, but as many fathers believe in being strict as believe in being lenient. Strict parents mean what they say. They never back down; they stick to their guns, and make no compromises. They act quickly, and demand immediate responses. They follow through, and keep after the child. Furthermore, they believe that beginning early and never giving in to the child will bring success. Some parents describe strict control as the method to use when other methods fail. Three typical sequences leading up to strict control are described by parents: "Ask them nice; tell them; walk in and give them the works"; "Expect them to do; remind them; yell"; and "Reason; threaten; punish." Some parents believe strictness is desirable even if there are only two children in the family; others consider such control imperative in a large family. One father said:

With a family this size [5 daughters], you've got to have discipline or they will drive you out of the house. . . . Never back down on them; they are always trying to get away with something. When you say something, really mean it, yes or no; be positive about it. . . . The best way is to say you are now going to do this, and if you can't do it under your own steam, I will stand right here until it's done today.

We have already noted the negative reaction of some parents to "permissive" control. Other parents are just as firmly opposed to the kind of control we label *authoritarian.* More parents (over half) discuss this level of control than any other, but not one espoused or approved of it. Although in some ways the descriptions of authoritarian control are similar to those of strict control, there are genuine differences. Authoritarian control demands undisputed acceptance of authority. It is militaristic in feeling: words like martinet, tyrant, and boss are used to describe the authoritarian parent.

Likening a parent to a martinet or to a tyrant indicates another aspect of authoritarian control: the parent is described as vindictive, angry, and hostile. His aggression takes various forms, all cruel: raising hell, yelling, hollering, shouting, slapping across the face, poking, hitting. Fear and force are part of his control, and such words as shove, force, and push too far are used often in the descriptions. This hostile element in "authoritarian" control definitely distinguishes it from "strict" control. The authoritarians are described as inflexible, allowing no leniency in any situation, no adjustment to the age, ability, or interest of the child. As one father said, such parents are "absolutely rockbound strict and consistent." Examples of authoritarian control follow:

> The concept of do-it-without-question, do not be curious intellectually or otherwise, because you'll find out later this is for the good of the corps. This is the army, it doesn't make sense to me in family rearing.

> Every time they start to do something, yell "no" or holler "no" or tell them they can't do this or can't do that. One person thinks he is the boss of the family and everybody else is supposed to jump.

More fathers discuss beliefs about authoritarian control than mothers. They not only give more specific details about it, but also tend to disapprove of it more vigorously than mothers, although the difference in percentage scores is not significant. It is possible that the fathers, more than the mothers, had suffered under this kind of control in their own childhoods.

What kind of control do the parents who disapprove of the extreme types of control—permissive or authoritarian—really approve of? We found that all mothers who disapprove of permissive control favor firm control, whereas the fathers who disapprove of permissive control are divided, some favoring firm, and some strict control. Mothers who disapprove of authoritarian control favor lenient or strict control about equally, whereas three-fifths of the codings of fathers who disapprove of authoritarian control are favorable to firm or strict control, and only two-fifths favor lenient control. From this analysis it is clear that when parents describe an extreme type of control, either permissive or authoritarian, they more often prefer firm control to lenient control (mothers, 71 per cent prefer firm; fathers, 60 per cent prefer firm and 12 per cent prefer strict). Therefore, about 70 per cent of the parents with beliefs about extreme permissive or authoritarian control seem to use them as a pretext to justify their beliefs in positive and firm control of children.

Comparison of control of mothers and fathers. Some parents express beliefs about the relative strictness of mothers and fathers, the amount of responsibility each parent takes in controlling his children, and parental disagreements over methods of control. Fathers are generally more concerned with such beliefs than mothers (see Table 7.1).

The parents who discuss the relative *strictness* of mothers and fathers are about equally divided between those who believe mothers are stricter and those who believe fathers are (18 and 21 per cent of mothers; 26 and 28 per cent of fathers). Fathers are believed to be stricter because women are small, more sympathetic and loving, or more patient. Mothers are believed to be stricter because they are with the children all day or have higher standards, or because fathers don't like to discipline.

Most of the parents who discuss beliefs comparing *the responsibility* of mother and father for disciplining children believe that the parent confronted with the situation is the one to care for it. Only a few mothers believe that a father should take care of the discipline of the day when he arrives home. All fathers and most mothers disagree consistently with this point of view.

All of the parents who compare the level or methods of control used by mothers and fathers believe that *disagreement over methods* leads to general confusion in the family. Each parent seemed to wish that his spouse were like him. The father who believes men are stricter than women is likely to be critical of his wife's more lenient methods, and to wish he could make her stricter. One father was obviously critical of the way his wife handled their eight-month-old son:

> Some time he's got to learn he can't just move furniture around when he wants to. It isn't fair for me to tell my wife how to handle him when she has to face him all day, every day; but even so she's going to have to face the responsibility. This is the wife's responsibility, like the man's is bringing home the bacon. When I tell him "No, no," he stops. She tends to take a lesser disciplinary attitude. I would like to see her on occasion try and deter him from taking every magazine and tearing it from cover-to-cover, and pushing the furniture, and eating all the plants.

Relation of Descriptive Beliefs to Demographic Characteristics

In Tables 7.3 and 7.4, the correlations are given between 30 descriptive beliefs and 7 demographic characteristics of parents; in the footnotes to the tables the significance of these correlations is shown. Of the 210 correlations for mothers, 42 (20 per cent) are significant at .10 or beyond; of those for fathers, 36 (18 per cent) are significant. The number of correlations at each level of significance for both mothers and fathers is greater than chance expectancy, the number significant at the level $<.10$ is half the total of significant correlations for fathers and more than half for mothers.

If we look at those characteristics that indicate the level of parental maturity (chronological age, size of family, and age of oldest child), we find that the less mature mothers emphasize beliefs about infancy, heredity and environment, readiness for learning, and the importance of consistency in controlling children. The more mature mothers stress beliefs about the characteristics of children at different ages, especially at adolescence. Mothers' beliefs about punishment show two trends: older mothers and those with older firstborns tend to disapprove of punishment; but mothers with larger families show strong tendencies to believe in punishment and strict control.

The less mature fathers stress beliefs about the characteristics of children (especially during infancy and early childhood), environmental influences, the process of learning, and the use of inhibitions in control. More mature fathers stress beliefs about the characteristics of children during late childhood and adolescence. More mature fathers also stress reasoning as a method of control, and tend to disapprove of physical punishment.

Strong relationships are shown between educational level and descriptive beliefs. More highly educated mothers tend toward leniency in control; mothers with less education lean toward strictness. However, fathers from lower levels of education and social position decry the use of punishment, particularly severe physical punishment.

TABLE 7.3. *Correlations between Descriptive Beliefs and Demographic Characteristics—Mothers*

	Age of parent	*Number of children*	*Age of oldest child*	*Consistency in religion*	*Education level*	*Social position*	*Social mobility*
Characteristics of children	.06	–.11	–.05	–.11	.25	.19	.17
In general	–.15	–.09	–.07	–.08	.36[b]	–.04	–.05
By age and development	.51[e]	–.21	.44[d]	–.05	.39[c]	.20	–.10
Infancy	–.18	–.50[d]	–.58[e]	–.10	.13	.06	.27[a]
Early childhood	.01	–.29[a]	–.25	.00	.23	.30[a]	–.16
Late childhood	–.01	.09	.21	.13	–.10	–.09	–.01
Adolescence	.37[c]	–.08	.51[e]	–.07	.23	.07	–.05
Heredity	–.04	–.32[b]	–.26	–.03	.15	.06	.15
Environment	–.35[b]	–.17	–.49[d]	.05	–.41[d]	–.31[a]	.18
Learning	–.21	–.10	–.32[b]	–.01	.14	.13	.00
Readiness	–.37[c]	–.14	–.45[d]	–.08	.12	–.02	.09
Process	–.05	–.08	–.18	–.07	.06	–.01	.05
Future	.17	.18	.32[b]	.18	.05	–.15	.07
Reward							
Approved	–.27[a]	–.09	–.27[a]	–.23	.04	.27[a]	–.02
Disapproved	–.01	–.02	–.12	–.11	.09	.16	.13
Punishment							
Approved	.10	.45[d]	.09	–.02	.00	–.18	–.07
Disapproved	.32[b]	–.12	.35[b]	–.16	.27[a]	.02	–.07
Physical (approved)	.11	.48[d]	.07	.09	–.15	–.22	–.14
Physical (disapproved)	.19	–.13	.18	–.22	.27[a]	.05	–.11
Social (approved)	–.15	.13	–.01	–.03	.05	–.13	.01
Method of control							
Reasoning	.16	.13	.24	.30[a]	.16	–.21	–.19
Consistency	–.57[e]	.05	–.13	.05	–.13	–.20	–.04
Inhibition (positive)	.27[a]	.01	.29[a]	–.10	.23	.15	–.27[a]
Inhibition (negative)	.07	–.10	.11	–.07	.11	.12	–.20
Insistence (negative)	.05	.13	.17	–.11	.23	–.13	–.10
Level of control							
Permissive	.22	–.06	.08	.05	.10	–.06	–.04
Lenient	.28[a]	–.08	.04	–.09	.46[d]	.34[b]	–.01
Firm	.13	.08	.14	.36[b]	.20	–.01	–.19
Strict	–.01	.45[d]	.14	.12	–.30[a]	–.37[c]	–.02
Authoritarian	.15	.02	.01	–.27[a]	.20	.24	.18

[a] $p < .10$; 11 expected by chance, 16 observed.
[b] $p < .05$; 6 expected by chance, 9 observed.
[c] $p < .02$; 2 expected by chance, 4 observed.
[d] $p < .01$; 2 expected by chance, 9 observed.
[e] $p < .001$; 0.2 expected by chance, 4 observed.

TABLE 7.4. *Correlations between Descriptive Beliefs and Demographic Characteristics—Fathers*

	Age of parent	*Number of children*	*Age of oldest child*	*Consistency in religion*	*Education level*	*Social position*	*Social mobility*
Characteristics of children	.03	.16	–.11	.09	–.36[b]	–.23	–.24
In general	–.02	–.07	–.32[b]	.22	.02	–.13	–.22
By age and development	.23	–.07	.30[a]	.08	.00	–.09	.18
Infancy	–.20	–.33[b]	–.34[b]	–.06	–.06	–.12	–.06
Early childhood	–.38[c]	.18	–.41[d]	.07	–.19	–.30[a]	–.31[a]
Late childhood	.15	.41[d]	.18	.35[b]	–.33[b]	–.24	.01
Adolescence	.33[b]	–.11	.44[d]	–.09	.09	.09	.23
Heredity	–.13	–.07	–.23	–.35[b]	.03	.04	–.05
Environment	–.27[a]	–.23	–.50[d]	–.09	–.13	–.15	–.20
Learning	–.22	–.02	–.24	.24	–.25	–.22	–.24
Readiness	–.02	–.22	–.22	.01	–.01	.12	–.19
Process	–.30[a]	–.06	–.27[a]	.20	–.30[a]	–.36[b]	–.26
Future	.01	.22	.18	.12	.10	.03	.15
Reward							
Approved	.21	.08	.23	.08	.00	–.03	.17
Disapproved	–.11	–.30[a]	–.24	.14	–.11	–.09	–.20
Punishment							
Approved	.13	.15	.27[a]	–.03	–.22	–.27[a]	.06
Disapproved	–.05	.27[a]	.20	.15	–.40[c]	–.45[d]	.01
Physical (approved)	–.15	.11	–.07	–.25	–.06	–.16	.00
Physical (disapproved)	–.12	.32[b]	.14	.21	–.48[d]	–.54[e]	.04
Social (approved)	.02	.07	.16	.04	.01	.03	.01
Method of control							
Reasoning	–.16	.42[d]	.14	.36[b]	–.54[e]	–.51[e]	–.07
Consistency	–.06	.19	–.13	–.13	.14	.15	–.15
Inhibition (positive)	.05	–.32[b]	–.30[a]	–.14	.03	.12	–.20
Inhibition (negative)	–.11	–.16	.02	–.08	.12	.05	.11
Insistence (negative)	.07	–.04	.10	–.01	–.15	.05	–.17
Level of control							
Permissive	–.03	.04	–.07	.01	–.12	–.07	.02
Lenient	.12	–.25	.10	.04	.02	.05	.41[d]
Firm	.24	.19	.10	.34[b]	–.04	–.06	–.06
Strict	–.15	.19	.05	.18	–.15	–.09	–.04
Authoritarian	–.11	.24	.06	–.12	–.12	–.12	–.24

[a] $p < .10$; 11 expected by chance, 12 observed.
[b] $p < .05$; 6 expected by chance, 12 observed.
[c] $p < .02$; 2 expected by chance, 2 observed.
[d] $p < .01$; 2 expected by chance, 7 observed.
[e] $p < .001$; 0.2 expected by chance, 3 observed.

Interrelations of Values and Beliefs about Control

We wished to find out to what extent the values and beliefs of parents about control are interrelated. It seemed possible that there might be some relation between parental values for control (Chapter IV), instrumental beliefs featuring control as means to goals (Chapter VI), and descriptive beliefs about reward, punishment, and control. To find out, we intercorrelated 23 values and beliefs (see Appendix Table D.5). Of the 253 correlations for each parent group, 31 (12 per cent) for mothers and 27 (11 per cent) for fathers are positive correlations, significant at the level of .10 or beyond. However, the numbers at the levels of $< .10$ and for mothers at the level of $< .05$ are less than would be expected by chance (see Appendix Table D.6).

One might assume that parents who said that parents should be lenient (parental value) would believe that child-oriented control is more effective in obtaining values (instrumental belief), and would emphasize beliefs approving reward and lenient control and disapproving punishment (descriptive beliefs). The correlations do not support such an assumption. Leniency, whether expressed as a value or a belief, shows little relation to other similar items. There is no overall pattern of significant correlations between values for lenience and beliefs about lenient control, child-oriented control, the efficacy of reward, and the disapproval of punishment.

Values for and beliefs about strictness are highly integrated for mothers, but for fathers the integration is not as strong. Table 7.5 gives a summary of the relevant correlations from Appendix Table D.5. Mothers who state that parents should be strict implement this value, not only with descriptive beliefs about strict control ($p < .01$) and approval of punishment ($p < .02$), but also with instrumental beliefs incorporating adult-oriented control ($p < .01$) and perhaps obedience ($p < .10$). This relationship is strengthened by the correlation between mothers' beliefs favoring punishment and favoring strict control ($p < .001$).

Fathers, on the other hand, show no non-chance relation between their values for strict control and their beliefs about it. The

TABLE 7.5. *Correlations between Values for Strict Control and Related Beliefs*

	Mo	*Fa*
Descriptive beliefs		
Strict control	.42	.07
Firm control	.11	.25
Reward (negative)	–.01	.13
Punishment (positive)	.37	.36
Inhibition (positive)	–.10	.28
Instrumental acts in beliefs		
Adult-oriented control	.47	.07
Obedience of children	.28	–.19

only consistency is the tendency for values for strict control to be associated with beliefs approving punishment ($p < .05$).

Fathers do, however, show a certain degree of internal consistency in their beliefs about strictness. Those who emphasize beliefs about strict control also emphasize instrumental beliefs favoring adult-oriented control ($p < .01$) and descriptive beliefs concerning disapproval of rewards ($p < .02$).

Scores for the two parent groups were obtained for various combinations of values, instrumental beliefs, and descriptive beliefs related to control. (See Appendix Table D.7.) For each combination, fathers' scores tend to exceed mothers', but in only one instance is the difference highly significant: fathers greatly exceed mothers in their emphasis on a combination of beliefs disapproving reward and approving punishment and strict control ($p < .001$). These integrated patterns are more highly related to demographic characteristics of mothers than those of fathers. (See Appendix Table D.8.) Two tendencies seem clear: mothers of higher education and those of higher social position emphasize gentler methods, whereas mothers with larger families and of lower social position stress the harsher values and beliefs. Although the correlations for fathers are relatively low, it appears that values and beliefs about strictness tend to be emphasized by older fathers, and those with older firstborns. Beliefs disapproving reward and approving punishment and strict control come from fathers of lower education and lower social position. There is a slight suggestion that fathers who are more socially mobile tend to lenient control in values and beliefs.

Differences between Mothers and Fathers

The difference between family-matched mothers and fathers in emphasis on descriptive beliefs is striking. Of the 61 categories in Table 7.1, 28 (46 per cent) show a difference significant at the level of .10 or beyond. Fathers' scores are higher in all except one category, beliefs disapproving of social punishment. The differences are outstanding ($p < .01$ or $< .001$), not only in the total category of descriptive beliefs but also in beliefs about learning, approval of punishment in general, disapproval of physical punishment, and approval of strict control. In addition, the combined score for beliefs about disapproving reward and approving punishment and strict control is significantly higher for fathers ($p < .001$).

Mothers show strong tendencies to have an integrated pattern of beliefs related to values for strict control, including beliefs favoring strict control, punishment, and the use of adult-oriented control. Fathers are more likely to have an integrated pattern related to values for leniency, but the relations are not significant.

Summary and Comments

The parents contributed a wide range of descriptive beliefs concerning the characteristics of children, heredity and environment, learning, reward, punishment, and control. We coded 3,294 descriptive beliefs, 66 per cent of all codings of beliefs, 15 per cent of the total number of codings in the study.

The tendency to be influenced by beliefs about the characteristics of children is widespread. Although there was considerable variation in the characteristics emphasized, certain ones were mentioned often: intelligence, impulsiveness, dependency, immaturity, development, and relations with parents. Parents were conscious of the fact that children change as they grow up. Their beliefs stress both the immaturities and the increasing development of infants and young children. During the period of late childhood, when children are in elementary school, parents seem more relaxed about their children and give relatively less emphasis to beliefs about their characteristics. They see them as full of energy, increasingly mature in making judgments, and seeking independence from their parents. The lack of emphasis on beliefs about late childhood may be due to the fact that this is the period in a child's life when the problems of early socialization are over, when the growth rate is relatively stable without the rhythmic fluctuations that precede and follow, when the immaturities demanding parental attention have been left behind. Indeed, the period of late childhood may be considered a relatively easy one for parents.

It is the period of adolescence that seems to concern parents most, even those parents whose children have not reached this stage of development. The stress on beliefs about adolescence is probably, to some extent, a reflection of parents' general concern about their own role during this period. It is possible that this concern stems from articles in newspapers and magazines, even though the parents who stressed beliefs about adolescence were not influenced greatly by communication sources. It seems clear that when most of these parents speak of adolescence they mean the latter part of the period. No parent gave any indication that he realized adolescence is a period of development, lasting from five to eight years, and including marked changes from onset to end. Adolescence to these parents is a point in time, heralded by the appearance of certain specific physical characteristics.

Many of these parents believe that all children "go through stages" in their development, and that there is very little a parent can do about these stages, except to wait for the child to outgrow them. The parents' beliefs about "stage" behavior were usually expressed in terms of behavior they disapproved of or considered unacceptable.

Even though parents talk about what they believe children are like, there are indications that they are really talking about their perceptions of their own children, or at least are basing their beliefs about all children on their experiences with their own. One finds, for example, that beliefs about infancy are stressed by parents with younger firstborns. Fathers with younger firstborns also stress beliefs about early childhood. On the other hand, older parents, with older firstborns emphasize beliefs about adolescence. The more experienced mothers (those who were older, and those with older firstborns) seem to have learned about the significance of changes in development, for they show an unusually strong tendency to emphasize beliefs concerning the age and development of children.

Although some parents report only beliefs about heredity, or only beliefs about environment, most believe that heredity is primarily responsible for some behavior and environment for other behavior. It is surprising to find that these parents had few beliefs which took into account the interaction of heredity and environment. We found very little consistency among the parents in the assignment of the effect of these factors to most of the behavior discussed.

By far the greatest interest was expressed in beliefs about how children learn, including practice, experience, and imitation. There was relatively little discussion of learning through explanation and reasoning, ways of learning that one would expect to receive more emphasis in a scientific age. The young mothers and those with young firstborns were particularly concerned with beliefs about readiness for learning. Some parents (particularly mothers with older firstborns) believe that learning now will lead to various rewards in the future. One is tempted to suggest that these parents concocted beliefs about future rewards in order to press children to learn what the parent wanted them to learn right at the moment. Certainly the interview material would lead to such suspicions.

Parents discussed beliefs about reward and punishment primarily in terms of getting children to do what they already know how to do, what they know is right, and what they know is expected of them. Reward received considerably less emphasis than punishment.

A variety of beliefs about punishment were discussed, some reflecting approval of punishment, others disapproval. Fathers were much more likely to emphasize the positive effects of punishment than mothers. Only mothers with larger families stressed the positive effects of punishment. Older mothers, more educated mothers, and those with older firstborns tend to disapprove of punishment. Fathers of lower educational level are strongly against it. Physical punishment was discussed more than other forms of punishment. Most of the parents who believed in physical punishment had qualifications about its use, some of which may help to mitigate the parent's feelings of guilt. Again, mothers with larger families approve of physical punishment, and those of higher education tend to disapprove of it. In contrast, fathers with larger families tend to disapprove of physical punishment, and those of lower social position were strongly against it.

On the whole, these parents favor firm control more than either lenient or strict control. Parents with higher social position favored lenient control. Few mothers believed in strict control (and these were mainly mothers from lower social position or those with larger families), but almost a third of the fathers did.

Permissive control, described as a complete lack of discipline, and authoritarian control, described as hostile and cruel discipline, wese disapproved by all who discussed them. Such extreme descriptions, however, seem to serve a distinct purpose: they apparently help parents define, and in some cases justify, the kind of control they do approve of. For example, by describing "permissive" control as a complete lack of any discipline, parents who believe in firm control can feel more comfortable about this belief. Among those who described authoritarian control, one senses something else: these parents seem to be describing realistically a kind of control that, during their own childhood, they had either experienced themselves, or had observed being meted out to their peers.

Intercorrelations between values, instrumental beliefs, and descriptive beliefs relating to control revealed some interesting relationships. Parents who state that parents ought to be lenient are not influenced by the instrumental or descriptive beliefs that would implement lenient values. On the other hand, values and beliefs about strictness show a much more integrated pattern.

Reasoning and consistency were the most emphasized and the most highly approved methods for controlling children. Younger mothers tended to stress consistency; whereas fathers of lower education and social position, and those with larger families, stressed reasoning.

There is evidence that parents change their beliefs about the development of children, and the factors that influence development, as their children grow older, their families become larger, and as they themselves become more mature. Maturity brings an emphasis on strict control, and the use of rules by mothers, and of reasoning by fathers.

Education and social position appear to be related to the descriptive beliefs that influence parents. Fathers of less education and lower social position show a strong tendency to be influenced by descriptive beliefs. It may be that the fathers who are less well educated, and therefore perhaps less psychologically sophisticated, feel freer to express their beliefs about what children are like, and to describe what they consider the best (or worst) ways for their learning and development. Or it may be that men of lower social position need the support of firmly held beliefs. These fathers have gained their beliefs from the school of personal experience, and they feel strongly about them, especially their disapproval of the use of physical punishment.

Fathers were definitely more influenced by descriptive beliefs than mothers. A combined score of beliefs (disapproving reward, favoring punishment, and approving firm control) was emphasized decidedly more by fathers than by mothers. It becomes increasingly evident that within families there is practically no difference in the parents' attitude toward lenient control, but that fathers tend to emphasize and favor strict control more than mothers do. Mothers tend to be hereditarians; fathers tend to be environmentalists. We wonder whether this particular sex difference is an indication that mothers are more concerned with family continuity than fathers, or whether it is an indication that mothers, because of their greater involvement in child-rearing, are more reluctant to believe that children are fundamentally affected by the way their parents rear them.

VIII
Family Members

In addition to values and beliefs, other influences operate to press a mother or father toward a particular practice with his children. These influences may affect a value or a belief, or they may affect a practice directly. In the next four chapters we will discuss some of the personal, situational, and experiential determinants that parents report in relation to child-rearing. The influences of the personality and behavior of self, of spouse, and of children are discussed in this chapter. Subsequent chapters discuss the subtle control exercised by the behavior setting in which the parent and child interact; the experiences in childhood and adulthood that parents want either to replicate or to avoid for their children; and finally the effect that communication sources, both mass and interpersonal, may have on child-rearing.

The characteristics of the people who make up a family unit (in this study, mother, father, and children) and their interaction with each other influence parental practices. The characteristics of the parents, which include both temporary conditions, such as being tired or busy, and more stable tendencies, such as being easygoing, or tense, influence how they raise their children. Sometimes, in spite of values or beliefs, other personal needs of parents determine what they do with their children.

The interaction of parents with each other modifies the behavior of each parent. It is probably safe to say that no mother would bring up her children in exactly the same way if she had married a different man, and the same holds true for the wife's influence on her husband's child-rearing practices. Finally, the child himself, with his idiosyncratic personality, his way of behaving, and his manner of responding to his parents, influences what a father or mother does. The interaction of a parent with a child may determine to some extent what a parent will do the next time with the same child, or what he will do when he has another chance with another child. Data concerning the influence of members of the family are presented in Table 8.1.

Characteristics of Parents

What a parent does with his children is weighted in some degree, at certain times, by what kind of person he is and how he feels at the moment. Practically all parents discuss such influences, mothers stressing them significantly more than fathers (see Table 8.1).

This discussion is limited to those characteristics that each parent recognized in himself—those which he could label and describe and which he thought accounted for some of his behavior with his children. Such characteristics are grouped in six categories, although we realize that the categories are not discrete and that the behavior of a parent may usually be caused by a combination of conditions rather than by a single one. For example, not feeling well, being tired, and becoming angry because of interruptions may combine to press a mother to be cross and punishing with her child.

Interests. A parent's interests are likely to affect what he does with his children. Interests are mentioned more by parents than any other characteristic. We are not discussing here the goals of a parent for his children, but rather his own personal likes and dislikes—what he enjoys doing, or what he does not like to do. Sports, entertaining, shop work, reading, gardening, jazz or classical music are some of the interests discussed by parents. Mothers stress such likes and dislikes significantly more than fathers. In the following quotation from the mother of a boy and two girls, we have an illustration of the effect of a mother's interests on certain child-rearing practices: "I like to be outside and sunning myself, so I like to take the children swimming. I like to play tennis, and that is why I want [So 10.1] to learn, but he doesn't

TABLE 8.1. *Influence of Family Members on Child-Rearing*

	Per cent reporting		*Number of codings*		*Mean percent-age score*		*Percentage score difference*	
	Mo	*Fa*	*Mo*	*Fa*	*Mo*	*Fa*	*t*	*p*
Characteristics of parents								
Interests	92	80	198	102	1.65	.96	3.04	<.01
Fatigued, sick	62	49	66	30	.55	.30	2.11	<.05
Angry	39	51	37	50	.30	.43	1.73	<.10
Anxious	62	39	50	21	.43	.21	2.09	<.05
Relaxed, easygoing	41	28	27	20	.22	.14	—	n.s.
Attitude toward children	12	31	18	21	.15	.19	—	n.s.
Other characteristics	46	41	27	25	.22	.23	—	n.s.
Σ Characteristics of parents	95	95	423	269	3.52	2.46	2.60	<.02
Spouse interaction								
Mutual interaction	69	92	84	80	.58	.78	—	n.s.
Agreement	64	62	73	67	.49	.65	—	n.s.
Disagreement	18	23	11	13	.09	.13	—	n.s.
Σ Mo influences Fa	49	59	33	52	.30	.51	1.73	<.10
Mo competent	10	31	6	23	.04	.24	3.06	<.01
Mo dislikes	10	26	4	18	.05	.15	1.82	<.10
Mo indisposed	10	15	5	8	.04	.08	—	n.s.
Mo criticizes Fa	31	5	18	3	.17	.04	2.33	<.05
Σ Fa influences Mo	56	15	46	12	.40	.10	3.27	<.01
Fa competent	39	8	26	3	.22	.04	3.81	<.001
Fa dislikes	8	5	5	3	.05	.02	—	n.s.
Fa indisposed	13	3	5	2	.04	.01	—	n.s.
Fa criticizes Mo	26	8	10	4	.09	.03	1.91	<.10
Σ Spouse interaction	92	82	163	144	1.28	1.39	—	n.s.
Behavior of children								
Aggression	100	97	326	254	2.69	2.63	—	n.s.
Orderly living	100	97	301	234	2.42	2.39	—	n.s.
Obedience	97	100	264	213	2.16	2.31	—	n.s.
Eating	92	85	235	213	2.13	2.22	—	n.s.
Dependency	92	80	184	130	1.43	1.26	—	n.s.
Fear	85	56	96	52	.83	.58	—	n.s.
Curiosity	62	39	61	29	.51	.31	—	n.s.
Sex	39	36	51	25	.38	.29	—	n.s.
Toileting	28	23	21	26	.22	.30	—	n.s.
Happy, unhappy behavior	49	44	31	24	.24	.25	—	n.s.
School	44	21	28	19	.25	.18	—	n.s.
Sleep	41	36	22	20	.18	.19	—	n.s.
Guilt	18	15	8	11	.07	.10	—	n.s.
Other behavior	95	90	288	221	2.31	2.26	—	n.s.
Σ Disapproved behavior	100	100	1,384	1,100	11.66	11.64	—	n.s.
Σ Behavior of children	100	100	1,916	1,471	15.90	15.27	—	n.s.

TABLE 8.1 *(cont.)*.

	Per cent reporting		*Number of codings*		*Mean percentage score*		*Percentage score difference*	
	Mo	*Fa*	*Mo*	*Fa*	*Mo*	*Fa*	*t*	*p*
Characteristics of children								
Motivation	100	97	395	271	3.35	2.75	1.97	<.10
Level of maturity	97	90	171	147	1.37	1.44	—	n.s.
Temporary condition	85	74	141	95	1.15	.95	—	n.s.
Abilities	62	64	61	68	.52	.63	—	n.s.
Physical development	64	49	61	39	.49	.40	—	n.s.
Individuality	44	39	30	33	.27	.31	—	n.s.
Birth order	31	15	22	14	.20	.20	—	n.s.
Similarity to parents	33	31	20	22	.16	.22	—	n.s.
Sex	23	13	12	10	.09	.13	—	n.s.
Σ Characteristics of children	100	100	913	699	7.60	7.03	—	n.s.
Parent-child interaction								
Interaction with sibling	69	59	94	76	.87	.69	—	n.s.
Practice repeated	51	39	25	29	.25	.25	—	n.s.
Practice changed	51	46	69	47	.62	.44	—	n.s.
Interaction with child	77	64	87	48	.69	.52	—	n.s.
Practice repeated	26	23	19	11	.14	.14	—	n.s.
Practice changed	77	56	68	37	.55	.38	—	n.s.
Interaction leading to repetition of practice	67	56	44	40	.39	.39	—	n.s.
Interaction leading to change of practice	92	77	137	84	1.17	.82	2.03	<.05
Σ Parent-child interaction	97	85	181	124	1.56	1.21	—	n.s.
Σ Influence of family members	100	100	3,596	2,707	29.86	27.36	2.01	<.10

know anyone to play with him. That is why I think the club we joined might be good for him."

An interest may be quite absorbing to a parent, and become in a sense part of his feeling of selfhood. He is then likely to resent interruptions or intrusions by his children. The following excerpt illustrates how a father's interest in his garden influences him to protect that part of his self:

I have the front lawn surrounded with flowers, and I am annoyed when they are trampled on by boys going after a ball and things like that. I have put a lot of time and effort into my garden. This is one of my outlets that I enjoy very much and take pride in. . . . My son and his friends trample through the flowers, just walk any place they want. This is when I become emotionally involved. I send them out on the street to play. About two minutes later here comes the ball through my flowers again, and I blow my stack.

There are other less consuming activities in which parents like to engage without interruption. When children interfere with such activities, a parent may respond with irritation and annoyance, and eventually with punishment. Interruptions when telephoning, noise when reading, a baby grabbing a newspaper the father is reading—such situations seem to instigate responses that stem from a parent's desire to protect himself from the intrusions of others. Such an occasion is well illustrated in the following excerpt from a mother of three girls under seven years of age:

I have said this when I am in a temper, "Just go, I don't care where you go, but I cannot stand to listen to you another minute." I have said this when I am lying down in my room and have to get away. I have tried to explain that everyone, even mother, has to get away all by herself just once in a while, and that it isn't that I don't love you or want you, it's just so that I can be better with you later.

Fatigue and illness. When parents are tired or not feeling well, they find it particularly difficult to adjust to the demands of active children. They cannot do what they know is right, or use what they believe is the most effective method, because they lack the physical energy necessary to cope with the total situation. Under such conditions, practices change—usually becoming more rejecting, more strict, more punitive. Mothers emphasize the effect of their physical condition on their practices with children significantly more than fathers.

Parents report illnesses due to minor upsets like colds, influenza, and indigestion, to operations, accidents, allergies, and overweight, and to pregnancy. Mothers are sometimes overwhelmed by the multiple tasks of housekeeping and child care when pregnant, and they are aware of this. Pregnancy, and conditions immediately following, account for about a third of the mothers' codings in this area. A mother of five children whose last baby was born when the oldest was under three years said: "I was pregnant with [Da 1.8] when the twins were just babies. I guess I was meaner when I was carrying her. I lost my temper quite a bit because I was pregnant and did not feel well. I think I insisted too much on them."

Closely related to pregnancy is fatigue. When a mother is pregnant or has recently had a child, she is more likely to become tired, especially if she is taking care of younger children. This tendency is illustrated in the following excerpt:

> My children were at a bit of a disadvantage. I had the four children in five and a half years, so I was always pregnant when they were little. I would always have one over my shoulder, and one in my stomach, and two or three around someplace, and I would get pretty tired. I realize that I was short with them often when I should not have been. . . . I was tired and if they would go through the house yelling, I would get upset and scold them and spank them. Now it does not bother me at all.

Mothers become fatigued for other reasons than pregnancy; for example, the stress of a menstrual period, holding down a full-time job, a series of exasperations during a day of housework and child care, or having house guests. It is not surprising that 80 per cent of the codings concerning the physical condition of the mother refer to fatigue. Fathers also stress fatigue (about 57 per cent of their codings), especially the tired feeling that comes after a day's work. At such times parents are likely to be more strict, to yell at children, or to punish them, even though neither their values condone, nor their beliefs support such behavior. This is illustrated in the following excerpt from an interview with a father:

> My training and background have made me believe in being permissive with children. When I come home tired, as I do on occasion, then I am not quite so permissive. But I am still basically oriented toward the permissive attitude in the rearing of children. My values are set this way. . . . My tolerance is diminished as the day goes on. Late in the day when I am awfully tired I do not care to have children arguing.

Anger. Day-to-day living with children brings frustrations that instigate anger in parents and incite them to be aggressive with their children. Children refuse to do what they are told, they spill things, they are careless, they quarrel, they get clean clothes dirty, and on and on. Parents are more likely to get angry when things go wrong, if other negative conditions are present. Fatigue is one of the conditions that reduces the control of parents over their emotions. The excerpt concerning a mother's behavior during pregnancy illustrates this. A parent is also more likely to lose his temper with children if there are strains in his life that make him feel insecure. A father of four children explained why he had slapped his first two children, but does not do it with the last two:

> I must confess that with [So 11.9] and [Da 10.5], when they were younger, if they wouldn't do what I thought they ought to do, if I lost my temper, I'd slap them. I don't think I approve of this idea. I'd always be profoundly sorry afterwards that I lost my temper in such a way. I wouldn't do it now, but I did it then. . . .
>
> During this period I was under a great deal of strain. I was building a house, working half-time, trying to accomplish a doctorate thesis, going to classes, doing my share of the housework. It all made life pretty difficult. All this time it was a terribly easy thing to reach the threshold of losing one's temper with little children. I feel that we were probably too hard with [So 11.9]. This might be one of the reasons why he is more introverted, perhaps less easily trusting, than [So 7.4].

The behavior of children can be "the last straw" that makes a parent express his aggressive feelings, or it can be a convenient scapegoat. One father says this quite clearly: "If we are a little short-tempered for other reasons, I think we are likely to maybe spank them instead of sending them to their room. I know that I've caught myself doing that."

When parents are angry, no matter what the cause, they are more punishing and more aggressive toward their children. Only rarely did a parent say that he never punished his child when angry. A few thought it should not be done, but under the stress of their emotions their values were pushed aside. More fathers than mothers discuss the effect of anger on their behavior with their children, and the difference in percentage scores is significant. As one reads these interviews, it seems that the fathers are more willing to admit that they get angry, or have a quick temper, while mothers hide their aggressive feelings (even from themselves) behind a mask of fatigue, or of "nervousness."

Anxiety. Very few parents use the word "anxiety" in describing their emotions. Usually they say "nervous and tense"; occasionally they speak of being "worried," "jumpy," or "afraid." Mothers stress such feelings and their effect on child-rearing more than fathers. Mothers appear to emphasize anxiety more than anger but the difference is not statistically significant ($t = 1.38$), whereas fathers emphasize anger significantly more than anxiety ($t = 2.29$, $p < .05$).

Parents tend to be unsure about rearing their first child. The following excerpt from a mother of four children illustrates the difference between rearing a first and last child. Learning through experience has reduced anxiety.

> Actually what's happened to me is that I feel more secure, and it is not necessary for me to be obeyed quite so quickly. I don't feel threatened now when [Da 3.3] does the horrid things she does. When [So 11.9] did this I would have been thrown into a panic. I would not have known how to handle it at all, and would be either too lenient or too severe. . . . I'm firmer with [Da 3.3] on certain things, and when I want to be firm I feel now that I know what a three-year-old could be expected to do, and how much pressure I can put on her without damaging her.

Not all parents decrease their anxiety through experience. For some anxiety is not a result of ignorance that can be gradually overcome, but rather is an integral part of personality that persists and is a part of the self of the individual. The following excerpt is from one such mother who had two preschool children:

> I'm rather nervous and high-strung and I think I'm a little stricter, perhaps, than other people would be. Certain things bother me that probably don't bother other people. Like an awful lot of noise and commotion makes me nervous. . . . I don't want them running up and down the hall—it just sounds like a clattering herd of elephants. I get very annoyed and nervous when I hear them just going up and down for not too much reason, like on rainy days. . . . I get after them, and I'll say they have to play separately; I put them in their rooms.

Anxiety can press a parent to be more punishing or more strict, but it sometimes works in the opposite way, as witness this report from a father about his adolescent boy.

> The only threat I can use now is to say that [So 13.9] cannot participate the next day in sport activity. Then he falls in line, usually resentfully, very resentful. . . . I know what sports mean to him, and whenever I have to exclude the sports I suffer considerably more than he does. My whole next morning is spoiled when I know what's ahead of him, and sometimes I break down and call the school to tell them he can stay after school for sports, because it depresses me more than I am able to say, it's on my mind, I just can't take it off my mind.

Relaxed. Parents sometimes state that they are easy-going or relaxed and therefore respond to their children in certain ways. Being relaxed indicates that they are not pressed by the emotions of fatigue, anger, or anxiety, or are not busy with other responsibilities. Mothers become more relaxed with their second or third child, because they are more experienced and feel more confident. An example is the mother quoted above. Another mother said of her third baby, "I am not bathing her as often as I did the others. I am not as frantic about keeping her well. With the others for instance, I gave them a daily bath, and now I bathe [DA 0.7] as I feel she needs it. I'm more relaxed with her."

When parents are "in a good mood," they are likely to be more lenient. The father of an eight-month-old firstborn stated this clearly:

> If he's crying because he wants attention, if we are in a good mood, he'll get it. Other times we let him cry. If he tugs at me when I get home from work, he can tug a pretty long time, but after I've been home awhile and relaxed then he can come up and play for a while. Generally speaking it's more a matter of convenience—how we are feeling—as to how we respond to him.

Attitude toward children. Some adults like children, enjoy being with them, and find playing with them relaxing and fun. Others find difficulty in adjusting to the different world of children, and feel either ill at ease with them or annoyed by them. Sometimes it is babies who bother them; sometimes it is boys who are a nuisance. Very few parents mention their attitude toward children in general, or children of a particular age or sex, as influencing their practices. Fathers mention only their delight in firstborn babies, whereas mothers also mention how satisfactory school-age children are. The following statement from a mother illustrates the effect on her practice of her difference in attitude toward younger and older children:

> When they were little and crawling around, and you had to watch them every second, they made me nervous. That is when I worked, and a lady took care of them. They didn't seem to miss me when they were with this baby-sitter who had other children. Now they don't get on my nerves the way they did when they were little. I feel now that I wouldn't want to work full-time now. Now maybe their problems are bigger, but I can talk with them, you know.

Other characteristics. The most frequently mentioned characteristic in this miscellaneous category is the temporary condition of "being busy." When a parent is concerned with other responsibilities, the needs of a child are sometimes ignored or refused. In a few instances parents report that they punish a child for demanding attention when they are busy, or they may indulge him to keep him quiet. Other characteristics mentioned by relatively few parents include being religious and being curious.

Spouse Interaction

Mothers and fathers influence each other's child-rearing practices in a variety of ways. Most mothers and fathers talk over with each other their plans for children, or discuss what they think is best to do in certain situations. The competency of one parent in a particular area of child-rearing is likely to influence the spouse. If one parent dislikes to do a certain thing with a child, the other parent may take over. If a parent is indisposed (busy or sick) the spouse must act. In addition, if one parent approves or disapproves of the child-rearing practice of the other, the practice is often changed. Data concerning the influence of spouse interaction are presented in Table 8.1.

Mutual interaction. In many situations involving their children, parents talk over what they should do, and usually come to some kind of mutual agreement. Only infrequently does the discussion end in disagreement, and when it does, more often the mother's opinion tends to prevail. Considerably more parents are influenced by this kind of mutual interaction than by their spouses directly.

About two-thirds of the parents state that their discussions end in mutual agreement. Fewer parents, though more mothers than fathers, report that either the father tends to convince the mother (26 per cent of mothers; 3 per cent of fathers), or the mother tends to convince the father (18 per cent of mothers; 10 per cent of fathers). Both mothers and fathers tend to report more influencing by, than influencing of, their spouses. One of the parents most influenced by talking matters over with his wife was Fa 1, and he reported only situations in which they came to an agreement. Usually, these decisions were mutually arrived at, but sometimes his wife was the one with whom he agreed; only once was the dominance reversed. He talked about such mutual decisions at length; the following is a brief summary:

> Interviewer: You mention over and over again, "My wife and I do this." How do you come to agreement on these matters?
>
> Fa 1: Oh, we've talked, talked, talked! Over a period of time, we have acquired a remarkably agreeable set of conclusions together. We don't have very many serious disagreements in any way. . . . I'm not sure that you can say whether one or the other of us is dominant; in fact, I think that there is very little disagreement between us on what should be done. I mean, that whenever a problem presents itself, we talk it over, and we both think along the same lines, and I can't say that one or the other has taken a dominant lead.

Relatively few parents report discussions with their spouses that end in disagreement, but a few more fathers than mothers did so (18 per cent of mothers; 23 per cent of fathers). Fathers are especially likely to state that the mother's ideas are dominant when disagreement occurred (23 per cent), whereas more mothers stress the father's dominance (13 per cent). A small percentage of mothers (5 per cent) report that the disagreements remained disagreements, even after discussion with their husbands.

Mo 29 told about her concern for her seven-and-a-half-year-old son, who was interested in quiet games, reading, or playing teacher. She said:

My husband was interested in sports, and he was very good at it. I tried to get [So 7.5] interested in football for a while. But my husband didn't want to press him. He said if he wanted to play football and things like that, he could do so later on, there wasn't any use to rush it; if he wanted to read and write, let him read and write.... That was sort of surprising. I thought my husband would really want him to play football and baseball and be interested in boxing. Well, so now we both let him do what he wants to.

This same mother also told how she influenced her husband, with the support of the teacher as authority figure:

We don't know much about children. I think most of my husband's ideas came from the talks we've had together. Maybe if I punished [So 7.5] for some reason and my husband didn't agree with me, we might talk it over at night and see why he didn't agree with it.... My opinion usually wins out. This doesn't happen very often, but most of the time I can tell my husband, "Well, the teacher suggested this." When [So 7.5] got so he wouldn't clean his teeth or straighten his room (when he was about six), my husband and I talked about it. He thought that the boy should be spanked for forgetting to do things. But the teacher didn't think he should be spanked, so I told my husband. She thought I ought to check up on him more often, to remind him. So my husband agreed to do it because the teacher said so.

Influence of the mother on the father. Fathers are more conscious of the mother's influence on them than the mothers are conscious of being influential. The difference in emphasis is statistically significant for the category as a whole, and is most marked concerning the effect of the mother's competency on the father (see Table 8.1). The following illustration is taken from the interviews with a father who had four children between three and nine years of age.

There's been lots of times I know for a fact that I've changed. I would take a more severe method of disciplining than she would. She'd use a little more psychology than I would. I'd talk it over with my wife and she'd tell me what her views are, and as a rule, her views are better than mine, as far as knowing what to do in raising the children.

About one-quarter of the fathers and a few mothers mentioned situations that the mother either disliked or did not want to handle, with the result that the father took over. The following excerpt from a father's interview is an example in point:

> My wife told me that our daughter had asked her about babies—and she seems to be at a complete standstill as far as being able to tell her. She doesn't know just what to tell her. So I said, while I was driving my daughter to school, I would tell her whatever she wanted to know.

If the mother is indisposed, busy, or ill, the father is often pressed to take responsibility to relieve the mother. One father discussed in some detail how his wife's condition affected both him and the children. This is a summary of a longer discussion:

> I come home, and I'm thinking about other things, and then I may be tired, and I hear some hassling between my wife and [Da 6.8], who has aggravated her; then I just take off right at the peak. I shouldn't really get into this business, because it is between [Da 6.8] and her mother. But my wife is tired and upset. I am beginning to wonder whether there isn't a relation between my wife's menstrual cycle and these problems in the home. I get into this situation to take the burden off my wife.

Only in one area do mothers discuss their influence on their spouses more than fathers do: situations in which the mother is critical of what the father does. The following excerpt from the interviews of a mother whose husband was a "diet fanatic" illustrates this point:

> I think a health diet is good but—; for instance, when it reaches the stage where all the kids in the neighborhood have Easter baskets full of candy, and my husband suggests that we cut off cubes of cheese and give it to our kids instead, I put my foot down. That is all right with him, if I suggest it, he will go along with it, but if he were doing it, he would give them the cheese, or some other unrefined food.

Influence of the father on the mother. In similar ways, fathers influence mothers. However, it is the mothers who are most conscious of their husbands' influence. Relatively few fathers have anything to say about their influence on their wives. The most outstanding difference between mothers and fathers, in their reports concerning the father's influence, has to do with the father's competence—mothers' scores are much higher. A mother was talking about her children's arguing and kicking each other under the table during meal times. She said:

> Well, the father handles these. I have let him handle them because he does a very good job of it. . . . Their father will say something like, "We will not have that at the table," and smooths it over, and starts a different conversation; he does very well with it. He doesn't believe in arguing at the table, and I don't either.

Only a few parents discuss the effect that the father's reluctance or inability to do certain things with the children has on the mother's behavior. This is somewhat surprising because experience tells us that mothers do many things with the children that fathers do not like to do or can do only awkwardly. Mo 6 complained that her husband forced her to be the disciplinarian: "My husband told me that he didn't want the children to hate him, and every time he said something, he didn't want to correct them, so he gives in to them. And I was always having to be real mean because he did not want to punish them."

Fewer parents mention that the mother is influenced because the father is busy or tired, or just not there. In one family, with four boys under six years of age, the mother said that when she was tired, she asked her husband to take over. Then she added: "My husband doesn't ask me to do it for him. I can just tell by his tone of voice, or his expression that he's tired or getting a little impatient, so I just step in and say, 'Come on, [So 5.8], do this, or do that.' "

Next to the father's competency, mothers state that his critical attitude toward their practices influences what they do. One mother told about her plans for her new baby: "I thought I would have a rocking chair and sing him to sleep. I've seen it in the movies—but that went out the window. I never got my rocking chair. My husband didn't believe in all that stuff, so I never got the rocking chair, and I never rocked the baby."

The Behavior of Children

Every parent in this study was influenced by his children: by the way the children behaved; by the characteristics they per-

TABLE 8.2. *Difference in Emphasis on Approved and Disapproved Behavior of Children*

	Mothers			*Fathers*		
	Higher	*t*	*p*	*Higher*	*t*	*p*
Aggression	D[a]	4.59	<.001	D	4.45	<.001
Orderly living	D	8.31	<.001	D	9.55	<.001
Obedience	D	6.08	<.001	D	6.51	<.001
Eating	D	4.81	<.001	D	3.80	<.001
Dependency	D	3.11	<.01	D	4.01	.001
Fear	D	2.40	<.05	D	—	n.s.
Curiosity	A[b]	5.07	<.001	A	3.86	<.001
Sex	A	—	n.s.	D	—	n.s.
Toileting	D	2.36	<.05	D	2.10	<.05
Happy, unhappy behavior	A	—	n.s.	D	—	n.s.
School behavior	D	1.90	<.10	D	—	n.s.
Sleep	D	1.93	<.10	D	1.74	<.10
Σ Behavior of child	D	11.53	<.001	D	9.93	<.001

[a] Disapproved behavior; [b] approved behavior.

ceived in their children; and by the responses of children to the methods parents use in bringing them up (see Table 8.1).

The specific behaviors of children that are described as influential factors cover a wide range. We grouped these behaviors into 13 specific categories and one miscellaneous category, as shown in Table 8.1. The kinds of behavior mentioned most by both parent groups are, in the order of emphasis: behavior related to aggression, to orderly living, to obedience, to eating, and to dependency.* It is noteworthy that the order of emphasis is the same for both mothers and fathers. Furthermore there is no difference between mothers and fathers in emphasis for any category that is greater than might be expected by chance.

Although mothers and fathers do respond to approved behavior in their children, disapproved or problem behavior is much more effective in stimulating parents to act. Almost three-fourths of the 3,387 situations discussed by the 78 parents refer to child behavior that parents sought to change (72 per cent of mothers'

* The emphasis on eating behavior and obedience may have been affected by the fact that the evening meal was chosen as a behavior setting, and obedience as a system of behavior, for discussion during the interview sessions. See Chapter I.

codings of child behavior; 75 per cent of fathers' codings). As can be seen in Table 8.2, the differences between the emphasis on approved and disapproved behavior are highly significant for both mothers and fathers, in the category of behavior as a whole, in eight of the 12 subcategories for mothers, and in seven subcategories for fathers.

Aggressive behavior. Both mothers and fathers respond more to aggression than to any other behavior of their children. We do not believe that this finding implies that children display more tendencies to hurt or injure than other kinds of behavior, but rather that parents have strong feelings about aggression. Parents differ widely in the amount or kind of aggressive behavior they can tolerate. Though practically all parents mention the influence of the child's aggression on them, they vary in their emphasis and in the degree they consider that it must be controlled and trained.

A high proportion of such behavior became the target for parental efforts to change it (69 per cent of mothers' codings of aggressive behavior; 70 per cent of fathers'). The difference in emphasis of parents on aggressive behavior that is accepted or ignored, and that which is disapproved or considered important to change, is highly significant statistically (see Table 8.2).

We compared the influence on parents of aggression directed toward parents, toward other children, toward property, and toward self. Aggressive behavior directed toward parents influences parents more than aggression directed toward children; for mothers the difference is statistically significant ($p < .01$). In addition the emphasis on aggression toward parents is more influential than the emphasis on aggression toward property for both mothers and fathers ($p < .001$). (See Appendix Table E.1.)

Mothers appear to emphasize children's aggression directed toward them slightly more than fathers do ($t = 1.80$, $p < .10$), perhaps because they are subjected to it more often. They especially emphasize verbal aggression, such as talking back or arguing. The following excerpt illustrates this tendency:

My children are allowed to talk back more than I was, but I still do not like outright rudeness. I am usually pretty abrupt when they are rude. [Da 10.5] is more of a problem this way than the boys. I think maybe girls are. Girls use their tongues, and boys use their fists. She usually picks an occasion when she has a friend, a sort of showing off, showing her friend how much she can get away with. I do not want to embarrass my children in front of their friends. On the other hand, I don't want to give her the impression that this is acceptable, so I usually reprimand her, and speak to her later about it.

Indirect aggression to parents (by pretending not to hear, sulking, or mumbling to self) brings responses from parents also. One mother said, "With [So 7.4], sulking is really a symptom that he is quite upset. If he goes to his room and flings himself on his bed and sulks, I usually try to search him out, because I can talk to him and I can get through to him."

Physical aggression, such as hitting or slapping a parent, is reported less often by parents, and mainly in relation to young children:

It used to upset me when a child would hit me. I really felt I was being attacked. Now [Da 3.3] does this constantly, and I simply hold her at arms' length, and it doesn't bother me at all. I think I do this because [So 11.9] was required to bottle up his hostile feelings too much, and I think he should have been allowed to hit back. If I am tired I tell her to stop, or try to divert her. . . . When I have to have my attention elsewhere, like talking on the telephone, I will put her in her room. Sometimes I have to do this to her.

Aggression of children toward other children, primarily their brothers and sisters, has about the same influence on fathers as aggression toward parents, but mothers stress it much less. Both parents stress aggression toward children much more than agression toward property (mothers $p < .001$; fathers $p < .01$). Hitting, fighting, quarreling, and teasing among siblings are annoying to both parents, and brought forth some response:

Occasionally at dinner there is some teasing, particularly between [So 11.9] and [So 7.4], who have a fair degree of rivalry. We don't allow them to kick at each other under the table, or to pinch or tickle while we are eating. . . . [So 11.9] has lost his temper with [So 7.4] many times, and we have lost our temper with him. I am beginning to feel that just ignoring it is not the proper answer from now on.

Aggressive behavior against self is responded to much less than aggression against parents (for mothers the difference is significant, $p < .001$). Head bumping and tantrums among young children (as expressions of aggression toward self) bring a variety of responses from parents, from ignoring to punishment. Most of these parents believe that the child outgrows such behavior, but in the meantime they feel compelled to try to control it. Fa 3 told about his second daughter, who banged her head and had tantrums. The following is an excerpt from a longer discussion:

> Along about three years of age, [Da 5.75] picked up an infernal habit of booming. It just drives you frantic. Just at the most unexpected times you hear this bang, bang, which would reverberate through the house. We consulted Spock, who assured us that this does not have any effect on her brains. We talked it over with other parents and asked our pediatrician. At first we let her do it, and she went ahead, and she did it, and did it, and did it. Then after she banged a hole through the wall, we told her she could not do it any more. We tried to think of something for her to do. We threatened her, but never did spank her for it.... At three years she also would throw tantrums for no real motive. We let her go ahead and have it. A few times I lost my temper and picked her up and paddled her little bottom. Sometimes I drove her into her room. I don't know which method we used most.

Orderly living. Parents seem strongly influenced by the behavior of their children that relates to orderly living in the home. This is emphasized more than any other category except aggression. The emphasis is almost entirely on behavior that parents want to change (89 per cent of mothers' total percentage score for behavior of children related to orderly living; 94 per cent of fathers' total percentage score). The preponderance of emphasis on disapproved behavior related to orderly living is shown in the highly significant difference (Table 8.2).

Parents are instigated to do something about such behavior as noisiness, fidgeting, getting underfoot, being messy or dirty, destroying property, not following routines, forgetting chores, being late for appointments, and childrens' manners. The following excerpt illustrates how a mother of preschool boys responded to one of the many problems that relate to orderly living.

I know these are boys and they are going to get dirty, but I like them to be clean. Now that they are running around more, I am not as strict as I was. I took care of that situation in this way. I put on their dirty clothes and say, "Now it is mud-playing time," and then they can go out and dig in the mud. They have dug a hole up to their necks practically, and filled it with water, and they will be covered with adobe. I just say, "Just call me when you are through playing." That seems to take care of it fine, because they have to have that dirty play. Otherwise they get a phobia, so I have read.

The most influential specific behaviors are the same for mothers and fathers: not being clean and neat, being careless or destructive of property, not coming home on time, and not letting the parent know where he is. Mothers emphasize this last behavior most highly, whereas fathers give greatest emphasis to the care of property. Manners, which was stressed as a value of parents, is only slightly emphasized in the actual behavior of children, except when there are adult guests in the home, or when the parents go visiting or to a restaurant.

Mo 19, who has the highest score in behavior related to orderly living, seemed to respond primarily to behavior having to do with cleanliness, doing chores, and knowing the whereabouts of her children. These were important considerations to this mother, who had a full-time job outside the home. The father with the highest score (Fa 6, an upward-mobile man) stressed the care of things: the children's toys and clothes, new furniture in their newly purchased tract home, and the garden in which he took great pride.

Obedience. Behavior relating to obedience or disobedience is third in emphasis by mothers and fathers. Again, the parents are more influenced by the problems they have in obtaining obedience than in the positive responses of their children (72 percent of mothers' codings and 73 percent of fathers' codings related to problems). The difference in emphasis on approved and disapproved behavior related to obedience is highly significant for both mothers and fathers (Table 8.2).

Many of the ways in which children refuse to obey can be recognized as forms of aggressive behavior, performed for the purpose of annoying the parent, even though both parent and child are sometimes unaware of the aggressive nature of the act.

We are discussing such acts here because parents perceived them as behavior related to obedience. Parents are most concerned when their children ignore their requests or demands (sometimes pretending not to hear), when they argue about requirements, when they try to wheedle out of obeying, or when they just plain disobey. Other less-emphasized problem behavior includes procrastination or dawdling, circumvention of parental requirements, and hostile reactions of children to parental requirements. One instance of the response of a mother to wheedling is illustrated by the following: "I detest wheedling and whining, and I am terribly arbitrary about that. I try to treat them reasonably and if I say, 'No, you cannot go,' it is because I have a very good reason for their not going. I explain that, and more teasing simply annoys me, and I usually shut it off very abruptly."

The positive behavior of children most frequently mentioned as influencing parents is cooperative obedience, but reasonableness and attempts of a child to reinstate himself into the good graces of the parent after disobedience are also mentioned. Mo 6, more than any other parent, stresses the influence of issues relating to the obedience of her two children, a boy about eleven and a girl of eight. She discussed disobedience 25 times in her seven interview sessions, but never mentioned the obedient behavior of her children. Most of these disobedient acts, which were performed mostly by her daughter, incited the mother to admonish or punish her child. A brief statement summarizes her response well: "If I tell them to do something, and they just absolutely, they just absolutely, disobey me, then they get a spanking."

Eating, toileting and sleep behavior. Mothers and fathers spend much time seeing that children eat properly, that they learn to control elimination, and that they go to bed on time, sleep well, and get up on time. These three areas of the socialization process are important during the early years of childhood, and if children do not learn the behaviors parents consider appropriate, there is great concern. Of the three, behavior related to eating influenced parents most. Parents are more concerned with the eating problems of their children than with their accomplishments, the difference being highly significant (Table

8.2). However, 66 per cent of mothers and 64 per cent of fathers discuss both. The accomplishments that motivate parents include weaning from the breast or bottle, eating well, and being skillful in eating. The problems relate to similar areas: delayed weaning, eating too little, refusing or vomiting specific foods, being messy when eating. In addition there are problems relating to conversation at meal times (talking too much, or talking with food in the mouth, or interrupting others), and to quarrels or teasing between children at the table. The behavior of her two children (So 7.3 and Da 4.1) at meal times, and the effect on the mother, is illustrated in the following series of excerpts.

Our evening meal is hectic and horrible! I would like them to eat without our having to remind them to eat the things they do not like and to have nicer manners. I think that is one of the reasons why it is so hectic, their manners are horrible, and it bothers us that we pester them. You just can't stand to see a child eat like a little puppy dog. They know they should not eat with their fingers and how to use a fork. . . . If they spill milk or something like that—if we are tired, we are cross about it, but if we are not, we ask them to wipe it up. . . . One of them will tease the other, and then we just make them be quiet; and if they won't then they have to leave the table, and they may come back when they feel like behaving properly. . . . We have a terrible time with dawdling, and we get so bored sitting there waiting. Sometimes we have our dessert and coffee and leave them to finish.

Only about a fourth of the parents report being influenced by the toileting behavior of their children, although there were 47 children under five years of age in the families in the sample, three-fourths of the families having such children. Most of the emphasis is on problems (wet bed, wet panties, playing with urine or feces); only 8 per cent of parents mention approved behavior such as the accomplishment of control. The difference in emphasis on approved and disapproved behavior is significant. The following excerpts are from interviews with a father of four sons between the ages of three and nine, and illustrate one father's response to the problems of bed-wetting:

Of the four children, we have got one that wets his bed every night. He's the second oldest one, [So 6.8]. I've tried getting him up at night, and found out that if I get him up at one or three o'clock in the morning, by seven o'clock he is sopping wet again. We tried buying him new pajamas and telling him he wouldn't want to wet something like that. . . . We are seriously thinking of buying one of those bed-wetting affairs with the alarm clock which we saw advertised in the paper. A friend of ours tells us that it was real effective with one of her kids who was a constant bed-wetter. She paid something like one hundred dollars to rent it for a month.

More parents discuss the behavior of children related to sleep and rest than discuss toileting behavior, but they do not stress it as much. Here again, problem behavior is discussed more than approved behavior by both mothers and fathers, but the differences are not as significant as they are for either eating or toileting behavior. The approved behavior mentioned includes: going to bed willingly, sleeping soundly, and getting up on time. The disapproved behavior is related to the same areas: not wanting to go to bed, interrupted sleep, and not getting up on time. The following excerpt illustrates the effect on a mother of a seven year-old who did not want to go to bed at night:

He is never very anxious to go to bed. He would like to linger and talk. Last night he tried to stay up a few minutes longer, but he did not succeed because we told him to go to bed. Then he wanted to have a story. We told him he had had a movie so no story—it was too late. Then he told me two or three things that happened during the day. Then I insisted he go to bed. But he didn't like his pillowcase. So we hunted for another one, but couldn't find it. Then he threatened to tear up his whole bed if I didn't find him his pillowcase. So I just ignored him and closed the door.

Sex behavior. Slightly more than a third of the parents discuss their children's interest in sex, and the problems presented in relation to immodesty, sex play, or masturbation (Table 8.1). The mother and father who discussed sex behavior most had a son who was entering adolescence. The mother stressed primarily this son's questions about the birth of babies, about physical differences of male and female, about reproduction. The father was more concerned with problems relating to petting, to any "extreme relationship with a girl," and to masturbation.

Dependency. All babies are dependent upon their parents for the satisfaction of their biological needs, and parents are highly indulgent of their dependency. Gradually, as children mature, they become less dependent in certain systems (dressing, toileting, eating, locomotion, etc.), but more dependent emotionally and socially.

Behavior of children related to dependency is fifth in emphasis as an influence on parents (Table 8.1). The parents in this study value independence highly (see Chapter V), and want their children to develop in that direction. However, they rarely respond unfavorably to such dependent behavior as seeking help from parents, wanting to be in parents' company, and seeking affection or seeking approval from parents (though the last two are seldom mentioned). A mother of three girls was somewhat ambivalent about her four-year-old daughter's dependent behavior:

> I have spoiled her because she is the baby. [Da 4.0] can get herself dressed with the exception of tying shoes, but she doesn't, just so she can get me in and do it for her. . . . I have threatened [Da 4.0] that if she did not start getting dressed we would just not be able to go where we were going. I should just go in and help her but I end up by doing it all.

In general, parents respond more to the kinds of dependent behavior they disapprove of, and wish to control or change, than they do to approved dependency behavior, the difference in emphasis being highly significant (Table 8.2). Fathers tend to stress change-worthy behavior more than mothers (64 per cent of mothers' codings; 70 per cent of fathers' codings on dependent behavior).

Parents stress negative attention-seeking behavior more than any other expression of dependency (61 per cent of mothers' total dependency codings; 50 per cent of fathers'). Such behavior, which was considered especially annoying when the parent was busy, includes: acting silly, clowning, whining, crying, and talking too much. A mother of four sons, born about a year apart, strongly emphasized the dependency behavior of her oldest child, and discussed how such behavior stimulated her to respond:

> After [So 4.9] was born, [So 5.8] was only eleven-and-a-half months old. He could barely walk, but he would pull at my skirt, and want to pull me away from the bassinet or the sink, where I was bathing the baby. I just had to ignore him when I bathed the baby, but it sure got on my nerves. . . . But when the baby was asleep I tried to play with

[So 5.8] and gave him a lot of my time. . . . But he was whiney, probably because when he whined I paid attention to him. . . . Later, I took this whining up with the preschool class I attended in the evenings.

The mother also discussed how she handled this child when he persisted in trying to get the attention of guests by interrupting or making noise, and when he persisted in crying loudly "over nothing, just to get attention." Seventeen times in her five interviews she talked about her annoyance and frustration with the dependent behavior of her firstborn son, and the punishment she increasingly meted out to him.

Some parents see thumb-sucking as a form of dependency. Mothers appear more likely to condone this, whereas fathers appear more likely to criticize and try to stop it. Dependency behavior in relation to other children is responded to in a similar way, acting silly is disapproved of, and seeking companionship usually approved of.

Fearful, anxious behavior. Parents are not as responsive to the fears and anxieties of their children as they are to their aggressions. Fewer parents discuss anxious behavior, and the difference between the emphasis on anxious and on aggressive behavior of children is highly significant (mothers $t = 6.97$, $p < .001$; fathers $t = 7.16$, $p < .001$).

Included in this category are not only specific fears of objects, animals, phenomena, and people, but also such anxiety manifestations as bad dreams, stuttering, tics. In addition, we included behavior related to anxiety; for example, being shy, overly sensitive, inhibited, tense or nervous, having inferiority feelings, and having tendencies toward perfectionism.

Few parents mention specific fears of children (23 per cent of mothers; 21 per cent of fathers); and manifestations of anxiety, such as bad dreams, stuttering, or tics, are reported by only 28 per cent of mothers and 18 per cent of fathers. Parents stress most their response to indirect expressions of anxiety (75 per cent of mothers' codings on fearful behavior; 67 per cent of fathers' codings). Most emphasized are being sensitive, perfectionist, tense, and shy. Mothers are more likely to try to change anxious behavior than to condone it, the difference being statistically significant. Fathers appear to tend in the same direction (see Table 8.2). The tendency of mothers to try to change anxious behavior is illustrated in the following excerpt:

[Da 9.3] is very sensitive. My goodness, if you bawled her out she would run down to her room and throw herself on her bed and cry. Very dramatic. . . . It reminds me of the way I acted when I was that age. I explain to her that she has to be a little tough about things, or she is not going to get along with people.

In several families a child was described at various times as acting shy, or being sensitive, or as feeling inferior, indicating that the parents sensed a relationship between such behavior, even though the word "anxiety" was never used. The following excerpts from the interviews of a mother of a six-and-a-half-year-old child illustrate this:

[Da 6.8] used to be real sensitive and shy, which I used to worry about. It probably was my own mistake in keeping her home too much by herself. That is why I started her in nursery school. For one quarter she was in tears every time I left her, but after that she was fine. . . . I often tell [Da 6.8] that I am proud of her if she has behaved well, because she is overly sensitive and shy. She would always feel she was inferior because she could not draw as well as Harold, one of her playmates. So I tell her that she can skate better than Harold, and she can read better.

Guilt and shame. Very few parents discuss the effect on them of a child's behavior related to guilt or shame, and those who do give little emphasis to such behavior. The discussions mainly concern a child's reactions to having disobeyed his parents. The father who emphasized such behavior more than any other parent said:

I told [So 6.3] he was not to get his boots wet in the creek. So when he came home with his wet boots, I said, "You remember what I told you?" He was shaking his head, he knew he had done wrong, and he was going to face the music. He said, "Spank me." So then he sprawls across my lap, and by golly he's waiting for his licking. So that just about takes everything out of you when he does that. I don't want to give him a spanking. But I give him a few licks because he deserved it.

Happy or unhappy behavior. Parents respond favorably to behavior indicating that the child's needs are satisfied: behavior indicating the child is cheerful, happy, contented, generous, and affectionate. The opposite kind of behavior, indicating unhappiness, selfishness, or discontentment, is responded to by efforts to change the situation, to console or offer advice, rarely to punish. There is about equal emphasis on approved and disapproved behavior, with mothers appearing to stress cheerful, happy behavior, and fathers appearing to give more emphasis to discontented and selfish behavior (Table 8.2). The difference between mothers and fathers in emphasis on disapproved behavior is significant at the level of $<.10$ ($t = 1.76$). A father said:

> My son is learning to dance now. One day he came home, and I saw he was bothered. Something was working on his mind and I asked him, "What's wrong?" "Oh, nuthin'," and he dragged his feet. So I told him, "If there is anything bothering you, son, you can tell Daddy, so as to see if I can help you out. I was your age once and probably the same thing happened to me."

Curiosity. Children's urge to know more about their world, as expressed in asking questions, exploring, and experimenting, brings positive responses from parents. Only rarely—when parents are tired or busy, or when they think there is danger to the child—do they respond unfavorably. Most of these parents gained a genuine satisfaction in being able to explain things to their children. A mother of five boys told about her third boy:

> When I was pregnant with my fourth child, I was pretty sick, and one morning the next older boy, who was five-and-a-half at the time, said, "Mother, what's wrong with you? I know that something is wrong because you are sick so much." I thought there is no use telling him now because it is so long to wait and I was not showing, so I said, "Mother is fine and I will tell you about it sometime." Then he said, "Well, Mother, I am five-and-a-half, and I am sure I can understand." So I told him I was going to have a baby.

Sometimes, questions are difficult to answer, as this father of an eight-year-old boy testifies: "He gets into technical questions like 'What makes a picture tube in television?' That is when we need help. We let him know we don't know the answer, but we have this World Book, and we look it up."

Behavior related to school. Although twice as many mothers as fathers discuss the influence of children's behavior related to school, the difference in emphasis is not significant. The issues discussed, in order of emphasis, are: academic success, attitude toward going to school, relations with the teacher, and interest in schoolwork.

Children's school problems are mentioned less frequently than problems in other areas (65 per cent of mothers' codings and 58 per cent of fathers' codings of behavior in school refer to problems). The difference in emphasis on approved and disapproved behavior reaches a significance of $<.10$ for mothers. The problems that influence parents most concern academic failure and not getting along with the teacher. Some parents sense a relation between problems in these two areas. A lawyer said of his eight-year-old son:

> When we moved to California, he was well behind in reading and phonics; and the teacher he had was not as satisfactory and he did not get along as well with her as with his present teacher, so we had him tutored. We felt that a child who did not learn well by the flash card method should be getting the basic foundations in phonics. So we had him tutored in spite of the public school's feeling that this was not necessary.

Other behavior. There are many actions of children to which parents respond that do not quite fit into the specific categories, and that do not have a sufficient number of codings for separate analysis. Most emphasis is given to motor achievements during infancy. Types of disapproved behavior mentioned by more than one parent include choosing friends whom parents do not like, taking things in stores, looking at television too much, hyperactivity, sophisticated behavior in adolescence, sex-inappropriate activities of boys.

Characteristics of Children

Parental practices are modified, not only by the behavior of children, but also by the characteristics of children as perceived and interpreted by parents. Johnny is stubborn, Lucy is so delicate and feminine, Tom loves to go fishing, Mary is the brightest one in the family—such opinions often in subtle ways determine what parents do. There are over 1,600 mentions by parents of the effect of their children's characteristics on their child-rearing practices (see Table 8.1).

The characteristics of children mentioned by parents as influencing them in rearing their children were grouped into nine categories: motivations, maturity, temporary conditions, abilities, physical characteristics, individuality, birth order, likeness to parents, and sex. Of all the characteristics of children that influence parents, three were particularly emphasized: the motivations of children, their level of maturity, and such temporary conditions as being tired, sleepy, hungry, or ill. Similar to the findings about the influence of children's behavior, there is unusual agreement between mothers and fathers in the degree and order of emphasis on the nine characteristics of children.

Motivations of children. What a child wants, desires, likes, or is interested in strongly affects the behavior of his parents, as reported by 100 per cent of mothers and 92 per cent of fathers. To a lesser degree, what a child dislikes, doesn't want, or is not interested in influences his parents (reported by 90 per cent of mothers and 69 per cent of fathers). Children who are bored, idle, disinterested, and in general lack motivation influence parental behavior to only a slight degree (reported by 18 per cent of mothers and 15 per cent of fathers). (See Appendix Table E.2.) Mothers and fathers place about the same emphasis on positive, negative, and no motivation, as indicated by the percentage of total codings of motivation that are found in each subcategory:

	Mo	*Fa*
Positive motivation	69%	71%
Negative motivation	29%	25%
No motivation	2%	4%

One family, with four boys under six years of age, responded to the desires of their children more than most families. The following is an excerpt from the mother's interviews:

[So 5.8] wants to carry the baby, and I always give him a pillow and place him on it. Sometimes I refuse if the baby is going to sleep, but if he is awake, I'll let him. . . . The children would get interested in TV programs; so often I would say, "All right, you may eat here in front of the TV set." For a while it went along fine. But after a bit they were more interested in the program than their food, so I put a stop to their watching TV at mealtime. . . . We allowed [So 4.9] to go without a bib when he was considerably younger than [So 5.8]—and it was just because he said, "I don't want to wear a bib."

They want to help with the meal preparation, so they can scramble eggs, or chop up wieners. Things that won't hurt them, I let them do. They get in the way, but I feel if they are not allowed to help now, they certainly won't help when they are adolescents. . . . We always made him take a nap until he was four-and-a-half, then he just said, "Can't I stay up? I don't feel tired. I'll just sit in this front room and rest for a while." So we let him do that and it's worked out fine.

Level of maturity of children. Parents have many beliefs about what children are like at different ages or development levels (see Chapter VII). They are also influenced directly by how mature or immature they perceive their own child to be. They judge maturity by the age of the child, or by his developmental level (infant, toddler, school age, or adolescent), or by more general terms such as little, old enough, or stage. Parents are more inclined to emphasize a child's developmental or maturity level than his chronological age, when discussing the child's influence on the parent.

Although parents are more influenced by beliefs about children's immaturity (see Chapter VII), in the characteristics of their own children, they are more influenced by the child's maturity than by his immaturity.

Temporary condition of child. When a child is tired or sleepy, hungry or thirsty, ill or injured, a parent's behavior is necessarily influenced. Such conditions are third in emphasis by parents. A mother, who discussed such adjustments more often than most parents, realized the difficulties she faced:

If they are really tired, I don't think I demand as much with regard to the routine of the day. I have found that if I let up at all because they say they are tired, then the excuse is, "Oh, Mommy, I'm tired and I can't do that"—particularly [So 5.7]. When he doesn't want to do something, he's just tired, his legs won't work—so I don't use that as a way of loosening any of the leash, so to speak. . . . But if they are really tired or they are sick, of course then they are excused from what they are supposed to do.

All parents who discuss the influences of these temporary conditions on child-rearing practices report that when the child is tired, ill, or otherwise temporarily indisposed, they lower requirements, adjust regimes, excuse or condone behavior usually unaccepted.

Abilities of child. About two-thirds of the parents indicate that they are influenced by the abilities, or lack of abilities, of their children. The abilities mentioned were grouped in three categories in the order of emphasis: intellectual (including academic abilities and knowledge), motor (including developmental skills, athletic skills, and motor coordination), and artistic (see Appendix Table E.3).

Intellectual abilities are discussed most often (by 39 per cent of mothers; 49 per cent of fathers), and mothers and fathers gave about equal emphasis to the presence or absence of these abilities. The following excerpt illustrates the influence on a mother of her six-year-old son's inability to learn as rapidly as his teacher expected him to:

> My little boy, the older one, is kind of slow in school, so I've been working with him at home. . . . The teacher sent a note home, so now I go and see the teacher every week, and she gives me work for him. I teach him the words, but he is kind of lazy and he don't want to do it, but I have to kind of push him. . . . The teacher wants to put him back, but I think he can do better if we work with him. We want him to pass if possible. . . . This summer, if she feels that she has to put him back, we're going to try and see if we can get a tutor for him. I would hate to see him put back. . . . We have to be patient with him, but it is hard; you kind of lose your temper when you see he is not catching on as fast as you want him to.

Motor skills and abilities in athletics are about equally emphasized, with mothers stressing positive abilities, while fathers give about equal emphasis to abilities and to lack of abilities. The parents of infants are interested in the emerging motor skills of their offspring, and they respond to each new accomplishment. This father of an eighteen-month-old firstborn said:

> I did not force the issue of walking at all. After he started walking and gave indications that he wanted to walk, I encouraged him to walk a few steps toward me, or I would hold him by his hand and let him take a few steps. . . . When he reverted back to crawling after he started walking, I'd put him on his feet. . . . If he gave indication that he wanted to take a few steps, I'd hold him by the hands, and walk behind him and support him more or less.

Very little is said about artistic abilities of children, but the four parents who discuss such abilities are strongly responsive to them. Such a tendency is well illustrated in the following excerpt from the interviews with a mother in an artistic, musical family:

I know [Da 10.5] is creative. She's extremely talented in drawing. She just showed me this morning a very charming Christmas poem, and it is full of word imagery. How can I take a child that is really productive, as she is, and say, "Leave your drawing and leave your writing and go clean up that room—it's a mess!" Or, "You can't spell 'choir' right. You must write it over again." Certainly talented children, and [Da 10.5] is one, need discipline probably, I guess, I don't know. But the women and men who want everything tidy won't be creative. I don't want her trained that way.

Physical characteristics. Many parents are quite sensitive to certain physical characteristics of their children and their behavior is accordingly influenced. The physical characteristics mentioned by these parents include: size, weight, sexual development, and, more than any other characteristic, physical defects.

As a child gets "bigger" a parent is likely to adjust his behavior toward him, especially in relation to control. The following excerpt from a mother illustrates this: "This little one [Da 6.7] is still at the age where a good spanking does her good. . . . But with [So 11.0] and [Da 8.9], both of them almost as big as I am, I'd feel kind of silly giving them a spanking."

A father said that he had not given his son, now almost fourteen years old, a whipping for at least two years.

Interviewer: Now, what made you stop licking your son?

Fa 34: Well, first of all, his size. . . . There was quite an experience three or four months ago, that gave me a little bit of a jolt, made me realize that life has changed in our house a little bit. I gave him [So 13.9] an order to do something which I thought was important for him to do—and I wanted it done at once. Well, he just stood up to me. I mean he was standing up ten inches away from me, looking me in the eyes. Here he was, as tall as me and strong—and I was facing the problem of physically forcing him to do it or giving it up. At the moment, I didn't know what to do, actually.

Most of the parents who talk about the weight of their children (23 per cent of mothers; 15 per cent of fathers) are concerned that their children are too fat. Usually this means a change of diet, not only for the child, but for the whole family, so that the overweight child will not be tempted by foods that increase fatty tissue. The following discussion concerned an only child, a six-year-old girl, who was "too fat":

> Well, the problem with [Da 6.8] is she is so fat. Dr. C. explains to her that when she started school, the children would tease her and make fun of her, and therefore she better cut out doughnuts and pastries, which she loves. . . . So I just tried to fix our menu so that we don't have a lot of things that she really likes. That way she doesn't feel too badly.

The emergence of somatic changes during adolescence stimulates some parents to explain their meaning to the child. In one family, there were two daughters who were only eighteen months apart in age. The younger of the two girls developed more rapidly than her older sister. The mother told how she prepared for this:

> I had been preparing both girls in case anything would happen. I have always taken advantage of a friend who is pregnant, or anything along that line, to try to point out all the different changes in life. Of course, before [Da 11.8] started her period, at ten-and-a-half years, her breasts had started to develop, and the pubic hair gets quite dark, and she was of course aware of this and knew that things were going on. I kept saying, "Of course, you know what the next step will be." And she knew, and she was prepared and we had supplies in her drawer. . . . I took her for a checkup with the doctor a couple of months before her period came, because I really didn't know if it was normal to develop quite so early.

More parents discuss defects in their children than any other physical characteristic (31 per cent of mothers; 26 per cent of fathers). These ranged from temporary developmental defects, such as facial acne during adolescence, to more serious abnormalities, such as cleft palate, congenital hip deformity, or strabismus. A father of an early developing adolescent said:

> A specific problem with [So 13.2] is the skin disorders that often accompany adolescence. He's had a little bit of a problem with that—not a serious one, but enough that we have helped him about it. We tried to reassure him and make him understand that it was a passing thing, that it is part of growing up. He seems to be accepting that as a nuisance, but thinking no more about it.

Serious physical defects in children press parents to make use of specialists and community resources. The following excerpt is less complicated than many:

> Our oldest child [So 7.3] was born with a cleft palate, and surgery was done before we left the hospital. It was very successful surgery. He's a nice-looking boy, and he will be able to have his teeth straightened later, and I don't think it will bother him or stand in his way in any way. He had difficulty to learn to talk, so we sent him to Stanford Village nursery school. He has had speech therapy. Then we have taken him to a private teacher for the last year, and we help him at home every day. He can speak very clearly except when he is tired. We have been fortunate in having good help and advice from Dr. "X," who has straightened out our attitude toward it. He has advised us, especially me, about my emotional feeling over all this—which was quite a problem.

Individuality. Parents find, sometimes quite gradually but often with surprise, that their children differ from children in the family or from other children the parent knows. Recognition of individuality tends to influence the parent to behave in different ways to different children. Many of these adjustments may be made unconsciously, for parents do not discuss these idiosyncratic differences as much as other characteristics of their children. However, some parents are extremely conscious of these differences. One mother, who stressed the differences between her little boy (So 4.3) and her little girl (Da 2.5) more than any other parent, said:

> I just think some children react differently than others. We are training our little girl to sleep all night without going to the bathroom and she is pretty good. But with my little boy, I had to wait a bit longer because he was just sopping. . . . I rarely spank my little girl because she gets all upset; you can slap her on the hand and she just screams her head off. My little boy, you can really give him a good wallop, and it doesn't seem to bother him very much. He will cry, but then it is all over with. It takes a lot more walloping to make an impression on my little boy.

Ordinal position in the family. Advantages and disadvantages seem to accrue to a child because he is the first baby, or the only grandchild, or the youngest nephew. Certainly, some parents (more mothers than fathers) give the first child a special kind of response. This is illustrated by the following excerpt from the interviews of a father of three girls:

> [Da 7.1], being our eldest child, received more attention than the other two. We were more concerned about her; we fretted more about her when she first came into the world. Right up until the second girl came, and I think perhaps since, [Da 7.1] has received our undivided attention. She was the eldest, she was more advanced, she was easier to handle, we appreciated her more than we did a second new baby in the house.

A mother talked a great deal about the differences between her three children, which she explained were due to the boy's being the eldest, the first girl's being the middle child, and the second girl's being the youngest.

> [Da 6.7] was the baby for a long time, and I babied her more and didn't make her do the things that the two others had to do when they were that age. . . . It seems like when there are three children, the one in the middle [Da 8.3] always gets the raw end of the deal all the time. . . . [So 11.6], being the eldest, has the most freedom and goes to bed latest.

Sex of the child. In our culture, parental behavior differs in many respects according to the sex of the child. Relatively few parents discuss the adjustments of their behavior to the sex of their children, although beliefs concerning sex differences were strongly emphasized (Appendix Table D.3). In general, those parents who mention this influence on their behavior stress the greater freedom given to a boy, and the more overt expression of affection given to a girl. One father told of his preference for the middle child in his family of three (in contrast to Mo 19, cited above). He said:

> I've always favored [Da 7.9] a little bit. I've always felt that [Da 7.9] was the prettiest and the smartest of the three—yet she isn't. I've always given her more love than I have [So 10.1]. I think it is because she is a girl. . . . I expect I will probably be more strict with my girls on dating and things of that sort when they go out than I will with [So 10.1]. . . . I spank [So 10.1] but I don't particularly care to spank the girls. It might be just because he's a boy. I might lose my temper a little quicker with him than I do with the girls. I raise my voice more to [Da 7.9] and [Da 4.4] but I very seldom touch them. I think it is probably because he is a boy, and he is older.

Similarity to parents. About a third of these parents mention how the similarity of a child to a parent influences child-rearing, but such characteristics are not strongly emphasized. Both mothers and fathers are more likely to discuss similarities between their children and themselves than they are to discuss likenesses between their children and their spouse. The tendency to see reflected in the offspring that which is seen in the self produces highly significant differences between the influences on mothers and fathers, a mother being more influenced by children perceived to be like her ($p < .02$), and a father being more influenced by children perceived to be like him ($p < .01$). A mother of two boys and two girls expressed her feeling this way:

> Another thing I did not mention last week about this eldest boy [So 10.4] is something I just think, I don't know whether it is right or not. He is just like me, or a lot like me, as far as his personality is concerned. I think I can see in him the things that should be changed, and they rub me the wrong way more because I know I do these same things. I am sort of taking it out on him when I really feel that these things are wrong within myself.

A father reported that there were no rules that the children had to eat everything on their plates, and explained it this way:

> I have tried sometimes forcing them to eat things, and I've seen [So 10.1] practically have to run out and spit it out because it is so distasteful to him. Whether he is putting it on or not, I don't know; I don't believe he is actually. I understand his problem because I am the same way. He is like me—there are things I just don't like.

As can be seen from these two excerpts, sometimes the perceived similarity between parent and child instigated an effort to change the behavior, and sometimes it caused the parent to condone the behavior of his child. We did not have enough codings to make a statistical analysis of such tendencies. We would also have liked to investigate the relation of sex of the child to the sex of the parent where likenesses were seen, if the data had been adequate for such an analysis.

Parent-Child Interaction

A parent learns by experience, not only with his spouse, but also with his children. As shown in the previous section, parents are continually responding to children's behavior, and children are responding to their parents'. By this interaction parents gradually build up generalizations concerning children and attitudes concerning specific methods of child-rearing. A mother or father acts in a certain way with his child; if the method used is successful in bringing about what the parent wants, then such behavior is reinforced, and the parent is likely to use this method again, not only with the child with whom it was successful but with other children in the family, especially those born later. If, on the other hand, the parent's method fails, he is less likely to use this method again with the same child, and he is also less likely to try it on other children in the family. In the process of experience, parents learn not only about the usefulness of their method, but they also gain insight into why it succeeds or fails. It is through interaction with a child that a parent often learns what to expect of a child and what behavior is appropriate for his stage of development.

Most of the parents discuss the influence of their interaction with their children on subsequent parental behavior, as shown in Table 8.1. Both mothers and fathers appear to emphasize the effect of interaction with one child on their behavior with a second child, more than the effect of interaction with one child on their subsequent behavior with the same child. However, these differences do not reach a statistical significance of .10 or beyond. In addition, parents stress parent-child interactions that lead the parent to change his practice, more than interactions that lead to repetition of the same practice. The difference in this emphasis is significant for mothers at the level of $<.001$ ($t = 4.65$), for fathers at the level of $<.01$ ($t = 3.35$). Mothers stress interactions with children leading to change in practice significantly more than fathers (Table 8.1).

The following excerpt illustrates the tendency for interaction with a sibling to influence later practice with another child, and also the tendency for failure to lead to changes in practice:

Interviewer: Do you think you will do anything different with [So 1.3] than you have done with [Da 5.6]?

Mo 22: Yes. This isn't so much a trial-and-error period as it was with [Da 5.6]; [Da 5.6] was my guinea pig. I have learned that certain things are not so important. I was very rigid, going along with the old idea of toilet training. My mother believed and told me that from the time when a child was old enough to sit up alone you start toilet training. Well, this, of course, is not reasonable. The child has to understand what it is. So I tried with [Da 5.6] and she was fine, and then all of a sudden she rebelled and the doctor told me, "Now listen, this is just a little person. You're doing more harm than good. Don't pester her so much. She'll come around to doing it again." And she did. . . . I was being very strict because my mother said this is the way it is done.

Relation of Influence of Family Members to Demographic Characteristics

The 41 categories relating to the influence of family members on child-rearing were correlated with seven demographic characteristics of parents. The correlations will be found in Appendix Tables E.4, E.5, E.6, and E.7. The significance of the correlations in relation to chance expectancy is shown in Appendix Table E.8.

TABLE 8.3. *Correlations between Influence of Family Members and Mothers' Demographic Characteristics ($p < .05$)*

	Age of parent	*Number of children*	*Age of oldest child*	*Consistency in religion*	*Education level*	*Social position*	*Social mobility*
Characteristics of parent							
Angry	—	—	—	—	—	.37	—
Fatigued	—	—	–.35	—	—	—	—
Anxious	—	—	–.32	—	—	—	—
Behavior of children	—	.42	.35	—	—	—	—
Problems (Σ)	—	.47	—	—	—	—	—
Obedience (Σ)	—	.34	—	.35	—	—	—
Obedience problems	—	.35	—	.39	—	—	—
Dependency problems	—	—	–.44	—	—	—	—
Aggression (Σ)	—	.44	.44	—	—	—	—
Aggression problems	—	.45	.38	—	—	—	—
Curiosity	—	.36	—	—	—	–.48	—
Characteristics of child	—	—	—	—	–.40	—	—
Motivations (Σ)	—	—	—	—	–.33	—	—
Motivations (positive)	—	—	—	—	–.37	—	—
Motivations (negative)	—	—	.32	—	—	—	—
Temporary condition	—	—	–.32	—	—	—	—
Parent-child interaction							
With sibling (Σ)	—	.35	—	—	—	—	—
Leading to change in practice	—	—	—	.32	—	—	—

NOTE: r .32, $p < .05$; r .37, $p < .02$; r .41, $p < .01$; r .51, $p < .001$.
Data taken from Appendix Tables E.4, E.5, and E.7.

Of the 287 correlations, 41 of those for mothers, and 44 of those for fathers, are significant at the level of .10 or beyond. The number of correlations significant at the level of $<.10$ is less than might be expected by chance for fathers. In Tables 8.3 and 8.4 are shown the correlations that are significant at the level of .05 or beyond.

Among both mothers and fathers, the education and social position of the parent, the number of children, and age of the oldest child are most highly related to specific influences of the family members.

Less highly educated mothers are more likely to be influenced

TABLE 8.4. *Correlations between Influence of Family Members and Fathers' Demographic Characteristics* ($p<.05$)

	Age of parent	*Number of children*	*Age of oldest child*	*Consistency in religion*	*Education level*	*Social position*	*Social mobility*
Characteristics of parent	—	—	—	—	.46	.37	—
Angry	—	—	—	—	.42	.40	—
Fatigued	—	—	—	—	.33	.48	—
Interests	—	—	—	—	.40	—	—
Spouse interaction							
Mo influences Fa	—	–.32	—	—	—	—	—
Fa influences Mo	—	—	–.41	—	.32	.32	—
Mutual interaction: agreement	—	—	.43	—	—	—	—
Behavior of children	—	.34	—	—	—	—	—
Problems (Σ)	—	.44	.34	—	—	—	—
Eating (Σ)	—	.35	—	—	—	—	—
Eating problems	—	.52	—	—	—	—	—
Obedience (Σ)	—	.36	—	—	—	—	—
Obedience problems	—	.39	—	—	—	—	—
Dependency	—	—	—	—	—	—	.35
Aggression (Σ)	.51	—	.52	—	—	—	—
Aggression problems	.48	—	.54	—	—	—	—
Characteristics of child	—	—	—	—	.38	.40	—
Maturity	—	—	—	—	—	.37	—
Temporary condition	–.43	—	—	—	—	—	—
Parent-child interaction							
With sibling leading to change	—	—	—	.33	—	—	—
With child (Σ)	—	–.32	—	—	—	—	—
With child leading to change	—	—	—	—	—	—	–.34

NOTE: r .32, $p<.05$; r .37, $p<.02$; r .41, $p<.01$; r .51, $p<.001$.
Data taken from Appendix Tables E.4, E.6, and E.7.

by the characteristics of their children, especially by their positive motivations, and those of lower social position respond to the curiosity of their children. Mothers of higher social position are more likely to change their behavior when they are angry.

Fathers show strong tendencies to emphasize their own characteristics if they are more highly educated and of higher social position. They report that their child-rearing practices are influenced by anger (as do mothers), by their own interests, and, to a lesser extent, by fatigue. Such fathers also respond to the characteristics of their children as they perceive them, especially in relation to maturity level. They appear to stress their influence on their wives.

In families with larger numbers of children, mothers and fathers respond to the child behavior they wish to change. Mothers particularly emphasize behavior related to aggression and, to a lesser extent, obedience and curiosity. Fathers in such families respond particularly to eating and obedience problems.

When firstborns are younger, mothers are somewhat influenced by their own fatigue and worries, and they are strongly concerned with dependency problems of their children. When firstborns are older, both mothers and fathers wish to modify aggression of their children. Fathers of younger firstborns tend to influence their wives, but fathers of older children are more influenced by decisions made through talking over problems and coming to some mutual agreement. Younger fathers respond to temporary conditions, such as fatigue or illness of their children; older fathers, to aggressive behavior.

Differences between Mothers and Fathers

Mothers and fathers differ quite markedly in their emphasis on some of the influences that husband and children, or wife and children, have on their respective child-rearing practices. The differences between fathers and mothers that reach a statistical significance of .10 or beyond are summarized in Appendix Table E.9. Appendix Table E.10 shows the level of significance in relation to chance expectancy.

Mothers are more likely than fathers to stress their own feelings and attitudes, especially their health, their anxiety, and their interests. They are much more likely to perceive the influence their husbands have on them, due to the husband's competence, and to a lesser extent to the husband's attitude toward his wife. The motivations of children appear to be emphasized somewhat more by mothers. Mothers stress the likeness of their children to themselves much more than fathers do.

Fathers stress two influences much more than mothers: the effect of the mother's competency (and perhaps her indispositions) on the father's child-rearing practices, and the effect of the child's perceived similarity to the father. In addition, they appear to be influenced more by their own anger.

The outstanding result of this analysis is the similarity of mothers and fathers in their emphasis on the effect of the behavior and characteristics of children, not only for the category as a whole, but for each specific category (except perhaps motivations of children), and on disapproved as well as approved behavior.

Summary and Comments

The kind of people who make up a family unit, and their interactions with each other, determine to some extent the rearing of children. No parent is a completely stable, inflexible person automatically acting out his values and beliefs in bringing up his children. He is a dynamic personality changing as his own inner needs change, molded by what his spouse does and believes, and pressed to respond directly to his child as he perceives him.

Parents differ at various times, in the intensity of their interests, in the level of tolerance for interruptions, in tension and anxiety. They realize that when they are busy, angry, worried, or tired, they tend to be less considerate of children's needs, more rejecting, and more punishing. One mother stated this clearly:

> If you're really the sort of person who, for her own needs, needs to be a little autocratic, it comes out whether your philosophy is one of extreme permissiveness or respecting the individuality of the child, and all those wonderful phrases, but, you know—if you really have to be boss, as I do very often, it turns out that this is what the sum total of your actions is, rather than your independently conceived philosophy, which sounded so good, and you even think is right!

The subtle interactions between husband and wife that influence child-rearing practices may be difficult for an outsider to recognize, but most parents are acutely conscious of them. In most families, one parent is not always dominant—not even the mother. There is much give and take, a lot of discussion to find mutual agreements, a shifting of responsibility back and forth because one parent is more competent, or is indisposed, or just plain does not like to do certain tasks.

Every parent in this study felt that his ways of bringing up his children were strongly affected by the nature and behavior of his children. Mothers stress the influence of children more than either their values or their beliefs; fathers emphasize beliefs slightly more. Parents' practices are modified by the characteristics they perceive in their children; by children's behavior; and by the way children respond to the child-rearing methods of the parent. Of such influences, the behavior of children is by far the most stressed.

The immediate stimulus for parental action is often the child's behavior. A parent's experience in his family of orientation may provide the prologue, and his values and beliefs the backdrop, but the behavior of the child is what actually raises the curtain on the drama in which the parent and the child are the performers.

Although parents are not unresponsive to, or totally ignoring of, behavior of their children of which they approve, they are much more conscious of the effect of behavior that they disapprove of and that they would like to change. Three-fourths of the behavior they discussed, they considered worthy of change. Every mother but one laid more emphasis on disapproved than approved behavior, and every father except three did the same. This strong emphasis on behavior parents do not approve of and therefore try to change is similar to the stronger emphasis given to beliefs related to punishment than to beliefs related to reward (Chapter VI), and perhaps is related also to the emphasis on parental control, more than any other instrumental act, as a means for obtaining desired goals (Chapter VII).

Parents are concerned about many aspects of children's behavior, but the areas they emphasize are behavior related to aggression, to orderly living, to obedience, and to eating. Less

attention is given to dependency, anxiety, guilt, curiosity, happiness, and to behavior related to toileting, sleep, and sex.

To a lesser degree parents respond to the characteristics they perceive in their children—especially their wants, likes, and interests. Children seem to subtly control the practices of their parents by their own strong motivations, by their abilities, or by their physical defects.

We regret that only about a third of the parents mentioned similarities of a child to his parents for this would be an interesting area to explore more extensively. There is convincing evidence that both mothers and fathers tend to see in their children more likeness to self than to the other parent. A parent may be stimulated to condone, or to try to change, behavior in a child perceived as similar to self, but we do not know from these data which tendency is stronger. Likeness was seen sometimes in a same-sex child, and sometimes in a child of the opposite sex, but we do not have enough data to determine which tendency predominated.

There is evidence that parents learn through experience in bringing up their children. If a practice brings a satisfactory response from a child, a parent is likely to repeat it, not only with that child but also with future siblings. But if the method fails, he is likely to change it. Parents are particularly conscious of interactions that lead to change.

The number and age of children in the family, and the education or social position of the parents, are most highly related to the influence of the family. Problems relating to aggressive behavior are emphasized when children are older, problems relating to dependency are stressed when they are younger. Parents with larger families are influenced by behavior they consider worth changing, mothers especially emphasizing aggression, whereas their husbands are concerned with eating problems and obedience. Parents of higher social position are more likely to stress their own characteristics, and these fathers also stress the characteristics of their children. However, it is the mothers of lower educational level who have more to say about the influence of their children's characteristics.

IX

Behavior Settings

Parents are influenced in their behavior with their children by the situation, or milieu, in which the interaction takes place. Being in church, or being in the living room, or having a guest for dinner, may alter to some extent what the parent expects of a child, the method he uses to obtain desirable behavior, the way he responds to what he considers appropriate behavior, as well as his manner of handling misbehavior. We used the term *behavior setting* to refer to the nonpsychological milieu in which parent-child behavior takes place and that influences not only the parent's behavior but the child's behavior as well. Barker and Wright, who are chiefly responsible for the development of the concept of behavior setting, state: "A behavior setting has two characteristics: it is a discriminable part of the non-psychological milieu, and it is generally perceived as being necessary or appropriate for the transaction of some particular behavior" (Barker and Wright, 1951, p. 8). A behavior setting, as we have used it in this study, represents an area that has general behavioral significance to parents in relation to their children.

Parents in the study were not highly conscious of the influence of behavior settings on their rearing of children, but all parents discuss them to some extent. Altogether there are 878 codings relating specifically to the effects of the setting on the parent's behavior with his child. As shown in Table 9.1, we have analyzed such influences under two subcategories: home settings, and settings outside the home. In addition, we have analyzed those characteristics of the settings emphasized by parents.

Mothers seem more conscious of the effect of the setting on

TABLE 9.1. *Influence of Behavior Settings*

	Per cent reporting		*Number of codings*		*Mean percent-age score*		*Percentage score difference*	
	Mo	*Fa*	*Mo*	*Fa*	*Mo*	*Fa*	*t*	*p*
Home settings	97	90	398	236	3.30	2.27	3.13	<.01
Activities	90	82	194	114	1.66	1.08	2.78	<.01
People in home	77	54	102	50	.83	.46	2.63	<.02
Furnishings	64	46	52	33	.41	.33	—	n.s.
Rooms	39	33	26	22	.19	.21	—	n.s.
Garden, patio, yard	23	39	24	17	.21	.19	—	n.s.
Settings outside home	85	82	153	91	1.29	.89	2.89	<.01
Neighborhood	69	67	62	48	.53	.46	—	n.s.
Public places	33	36	25	17	.20	.18	—	n.s.
Others' homes	41	15	28	8	.26	.08	2.50	<.02
Recreation	36	21	21	11	.18	.11	—	n.s.
School	33	15	17	7	.12	.06	1.78	<.10
Σ Behavior settings	100	100	551	327	4.59	3.16	3.49	<.01

their behavior than fathers, and the differences in emphasis are statistically significant for each main subcategory, as well as for the category as a whole.

HOME SETTINGS

There are three kinds of home settings parents discuss as influencing their behavior: the physical plant of house and garden, certain activities in the home, and people in the home. Mothers and fathers emphasize the effect of activities and of people in the home more than other aspects of home settings.

Home activities. The behavior settings related to home activities mentioned as influential on parental behavior include both routine activities (such as mealtime, going to bed, getting up, toileting) and special occasions (such as birthdays, Christmas, and other holidays). These activities are stressed more by both parent groups than any other aspect of home settings.

Relatively few parents (36 per cent of mothers; 15 per cent of fathers) recognize that the settings of routine activities influence their behavior. The following excerpt is from the interviews with a mother of four children, who usually does not emphasize promptness, except at mealtime:

When I was a child, we always ate on the dot. Six-thirty and the bell rang, and we washed our hands and came down. There are times when I give the children a few minutes' leeway, but I have reached a point where I will not call the older ones more than once. I have a bell, and I will ring the bell, rather than yell, and if they don't come and they are late, they may get a little bit to eat, but they certainly don't get dessert, if they don't come on time.

Special occasions, such as birthdays, Christmas, and other holidays, cause parents to modify their usual practices, mainly in the direction of indulgence and permissiveness. Over half of the parents (51 per cent) recognize and discuss such settings.

People in the home. The home setting depends in part upon the people in the home. The absence of either father or mother because of business or illness, the presence of maternal or paternal grandparents, of other guests, of a nurse or a servant, as well as the number of children in the family, contribute in one way or another to modification of the home setting, and therefore may influence parental behavior. Only a few parents mention these influences.

More parents (31 per cent of mothers; 21 per cent of fathers) mention the effect of the number of children in the family on their goals and practices, than mention other settings in this category. The following excerpt from the interviews of a mother of four boys, between the ages of one month and six years, illustrates this point:

We were all alone with [So 5.8]. He was the only one for a while, and [So 4.9] was still young then, so we would have the time to tell [So 5.8] how to hold his spoon, how to eat. . . . We just had the time, and so we expected him to do things. With each successive child you just don't have the time, so you don't require them to do something, or you just don't look for things. With the first one you have the time to look for those little things.

The effect of visitors in the home is strongly emphasized by mothers (64 per cent) and by some fathers (44 per cent). The home setting becomes changed when there is a visitor, and parents are pressed to modify their requirements, to change routines, or to become more lenient or more strict with their children. This is true when a child has his playmates visit him, but it is more emphasized, by both mothers and fathers, when adults are being entertained in the home. A parent may become more lenient at such times, as illustrated in the following excerpt from a father of two girls, six and four-and-a-half:

> I think with children our children's ages, they resent having company around. There are outsiders in the home and they are not getting the attention, so they tend to go overboard and show off. We just expect that when we have company, they are going to do something that they know they aren't supposed to do, primarily to attract attention, or because they are jealous. So unless it is too bad and unpleasant for the company, we'll just ignore them.

Mothers often try to make things run as smoothly as possible when they have child or adult guests. The following excerpts are from a mother who was particularly resourceful in this way. She needed to be, with four young sons:

> Mo 33: If there are other children who come for dinner, we found it works better if the children eat at a separate table.
>
> Interviewer: But if there are just adult guests how do you handle the situation?
>
> Mo 33: It depends on the guest we have asked. If we know it is someone who doesn't mind children, and enjoys them in fact, we allow the children to eat with us. But if we know it is somebody that might be a little fussy, we feed the children first. . . . I let them talk to my friends before they go to bed, show their toys, and so forth.

There are other women who are less adept at handling their children when company comes:

> Sometimes if we have company, I'll use bribery; I'll offer them the moon, to make them behave, and not disrupt everything. . . . Sometimes I'm kind of up a tree, I will put them in their rooms, and they will start screaming, and then I have to leave the company and go in, and tell them to stop screaming.

Rooms, garden, and furnishings. Restrictions and freedoms, requirements and permissions, punishments and rewards, are sometimes related to a certain room in the house (living room, parent's bedroom, child's own room, the hall, kitchen) or to the patio or garden. Such situations are not highly stressed by parents, but about one-half mention them. One of the mothers who emphasized home settings said:

Having so many windows in the house, we don't play football or baseball in the backyard or the front yard. We do not ride things down the driveway. It is a blind driveway that is extremely steep, and in the past we have really had to lay down the law. They don't play in the music room. We don't paint with water on the hardwood floors. We do that in the bathroom.

Another mother was strict about the back yard, as illustrated in the following excerpt.

We have an awfully large yard, and they can play anywhere in the yard, it doesn't matter. Except the back—I don't want them in the back, because there is nothing out there for them to play with, and they aggravate the dog. There is no reason for them to go there. They go out there and they climb—my husband has some lumber stacked back there, and he has it stacked so that it won't get warped, and he does not want them crawling on it. They climb all over it, and we put a new fence across the back, and they climb on that, and there is just nothing back there for them to play with.

Settings Outside the Home

Table 9.1 also presents the analysis of the settings outside the home that are mentioned as influencing parental practices. They are mentioned less than half as much as settings within the home. Neighborhood, school, restaurants and stores, picnics, camping, automobile trips, and visiting, all are mentioned by some parents as situations affecting parental behavior.

Neighborhood settings. Settings within the neighborhood are mentioned by two-thirds of the parents as influencing their behavior. The behavior settings mentioned include the following: a deep creek bed, automobiles parked on the street, traffic, decorative pebbles in a neighbor's garden, poison oak in the hills, a vacant lot, the railroad tracks, construction in progress. Such settings are stressed more than other settings outside the home by each parent group. And of these, traffic on the streets, especially in conjunction with children riding bicycles, is stressed most; the following excerpt is from a mother:

They are not to go on Willow Road on their bicycles, and they go on Willow Road. I have told them they are not allowed on the road, because there is so much traffic coming off the Bayshore Freeway. After I told them why they cannot go on the road, they still go. [Da 7.1] had to put her bicycle in the garage for three days because she went on Willow Road.

The following excerpt from the interviews of one father (with four children) illustrates the effect of the California countryside on his practices:

Because we live in the country, we are very careful about fire. Especially in the dry season, we do not allow the children to play with matches or candles or anything like that. And we have found it essential to require every child who has been playing in the creek bed to take a shower bath immediately upon coming home, because of the difficulty with poison oak. We recommend that they stay out of it, but if they want to go ahead and do it, they must shower.

Public settings. About a third of the parents make some mention of public settings, such as restaurants, stores, or public conveyances. The following excerpt emphasizes the change in a father's practices when he takes his children out.

Definitely, we require better manners of them when we are out than when we are at home. I think they understand that. For one thing, they are dressed up a little specially. We tell them around three or four o'clock that we are going to take them to dinner. They realize something special is going to happen. . . . Most of the time it works out pretty well. Occasionally, the kids start acting silly, creating a little disturbance. I get a little perturbed because we feel that we cannot tolerate screaming, or naughty behavior, teasing, or whatever, when we are out. I might threaten to put them in the car, if they don't behave. If they continued to act up, we might take one of them and put him in the car.

Visiting. Mothers, more than fathers, are concerned with their children's behavior when they are in other people's homes. In such situations parents often become more strict, as illustrated in the following excerpt:

Some parents send their children out of the room if they get too out of line. But I usually very quietly sit down next to them, and tell them to be quiet and sit down. And they do, because if they don't, when I get home I really lay the law down to them, and I won't take them again to visit if they act like that.

Recreation settings. Few parents discuss the effect of such recreation settings as parties, picnics, camping, or automobile rides on their behavior with their children. The following excerpt is an illustration of the effect of one recreation setting on the behavior of a father.

> [So 11.0] has been going fishing with me now for about five years. Every time I take him out fishing, we go through all the safety rules. I show him how to bait a hook, explain to him to be cautious, so that when he throws his line out he won't hook himself or me or somebody else. When we are out at the ocean, he has to follow me. He can't wander off. While we are sitting there and the fish are not biting, I will talk to him about the rules of fishing, the limits in size of fish, and so on.

School settings. Situations in school, although not strongly stressed by these parents, deal mainly with classroom settings and concern the relation of the child to the teacher and the child's success in school. The following is a summary of a much longer discussion by a mother concerned with the schooling of her seven-year-old son.

> I have just arranged today that [So 7.4] go to the "X" school. I am sorry I did not do this earlier. I have been unhappy this year because I felt [So 7.4] was not being stimulated in his present school. He was bored at the kind of work they have to do. It is a large class, and in talks with the teacher, I felt that she had no understanding of [So 7.4] as a person, or of his particular abilities. She is unhappy because he gets dirty at play and gets the school dirty. He is left-handed and is not neat about writing. These are the sorts of things I think are unimportant.

Characteristics of Behavior Settings

There are five characteristics of behavior settings in the home, the neighborhood, and the community that parents identify as influencing their behavior with their children. Most emphasized are situations that a parent considers dangerous. In addition, the amount of time available, the weather, and the importance of the situation to the parent are mentioned. The relation of certain aspects of the occupational life of parents to the setting is also discussed. These data are presented in Table 9.2.

TABLE 9.2. *Characteristics Emphasized in Settings*

	Per cent reporting		Number of codings		Mean percentage score		Percentage score difference	
	Mo	*Fa*	*Mo*	*Fa*	*Mo*	*Fa*	*t*	*p*
Danger	82	69	87	63	.73	.68	—	n.s.
Time	74	49	78	40	.67	.36	2.50	<.02
Occupation	54	49	40	39	.34	.38	—	n.s.
Weather	41	23	27	11	.27	.11	1.82	<.10
Importance	21	10	14	5	.12	.03	2.06	<.05
Σ Characteristics of settings	100	92	246	158	2.13	1.56	2.65	<.02

Danger to child. Settings that a parent considers to be dangerous to his child brought forth a variety of behavior: explanation and protection for the young child, admonitions and punishment for the older child. Children playing in, or crossing, the streets where dangerous traffic conditions exist are mentioned most often. Playing with sharp knives or tools, hitting and breaking glass, running on slippery floors, getting into medicine, turning on the gas stove, and playing with electric cords, outlets, and equipment, are mentioned as dangerous aspects of home settings. Starting fires, especially during the dry California summers, and playing in the creek bed on rampage in the spring, also are considered dangerous settings, and parents reacted in terms of the hazards they perceived for their children.

In the following excerpt the mother is talking about how she disciplines her children. She believes that in situations with potential danger a parent should spank. She said:

A lot of people don't believe in spanking but I do. Sometimes I think they have to have a spanking.... I'll tell you something that happened tonight. One of the twins [So 2.8] went into the kitchen and turned on all the burners on the stove. So I had to spank him then.... I made him turn the burners off himself, and I spanked his hand, and sent him back in the bedroom.... Usually if I see them running out in the street, I go spank them.... Like playing with matches. One morning we were in bed, and [Da 3.5] had struck one, and threw it in the trash box. Our roomer saw it smoking and told me, and I spanked her for it. Medicine we put out of the way. But other things that are not dangerous, we usually tell them not to bother it. We don't hide it from them.

Time. Time as an aspect of a setting is mentioned by about three-fourths of the mothers, and half of the fathers. The greater emphasis by mothers is significant. Most of these influences (42 per cent of the codings about time) are related to the time available, as indicated in such expressions as "It was early," "We were late," "There just was not time enough." Slightly less emphasis was given to the time of day (36 per cent of mothers' codings; 38 per cent of fathers'); and the least emphasis was given to the influence of the day of the week or time of the year; for example, weekend, school days, vacation (22 per cent of mothers' codings; 20 per cent of fathers').

Time is an important element in most routine settings for mothers, as indicated in these excerpts from the interviews with a mother of five young daughters between the ages of six months and seven years.

They're in bed by 7:30 on school nights. On Friday and Saturday they usually go to bed at 8:30. And then on Sunday they go to Sunday school. If we go somewhere, we take the kids with us, unless we go out in the evening. I don't like to have them out late, they're so used to going to bed at 7:30. . . . Usually on weekends or Sunday we go somewhere. Sunday we went, it was pretty nice, to Coyote Point Yacht Harbor.

Occupational life. Certain characteristics of the occupational life of a parent modify the settings that influence child-rearing; these are mentioned by about half the parents. The hours of work, the kind of work, nearness of the job to home, as well as the income derived, may directly affect the behavioral settings of family life. The effect of the father's job is usually mentioned, and in the few families where the mother worked, the mother's job is also mentioned as influencing settings. The time of meals, the extent to which parents and children have meals together, the use of free clinics instead of private pediatricians, these and other specific aspects of settings seem related to the exigencies of the father's or mother's job. A wife of a physician said:

We try to have dinner at six—if my husband is home at six, and he tries very hard to come. If not, we wait until 6:30 for him, and if he isn't there then, we go ahead. Monday night is the one exception to this. He is never there on Monday night, so we have dinner promptly at 5:30 in the television room.... When my husband is on call, and the telephone is going to disturb the children all during the evening, we let them go to sleep in our bed, and then pick them up and put them in their own beds when they are asleep.

Probably the most important effect of the father's work is the way it affects him; his attitude toward his job may influence all family settings. One mother discussed this effect at length, comparing family life when the father had a job he did not like with life when he had a job he did like. The following excerpts are from a much longer discussion.

I think my husband's job has definitely set the pattern of our lives. He has a very creative mind. If he isn't happy in his work, he's absolutely miserable in every way, bored and restless.... To be restless and bored certainly makes you a less pleasant person to have around. Now he works all the time, Saturdays and at home every night, but he's excited about it.... And we are all happier.

Weather. Weather, even in California, modifies settings. Warm weather in summer means playing and eating out of doors, going camping, having picnics at the beach; rainy and cold weather in winter means letting the children undress by the fire, seeing that they wear warmer clothes, putting them to bed earlier, letting them play indoors.

Importance to parent. When a parent considers that behavior in a situation is important, he is likely to insist upon conformity or immediacy from a child, although relatively few parents mention this. One father of four children stated:

If it is an occasion when we need obedience and think it is essential, we don't allow them to talk back. If they start to do this, we will threaten them with a little physical punishment, or something of the kind. But if it is an occasion of no particular importance, talking back is part of the game sometimes.

Relation to Demographic Characteristics

Tables 9.3 and 9.4 present the correlations between the emphasis parents place on the influence of behavior settings and seven demographic variables. Table 9.5 gives the significance of

TABLE 9.3. *Correlations between Emphasis on Behavior Settings and Demographic Characteristics—Mothers*

	Age of parent	*Number of children*	*Age of oldest child*	*Consistency in religion*	*Education level*	*Social position*	*Social mobility*
Home settings	.06	.31[a]	.00	.09	–.04	.14	.27[a]
Activities	–.05	.32[b]	–.12	–.06	.06	.05	.18
People in home	.13	.24	.07	.16	.03	.27[a]	.14
Furnishings	.01	–.03	–.18	.19	–.21	.06	.35[b]
Rooms, garden	.13	.06	.24	.07	–.11	.05	.06
Settings outside home	–.04	.24	.29[a]	–.24	–.16	.14	.06
Neighborhood	–.16	.17	.22	–.23	–.15	–.02	–.04
Public places	.07	.16	.02	–.05	–.04	.19	.27[a]
Characteristics of settings							
Danger	–.19	.12	.07	.14	–.48[d]	–.28[a]	.34[b]
Weather	–.29[a]	.08	–.20	–.22	.03	.09	–.05
Time	.06	.18	.00	–.11	.21	.14	.25
Occupation	.14	–.02	–.08	–.08	.00	.12	.07
Σ Behavior settings	.08	.29[a]	.13	–.04	–.09	.23	.19

[a] $p < .10$; [b] $p < .05$; [c] $p < .02$; [d] $p < .01$.

TABLE 9.4. *Correlations between Emphasis on Behavior Settings and Demographic Characteristics—Fathers*

	Age of parent	*Number of children*	*Age of oldest child*	*Consistency in religion*	*Education level*	*Social position*	*Social mobility*
Home settings	–.21	.56[e]	.04	.15	.06	.05	.09
Activities	–.15	.38[c]	–.12	.03	.37[c]	.27[a]	.12
People in home	–.10	.09	.02	–.09	.22	.20	.11
Furnishings	–.04	.48[d]	.16	.29[a]	–.27[a]	–.25	.12
Rooms, garden	–.21	.46[d]	.11	.18	–.40[c]	–.26	–.20
Settings outside home	.07	.08	.10	–.15	.02	.02	.00
Neighborhood	.02	.10	.12	–.07	.01	–.09	.03
Public places	.01	.11	–.07	–.02	.07	.18	–.02
Characteristics of settings							
Danger	–.02	.45[d]	.16	.31[a]	–.32[b]	–.37[c]	.06
Weather	–.10	.13	–.19	–.02	.01	–.09	–.16
Time	–.08	.22	–.11	–.13	.38[c]	.24	.07
Occupation	–.15	.18	.03	–.07	.07	.15	–.05
Σ Behavior settings	–.14	.49[d]	.10	.07	.03	.04	.06

[a] $p < .10$; [b] $p < .05$; [c] $p < .02$; [d] $p < .01$; [e] $p < .001$.

TABLE 9.5. *Significance of Correlations between Behavior Settings and Demographic Characteristics*

Level of significance	Number expected by chance (91 r's)	Number observed Mo (91 r's)	Fa (91 r's)
<.001	.09	0	1
.001 to .01	.82	1	4
.01 to .02	.91	0	5
.02 to .05	2.73	3	1
.05 to .10	4.55	7	4

these correlations, in relation to chance expectancy. For mothers, the correlations are relatively low, with only one exception: dangerous settings are definitely emphasized by mothers of lower education (and perhaps of lower social position and higher mobility). There appears to be a slight tendency for mothers with more children to stress settings in general, particularly activities in the home. Women who are more highly mobile in social position also appear to stress the importance of home furnishings and proper behavior in public places.

The fathers' emphasis on behavior settings reveals strong and statistically significant relationships to several demographic characteristics. Fathers of larger families stress behavior settings as a whole, particularly those relating to home settings (such as rooms, gardens, furnishings, and activities), and those involving danger. Those fathers who stress rooms or garden tend to be from lower educational levels, and those emphasizing dangerous settings are also from a lower social position. In contrast, fathers who stress activities in the home are of higher education and perhaps higher social position. Such men also tend to stress the importance of the time element in behavior settings.

Differences between Mothers and Fathers

From the data presented in this chapter, it seems clear that mothers are more conscious of the influence of behavior settings on their behavior with their children than are fathers. Mothers have higher scores than fathers for 17 of the 19 categories under behavior settings, and 11 of these differences are statistically significant at a level of .10 or beyond. Therefore 57.9 per cent of the categories of analysis of behavior settings show a statistically significant difference in favor of mothers (see Tables 9.1 and 9.2). The number of observed differences at each level of significance is greater than chance expectancy.

Mothers emphasize significantly more than fathers the sum of behavior settings, and the two main subcategories of home settings and settings outside the home. In home settings they give greater stress to the influence of persons in the home and activities in the home. Among behavior settings outside the home, school and visiting in the homes of other people are given more emphasis by mothers than by fathers. The characteristics of settings that mothers stress significantly more than fathers are the time element, weather, and the importance of the setting to the mother.

In the families with larger numbers of children, the fathers are much more emphatic than their wives about the influence of behavior settings in the home and about the dangers inherent in settings. Fathers of higher education are likely to stress behavior settings in the home relating to activities and the importance of time in behavior settings, but mothers of higher education show no tendency to emphasize any particular behavior setting. Mothers who have moved up the social ladder appear to emphasize home settings, public places, and the danger in settings, but upward-mobile fathers show no particular tendencies in relation to the influence of behavior settings.

Summary and Comments

The ordinary daily life of a parent with his children might be described as a series of interlocking and overlapping behavior episodes, each determined to some extent by the attributes of the setting in which it takes place. Behavior settings not only influence the behavior of children but also affect the rearing of children by parents. Part of a parent's job is to teach children how to behave in different settings. The behavior setting coerces the parent to teach and control children so that they will behave appropriately.

All of the parents in this study discussed to some extent the influence of the milieu, or the behavior setting, of which the parent-child interaction is a part. However, the relative emphasis given to the effect of behavior settings was slight compared to the emphasis given to other determinants of child-rearing. In general, two characteristics of a behavior setting seem to bring it to the consciousness of the parent: an issue involved (struggling to get children to bed on time, or making children behave properly at the evening meal), or special visible characteristics of the setting (such as danger—cutting an apple with a sharp knife; weather conditions—going out to play in winter; a time limit—getting off to school on time).

Behavior settings in the home were emphasized more than twice as much as settings in the neighborhood or community. This difference probably reflects the greater amount of time parents spend with children in the home. Children have to be taught behavior that is appropriate for the routine situations of life, as well as behavior that fits the cultural rituals of birthday parties, Christmas dinner, and Easter egg hunts.

Home settings are repleat with physical structures, furnishings, equipment, utensils, and gadgets that force parents to interfere with children's activities, to make rules, and to train children in necessary skills. It is not surprising to find that fathers of larger families are particularly concerned with appropriate behavior in relation to house and garden.

Guests in the home are both a pleasure and a problem, for parents must help children learn that a guest changes the situation and that out-of-the-ordinary behavior is expected: a change from ego-centered to other-centered behavior. Parents also are conscious of the control and socialization necessary when children visit others' homes. Mothers are particularly sensitive to children's behavior in both of these settings.

Except for situations in the immediate neighborhood, parents gave relatively slight emphasis to the influence of behavior settings outside of the home. In Midwest, a town of 700 people, investigators identified 107 general categories, and 585 subcategories, of behavior settings that modified child behavior. Many of these settings exist in the Stanford community but they were not mentioned at all by the parents in this study; for example, churches, theaters, post offices, hardware stores, department stores, athletic contests, hotels, barber shops, banks, school parties, shoe shops, doctors' offices, laundries, gas stations, bakeries, libraries (Barker and Wright, 1955, Chapter IV). Probably there are two causes of the lack of data concerning behavior settings outside the home: the parents were not highly sensitive to the effect of behavior settings outside the home; and our interviewers did not probe adequately to elicit the information.

X

Previous Experiences

Every parent has had experiences in the past, that he can remember, identify, and label, that influence to some extent the way he brings up his children. Three categories of past experiences reported by parents as influential on child-rearing are discussed in this chapter. They are: experiences during childhood with the respondent's own parents; other childhood experiences; and experiences during adult life.

Parents in Family of Orientation

The experiences a man or woman has with his own parents in his family of orientation are particularly crucial. They are emphasized more than other childhood or adult experiences (see Table 10.1). The remembered experiences with father or mother, and the remembered feelings about the practices, beliefs, or values of parents, affect to some extent the rearing of children by the respondents. A father may remember with great resentment the punishment he received from his own father, and therefore consciously strive never to treat his child in a similar way. A mother may remember with admiration her mother's guidance, and try to emulate her mother in bringing up her own children. Although other factors may press a parent to take a direction other than the one he consciously wishes to take, the fact that he inclines toward a certain course probably brings about compromises and perhaps conflicts that otherwise would not occur.

Identification of parent. In discussing how the experiences in

TABLE 10.1. *Previous Experiences of Parents*

	Per cent reporting		*Number of codings*		*Mean percentage score*		*Percentage score difference*	
	Mo	*Fa*	*Mo*	*Fa*	*Mo*	*Fa*	*t*	*p*
In family of orientation								
Respondent's mother	87	44	145	64	1.19	.61	2.33	<.05
Positive influences	69	33	78	40	.60	.37	—	n.s.
Negative influences	62	39	67	24	.59	.24	2.49	<.02
Respondent's father	44	56	34	75	.28	.72	2.88	<.01
Positive influences	31	49	20	41	.16	.40	2.33	<.05
Negative influences	26	36	14	34	.12	.32	1.99	<.10
Respondent's folks	92	85	187	139	1.61	1.48	—	n.s.
Positive influences	72	74	109	79	.83	.83	—	n.s.
Negative influences	80	64	78	60	.78	.65	—	n.s.
Σ Respondent's family of orientation	100	92	366	278	3.08	2.81	—	n.s.
Positive influences	85	87	207	160	1.59	1.60	—	n.s.
Negative influences	92	80	159	118	1.49	1.21	—	n.s.
Other childhood experiences								
Experiences with people	44	44	32	43	.29	.42	—	n.s.
Positive	36	28	19	24	.18	.25	—	n.s.
Negative	28	31	13	19	.11	.17	—	n.s.
Experiences in settings	41	56	27	42	.24	.46	1.75	<.10
Positive	28	31	14	17	.12	.21	—	n.s.
Negative	23	44	13	25	.12	.25	2.59	<.02
Self-characteristics	72	69	66	63	.62	.61	—	n.s.
Positive	51	46	31	39	.29	.39	—	n.s.
Negative	46	44	35	24	.33	.22	—	n.s.
Σ Other childhood experiences	90	80	125	148	1.15	1.49	—	n.s.
Positive	77	56	64	80	.59	.85	—	n.s.
Negative	62	64	61	68	.56	.64	—	n.s.
Adult experiences								
Teaching, caring for children	44	18	57	15	.39	.14	2.77	<.01
Positive	41	18	47	15	.33	.14	2.40	<.05
Negative	13	0	10	0	.06	.00	—	n.s.
Observing parents with children	95	92	203	160	1.75	1.68	—	n.s.
Positive	80	80	88	71	.71	.77	—	n.s.
Negative	85	72	115	89	1.04	.91	—	n.s.
Other experiences	28	57	26	56	.20	.59	2.61	<.02
Positive	26	54	18	44	.15	.49	2.67	<.02
Negative	13	23	8	11	.05	.10	—	n.s.
Σ Adult experiences	95	97	286	230	2.34	2.41	—	n.s.
Positive	90	90	153	130	1.19	1.40	—	n.s.
Negative	85	74	133	100	1.15	1.01	—	n.s.
Σ Previous experiences	100	100	777	656	6.57	6.71	—	n.s.

the family in which they grew up affect their present-day behavior with their children, parents sometimes refer to the influence of their mother and sometimes to the influence of their father, but often they use more general terms, such as "parents," "the family," or "the folks at home." Table 10.1 presents data on the influence of the respondent's mother, father, or "folks." The following three excerpts from the interviews of one mother illustrate the tendencies of a respondent to refer to the influences of mother, father, or, in more general terms, family and folks.

> I guess I got my ideas of what children should eat from my mother. She always said you should have a green vegetable with every meal—she was a nurse.
>
> Well, they are pretty prompt because they know I am very impatient. If [Da 8.0] doesn't come, then she gets punished, she knows I get mad about it. . . . I think it is important; it's just the way I was brought up. My father was always prompt, and he was impatient.
>
> Lots of times when the children are asleep I'll whisper "I love you," and maybe their subconscious mind will hear that; and they will know that their mother loves them, because my family never told me that.

Positive and negative effects. The respondents also indicate in their discussions whether the experiences in their family of orientation affected them positively or negatively; that is, whether they try to do with their own children what had been done with them, or whether they strive to change the pattern and to bring up their children in a different way.

In Table 10.1, positive and negative influences are reported. In general, these parents appear to stress positive influences more than negative influences, but the differences do not reach a significance of .10 or beyond, as will be shown in Table 10.2.

The distribution of parents who report only positive influences, only negative influences, or both positive and negative influences of their own parents is shown in Appendix Table F.1. Seventy-seven per cent of the mothers and 74 per cent of the fathers tend to see both good and bad in their own childhood experiences with their parents. More parents emphasize both positive and negative effects of their own parents than report either positive or negative effects alone. The only exception to this generalization lies with the reports of mothers about their fathers: 21 per cent of mothers mention only positive influences, 13 per cent report only negative influences, and 10 per cent mention both positive and negative effects. The tendency toward emphasizing the positive as well as the negative influences of the family of orientation is illustrated in the following excerpts from interviews with a father of three girls:

> I know that while I believe in giving my children a lot of overt affection, I believe I did not get it as a child. . . . I feel that my parents were cold to me, much colder to me than I am toward my own children. Isn't that strange? . . . My mother never did love us up very much. I don't think as much as Dad did. This may be where I get the idea that you should be more demonstrative towards your children.
>
> I am intent not in raising my children in a particular religious affiliation, but in raising them first as Christians, rather than for a particular religious sect. I believe that will make them more tolerant. . . . This is very much influenced by my own early training. . . . Both my parents are Christians, and they are really, I think, religious; rather deeply religious, but not ostentatious in their religion, and not intolerant of other religions. I have felt, seeing them, that this has been a fairly successful adjustment to the whole problem.

Source of influence. A parent may modify his child-rearing practices because of the characteristics, values, beliefs, or practices of one of his own parents. Appendix Table F.2 presents an analysis of these four sources of influence. Over 90 per cent of the parents in this sample recognize the practices of their own parents as most influential. Much less influence is reported to come from the characteristics of the parents of these mothers and fathers. Least of all recognized as influential are the values and the beliefs of the respondent's parents.

The respondent's mother. Both women and men report that their own mothers influence them in raising their children. However, about twice as many mothers as fathers discuss such influences, and they emphasize them significantly more (Table 10.1). Some of the parents report that they had endeavored to emulate their own mothers in rearing their children. Such positive influences are mentioned by twice as many women as men.

The most outstanding example of a woman consistently influenced by memories of her mother's ways of bringing up children is Mo 19, an employed woman with three school-age children. She had grown up in a lumber camp, and remembered with affection and admiration how her mother had brought up a large family in this difficult environment. Seventeen times in the interviews, Mo 19 referred to the practices and, to a lesser extent, the values, beliefs, and personal characteristics of her mother as positive influences on her own life as a mother. The following excerpts from an interview illustrate the influence of her mother's practices on Mo 19:

Interviewer: From what you said I gather you have a rule that no outsiders can come into your home when you are not there.

Mo 19: Definitely. No one is to come in the house if we're not there.

Interviewer: Could you tell me why you have that rule?

Mo 19: It's just a matter of routine with me. My mother would never allow anyone in the house when she wasn't home, and we always knew when we could ask somebody to come in the house, or when we couldn't ask somebody to come in the house. . . . I never did care for children running in and out of the house.

Mo 19's interviews contained many such references. Her beliefs were also influenced by her mother's beliefs, as witness this statement: "I don't think you should give girls too much freedom. My mother always said that you'll never have a bad child if you keep him occupied—she said it's the ones that don't have anything to do that get into trouble." Mo 19's values were also influenced by her mother: "The main thing I remember in my childhood which was understood, without my mother commenting on it, was to have respect. As long as you have respect for everyone, everything else just sort of takes its course. That is always the main thing—to have respect." Toward the end of the fifth and final interview with Mo 19, we find this statement:

Interviewer: Suppose something came up now that you needed help about, something concerning the behavior of one of your children, where would you go to get help?

Mo 19: Well, I think first of all I would talk to my mother. I would just talk to her and see what she has to offer, because I know, in talking to her, that she would sincerely say anything that she thought would help, but on the other hand she wouldn't expect me to do what she would say. She would leave it up to me as to what to do with her suggestion.

There are, however, about as many parents whose experiences in their family of orientation either made them want to do just the opposite of what their own mothers had done, or, at least, incited them to make a conscious effort to raise their own children differently. Mothers emphasize such negative influences of their own mothers significantly more than fathers (see Table 10.1). Such a negative attitude is illustrated in the following excerpt:

> The only thing that I think made me oversensitive with my first child was the fact that for the first five or six years of my life I had an English nanny—and mother was a "queen." I didn't feel she was "mother" and I was determined that I would give more of myself to my child than I had had of my own mother. . . . I told my mother, and she agrees with me. My sister is nine years older than I am, and when she was born, my family was not as comfortably situated as when I was born. My mother raised my sister. My sister was happier, she didn't have as many emotional problems to resolve. She had more of mother. Consequently, she is closer to mother. I never was that close to my mother, so I feel that this was a very sad mistake, and I was determined that I would never have a nurse for my children, that I was going to be there.

The respondent's father. About half the parents are influenced in their relations with their children by the experiences they had during childhood with their own fathers. Men, more than women, report being influenced by their fathers, both positively and, to a lesser extent, negatively (see Table 10.1). As did the influence of the parent's mother, the influence of the parent's father appears to have more positive than negative effects, but the differences are not statistically significant. The tendency to stress positive influences of the father is well illustrated in the interviews with Fa 7, who only mentioned positive influences of his father:

> One point in my background that I didn't mention was the Spanish influence, the fact that we hope that [So 4.25] and [Da 2.5] will both be able to speak Spanish. We were taught to speak Spanish when we were children. Dad placed a certain amount of emphasis on that. . . . I think it is part of their heritage. They're half Spanish.

In contrast to the above, the following excerpt is from the interviews of a father who made it clear that there was little about his childhood family that he wished to emulate.

> And when I was growing up, the thing I remember most vividly was that I never could seem to do a job in a way that would satisfy my father. Or if it did, he wouldn't say anything about it. Ninety-nine percent of the time it didn't satisfy him, and so there would be clashes. Naturally I was the weaker, and I couldn't win any of the clashes. So my own defense mechanism was to withdraw into myself and simply sulk—refuse to talk to anyone, keep still for as long as I could, things like that. That was, at the time at least, the only thing I could do—the only way I could express my own rebellion. Before I was ever married, I resolved that if I married and if I had any children, that was one thing I was going to not do. I planned to express a positive stand, I was going to try to let my children know when they did something well, and let them know when they didn't do it well too, but give them a sense of accomplishment when they had done it. Human frailties being what they are, of course, I haven't carried it out as completely as I would like to, but I would like to think that I do, and make a definite effort to.

The respondent's parents or "folks." A high percentage of mothers and of fathers do not distinguish between their mother and their father when they discuss the influences of their family of orientation, but instead use some general term like "parents," "folks at home," or "family." About one-half of each parent group report both positive and negative influences of their "folks" (see Appendix Table F.1).

Both mothers and fathers discuss the influence of practices decidedly more than the influence of the values, beliefs, or personal characteristics of their "folks." This is similar to the emphasis on practices of the respondent's mother or father specifically (see Appendix Table F.2). The following excerpts from interviews illustrate the effect of the respondent's "family" or "folks" on child-rearing. A mother, in discussing how she was rearing her first baby, said:

> I think he can do with all the affection I have to spare, and I don't hold back on that at all. . . . It just comes from my family—the way I was brought up. I could always count—no matter how bad I was—I could count on my parents' affection. I never was scared of losing that. I think the love you can give a child is the best thing in the world.

Another mother told about the belief she had learned in childhood from her family, and was now passing on to her children:

> I told my children that any lie, everything they do that is bad, is just building bricks in Hell, is building like a furnace, and every lie adds another brick to the furnace in Hell. . . . In Heaven it's the golden bricks, but in Hell it's the bricks of badness that makes the furnace. . . . That's the story I've told them and the one I was raised on in my family.

The mothers and fathers who talk about their childhood "folks" emphasize the negative influences almost as much as the positive influences. The husband of the mother quoted above said several times that he wanted to bring up his children in a different way from the way he was brought up. In the following excerpt, he emphasizes the difference in values:

> I think the basic reason is I want them to be happier. When I was a kid I was always clean and neat, and we always had enough to eat but I can't remember being really happy as a child. Everything was the bare essentials. . . . I guess you do act a lot by the way you were taught by your parents, or the way your parents acted around you. I can see why they acted as they did, living in Europe they probably

TABLE 10.2. *Differences in Emphasis on Influence of Family of Orientation*

	Higher	*t*	*p*
MOTHERS			
Mo Mo vs Mo Fa (total)	Mo Mo	4.01	<.001
Mo Mo vs Mo Fa (positive)	Mo Mo	2.85	<.01
Mo Mo vs Mo Fa (negative)	Mo Mo	3.42	<.01
Mo Mo (positive) vs Mo Mo (negative)	Positive	—	n.s.
Mo Fa (positive) vs Mo Fa (negative)	Positive	—	n.s.
Mo Pa[a] (positive) vs Mo Pa (negative)	Positive	—	n.s.
Σ Mothers' family of orientation (positive) vs (negative)	Positive	—	n.s.
FATHERS			
Fa Mo vs Fa Fa (total)	Fa Fa	—	n.s.
Fa Mo vs Fa Fa (positive)	Fa Fa	—	n.s.
Fa Mo vs Fa Fa (negative)	Fa Fa	—	n.s.
Fa Mo (positive) vs Fa Mo (negative)	Positive	—	n.s.
Fa Fa (positive) vs Fa Fa (negative)	Positive	—	n.s.
Fa Pa[a] (positive) vs Fa Pa (negative)	Positive	—	n.s.
Σ Fathers' family of orientation (positive) vs (negative)	Positive	—	n.s.

[a] Pa refers to the parents or "folks" of the respondent.

never had too much. As long as you had enough to eat and a house, forget about the fun. Just bring the children up right. I'd like to bring the children up right but I would like them to have a lot of fun.

Differences in influence. In Table 10.2 we present an analysis of differences in the emphasis mothers and fathers in this study place on the influence of the parents in their family of orientation. Mothers in this study are influenced by their own mothers decidedly more than by their fathers. The differences are highly significant, both for total mentions and for mentions of both positive and negative effects. In contrast, fathers appear to be influenced more by their fathers, both positively and negatively, but the differences are not statistically significant.

Other Experiences in Childhood

Experiences during childhood and adolescence outside the family of orientation also modified the rearing of children by the mothers and fathers in this study. In Table 10.1 we see that such experiences are emphasized only a little more than half as much as those in the family of orientation, but a large percentage of both mothers and fathers mention them.

The other experiences that parents report are grouped under three headings: experiences with people; experiences in settings; and remembered self-characteristics (see Table 10.1). Table 10.1 also reports whether such experiences motivate a parent to try to provide similar experiences for his own child (positive), or to try to protect his child from such experiences (negative).

With people. The persons other than parents who are mentioned most often in connection with childhood experiences are siblings, playmates, relatives, teachers, and leaders of youth groups. Mothers speak about their experiences in caring for younger siblings, as witness the following excerpt from the interviews of a young mother:

I've got three sisters and two brothers. I'm the oldest. My next sister is sixteen, and then they run down to about four months. I've had a little bit to do with all of them—bringing them up. I wasn't afraid of not doing the right thing with my baby, because I had the experience before.... I am trying to wean my baby now. If I remember correctly, my little brothers and sisters, when they were about nine months old, they were drinking out of a cup . . . and it didn't hurt them any.

Fathers tend to mention their experiences with children outside the family more than experiences with siblings or adults. The following excerpt from the interviews of a thirty-year-old father illustrates the influence of a childhood playmate and his family:

> I spent quite a bit of time with a friend that I met when I was five years old. His parents had a home that I have always considered, ideal, and I see them as a guide to what I should do. I probably learned more on how to raise children from them than any place. I really worshipped their home life. . . . It seemed very tranquil. The husband brought home an excellent income, made things as pleasant for his wife as possible, did all the repair work around the house. . . . They expected an awful lot of their children: they were expected to partake in the functioning of the home. . . . They were a team, the wife had her responsibilities, and the husband had his, and they brought up their children thinking the same way. . . . My wife and I are this same way. We are dependent upon each other, and we hope that [So 0.7] will take the same feeling. But we want him to be very sociable too, like my friend and his family.

The following excerpt, from the interviews with a father of three boys, illustrates how childhood experiences can stimulate a man not to act in certain ways with his own children:

> One of the things that I know influences me—we had some very good friends across the street when I was a child. The couple were contemporaries of my parents, and they were good friends. They had two boys, about the same age as myself and my sister. On occasions the father was the sternest man. If his kids wouldn't do something, he'd just snap them right at that point; he'd grab them by the ear, haul them back out to the garage, and just beat the tar out of them. . . . This is one of the images of a father that I want nothing to do with.

In settings. Almost half of the parents discuss the influence of certain settings in their childhood, without identifying, or sometimes perhaps without knowing, the persons who were involved in these settings. School is mentioned more often than any other setting, but living on a farm, in a congested area of a city, in a fishing village, or in an apartment are mentioned. In addition, experiences in Scout activities and in other organizations are discussed. Parents lay about equal emphasis on positive experiences, those they want their children to have, and on negative experiences, those they do not want their children to have. The following excerpt from a father's interviews illustrates the tendency of parents to react negatively to school experiences: "They pushed me along in school too fast. We won't let our children do that. Both [Mo] and I were pushed too fast, skipped grades, and wound up way out of our peer group." Fathers have twice as many negative as positive codings in relation to school; mothers have more positive than negative codings. These figures are too small to warrant statistical treatment.

The emphasis that some parents place on the community in which they grew up is illustrated in the following excerpt from the interviews with a father.

> I was raised in Kansas City—on the third floor of a three story walk-up, and it wasn't a slum by any means, but still we never owned a home. We never had a backyard to play in; you had to go to the park and be supervised. We just didn't want it for our kids. We wanted a place where they could stretch out and grow up.

Experiences during childhood in a Scout group and their effect on a father's level of control with his children are illustrated in the following excerpt.

> We have been rather strict with our children. . . . I can't really say where I get this from really. I can remember back in my own experience, as a Boy Scout. The one Scoutmaster that stands out most in my mind made us all toe the line, but we got a lot accomplished and we liked him very, very much. We were very proud of ourselves, proud of our troop. I sometimes wonder whether being strict does net you dividends, and I've always looked back to that person—how I felt about him and how other boys felt.

Self-characteristics. Parents are influenced more by their memories of what they were like when they were children than by either their experiences with people or their experiences in settings. The difference between emphasis on self-characteristics and emphasis on experiences with people is significant for mothers

($t = 2.36$, $p < .05$), but not for fathers. Mothers emphasize self-characteristics in childhood even more strongly than settings ($t = 2.72$, $p < .01$), but the difference for fathers is not significant. If experiences with people and in settings are combined, parents appear to emphasize them more than self-characteristics, especially those they respond negatively to.

The remembered interests, likes, dislikes, and feelings about activities and experiences during childhood modify the way some parents bring up their children. Mothers and fathers appear to show little difference in positive or negative effects of their remembrances of self-characteristics during childhood. The following excerpt illustrates how a mother's discipline is affected by her childhood memories: "If my child should hit me, I wouldn't spank him. It would be better to sit down and talk to him. I know when I was a child, a talking did me more good than a spanking, because I would remember it longer. . . . I do remember every talk I ever had."

There are parents, however, who want their children to have a life different from the one they had when they were children. Some parents remember their confusion about sex, and want to give a better sex education to their children. A father who learned Japanese and English at the same time, and got them mixed up, does not want his child to learn a foreign language until he knows English well. The following excerpt from the interviews with a father of an eight-month-old firstborn illustrates the tendency of some parents to want their children to have experiences in childhood that are different from their own remembered ones.

> I hope [So 0.7] is more athletic than I was. I always was at the end of the class athletically. When you are young, this is painful. I don't want him to be outstanding. If he is, all well and good, but I'd like him to be average, so he can keep up with the group. The only pain I ever had in childhood was the fact that I was not athletically inclined. Though I liked it, I really wanted to, I just wasn't capable. I hope he doesn't face this problem.

Experiences in Adulthood

Most of the parents modify their child-rearing in some ways on the basis of experiences they have as adults. Such influences are emphasized by mothers and by fathers almost as much as experiences with their own parents, and more than other experiences during childhood (see Table 10.1). The difference between emphasis on adult experiences and on childhood experiences not related to parents is highly significant for both mothers and fathers (mothers: $t = 4.55$, $p < .001$; fathers: $t = 3.06$, $p < .01$).

In Table 10.1, experiences in adulthood are presented under three headings: teaching and caring for children other than one's own; observing other parents and their children; and other experiences (including those in college, military service, and jobs). Mothers gave about equal emphasis to experiences having positive effects and those having negative effects; fathers stress positive effects more, but the difference is not significant.

Experiences with children. Some parents gain ideas that modify their child-rearing from experiences as teachers, or from taking care of children not their own. As one might expect, mothers stress such experiences significantly more than fathers. Most of the parents' experiences with other children come from teaching, and are primarily positive influences. Those parents who either had been or were teachers incorporated some of their teaching experiences into their values, beliefs, or practices concerning child-rearing. The following excerpt from the interviews of a mother who had taught five years before her marriage illustrates this tendency.

> There are many things from the teaching that I carry over with my children. Things that I used in the classroom that make them interested in music and rhythms, I use with my own children now. . . . I do most with the things that most children had difficulty with in school. Numbers specifically. They might be able to count to a hundred, and not have the concept of the number five. So I consciously work with our children on the meaning of numbers.

Relatively few mothers or fathers are influenced by experiences in caring for other people's children (15 per cent of mothers; 8 per cent of fathers), and all but one of these parents stress the positive nature of the experience.

Experiences with other parents and children. Contacts with, and observations of, other parents interacting with their children are by far the most influential experiences of adult life. More of these experiences appear to stimulate mothers and fathers not to do as they observed, rather than to emulate, but the differences in percentage scores do not reach a difference of .10 or beyond. The following excerpt from a mother of a son and two daughters illustrates how a specific practice may be influenced by these contacts:

One couple had two small children, and when they came to visit you the children would be turned loose in the house. If there was any admonishing done it would always be by the host or hostess. My husband and I often discussed it. We didn't want this to happen with our children. When we went visiting we would certainly take the responsibility for them. If the children did not behave in another home the way we thought they should, then we would not go visiting.

Values, beliefs, as well as practices were influenced by contacts with other parents, as shown in the following excerpt:

I think I am always influenced by other families. I am afraid I am a sort of a chameleon, and take on the color of the surroundings.... When our son was little one of the families in the apartment was completely arbitrary about demands, and slaps and spankings were the rule. The comments were all directed toward "give him a good spanking and straighten him out"—that sort of thing. If I had been in a different situation I might have handled him differently.... When we moved, the people were quite a different type, then I began to see much more the logic of the more permissive, understanding behavior.

Other adult experiences. Experiences at college, during military service, or on the job can modify to some extent the way parents bring up their children. Fathers emphasize such experiences more than mothers. They appear to influence parents primarily in a positive manner. Parents report that they have been influenced in child-rearing by a variety of experiences in college: roommates, friends, professors, curriculum, and the content of courses. (If the content of a course relates directly to ways of rearing children we have coded it under communication sources, which will be discussed in Chapter XI.)

About two-thirds of the mothers and fathers in the study had some college education (see Appendix Table A.3), but few of them mention any influence that college experience had on the rearing of their children (18 per cent of mothers; 26 per cent of fathers). Mothers appear to give about equal emphasis to positive and negative influences of college; fathers appear to stress positive influences primarily. (The number of codings is too small for statistical analysis.) Mothers are likely to discuss the courses they took, or their attitude toward academic pursuits, as illustrated in the following excerpt from a mother of four:

> As far as formal education, I certainly wasn't trained to be a mother. . . . I was a physics major, not because I particularly had any bent that way. It was a silly waste of time, except that it eventually threw me into a place where there were a lot of unattached men. The whole sum of that experience is that I shall be very careful not to repeat it with any daughter of mine. Let girls stick to the silly things girls like.

Fathers appear more likely to discuss the people they knew in college, and the impressions various persons made on them—both professors and fellow students.

Experiences in military service affect the way about one-fourth of the fathers and a few mothers bring up their children. Some fathers emphasize the broadened horizons gained in the Service, but more fathers stress military discipline. One father, who had been in the Marines during the war, was influenced more by this experience than any other in his life, referring to it in relation to his values for traveling, his goals for a relaxed evening meal, his rejection of psychiatrists as communication sources, and his beliefs in discipline. The following excerpts illustrate the influence of the Marines on the father's methods of discipline and punishment:

> Fa 22: I don't know whether I am a little bit sadistic or not. I don't think I have spanked [Da 5.6] more than three times in her life, but I made each one of those spankings count by playing on her. I say, "You are going to get spanked" and "You are going to get spanked" for quite a while before the actual event occurs, and it seemed to have a lasting impression on her.
>
> Interviewer: Where do you suppose you picked up the idea of "playing on her"?
>
> Fa 22: Probably from the Marines. All discipline seems to be inspired by fear, I would say, and that seems to be half the battle. . . . About seven months ago [Da 5.6] had been particularly unruly all day long. I came home probably with a chip on my shoulder from

business. I warned her I would have none of it. Finally we got to the dinner table—and dinner is one thing the Service taught me should be a time of complete relaxation. [Da 5.6] continued being unbearable at dinner. I had my wife put her in bed . . . and bring her a slice of bread and water for her dinner. . . . I don't know what kind of permanent impression it left on her, but I recalled it to her on several occasions, and she remembered it well.

Interviewer: How did you happen to think of doing this?

Fa 22: Well, when the uniform code of military justice came in, bread and water was the standard punishment for doing just about anything in the Marines, up to 30 days of it. That's probably what was in the back of my mind at the time.

Fathers and mothers have experiences at work that influence what they do at home with their children. Over a fourth of the fathers discuss these experiences, but less than half that many mothers do. Although there are a few negative experiences, most of the parents report positive ones. A supervising engineer in a large industrial plant discussed such influences in his interviews:

Various things on my job that have to do with dealing with people have influenced how I deal with the children. I have learned the importance of explaining things to people, even the ones that are not directly concerned with the work, giving them an overall picture so that they will feel a part of the project. . . . When we decided to move up here, I told the children why I was leaving the former firm, and what I hoped to do with the new company; why we were moving, and what kind of an area it would be; and how we felt about moving and so forth.

Relation to Demographic Characteristics

In Tables 10.3 and 10.4 we present the correlations between the emphasis mothers and fathers place on 19 categories of previous experiences and seven demographic characteristics. In the footnotes to these tables the significance of those correlations in relation to chance expectancy is given. The correlations for fathers include few of high order significance; those beyond chance expectancy are at the levels of .05 and .10, as shown in Table 10.4.

Family of orientation. Women from families consistent in religion appear to be critical of their parents. Mothers of low social mobility tend to emphasize the positive influences of their par-

TABLE 10.3. *Correlations between Influence of Previous Experiences and Demographic Characteristics—Mothers*

	Age of parent	*Number of children*	*Age of oldest child*	*Consistency in religion*	*Education level*	*Social position*	*Social mobility*
Experiences, family of orientation							
With mother	–.21	–.06	–.04	.08	–.21	–.38[c]	–.14
With father	.18	–.07	.16	.13	.18	.12	–.21
Σ Experiences, family of orientation	–.05	.10	.04	.15	–.04	–.22	.–34[b]
Positive	–.05	–.02	.03	–.06	.06	–.13	–.35[b]
Negative	–.02	.20	.03	.29[a]	–.12	–.19	–.14
Other childhood experiences							
With people	–.03	.18	–.16	.10	–.21	–.34[b]	–.26
In settings	–.23	.17	–.07	–.06	–.20	.22	–.28[a]
Self-characteristics	.08	–.09	.26	.24	–.24	–.23	–.09
Σ Other childhood experiences	–.03	.07	.12	.22	–.37[c]	–.25	–.29[a]
Positive	.14	.24	.17	.10	–.02	–.13	–.29[a]
Negative	–.06	–.09	.08	.18	–.36[b]	–.20	–.14
Experiences in adulthood							
With children	–.03	–.36[b]	–.29[a]	.03	.24	–.02	.07
With parents and children	.15	.01	–.06	.28[a]	–.05	–.32[b]	–.16
Positive	.18	–.05	–.07	.02	.09	.17	.05
Negative	.10	.01	.00	.30[a]	–.08	–.43[d]	–.21
Other experiences	.21	–.04	.14	.03	.24	.03	.07
Positive	.24	–.30[a]	–.15	.03	.31[a]	.14	.03
Negative	.05	.02	–.07	.31[a]	–.07	–.44[d]	–.14
Σ Experiences in adulthood	.18	–.15	–.14	.28[a]	.11	–.30[a]	–.10

[a] $p < .10$; 7 expected by chance, 12 observed.
[b] $p < .05$; 4 expected by chance, 6 observed.
[c] $p < .02$; 1 expected by chance, 2 observed.
[d] $p < .01$; 1 expected by chance, 2 observed.

ents, and those of lower social position (as determined by their husband's rating) stress the influence of their own mothers. Similarly, fathers who stress the influence of their mothers are of lower social position, tend to be less socially mobile, have larger families and tend to be younger. Men who emphasize the influence of their fathers are more highly educated, apparently of higher social position, and have younger children. There is also a tendency for men from families of low consistency in religion to stress the negative influence of their families of orientation,

TABLE 10.4. *Correlations between Influence of Previous Experiences and Demographic Characteristics—Fathers*

	Age of parent	*Number of children*	*Age of oldest child*	*Consistency in religion*	*Education level*	*Social position*	*Social mobility*
Experiences, family of orientation							
With mother	−.31[a]	.32[b]	−.13	−.09	−.19	−.32[b]	−.27[a]
With father	.12	−.20	−.32[b]	−.15	.37[c]	.29[a]	.01
Σ Experiences, family of orientation	.06	.02	−.02	−.27[a]	.16	.12	.01
Positive	.08	.04	−.04	−.11	.17	.17	−.16
Negative	.00	−.03	.03	−.33[b]	.06	−.03	.23
Other childhood experiences							
With people	.02	.03	.21	.03	−.01	−.11	.27[a]
In settings	.14	−.02	.14	−.36[b]	.10	.06	.28[a]
Self-characteristics	.09	−.08	−.05	−.32[b]	.28[a]	.23	.11
Σ Other childhood experiences	.12	−.03	.12	−.31[a]	.17	.09	.29[a]
Positive	.14	.02	.14	−.33[b]	.23	.18	.20
Negative	.00	−.12	.02	−.09	.05	−.13	.29[a]
Experiences in adulthood							
With children	−.18	.08	−.22	.07	.35[b]	.16	.23
With parents and children	−.13	−.32[b]	−.28[a]	−.01	−.23	−.20	−.21
Positive	−.02	−.19	−.22	−.14	−.10	.09	−.17
Negative	−.12	−.25	−.16	.13	−.23	−.32[b]	−.12
Other experiences	.10	−.08	−.03	−.12	.28[a]	.22	.17
Positive	.04	−.17	−.20	−.15	.20	.24	.02
Negative	−.14	−.25	−.19	.10	−.20	−.28[a]	−.08
Σ Experiences in adulthood	−.07	−.31[a]	−.29[a]	−.05	.02	−.01	−.04

[a] $p < .10$; 7 expected by chance, 15 observed.
[b] $p < .05$; 4 expected by chance, 10 observed.
[c] $p < .02$; 1 expected by chance, 1 observed.

which may indicate a rejection both of family religion and practices in child-rearing.

Other childhood experiences. Women with less education stress childhood experiences other than those with their parents, and such experiences tend to have a negative effect. Women of lower social position emphasize experiences with other people during childhood. Those less socially mobile appear to have positive attitudes toward childhood experiences, especially those in settings. There seems a tendency for men from heterogeneous religious backgrounds (who express negative attitudes toward their family of orientation) to stress positive childhood experiences, both in settings and in relation to self-characteristics. Men of higher social mobility appear to stress childhood experiences, but their attitude toward them seems to be negative.

Experiences during adulthood. The most highly significant correlations ($<.01$) for mothers point to the strong tendency for mothers of lower social position to emphasize observations of other parents and their children, and other experiences during adulthood, both of which bring a negative reaction. There appear to be tendencies for mothers of smaller families to stress experiences with other children and positive experiences at college or at work. Mothers from a homogeneous religious background appear to have a negative reaction to experiences during adulthood.

Less mature fathers (with fewer or younger children) tend to emphasize experiences during adulthood, especially those with other parents and their children. Fathers of higher educational level appear to stress experiences with other children and experiences at work, at college, or in the Service. Men of lower social position tend to stress the negative aspects of their observations of other parents with their children and of their experiences at work or in the Service.

Differences between Mothers and Fathers

In Appendix Table F.3, we have summarized the categories relating to previous experiences for which we obtained significant (.10 or beyond) percentage score differences between family-matched mothers and fathers. The number of differences at each significance level is greater than chance expectancy. Of the 14 differences, seven show mothers higher, and seven show fathers higher.

Compared with their husbands, the women in this study are influenced more by their mothers, especially by maternal practices and perhaps by maternal characteristics and the characteristics of "family" or "folks" as well. Women also show more negative attitudes toward the example set by their mothers. The men, on the other hand, lay greater stress on the influence of their fathers, both their positive attitudes toward their fathers' influence and perhaps also their negative attitudes.

The men in the study appear to stress, more than their wives do, other childhood experiences, and to emphasize particularly their desires that their children should not have these same experiences. In experiences during adult life, the wives are influenced positively, more than their husbands, by teaching and caring for other children; whereas the husbands exceed their wives in stressing positively experiences at college, at work, or in the Service.

Summary and Comments

The way a parent brings up his child often has roots in the previous life experiences of the parent, some of which he can identify and recall. All of the 78 parents in this study report such experiences, which occured either during their childhood or during their adult life. Almost twice as much emphasis was placed on happenings in childhood as on happenings in adulthood.

The characteristics, values, beliefs, and, most of all, the practices of the respondents' own parents had the greatest influence on their child-rearing. Some of the women and men remembered only what they liked, what they approved of, and what they wanted to emulate in their own parents; a few recalled only what they did not like and what they wanted to avoid doing with their own children. But most wives and husbands saw both good and bad in their experiences with their own parents, some of which they tried to repeat, some of which they determinedly tried to change. Generally, however, parents appear to tend to respond to their upbringing more positively than negatively, endeavoring to preserve the continuity of child-rearing practices, and, to a lesser extent, values and beliefs, from generation to generation.

Although parents modified their practices according to the model of both the father and the mother in the family of orientation, for women the dominant line of transmission is from mother to daughter, whereas for men it is from father to son. There is one interesting exception to this general finding: although men of higher education and social position are strongly influenced by their fathers, men of lower social position stress the influence of their mothers. The father's father in lower-position families may have been absent or incompetent, or both. One father from such a family said, "I ain't never seen my father and I don't know nothing about him."

Other experiences during childhood also modified the rearing of children by these mothers and fathers, but none did so to the extent of the experiences with their own parents. By taking care of younger children or observing what went on in their playmates' homes, or through contacts with youth-group leaders, some parents had learned or had found models for their later roles with their own children. Experiences in certain childhood behavior settings might also modify a parent's child-rearing practices. Being skipped a grade in school, or living in cramped quarters in a city, may make a parent try to avoid similar experiences for his children; whereas the remembered freedom and excitement of living on a farm, or adventures in a summer camp, may press a parent to provide similar opportunities for his children.

Parents also recall and are influenced by certain self-characteristics during childhood. Some parents tend to become more indulgent when they perceive similar characteristics in their children. The father who always went to bed with his teddy bear is more understanding of his first-born's need for a "security symbol." The man who, as a boy, pretended not to hear his parents says he is patient when his son does this. The mother who remembers that she was always hungry after school believes her children should have a snack in the afternoon.

Other parents try to prevent their children from being what they were, or feeling as they did, when they were children. The father who was a poor athlete tries to help his son develop skill in sports. The boy who was called a "wop" grows up to be a man who tries to make his child "all American." The mother who felt different because she did not get an allowance sees that her child gets one.

Experiences during adulthood were believed to be, by these parents, almost as influential as the parent-child relations in their family of orientation. They learned a great deal from observing other parents interact with their children, apparently more about what they did not want to do with their own children than about what they did want to do. By teaching children, mothers—and a few fathers—learned many practices and gained some values, which they carried over into their relations with their own children. In college, at work, and in military service, the men and the women had gained insights, values, or techniques that they wished to use in connection with rearing their children.

There is convincing evidence that women of lower social position and less educational background do not look back on their past experiences with feelings of satisfaction. They do not want their children to suffer as they did in childhood; and they look skeptically at what other parents do with their children, as well as at what they have learned from other experiences in adult life.

XI
Communication Sources

Since the study of the development of children began in the early 1920's, a vast amount of information has accumulated: normative data; data on developmental sequences and many aspects of child behavior; descriptions of how children are socialized and how specific child-rearing practices relate to children's behavior and personality; information concerning the influence of cultural behavior settings on the learning and behavior of children. The results of these many investigations, though in no sense definitive, have provided a store of facts, information, and suggestions that might be useful to parents in the upbringing of their children. The vital question is one of transmission.

Many individuals, organizations, and agencies are at present engaged in the communication of relevant information and advice to parents, through individual conferences, group meetings, or through the written word. They are attempting to transform "the parental role from one guided by cultural tradition and internalized values to one in which the parent must become, in part, his own judge of good and evil, and seek to develop a highly conscious, rationally determined role performance." (Brim, 1959, p. 19.)

The parents in this study made use of a variety of communication sources in their efforts to become better parents, to solve problems with their children, or to gain reassurance in the difficult task of bringing up children in an increasingly complex world. Communication sources are referred to as influences on parental behavior in 22.8 per cent of all codings for mothers,

TABLE 11.1. *Communication Sources Reported by Parents*

	Per cent reporting		*Number of codings*		*Mean percent-age score*		*Percentage score difference*	
	Mo	*Fa*	*Mo*	*Fa*	*Mo*	*Fa*	*t*	*p*
Interpersonal	100	100	1,471	729	11.68	7.64	4.54	<.001
Mass media	100	100	945	474	7.24	4.86	3.82	<.001
Organized education	95	85	333	163	2.55	1.61	2.77	<.01
Cultural milieu	31	33	24	17	.17	.21	—	n.s.
Σ Communication sources	100	100	2,773	1,383	21.64	14.35	5.46	<.001

and 14.4 per cent of those for fathers (see Table 3.2, p. 28). Only the effect of children and husband are mentioned more by mothers; but fathers discuss values and beliefs, as well as the effect of children and wife, more often. The percentage scores on communication sources for mothers range from 49.9 to 9.2; for fathers, from 37.4 to 5.5.

Communication sources, as shown in Table 11.1, are organized into four categories: interpersonal sources, mass media, organized education, and influences derived from the cultural milieu of the parent. Mothers exceed fathers in their emphasis on the sum of all communication sources, as well as on each specific category except cultural milieu, and the differences between matched husbands and wives in percentage scores are statistically significant. As parents discussed these communication sources, they indicated whether they had accepted the advice or used the information they received, whether they were critical in any way of either the source or the content, or whether they rejected either source or content. Of all mothers' communication codings, 83 per cent indicate acceptance, 6 per cent are critical, and 11 per cent are rejecting. Of fathers' codings 77 per cent are accepting, 5 per cent critical, and 18 per cent indicate rejection of either content or source.

INTERPERSONAL COMMUNICATION SOURCES

Parents used interpersonal sources more than any other form of communication; in fact, these sources constitute more than half of the total. The interpersonal sources of communication

TABLE 11.2. *Interpersonal Communication Sources*

	Per cent reporting		*Number of codings*		*Mean percent-age score*		*Percentage score difference*	
	Mo	*Fa*	*Mo*	*Fa*	*Mo*	*Fa*	*t*	*p*
Professional people	100	100	841	438	6.78	4.72	4.34	<.001
Physician	100	95	464	224	3.70	2.43	3.82	<.001
Teacher	95	82	227	105	1.87	1.13	3.05	<.01
Psychologist	51	51	58	46	.44	.45	—	n.s.
Psychiatrist	39	49	38	34	.28	.38	—	n.s.
Clergyman	41	36	32	22	.28	.24	—	n.s.
Nurse	21	10	22	7	.21	.09	—	n.s.
Clinics	80	41	91	32	.83	.32	2.62	<.02
Psychological	41	10	44	8	.38	.07	2.08	<.05
Medical	15	21	33	12	.31	.12	2.28	<.05
Educational	26	21	14	12	.14	.13	—	n.s.
Acquaintances	97	90	351	181	2.68	1.80	2.25	<.05
Relatives	74	49	172	67	1.26	.70	2.20	<.05
Of mother	59	36	113	27	.79	.27	3.12	<.01
Of father	46	49	59	40	.47	.43	—	n.s.
Other	31	15	16	11	.14	.13	—	n.s.
Σ Interpersonal sources	100	100	1,471	729	11.68	7.67	4.54	<.001

that influence parents are listed in Table 11.2. Interpersonal sources include members of various professions, persons who work in clinics but who are not identified specifically, relatives, acquaintances, and various miscellaneous sources (for example, stories or rumors heard about parents and children). Mothers accepted 86 per cent of the advice; fathers accepted 83 per cent.

Professional people. The professional people mentioned by parents as most influential include, in this order of emphasis: physicians, teachers, psychologists, psychiatrists, clergymen, and nurses. The family *physician,* or the child's pediatrician, is relied upon for advice more than any other person. Mothers mention the doctor significantly more than fathers do, but fathers still put him in first place. Most of the advice from doctors is accepted without question (93 per cent of mothers' codings; 88 per cent of fathers' codings). Parents not only seek advice from doctors about illness, nutrition, overweight, and general health; they also want advice about development, eating problems, bedwetting, excessive crying, discipline, and extreme emotional problems.

The mother who stressed the influence of doctors most is the one who had the highest percentage score in communication sources. She took the doctor's advice on books to read, on nursing her baby, on feeding him, on thumb-sucking, and on giving the baby affection and attention. She summed up her relationship in the following statement: "As a matter of fact, I did everything the pediatrician said just right down the line. I felt that he was the one who knew, and therefore that I should follow all his directions." There were only two ripples of discontent in this happy relationship. The nursing service from the mother's church recommended orange juice, but the pediatrician did not. The mother said, "I really would have liked to give him orange juice, simply because I like it myself; but I didn't, because of the pediatrician." Although the doctor gave many suggestions about how to stop the baby's incessant crying, none of them worked; but "it wasn't his fault," the mother hastened to add.

As children become older, and emotional disturbances cause problems for parents, some are likely to consult their doctors. A mother of four children was concerned about her oldest, and talked to the doctor:

> When things don't go right, and when they don't go her way, [Da 8.3] just goes and sits on the couch and bounces. . . . I feel we made an issue of this bouncing when we should not have. She was embarrassing us. . . . The last time we went to the pediatrician's office I mentioned it to him, and asked if he had any suggestions as to how we can work this out with [Da 8.3]. He said to just sit down with her and talk it out with her. She is old enough to reason with, and that's what we have to do. . . . Make her aware of her actions and why she is doing it.

This family had confidence in the doctor's advice. When there was a conflict between the advice of the grandparents and that of the doctor, the parents followed the doctor. The following episode was related by the husband:

> When our oldest child was a baby, she had a high fever. The grandparents were there visiting. My wife telephoned the doctor, and he said, "Pack her up and bring her down here and let me take a look at her." And the grandparents went up in the air, because the doctor didn't come out to our house. When the doctor saw her he told my

wife to put the child in a cold tub of water to get the fever down. Of course this was contrary to the grandparents' belief. So then the doctor finally got on his high horse and told them, "We knew for 70 years that this would bring the fever down, and it is just grandparents like you that have kept us from using it." So since that time we have used it three or four times with the other children—and it works.

But there is a small percentage of parents who would not seek the advice of doctors concerning anything other than health or illness. When one father of two young children was asked his reasons for this attitude he said:

It seems like all the doctors we know, their kids are strictly unmanageable, particularly pediatricians. I don't know why it is, unless they are so busy they don't have time to practice what they preach. But I certainly couldn't see myself going to a pediatrician for advice on raising my child, when I have seen the job he has done on his.

A mother who had severe problems with a five-year-old daughter (head bumping, tantrums, thumb-sucking) said, "I have never discussed any of my difficulties with my doctor, because I don't feel he is any more capable of solving those problems than I am."

In the category of *school teachers,* we have included not only classroom teachers but also nursery school teachers and directors, counselors, and principals of elementary and secondary schools. A large percentage of parents sought advice from such people, but the emphasis is only about half that given to the influence of physicians. Mothers stress the use of teachers significantly more than fathers. Many of the suggestions that parents receive from teachers or from other school personnel relate to success or failure in school subjects, or to the behavior of a child in school. But the influence of teachers is by no means limited to the school-connected behavior of children. Nursery school, kindergarten, and first-grade teachers are consulted about a wide range of behavior, including anxiety, inattention, jealousy, irresponsibility, immaturity, and so forth. Junior high school counselors and principals are asked for advice about sex education, boy and girl relations, appropriate dress, friends and associates of children. Behavior of children that is manifested both at school and at home, though perhaps in different ways, may become a matter of concern for parents and teachers. This was discussed by a mother, in the following excerpt:

> When I talk with the teacher, these are mostly things that she is having problems with at school. As it turns out, some of the time I am having the same problems at home, and we get around to discussing these. She will help me with the problems I am having at home.... The teachers have been very, very good. I have an awful lot of respect for them.

Most of the parents, like the mother quoted above, are quite satisfied with the help they receive from teachers (89 per cent of mothers' codings; 92 per cent of fathers' codings). Only 4 per cent of mothers' codings, and 1 per cent of fathers', are critical of the advice from school personnel, and only 7 per cent of the codings indicate rejection of specific advice. The confidence that parents have in the opinion and advice of educators is well illustrated in the following quotation from the mother who spurned the advice of doctors about emotional problems.

> You know I think the sun just rises and sets in [the director of the nursery school]. If anyone were really having a terrible problem I would suggest that they talk to her.... When I was having so many problems with [Da 5.8], she reassured me immediately that there was nothing wrong with [Da 5.8], which was really what I wanted. I wanted someone who knew to tell me that mentally there was nothing wrong with my child.

The fact that teachers can offer practical suggestions to parents about children's activities makes them particularly effective as communication sources. This is well illustrated in the interviews with a lower-middle-class mother, whose oldest son was in the second grade. The following are brief excerpts from much longer discussions:

> The teachers have helped me so much with [So 7.5].... When he was in the first grade, and his brother was a baby, the teacher told me, "Your son talks about the baby a lot, and about how much attention you pay to the baby." She said he wanted so much attention from her, and asked how he acted at home.... She told me to have the baby down when he came home from school, so I'd be free to talk to him about whatever he wanted to talk about. She suggested his Daddy take him someplace, all by himself. And we did these things, and it must have helped.... His father reads with [So 7.5] at night. This came

from the school, a suggestion from the teacher. . . . She suggested we let him bring some books home from the library every week, and help him to read those, and then that would help him in his schoolwork.

There are many other specific suggestions that the teachers gave this accepting mother: about the degree of responsibility a five-year-old can be expected to take for his own room; about how to help him learn not to interrupt when others are talking; about giving him experiences, such as a trip to the zoo or a picnic at the beach.

The mother and father of two adolescent girls consulted the counselor and the principal in the junior high school about a sex-education film, about the younger daughter's inferiority feelings, about the older girl's going steady, about the kind of parties to have for teenagers. Both parents said that if they were ever having any problems with their children, they would consult the school counselor first of all. There are rare occasions, however, when parents are critical of the counsel teachers give them, as illustrated in the following excerpt from a father:

When we came here [So 8.3] was behind in the second-grade reading and phonics. The teacher was not as satisfactory as his current teacher. So we had someone tutor him, despite the public school's feeling that this was not necessary. They actually discouraged us in doing this. We felt he was not getting the basic foundation in phonics that he seemed to need. This has been confirmed, and he is doing much better in his reading.

About half of the parents had had some contact with a *psychologist.* Parents' experiences with psychologists include going to the school psychologist to discuss learning ability, academic failure, or school behavior; talking over general and sometimes specific problems about children with friends who are psychologists; seeking reassurance and advice from a psychologist connected with a nursery school; consulting a child psychologist about mental abilities and severe emotional disturbances. In general, the parents are satisfied with the help they receive (83 per cent of parents' codings), but there are more rejections than for either doctors or teachers (16 per cent of mothers' codings; 15 per cent of fathers' codings).

One mother reports conferences with the nursery school psychologist, the school psychologist, and a psychologist friend. She discussed the influence of the school psychologist:

> One thing that came up was the psychologist felt that [Fa] was not strict enough with our daughter.... My husband said, "It hurts me to be rough with her." ... The psychologist thought that was where one of the mistakes has been made.... I think my husband thought it over, and I see some difference.... Now I find he will say to her, "I don't want to hear any more about it. You go to your room and when you want to come out and talk about it, you come."

There are some criticisms and rejections of psychologists. One father had a limited concept of their services and dismissed them quite cavalierly: "I find that what a psychologist does, that is, testing, only sort of confirms what already my own impression has suggested."

Parents mention *psychiatrists* as sources of help less than they do psychologists. Those who mention psychiatrists are sometimes accepting of them (76 per cent of mothers' codings; 68 per cent of fathers'), but they are also relatively often rejecting (21 per cent of mothers' codings; 26 per cent of fathers'). One reason given for hesitancy in using psychiatric help is the financial obligation involved. The following excerpt is taken from the interviews with a mother of four, the oldest of whom was nearly ten years old.

> [Da 9.8] had been doing some stealing at the store, and from us, too. I talked to my pediatrician and he recommended a psychiatrist. [Da 9.8] had one visit with him, and I guess I had two. He thought we would need an hour a week. I felt that financially it would be such a terrific burden.... I felt that the burden would be such that my husband might get a little resentful about it and take it out on the kids. He wouldn't have done it consciously, but it might have happened. ... I didn't feel any real confidence in the psychiatrist. He is undoubtedly good, but I did not feel that I could really talk to him without reservations, and that really was not a good situation.

There is some evidence that a few parents feel it is a disgrace to go to a psychiatrist, but most of the parents indicate that they would go to a psychiatrist if they needed one, especially if their doctor recommended it.

Rabbi, priest, minister, and ward bishop are each mentioned by at least one parent as a source of help in child-rearing. Two-fifths of the mothers, and fewer fathers, discuss the *clergy*, and in general they consider them useful (81 per cent of mothers' codings; 86 per cent of fathers'). The following excerpt, from the interviews of a mother illustrates this:

> We had a minister who talked a great deal about family life, and I think it has given us a better attitude. He had sermons on the place of the mother and the father in the home. I remember one sermon about disciplining children. He felt that you should make them mind—but they should be able to assert themselves. They were simple, down-to-earth sermons, but they were very effective. . . . I think we have both improved tremendously.

Most of the rejections of the advice of the clergy relate to such matters as thumb-sucking, disobedience, and emotional problems.

Only a few parents discuss the influence of the professional *nurse*. Reference is primarily to the maternity-ward nurse, but there is also some mention of the nurse in a doctor's office. Mothers are somewhat critical of their usefulness (23 per cent of mothers' codings). Fathers rarely mention them, but are as critical as they were of advice from clergymen (14 per cent of codings). The following excerpt from the interviews with a thirty-year-old mother of a first baby is typical of the kind of influence a baby nurse can have on a young mother, "The nurse brainwashed me about crying. She said it was good for babies; they needed it to develop their lungs; it made them good and hungry. So when I hear him cry, I think he's hungry. So it didn't bother me any more."

A new mother was critical of the nurses in the hospital where her baby was born. She said, "The nurses were cold. They don't seem particularly pleased with what they are doing. . . . I asked them many questions, and I wouldn't get too many answers. They were not helpful at all."

Clinics and agencies. In this category we included the references that parents make to clinics or agencies giving professional services, without specifically identifying the person or persons with whom contacts were made. The services mentioned include medical (health centers, well-baby clinics, medical clinics); psychological (diagnostic centers, child clinics, school psychological departments, psychological-social service agencies); and educational (remedial-learning agencies). Such centers or clinics are referred to by a large percentage of mothers, but by less than half of the fathers. The difference between the emphasis of mothers and fathers is statistically significant ($p < .02$) for the category as a whole, and also significant at a lower level ($p < .05$) for the subcategories medical and psychological.

The clinic or agency not only advises and reassures the parent, but sometimes refers the parent to other agencies that prove helpful. Often books and pamphlets are given, loaned or recommended, and these modify the parents' practices. The following excerpt from a young mother of four preschool children illustrates such an influence:

Mother: If the children pull on the baby's finger too hard or something, I never spank them for it. I just keep telling them how to play with the baby's finger. I let them sit on the couch and hold the baby. I think that is the best way, because I know my sister used to spank the kids if they did something to the baby. I think that made resentment.

Interviewer: Now where did you get the idea of doing differently from the way your sister did?

Mother: I read about it out of a book really. . . . I had a couple of pocket books that they give you at the clinic. The clinic recommended it and gave it to me.

Parents are unanimous in accepting the advice from educational agencies. Mothers accept 100 per cent of the advice from medical clinics, but fathers reject it in 8 per cent of their codings. Advice from psychological clinics did not fare as well: only 77 per cent of mothers' and 75 per cent of fathers' codings are without criticism.

Acquaintances. A great deal of information on how to raise children is passed back and forth between neighbors and friends; some of it affects what parents do. All but a few parents report being influenced by such acquaintances. The emphasis is much less than that given to professional people as a whole, but greater than that given to any specific professional group, with the exception of physicians. Mothers emphasize the effect of acquaintances significantly more than fathers. They also are somewhat more accepting of their advice than fathers are (84 per cent of mothers' codings; 75 per cent of fathers').

An illustration of the continuous and pervasive influence of a neighbor is found in the interviews of the mother in the second case summarized in Chapter II. Eighteen times in the interviews, this mother of two children refers to the helpfulness of one neighbor. The neighbor had formerly been a schoolteacher. Married to a man whose job kept him away from home several days at a time, and having no children of her own, she was available and willing to discuss with the mother in this study the problems she encountered in bringing up her son and daughter. In each instance, the mother reports a specific problem that her neighbor had given her advice on; she used the suggestions and had immediate success. It equals the miracles of television advertisements. The following excerpt is one of many that could be cited to illustrate the influence of her neighbor.

> I had trouble with [Da 8.0] always running out of the house without her sweater. Every time she goes out the door I say, "[Da 8.0], you haven't your sweater on. [Da 8.0], put your sweater on!" I was saying to my neighbor . . . , "I'm tired of telling her." And she says to me, "Well, just tell [Da 8.0] if she goes out without her sweater, she's not allowed to go out and play any more." So I did, and ever since I've had no more trouble.

For the most part, the advice given by neighbors or friends refers to small everyday situations like the one quoted above. Less often do acquaintances discuss more general beliefs (for example, beliefs about firmness or leniency in control), and rarely do such contacts influence parental values.

Relatives. Under this category, we included present-day communication with relatives concerning child-rearing. Experiences in the past in the family of orientation are discussed in Chapter X. More mothers than fathers report the influence of family relatives; and the difference in emphasis is statistically significant for the category as a whole, and for relatives of the mother. Each parent group gives greater emphasis to the influence of own parents than to the influence of spouse's parents. Mothers accept 73 per cent of the advice from relatives, and fathers accept 69 per cent. Fathers tend to accept less advice from their in-laws (56 per cent) than from their own family (78 per cent); whereas mothers tend to respond with about the same degree of acceptance to their own relatives as to those of their husbands. The following excerpt from the mother of two children illustrates her usual positive response to one of the many suggestions her own mother gave her:

> We never discuss finances in front of the children. When we were considering giving [Da 12.8] an allowance I discussed it with my mother. She said, "Well, it is a good idea, but if you have anything to discuss about business that you don't want children to overhear, always discuss it after you have gone to bed at night." And we always do, we wait until the children are asleep.

The positive responses of the mother quoted above to the suggestions of her mother are unusual because her mother was reared in a foreign country. Her husband was not nearly as receptive of suggestions from his mother (also reared abroad), as illustrated in the following excerpt from one of his interviews:

> My mother says, "You are not bringing up your child right," but I tell her, "Well, you brought your child up the way you thought you should bring him up, and I'll bring up my child the way I think is right." . . . Because our parents are from the old country, and they have the old country's ideas, where we are more or less being westernized, and it is a different position from our parents.

A young Negro man, with four children under four years of age, felt that his mother, who had raised eight children of her own, was a great help to him. His wife mentioned her own mother more, but her one reference to her mother-in-law was positive. The husband said:

> Every time the children get sick or anything is wrong, I call my mother, and whatever she tells me to do for them, I do it. It seems to help them a whole lot. If it wasn't for my mother, there's a lot of things I wouldn't know about how to take care of my kids. . . . She has helped me a whole lot in raising the kids.

Mass Media

Communication from the mass media is emphasized less than that from interpersonal sources, but it is about equal to the em-

TABLE 11.3. *Mass Communication Sources*

	Per cent reporting		*Number of codings*		*Mean percentage score*		*Percentage score difference*	
	Mo	*Fa*	*Mo*	*Fa*	*Mo*	*Fa*	*t*	*p*
Literature	100	100	844	397	6.49	4.06	4.08	<.001
Books for parents	95	82	293	112	2.31	1.13	4.00	<.001
Pamphlets and unidentified	90	90	313	138	2.35	1.46	2.57	<.02
Magazines	92	74	148	71	1.20	.68	3.15	<.01
Newspapers	56	54	61	50	.44	.47	—	n.s.
Fiction, cartoons, ads	31	33	29	26	.19	.32	—	n.s.
Television	59	56	62	43	.48	.45	—	n.s.
Radio	44	44	33	27	.23	.29	—	n.s.
Cinema	15	13	6	7	.04	.06	—	n.s.
Σ Mass communications	100	100	945	474	7.24	4.86	3.82	<.001

phasis given to professional people and to those in clinics. (See Table 11.2.) Mass media include printed literature, radio, television, and cinema. The data for these sources of influence are presented in Table 11.3. Mothers emphasize the influence of mass media on their child-rearing decidedly more than fathers. They also appear to be somewhat more accepting of suggestions from such sources (79 per cent of mothers' codings; 68 per cent of fathers' codings).

The difficulty in identifying the specific influence of mass media, but the recognition that it is at work, is well illustrated in the following excerpt from the interviews with the father of three little girls.

Father: I am generally dissatisfied with the fact that we don't do more with them as a family group. Although I am not really quite sure what to do with them.

Interviewer: Where have you gotten the idea that it is of value to do things as a family?

Father: I'm not sure exactly what the specific source was. There seems to be quite an emphasis in the movies, and in literature, in newspapers, and in advertising. In almost all the communication media, there is emphasis on doing things as a family, almost without exception. "A family that prays together, stays together." . . . There is endless advice of doing things with the family from the comic strips, too. I think all of these things probably enter into it.

Literature. In this category we included influences derived from columns or articles in newspapers, articles in magazines, books for parents, pamphlets for parents, and what is vaguely referred to as "something I read." We also included the few references to fiction, cartoons, comics, and advertisements. Every parent had, to some extent, modified what he did with his children on the basis of what he read. Mothers emphasize such sources more than fathers. The differences between mothers and fathers are statistically significant for all kinds of reading material except newspapers and the category including fiction, cartoons, and advertisements. Mothers also appear to be somewhat less critical or rejecting of what they read than fathers (22 per cent of mothers' codings; 32 per cent of fathers' codings).

About 34 per cent of the references mothers make to reading material, and 30 per cent of the references made by fathers, concern *books* written for parents. The two authors most frequently mentioned are Spock (69 per cent of mothers; 39 per cent of fathers), and Gesell (41 per cent of mothers; 21 per cent of fathers). One mother certainly made use of books for parents in rearing her children. She owned several: *New Ways in Discipline* by Baruch; *Psychology of Women: Girlhood, Motherhood* by Deutsch; *Painting and Personality* by Alschuler and Hattwick; *The Rights of Infants* by Ribble; *The Inner World of Childhood* by Wickes; and *Baby and Child Care* by Spock. She referred to the influence of specific books written for parents 12 times in the interviews (percentage score, 3.24), and, in addition, mentioned "reading" or "books" without giving titles several times (score, 4.86). The following excerpts show how the material in certain specific books influenced this mother.

Mother: I don't know why people go around having babies without having given it any thought whatever. . . . Suddenly I was faced with the desire to have some sort of philosophical attitude toward this thing I was involved in.

Interviewer: What did you do in trying to figure out what being a mother is?

Mother: People gave me books. A perfectly horrible book, schedules and such: "Don't let them ever get the upper hand or you will regret it." I read it and it all sounded logical, but it sounded as if I were in for a life of one long combat. It was depressing. . . . Then one young mother gave me a book that really changed my whole attitude, the most valuable thing I have read, that was written by Margaret Ribble. The book said I could go ahead and do what I felt like doing with my child. . . . I think Baruch's *New Ways in Discipline* had quite an effect on me. I think that if someone asked me what book I would recommend to read if she were having difficulty with discipline, I would unhesitatingly recommend that one.

There are many *pamphlets* written for parents, and these parents report that some affected how they raised their children. Few parents could remember the titles or the authors of these pamphlets, but they got hold of them through obstetricians, pediatricians, hospitals, well-baby clinics, adoption agencies, insurance companies, the U.S. Government, American Medical Association, church groups, Red Cross, family magazines, and parent-teacher associations. We grouped pamphlets with other reading material that parents could not specifically identify. Most of the parents discuss the effect of such literature on their child-rearing practices; and 79 per cent of mothers' and 68 per cent of fathers' references indicate the usefulness and acceptability of the material.

One mother and father, with a first baby, read so much that it was difficult for them to identify specifically what literature had influenced them. In talking about why she breast-fed her baby, the mother said: "I did read somewhere, I couldn't begin to tell you where, that cows' milk or . . . homogenized milk is a little bit difficult for a baby's stomach to digest. It is so different from breast milk, and most babies' stomachs up to three months are just unable to take it." This mother told of receiving a little circular from the clinic when her baby was born.

Interviewer: Did you find the pamphlet helpful?

Mother: Oh, the greatest joy in the world. When you first go home from the hospital, you are faced with diapering the baby; you are thinking with horror of bathing it, and just handling it is a problem. All those little things—it just told you point by point what to do, even how to put the nipple on the bottle. It was just a very great aid. . . . I followed these instructions to the letter.

Whenever this mother and father faced a decision, they sought help through reading: about diet and regime during pregnancy, about natural childbirth, rooming-in, breast-feeding, physical care of infant, demand-feeding, persistent crying of infant, starting baby on solid foods, thumb-sucking, toilet-training, cuddling and spoiling the baby, normal motor development, baby's playing with genitals and putting things in his mouth, parents' response to serious accidents, expression of affection, rules and obedience, spanking, thwarting children, sex differences, and the age when a child knows right from wrong. In summarizing her attitude toward literature for parents by experts, the mother said:

> Articles by experts have a great influence on me. I have a healthy respect for people who have made their lifework the study of a phase of child's behavior, or his nutritional needs. I feel they are bound to know a great deal more than I could, or my friends or relatives could, from just common experience. I read a lot of articles that are about children, but I think books are the most informative. *The Rights of Infants* by Margaret Ribble is a must. I found a great deal of help in Gesell's *Child Development*. . . . Articles in the newspaper, as well as the *Ladies' Home Journal*. If there is an article in *The Reader's Digest* on babies, I read that. My husband brings home medical journals now and then; and sometimes there are excerpts from some article, and I do read those.

Most of the mothers and three-fourths of the fathers report reading *magazine articles* that influence to some extent how they raise their children. Mothers emphasize these more than fathers, and appear to be more accepting of the content than fathers (84 per cent of mothers' codings; 70 per cent of fathers'). The husband of the woman quoted above, the mother who had such admiration for the writings of experts, expresses the fathers' more critical attitude in the following excerpt:

> These stores have a magazine called *Your Baby,* and there is another one. They are free. They have a lot of advertisements, but they have four or five articles that deal with child-rearing. My wife read all of them, and I glanced at most of them. I don't know if they are particularly educational. I cannot say I have any ideas I can credit to them. Sometimes I think I might have found an idea that confirmed and made me feel better, but I don't think I came away with anything new.

Only about half of the parents mention the effect of what they read in *newspapers* on their child-rearing practices, but they are on the whole highly accepting of the material (98 per cent of mothers' and 85 per cent of fathers' codings). Like any other communication source, a newspaper article may reinforce methods the parent is already using. This is illustrated in the following excerpt from the interviews of a father of three preschool boys:

> There was an article in the Sunday Supplement about three weeks ago by a man from Columbia. He told about an analysis of the behavior of children in school who had been raised in permissive homes, and some who had been raised in authoritarian homes. He pointed out that greater creativity and greater accomplishment came from children raised in permissive homes. This gave us a little spur to develop this type of relationship, rather than falling back on authoritarian methods, which seem to be the last straw after you exhaust all the other possibilities.

Only a few parents (21 per cent of mothers; 18 per cent of fathers) mention the effect that *fictional literature* has on their rearing of children, and a large percentage of the material from these sources is rejected (30 per cent of mothers' codings; 60 per cent of fathers' codings). Fictional articles referred to were usually stories in magazines, especially women's magazines. *Cartoons* or "*comics*" are referred to by a few parents (18 per cent of mothers and 21 per cent of fathers), and parents are highly rejecting of them (50 per cent of mothers' codings; 40 per cent of fathers' codings). One father mentioned that he read several comic strips that dealt with families: "I have read *Gasoline Alley* occasionally, although all the children in that strip have grown up. They have grandchildren, so we don't feel the empathy that we do toward *Peanuts*. We can see the foibles of our own children in *Peanuts*."

Few parents discuss the influence of *advertisements* on their child-rearing behavior (8 per cent of mothers; 13 per cent of fathers). The few codings are somewhat critical, but not completely rejecting. Here again, we find that parents believe advertisements may reinforce a tendency, but rarely provide the primary incentive for behavior. The following statement shows how an advertisement stimulated the father to buy a gadget for toilet-training that had already been enthusiastically recommended by a neighbor: "I am seriously thinking of trying one of those bed-wetting kits with the alarm clock which my neighbor used. There's a cheaper one advertised in the Peninsula Living section of the Redwood City *Tribune*. That's where I saw it. They show a baby sleeping and the bright light coming on."

Radio. Less than half of the parents mention radio programs as a source of help in raising children. Few of the mentions indicate an acceptance of the material (21 per cent of mothers' codings; 33 per cent of fathers' codings). We had hoped to analyze the codings separately by content of programs (for example, lectures by specialists, dramatic fiction, and advertisements), but there were too few references. One mother mentioned the radio when she was discussing feeding her children. She said, "Well, you get a few ideas about nutrition from radio. You hear all this, but I'm not carried away by all these things that they tell us."

Television. More parents mention television than radio, and are somewhat more accepting of the material (50 per cent of mothers' codings; 56 per cent of fathers' codings). A mother of two children listened to suggestions about food on a television program:

> We have the book by ——. He's on TV, you know. He talks about food. He doesn't believe in cooking vegetables very long. He eats them raw! I try to cook them as he says—like, not put a whole lot of water in it. It cooks out all your vitamins. He makes you think, boy! He told about Yami Yogurt, and I went out and got that. We tried it but it just wasn't very good. I guess it's good for you, but we just couldn't like it.

Cinema. Motion pictures are rarely mentioned as modifiers of parental practices. Over a third of the mentions are critical or rejecting.

Organized Education

Parents report six kinds of educational experience that influence the way they bring up their children: college courses, lectures, adult education classes, church groups, parent-teacher groups, and nursery school participation. (See Table 11.4.) Mothers stress such influences significantly more than fathers.

College courses. About two-thirds of the parents in the study

TABLE 11.4. *Organized Education as a Source of Communication*

	Per cent reporting		*Number of codings*		*Mean percent-age score*		*Percentage score difference*	
	Mo	*Fa*	*Mo*	*Fa*	*Mo*	*Fa*	*t*	*p*
College courses	64	46	109	72	.78	.60	—	n.s.
Adult classes	62	39	67	22	.50	.26	1.96	<.10
Lectures	54	39	51	24	.42	.25	1.69	<.10
Church groups	51	44	38	31	.32	.33	—	n.s.
Parent-teacher groups ..	46	23	31	10	.24	.13	—	n.s.
Nursery school participation	23	8	37	4	.29	.04	2.55	<.02
Σ Organized education sources	92	80	333	163	2.55	1.61	2.77	<.01

had some college education (64 per cent of mothers; 67 per cent of fathers). As shown in Table 11.4, all of the mothers, but not all of the fathers, who had gone to college report some influence from college courses. The content of the courses these men and women had taken in college is more influential than the content of other educational programs. College courses are the topic of 33 per cent of the codings of communication through organized education for mothers, and 44 per cent of those for fathers. There is a high degree of acceptance of information received from college courses (89 per cent of mothers' codings; 82 per cent of fathers' codings). One father had been greatly influenced by a professor whose courses he took as an undergraduate. The following excerpts are taken from a much longer discussion:

> I did my work in a small liberal arts college, with a man who headed the psychology department, who perhaps is the man who has influenced me in my life more than any other person has, or ever will. . . . I took undergraduate work in psychology, and he influenced me tremendously. He tended to be favorable toward this permissive, nonauthoritarian kind of atmosphere with child raising. . . . What is really significant to me, in terms of my own child-rearing practices, is the work that I did with him.

A father of three little girls mentioned the general influence of a college education, and the specific influence of several courses—psychology, philosophy, and aesthetics. The following illustrates the effect a college course had on him: "We were discussing last time my insistence on [Da 5.8] at least tasting her food . . . , and I pointed out that I thought it was necessary to experience different sensations and to become accustomed to them and to enjoy them. This dates back specifically to an aesthetics course I took in college."

A young mother of two preschool children indicated how courses she took in preparation for teaching helped her.

Mother: [Da 5.6] is beginning to be jealous of [So 1.25]. She gets that look on her face. I am glad that she expresses it, instead of keeping it to herself. . . . I just don't think you should keep these resentments to yourself. They tend to grow, and become large out of all proportion. It is much easier to talk it out to clear the air.

Interviewer: Where did you get this idea?

Mother: A certain amount of this I got from my work at the university, and again I found these same ideas repeated when I was taking adolescent psychology, when I was going into the teaching field. It all related to those very basic things I had learned, and somehow I tucked them away in my mind.

Lectures. Mothers appear to attend more lectures related to child-rearing than fathers do. However, both parent groups are somewhat critical or rejecting of the information they receive (35 per cent of mothers' codings; 67 per cent of fathers' codings). One reason for the high percentage of rejection is well illustrated by the following quotation from the interviews of a mother of four boys: "I've gone to the lectures at the Y. This last one was on shyness. It didn't apply. I don't have any shy children. It didn't really interest me; it didn't hit home."

Special classes for parents include: *adult education classes, church groups, parent-teacher groups,* and *nursery school participation.* Mothers appear to emphasize the influence of such groups more than fathers, but the only significant differences in emphasis are on adult classes and on nursery school participation. The relative usefulness of these experiences is as follows: nursery school experience (92 per cent of mothers' codings; 100 per cent of fathers'); parent-teacher groups (81 per cent of mothers'; 80 per cent of fathers'); church groups (68 per cent of mothers'; 74 per cent of fathers'); adult education classes (64 per cent of mothers'; 55 per cent of fathers').

Cultural Milieu

We had hoped in this section to be able to show the influence of the neighborhood the family lived in, of the hospital where the baby had been born, of the school the children attended, and, in general, of what parents considered "the thing to do." We are convinced that such atmospheres, attitudes, and practices, within various neighborhoods and institutions, may influence parental practices. However, these parents were not highly conscious of such pressures. Because less than a third of the parents mention the influence of cultural patterns, we cannot analyze the codings except generally.

There are several parents who refer to the influence of neighborhood patterns, but they usually modify neighborhood pressures in terms of their own values or beliefs. This tendency is illustrated in the following excerpt from the interviews of a mother of four children:

> I think we have given the kids a little more leeway as to going calling on other children because our neighbors do, but when they do, I know exactly where they are going.... I let the kids join the Brownie group, because the other children in the neighborhood are doing it, but also because I think it's a very important phase of their group activity.

Parents also refer to the effect of certain cultural traditions in their family background on their ways of raising their children: Jewish traditions, Italian traditions, Mexican traditions. The following statement came from a new mother, who had lived in the United States only about six years: "As soon as possible children get trained to go to the toilet after breakfast, and get in the habit of passing a movement then. That is good English training, and we feel it is a good idea."

References are also made to the more general concept of cultural expectancy, as witness the following statements:

> And that was the thing I felt was expected of all good mothers, that they nurse their babies.
>
> I started to train my first baby for the toilet when he was pretty

young. He was awfully little. I think it was because everyone else was doing it.

I think that a girl is expected to conform more than a boy, and that would seem to play a part in my own behavior in letting the boy have more individuality.

Critical Attitude toward Communication

In Table 11.5, we give the percentage of parents who are critical of interpersonal sources, mass media, and the sum of communication sources. We also give, for each category, the percentage of codings that indicate a critical attitude toward either the source or the content of communication. For these three categories, the same parents who are critical sometimes, are accepting at other times. There is no one parent who is only critical of communication sources; each parent is more accepting than critical. More mothers than fathers indicate critical attitudes, but the fathers appear to have a higher percentage of critical codings. Both groups of parents appear to be more critical of mass media than they are of interpersonal sources.

Table 11.5. *Critical Attitude toward Communication Sources*

	Percentage of parents reporting	*Percentage of parents critical*		*Percentage of codings critical*	
		Mo	*Fa*	*Mo*	*Fa*
Σ Communication	100	97	90	17	23
Interpersonal	100	77	33	14	17
Mass media	100	92	77	21	32

Relation to Demographic Characteristics

The percentage scores for the 13 categories of communication sources were correlated with the seven demographic characteristics (see Table 11.6). The significance of these correlations in relation to chance expectancy is shown in Table 11.7. Of the 91 correlations for mothers, 26 per cent are significant at the level of .10 or beyond; of those for fathers, 25 per cent are significant.

The outstanding finding of this analysis is that mothers and fathers with smaller families, and those with younger firstborns,

TABLE 11.6. *Correlations between Communication Sources and Demographic Characteristics*

	Age of parent	*Number of children*	*Age of oldest child*	*Consistency in religion*	*Education level*	*Social position*	*Social mobility*
MOTHERS							
Professional	–.21	–.31[a]	–.40[c]	–.08	–.04	–.05	.06
Physicians	–.31[a]	–.26	–.55[e]	–.11	–.03	–.05	.04
Teachers	–.04	–.16	.06	.13	–.11	–.10	–.02
Acquaintances	.11	–.47[d]	–.22	–.09	.17	.09	.22
Interpersonal	–.11	–.43[d]	–.40[c]	–.13	.03	.02	.13
Critical	–.19	–.26	–.09	–.14	–.04	–.09	–.30[a]
Mass media	–.15	–.45[d]	–.41[d]	–.15	.04	.14	.30[a]
Accepting	–.08	–.37[c]	–.36[b]	–.14	.17	.20	.38[c]
Critical	–.23	–.30[a]	–.22	–.18	–.03	–.01	–.25
Mass media, literature	–.11	–.43[d]	–.35[b]	–.16	.04	.17	.30[a]
Organized education	.05	–.06	.05	–.08	–.17	–.12	.20
Σ Communication sources (Mo)	–.15	–.50[d]	–.47[d]	–.14	.05	.09	.32[b]
Σ Critical (Mo)	–.33[b]	–.32[b]	–.41[d]	–.22	–.14	–.02	–.18
FATHERS							
Professional	–.18	–.29[a]	–.47[d]	–.12	–.03	.09	–.29[a]
Physicians	–.17	–.36[b]	–.56[e]	–.01	–.01	–.05	–.31[a]
Teachers	–.03	–.13	.06	–.20	–.06	.07	.02
Acquaintances	–.24	–.13	–.33[b]	–.09	.00	.05	–.10
Interpersonal	–.25	–.24	–.49[d]	–.07	–.05	.04	–.31[a]
Critical	–.05	–.36[b]	–.24	.01	–.05	.04	.01
Mass media	–.19	–.47[d]	–.45[d]	–.25	.05	.07	–.17
Accepting	–.23	–.37[c]	–.37[c]	–.13	.06	–.02	–.09
Critical	–.06	–.38[c]	–.38[c]	.02	.04	.12	–.17
Mass media, literature	–.12	–.34[b]	–.29[a]	–.28[a]	.10	.09	–.22
Organized education	–.21	–.18	–.28[a]	–.07	–.05	.00	–.10
Σ Communication sources (Fa)	–.30[a]	–.36[b]	–.61[e]	–.18	.05	.09	–.26
Σ Critical (Fa)	–.01	–.24	–.26	.15	.00	.12	–.19

[a] $p < .10$; [b] $p < .05$; [c] $p < .02$; [d] $p < .01$; [e] $p < .001$.

are highly influenced by communication sources. They are critical of some of the advice they receive, but are also receptive and accepting. Parents of younger firstborns make use of mass media and of interpersonal sources, primarily physicians. Fathers of younger firstborns also consult acquaintances. Parents with smaller families make use of mass media (including literature). Mothers with smaller families are also high in the use of interpersonal sources (especially acquaintances). In addition, fathers with smaller families make use of doctors. Only one other rela-

TABLE 11.7. *Significance of Correlations between Communication Sources and Demographic Characteristics*

Level of significance	*Number expected by chance (91 r's)*	*Number observed*	
		Mo (91 r's)	*Fa (91 r's)*
<.001	.09	1	2
.001 to .01	.82	8	4
.01 to .02	.91	4	4
.02 to .05	2.73	5	5
.05 to .10	4.55	6	8

tion should be mentioned: mothers who are socially more mobile tend to make use of communication sources, and tend to be highly accepting of material from the mass media.

As can be seen in Table 11.6, mothers who are in general critical of communication sources are also younger, with younger firstborns, and smaller families. However, these women are not critical of interpersonal sources. Among fathers, no demographic group is significantly related to critical attitude of sum of communication sources, but fathers with younger firstborns and smaller families tend to be critical of mass media, and those with smaller families of interpersonal sources.

Relation to Other Influences on Parent Behavior

We analyzed the relation of nine categories of communication sources to 144 categories of other sources of influence on parental behavior. The nine categories of communication sources include the following general and specific categories (the percentage of parents reporting is noted in parentheses):

General	*Specific*
Communication sources (100%)	Physicians (Mo 100%; Fa 95%)
Interpersonal sources (100%)	Teachers (Mo 95%; Fa 82%)
Professional sources (100%)	Acquaintances (Mo 97%; Fa 90%)
Organized education (Mo 92%; Fa 80%)	Literature (100%)
Mass media (100%)	

Of the 1,296 correlations between communication sources and other influences for each parent group, 26 per cent of those for mothers and 15 per cent of those for fathers are significant at the

TABLE 11.8. *Significance of Correlations between Communication Sources and 144 Other Influences on Parental Behavior*

Level of significance	Number observed Mo (1,296 r's)			Number expected by chance (1,296 r's)	Number observed Fa (1,296 r's)		
	+	−	Σ		+	−	Σ
<.001	3	12	15	1.30	8	4	12
.001 to .01	22	46	68	11.66	18	21	39
.01 to .02	15	43	58	12.96	9	15	24
.02 to .05	14	69	83	38.88	21	27	48
.05 to .10	29	86	115	64.80	33	43	76

level of .10 or beyond. The significance of these correlations in relation to chance expectancy is shown in Table 11.8. Of the correlations that are significant at .10 or beyond, 24 per cent of those for mothers, and 45 per cent of those for fathers, are positive, indicating a direct relation between influences of communication sources and certain other categories of influence on parental behavior. The remainder (76 per cent of mothers' significant correlations; 55 per cent of fathers') are negative, indicating an inverse relation between the correlates. It should be noted that the positive correlations for mothers at the significance levels of <.05 and <.10 are less than 50 per cent of total chance expectancy, and that those for fathers are just about 50 per cent of chance expectancy. Therefore, this discussion will emphasize correlations at the levels of .02 or beyond.

High communicators. In Table 11.9 we list the categories of influence that show a direct relation with the sum of communication sources; and we also present the correlations between these categories and eight specific categories of communication sources. It is well to remember, in looking at Table 11.9, that the parents who are high in scores on use of communication sources as a whole have younger firstborns and smaller families.

High communicators among both mothers and fathers are more influenced by descriptive beliefs than by any other category (see Table 11.9). Both parent groups are influenced by beliefs about infancy and, perhaps, learning; mothers, by beliefs about heredity; and fathers, by beliefs about environment and about rules and other inhibitions. When their children show dependent behavior (especially whining and crying), mothers and perhaps fathers who are high communicators try to change it.

TABLE 11.9. *Direct Relations between Communication Sources and Other Influences (p .10 or beyond)*

	Σ Communication	Interpersonal	Professional	Physician	Teacher	Acquaintance	Organized education	Mass media	Literature
MOTHERS									
Values for parenthood, to nurture	.28	—	—	.39	—	.41	—	.44	—
Basic values, biological	.28	.28	.40	.48	—	—	—	—	—
Descriptive beliefs									
Maturity	.34	.35	.36	.46	—	—	—	.27	—
Infancy	.55	.47	.46	.64	.37	.28	—	.48	.41
Heredity	.39	—	—	—	—	—	—	.46	.42
Learning	.34	.39	.28	.30	.41	—	—	—	—
Process of learning	.44	.40	—	.33	—	.38	.33	.29	—
Child behavior									
Dependency	.29	.31	.33	.35	.35	—	—	—	—
Dependency problems	.40	.41	.43	.55	.31	—	—	.27	—
Adult experiences									
With children	.41	.35	.28	.27	.32	—	—	.42	.41
Other (positive)	.28	—	—	—	.30	—	—	.37	.37
FATHERS									
Basic values									
Emotional security	.28	—	—	.40	—	—	.36	.30	—
Biological	.29	.28	—	—	—	.37	—	—	—
Instrumental beliefs about family values	.30	—	—	—	—	—	—	.35	.39
Descriptive beliefs									
Infancy	.57	.44	.39	.44	—	—	.44	.44	.28
Environment	.61	.53	.56	.53	—	—	.28	.39	—
Learning readiness	.33	.36	.42	.29	.28	—	—	—	—
Inhibition	.52	.40	.45	.45	—	—	—	.55	.46
Parent characteristics, fatigue	.37	.41	.43	.41	—	—	—	—	—
Child behavior, dependency problems	.30	—	—	.29	—	—	—	—	—
Parent-child interaction	.30	.42	.37	.43	—	—	—	—	—
Adult experiences									
Parents and children	.30	.29	.31	.31	—	—	—	.33	.34
Positive	.33	.41	.41	.41	.27	—	—	—	—

r .27, $p < .10$; r .32, $p < .05$; r .37, $p < .02$; r .41, $p < .01$; r .51, $p < .001$.

Mothers find their previous experiences in teaching or caring for children useful in rearing their children. Fatigue is likely to influence the way these fathers respond to their children.

High seekers from physicians. High use of physicians is related to similar categories of influence as high use of communication sources in general, but there are some differences in emphasis (see Appendix Table G.1). Among mothers who stress physicians two values receive emphasis; values for nurturance and biological goals (particularly health and nutrition). Two categories of descriptive beliefs are stressed: maturity of children and infancy. Beliefs concerning environment rather than heredity become important. Dependency behavior is emphasized more. The correlations for fathers indicate that high seekers from physicians are similar to high seekers in general, with two exceptions. High seekers from physicians are guided by values for emotional security, and by instrumental beliefs related to such values. They are also influenced more by their experiences in raising their own children, and by observations of other parents and children they wish to emulate.

High seekers from teachers. A large percentage of mothers and fathers modify the rearing of their children on the basis of advice or suggestions received from teachers (see Table 11.2). The parents who have relatively high scores in communication with teachers were not from any particular demographic group. The positive correlations between emphasis on teachers and other categories of influence are shown in Appendix Table G.2. Here, we find relations that are different from those found for parents who are high seekers from physicians. Mothers who seek help from teachers strive to make use of community resources; and they have strong economic goals for their children. They tend to be guided more by beliefs about learning than are mothers who are high in use of physicians or in use of communication sources as a whole. They do not believe in extreme permissive control, and, in fact, show a slight tendency toward strict beliefs ($p < .10$). Beliefs about infancy and the dependency behavior of their children are stressed less by these mothers than by mothers who seek help from physicians. These mothers also appear to be guided by their previous experiences with children, mainly in teaching ($p < .05$). Fathers who seek help from teachers think parents should control their children in an authoritative manner. There is a slight indication that these fathers are concerned with older children, because they appear to discuss beliefs about adolescence ($p < .05$).

High seekers from professionals. References to all the specialists who are consulted by parents (physician, teacher, psychologist, psychiatrist, clergyman, and nurse) were grouped together, and relations between the scores on specialists and other categories of influence were investigated. In general, the relations with professional people mirror those with physicians. The dominant scores for physicians account for this (Table 11.2).

In addition to the relations shown in Table 11.9, mothers who emphasize the influence of specialists appear to stress three categories not related to physicians, though the correlations are relatively low: value to rear children well ($r = .33$, $p < .05$); beliefs concerning readiness for learning ($r = .29$, $p < .10$); physical characteristics of their children ($r = .30$, $p < .10$). For fathers, there appears to be a relation between the use of professionals and beliefs concerning heredity, but the significance level is also relatively low ($r = .32$, $p < .05$).

High seekers from acquaintances. Emphasis on the helpfulness of acquaintances shows a different pattern of relations with other influences than that shown by the sum of communication. (These correlations are shown in Appendix Table G.3.) Mothers who find acquaintances helpful tend to stress the influence of values for providing nurturance, beliefs about environment and learning, as well as the influence of the temporary condition of their child. Fathers who are influenced by their acquaintances stress biological values and the influence of the temporary condition of their child. Their practices are modified by experiences with previous children. They mention the influence of the weather on their child-rearing.

High seekers from interpersonal sources. We summarized in one score all references to interpersonal sources including relatives, acquaintances, specialists, clinical personnel, and others. As shown in Table 11.9, relations with interpersonal sources are similar to those found for the sum of communication sources. Mothers who use interpersonal sources stress beliefs concerning infancy and learning, and the dependency problems of their children. Fathers stress the influence of beliefs about infancy and environment, inhibition as a method of control, and fatigue of parent—all of which are related to the sum of communication. They modify practices according to the responses of their children. In addition, they emulate the observed practices of other parents.

High seekers from educational sources. The emphasis that these parents place on various forms of organized education (lectures, college courses, study groups, etc.) is low in comparison with the emphasis on interpersonal sources, or mass media (see Table 11.1). The correlations are summarized in Appendix Table G.4. The mothers who do attend meetings for parents stress primarily the influence of instrumental beliefs, beliefs concerning regulation of sexual behavior, the usefulness of child-oriented control and of peer groups for children. Fathers who attend educational meetings stress beliefs about infancy. To a lesser degree they appear to stress values and instrumental beliefs relating to emotional security, beliefs concerning adult-oriented control and parental love as means to goals, and descriptive beliefs concerning learning, and consistency in control (all at the level, $p < .05$). It is noteworthy that no overlap occurs between the influences related to organized education and to teachers for either parent group.

High seekers from mass media. As can be seen in Table 11.9, all but three of the categories stressed by mothers who were generally high seekers are also stressed by mothers high in use of the mass media. The goal of nurturance, beliefs related to heredity, and the influence of experiences at work or at college are more highly stressed by those using mass media. Beliefs about learning and dependency problems are stressed less. Mothers also stress instrumental beliefs about the regulation of sexual behavior (see Appendix Table G.5).

Fathers who stress the use of mass media have fewer categories of influence in common with high seekers in general (see Table 11.9). Descriptive beliefs about infancy, environment, and inhibition are most strongly emphasized. In addition, fathers who are high seekers from mass media show tendencies to stress a number of instrumental beliefs; for example, beliefs about play values

TABLE 11.10. *Inverse Relations between Communication and Other Influences (p .10 or beyond)*

	Σ Communication	Interpersonal	Profesional	Physician	Teacher	Acquaintance	Organized education	Mass media	Literature
MOTHERS									
Values for parenthood	–.36	–.33	—	—	—	–.30	—	–.28	—
Provide emotional security	–.39	–.45	–.35	–.31	–.35	—	—	—	—
Control authoritatively	–.27	—	—	—	—	—	—	–.35	–.35
Control	–.31	—	—	—	—	—	—	–.39	–.39
Educate	–.42	–.45	–.30	–.43	–.42	—	—	—	—
Basic values	–.59	–.50	–.30	–.32	—	–.51	–.32	–.36	–.31
Family	–.52	–.42	–.37	–.39	—	–.37	–.30	–.44	–.40
Orderly living	–.38	—	—	–.27	—	–.27	–.52	–.30	–.27
Moral	–.38	–.38	—	—	—	–.28	—	–.30	–.29
Education	–.31	—	—	—	—	—	—	–.34	–.32
Instrumental beliefs	–.32	—	—	–.30	—	–.35	—	—	—
Descriptive beliefs									
Reasoning	–.36	–.42	–.35	–.38	–.29	–.28	—	–.28	—
Insistence (negative)	–.36	—	—	—	—	—	—	–.27	–.27
Parent characteristics, angry	–.29	–.31	—	—	—	—	—	—	—
Child characteristics	–.27	—	—	—	—	—	—	—	—
Motivations (negative)	–.37	–.35	–.45	–.47	—	—	—	—	—
Child behavior	–.51	–.38	–.35	–.34	—	–.38	—	–.57	–.55
Problems	–.56	–.42	–.29	–.31	–.28	–.40	—	–.56	–.55
Eating	.–29	—	—	–.33	—	—	—	–.30	–.29
Eating problems	–.30	—	—	–.39	—	—	—	—	—
Obedience	–.41	–.36	–.35	–.35	—	–.36	—	–.48	–.48
Obedience problems	–.42	–.38	–.31	–.32	—	–.41	—	–.50	–.49
Aggression	–.43	–.36	–.32	–.27	—	–.33	—	–.38	–.37
Aggression problems	–.47	–.40	–.28	—	–.34	–.38	—	–.38	–.36
Parent-child interaction	–.35	–.42	–.41	–.38	–.28	–.43	—	—	—
With sibling	–.47	–.51	–.51	–.50	–.42	—	—	–.32	—
With sibling (repetition)	–.35	–.45	–.41	–.39	–.37	—	—	—	—
With sibling (change)	–.40	–.39	–.41	–.39	–.33	—	—	–.31	—
Σ Change	–.33	–.36	–.36	–.37	–.35	—	—	—	—
Behavior settings	–.47	–.46	–.47	–.36	–.33	—	—	–.33	–.29
Home	–.42	–.40	–.40	—	—	—	–.29	–.35	–.33
Rooms	–.29	—	—	—	—	—	—	—	—

TABLE 11.10 (*cont.*).

	Σ Communication	Interpersonal	Professional	Physician	Teacher	Acquaintance	Organized education	Mass media	Literature
People	–.31	–.37	–.41	–.34	—	—	—	—	—
Activities	–.36	–.30	–.28	—	—	—	–.34	–.34	–.36
Outside	–.37	–.41	–.42	–.46	—	—	—	—	—
Neighborhood	–.29	–.30	—	–.30	—	—	—	—	—
Past experiences, family of orientation	–.50	–.43	–.44	–.41	—	–.41	–.31	–.39	–.37
Positive	–.30	—	—	—	—	—	–.34	–.28	–.27
Negative	–.43	–.45	–.44	–.41	—	–.45	—	–.28	—
Father	–.33	–.28	–.33	–.27	—	—	—	–.28	—
Childhood experience	–.28	—	—	–.27	–.32	—	—	—	—
Positive	–.35	—	—	–.27	–.37	–.27	—	–.42	–.41
FATHERS									
Values for parenthood	–.36	–.35	–.31	–.42	—	—	—	—	–.27
Control	–.27	—	—	—	—	—	—	—	—
Control permissively	–.27	–.34	–.29	—	—	—	—	—	—
Educate	–.31	–.32	—	–.37	—	—	—	—	—
Basic values	–.42	–.46	–.44	–.46	—	—	–.37	—	—
Egoistic	–.28	–.38	–.35	–.29	—	—	—	—	—
Interpersonal	–.45	–.52	–.45	–.31	—	–.45	–.33	—	—
Moral	–.34	–.33	–.31	–.32	—	—	–.38	—	—
Education	–.35	–.35	–.40	–.35	—	—	–.33	—	—
Descriptive beliefs									
Punishment (negative)	–.32	—	—	–.32	—	—	—	–.39	–.38
Physical punishment (negative)	–.29	—	—	–.29	—	—	—	–.38	–.41
Permissive control (negative)	–.30	–.34	—	–.34	—	—	–.42	—	—
Reasoning	–.30	—	—	—	—	—	—	–.36	—
Child behavior	–.40	—	–.31	–.28	—	—	–.42	–.41	–.30
Problems	–.39	—	–.29	—	—	–.27	–.39	–.42	–.29
Obedience	–.41	—	–.33	–.38	—	—	–.40	–.56	–.46
Obedience problems	–.44	–.27	–.33	–.39	—	—	–.42	–.56	–.46
Behavior settings	–.31	—	–.33	–.31	—	—	—	—	—
Home	–.27	—	–.28	—	–.27	—	—	–.31	—

r .27, $p < .10$; r .32, $p < .05$; r .37, $p < .02$; r .41, $p < .01$; r .51, $p < .001$.

($p < .05$) and the use of obedience in obtaining values ($p < .05$) (see Appendix Table G.5).

Mothers who make use of reading material about child-rearing tend to stress the same categories of influence stressed by mothers who make use of mass media as a whole—beliefs about infancy and heredity, and adult experiences. Fathers emphasize fewer categories of influence in relation to literature compared with mass media. They stress instrumental beliefs related to family values, and beliefs concerning the use of inhibitions in control (Table 11.9). In addition, instrumental beliefs about the use of obedience ($r = .50$, $p < .01$), are strongly emphasized. Beliefs about play values ($r = .32$, $p < .05$) appear to be related also.

Low communicators. As the opposite of high communicators, those parents who are affected little by communication sources tend to have larger families and older firstborns (see Table 11.6). In Table 11.10 we report the correlations between the 9 categories of communication sources and other categories of influences on parental behavior that show an inverse relation with the sum of communication sources. The negative correlations, with specific categories only, for mothers (50) and for fathers (27) are of relatively low significance. They are given in Appendix Tables G.6 and G.7, and will be mentioned only if significant at the level of .02 or beyond.

Although mothers who are low seekers emphasize significantly more than twice as many other categories of influence as fathers (42 compared with 19), there are certain similarities between the two groups of parents. They both tend to stress the influence of values (both values for parenthood and basic values) and the problem behavior of their children. However, the more specific items under these three categories differ somewhat for the two parent groups.

Low seekers among mothers emphasize the importance of educating, of providing emotional security, and, perhaps, of controlling children. They have strong family values, moral values, and goals for orderly living. They are influenced by the negative motivations of their children, and by behavior they want to change, especially behavior concerning obedience and aggression. These mothers stress what they have learned from bringing up their children. Settings both inside and outside the home are emphasized. They are likely to strive to rear their children differently from the way they were raised (Table 11.10). In Table G.6 we find that mothers who read relatively little material for parents stress beliefs approving of punishment. Those who do not go to meetings for parents emphasize the influence of temporary conditions of their child; those who consult teachers relatively less often stress the influence of their own characteristics.

Fathers who are low seekers tend to emphasize only a few categories of influence. They tend to stress both parental and basic values, especially interpersonal values (see Tables 11.10 and G.7). They respond to problem behavior of their children, especially that related to obedience. Those who read little of the material directed to parents do not believe in punishment, especially physical punishment, but stress beliefs favorable to the use of social punishment (Table G.7). Those who seldom attend lectures or take advantage of other organized educational opportunities stress moral values, beliefs in heredity, and negative beliefs about permissive control. Those who do not make use of specialists tend to stress educational and interpersonal values.

Summary and Comments

To bring up children today, parents sometimes need help, guidance, or reassurance, and are thus motivated to seek information, ask advice, or look for emotional support from a variety of sources. They talk over their problems with relatives and acquaintances. They consult physicians, teachers, psychologists, psychiatrists, clergymen and nurses. They go to clinics of various kinds. They read books, pamphlets, magazine articles, and newspaper columns written for parents. A few gather ideas from novels, cartoons, or advertisements. Some get help from the radio, television, or cinema. Mothers make use of these sources more than fathers do. The mothers and fathers who emphasize the influence of communication sources most are those with younger firstborns and smaller families. Mothers who are more socially mobile also tend to stress communication sources, primarily mass media.

Communication sources were analyzed under four general categories, and these were emphasized by both parent groups in the following order: interpersonal sources, mass media, organized education, and cultural milieu. Among interpersonal sources, specialists are sought more than lay people, and physicians are the ones most depended upon, especially by parents with younger firstborns. The parents in this study consulted their friends and acquaintances more than their relatives or their children's teachers. Information and suggestions gathered from reading had more effect on child-rearing than radio, television and cinema combined. Most of the parents had at some time attended lectures or been members of study groups, or participated in nursery schools. According to the parents, however, such experiences in organized education had much less effect on bringing up children than either interpersonal sources or mass media. The parents who emphasized the influences of organized education, as well as those who stressed teachers as a source of help, were not distinctive with respect to any of the seven demographic variables.

The effect of what we termed the cultural milieu was seldom mentioned by these parents. It is possible that the general environment of a hospital, or the habits and practices in a neighborhood, or the atmosphere of the school the children attend, have subtle effects, not recognized by parents and therefore not reported. There is some indication that mothers who are socially mobile are more conscious of "the thing to do" than other parents, but the data do not warrant statistical treatment.

High and low seekers. There are definite differences between parents who report that they are highly influenced by communication sources and parents who give relatively slight emphasis to such sources. The high-seeking mothers, women with younger firstborns and smaller families, stress beliefs rather than values: beliefs about infancy, heredity, and learning. They respond to the dependent behavior of their children. They are influenced by their previous experiences with children. In contrast, the low-seeking mothers, women with older firstborns and larger families, emphasize values (family, moral and orderly living), but few beliefs. They are consciously trying not to raise their children as they were raised. They want to educate and control their children, as well as give them a basis for emotional security. They are concerned with the negative motivations of their children, and with making them more obedient and less aggressive.

Fathers who are high seekers, like mothers, stress beliefs rather than values. They, too, are influenced by beliefs concerning infancy, which seems appropriate for fathers of younger firstborns and of smaller families. But unlike mothers, who stress heredity, these fathers stress beliefs about environment. These fathers, perhaps because they are just learning their roles, are likely to be irritable and short with their children when tired, and to stress beliefs about using inhibition as a method of control.

In contrast, the fathers who were relatively low seekers stress values (interpersonal, moral, education). They are just as concerned about problems of obedience as mothers are, but they do not believe in punishment, especially physical punishment.

A correlational analysis, such as we have made here, does not tell us which of the two related categories is cause and which is effect, or indeed whether there is any causal relation between the two. But we might hazard the suggestion that those parents who know what their goals are, and what they want their children to be and do, feel less need for advice or help from communication sources. This may be one reason why fathers use communication sources less than mothers, for they emphasize the values that guide them more than mothers do. Communication sources seem to have little to do with the development of values in parents, which seems to be more a function of experience in family life, and the changing needs of parents and of children as perceived by parents. Parents who are low communicators show this clearly in their strong emphasis on basic values as well as on values for parenthood. The parents who do make use of communication sources (especially physicians and mass media) stress descriptive beliefs, which may be what these sources are concerned with (Brim, 1959, Chap. 6).

The impetus for communication-seeking behavior does not seem to be a specific problem confronting a parent in rearing his child, but rather the parent's feelings of inadequacy to handle the problem. With the first baby, a parent, especially a mother, is faced with new situations, and unless she has had experiences with babies before, she is driven to seek advice from a variety of sources. But through experience as a parent, as his family grows and his children become older, the parent feels more adequate, and can face his own problems with less dependence on either specialists, acquaintances, or mass media. It is noteworthy that parents who are pressed by dependency problems of young children are high seekers, whereas parents of older children, pressed by problems of obedience and aggression, are low seekers. The lack of time available for reading and consulting may prevent parents with larger families from using communication sources, even though it has been said that one baby takes all of a mother's time, and four children can take no more.

This discussion should not lead one to conclude that parents with larger families and older children make no use of communication sources; it is only that they seek them less than those with fewer and younger children. When a problem arises that the parent considers extreme or feels himself inadequate to handle, a great deal of seeking behavior may occur.

XII

Discussion of Influences on Parent Behavior

In this study we have described the influences that 78 parents ascribed to their behavior with their 111 children. These parents were ordinary people, and they discussed with us the ways they met the ordinary situations of daily living with their children, and searched for the influences affecting their behavior. The sample of parents, although relatively small in number, varied widely in age, in length of marriage, in number and age of children, in education, in social position, in degree of social mobility, and in religious and national background.

Causes of parent behavior are difficult to ascertain. The motivation, memory, insight, and self-protection mechanisms of the respondent may either facilitate or hinder the process of recall and analysis. Memory did not play as large a part in these interviews as it does in many child-rearing studies, because the parents were asked mainly to discuss current practices. Only with the data presented in Chapter X (the influence of past experiences) does memory play an important part, and we do not know whether the recall of influences on practices is subject to the same errors as recall of practices in child-rearing (Robbins, 1963).

The skill of the interviewer and the relation he is able to establish with the respondent also affect the results of a study. Our professional interviewers varied in their skill in building facilitating relationships, and in eliciting the material we wanted. The parents varied, too, in their ability to recall episodes and to tease out influences on their child-rearing. Heider (1967, p. 25) suggests that "the most complexly interwoven cognitive patterns occur when people try to give an account of social situations."

We hold no illusions, therefore, about the limitations of data gathered through interviews. Nevertheless, the technique of interview is, perhaps, the only way we have at present to gather relevant descriptive material concerning the causes of parental practices. The 78 respondents, in an average of four interviews each, contributed material that yielded over 21,000 codings for analysis. The influences on parent behavior, as perceived and reported by the parents, were grouped in the following general categories:

1. Past experiences in childhood and adulthood.
2. Information and advice from communication sources, such as relatives and friends, professional people, mass media, and organized education.
3. Values and beliefs held by the parents.
4. Current elements of situations affecting parents, including: physical and emotional condition of parents; spouse interaction; characteristics and behavior of children; behavior settings within and outside the home.

The preceding chapters, which report the findings on the above influences, bear witness to the fact that the way a parent brings up his child depends upon many pressures that impinge upon him. Certain of these pressures are an intrinsic part of the personality of the parent. But the fundamental urges, values, and beliefs of any parent may become abeyant because of critical elements in the immediate situation—a mother's fatigue, a visitor in the home, a child running out in the street. And they may be modified by conversations with neighbors, or changed drastically by strict directives from a physician, or rendered less dogmatic by exposure to a variety of ideas in magazines or books.

Parents operate within a milieu of psychological pressures. In any parent-child interaction sequence, we find a variety of factors at work, which we have tried to illustrate schematically below. The schema represents a parent and child in a behavior setting. The parent has immediate urges, goals, and perceptions that are determined by his personal characteristics, and his values and beliefs about child-rearing that have developed from past experiences. The child also has goals and beliefs, and perceptions of his parent, stemming from past experience (which are not illustrated here). The parent-child interaction may be initiated either by the child or the parent. In either case the parent acts, and this act may be labeled a child-rearing practice. The patterning of influences recorded by one parent varies from that recorded by any other parent, for each has had his own idiosyncratic history of learnings.

Factors Operating on the Parent in a Parent-Child Interaction Sequence

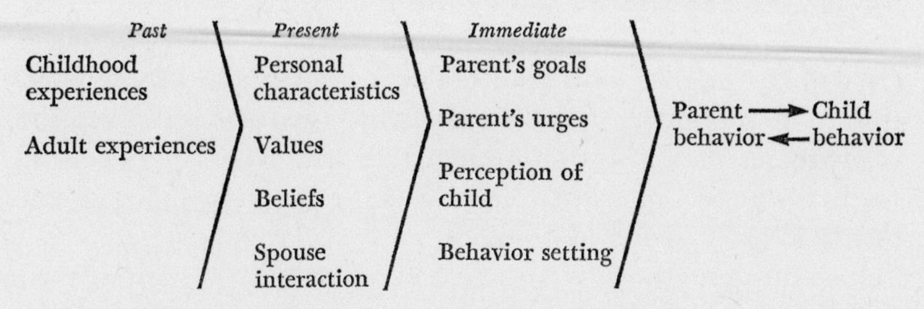

We shall not attempt in this final chapter to summarize the findings reported in the preceding chapters. The reader will find at the close of each chapter a summary that points out the most important findings. At this time we want to examine some of the findings, and to discuss certain implications that may be of special interest to those contemplating research in this area, and that may prove useful both to those informing, directing, or advising parents, and to some parents themselves. There are many persons engaged in services to parents either through direct personal contact, through lectures or discussions with groups, or through publication of literature for parent consumption. Most of these persons are trained in some profession, and they try to influence the way parents rear their children, either by telling them what is fact, directing them what to do, or helping them gain insight into their own behavior and the responses of their children. We are concerned with the implications of this study for the education of parents rather than for therapy.

Multiple Determinants of Child-rearing

When we contemplate the variety of influences that operate in any parent-child interaction sequence, we can understand why the efforts of psychologists to relate a specific child-rearing practice of parents to a specific personality characteristic of children have for the most part shown a paucity of definitive results. A question arises, for example, whether the acknowledged beliefs or values of a parent (the basis of many antecedent-consequent child-rearing studies) can be assumed to be consonant with his practices. If a parent reports that he believes physical punishment is wrong, can we be sure that he will not spank or slap when provoked by danger, interruptions, disobedience, or independence? Or will the mother who reports that parents should show affection to their children be able to be affectionate herself when she is pregnant, or has several young ones underfoot, or is getting ready for guests, or is just plain tired, or is perhaps all of these things at once? Interruptions of the translation of values and beliefs into practices may occur not rarely, but constantly, even daily or hourly. Individual parents vary in their reactions to the fluctuations of their own feelings, their spouse's actions, the moods and behavior of their children, the behavior setting—but each in his own way makes subtle or drastic changes in his child-rearing practices because of them.

The multiple determinants of parent behavior result in child-rearing that is organically human rather than mechanistically automatic. This compounds the problems of investigators. The variety of causes of parent behavior that have been described should serve as an antidote to oversimplification in research, and as a warning that an intricate network of influences operates to determine parent practices. The outline of values, beliefs, and other influences may serve as a schema for future investigations, and the data presented may serve as a base line for comparing other groups of parents.

Values of Parents

Out of a wide variety of life experiences, parents gradually develop values related to child-rearing. In spite of the many recent studies focusing on the rearing of children, we know relatively little about the value preferences that motivate and guide a parent in his contact with children. White (1951) states that our value-system is so completely taken for granted in our culture that we seldom focus attention on values. Brim (1959, p. 134), in his discussion of parent education, also comments on this: "It is remarkable that there is almost no research describing what parents seek to achieve through child-rearing." The 4,000 statements of parents' values analyzed in this study should open the door for further investigations.

Of the eight categories of values relating specifically to the parental role, three were stressed considerably more than the others, and discussed by nearly all the parents .These "oughts" for parents are: to teach a child; to provide a child with situations conducive to emotional security; to control a child. The parents were conscious of the fact that their role involved socializing their children, both controlling and teaching them, but they wanted to exercise these functions in ways that would insure their children's emotional health. The parents' concepts of mental health were often vague, as indeed they are often found to be in the literature for parents (Brim, 1959, p. 83). Here is an important opportunity for those working with parents to help them find ways to teach and control children that will not jeopardize a child's sense of self-esteem, or engender hostility toward authority figures, or create overwhelming anxiety within him.

Three-fourths of the 4,000 values categorized referred to the basic values that guide parents in rearing their children. Altogether, 55 specific subcategories of values were reported, but no one category was mentioned by every parent. There are, however, a number of goals that were discussed by two-thirds or more of the parents, and which stand relatively high in the hierarchy of emphasis. Specifically, parents want their children to be obedient, to behave courteously, to be independent, to feel close to the family group, and to be religious. Fathers also strongly emphasize the importance of children having knowledge and being responsible, whereas mothers strive to have their children get along well with others.

A factor analysis was made of the 18 subcategories of most highly emphasized values, isolating one set of eight factors for mothers and another set of eight factors for fathers. We compared the factors we obtained for mothers with factors for mothers discussed in two previous studies that report traits or clusters related to child-rearing practices (Sears *et al.*, 1957; Miller and Swanson, 1958). There are no similarities between the clusters we found and those reported in the other two studies. As we have stated, the number of our cases is small, and the correlations on the whole are relatively low. The best we can say for the factors presented is that they describe this group of parents, and may be suggestive for future investigations.

There are other basic differences in the three studies that probably would preclude comparable results. We should point out that in the previous studies, the values, or goals, of mothers were not analyzed separately as they were in this study but were combined with practices. This fact raises a question about the variability of these two aspects of child-rearing. It is possible that the clustering (correlations and factors) of variables at the level of goals may differ from the clustering at the level of practices. If empirical evidence should prove this to be so, then in the future the separation of values and practices in child-rearing studies may be desirable. Another difference lies in the basis of selection of variables. The two previous studies selected their variables on the basis of theoretical significance; we selected ours on the basis of emphasis by parents. Half of the 18 most-emphasized values in the present study did not appear in Sears *et al.*, and only two seem related to those in the Miller and Swanson study.

The values that parents hold depend in some measure upon the circumstances of their lives. We have some indications of the experiences in life that contribute to the development of values relating to child-rearing. Some are learned from experiences during childhood in the family of orientation, the period when the parent's parent becomes the model for later imitation or rejection. Other experiences in childhood, adolescence, and adulthood raise issues of good and bad, and new values may either become interwoven with or replace earlier family-learned values. As an individual matures, his own personal needs may press him to value, for example, dependency in children, or a quiet household, or orderliness. With marriage, interaction with one's spouse may bring about revision of old values or exposure to new ones. The experience of raising a child is the reality testing and may result in reorganization of values; and values may be changed again by experiences with the second, third, or fourth child.

There is some evidence, too, that values may be related to the developmental process of life: the age of parents and the age of children. The sheer weight of numbers in a family affects values —what seems good in a small family may seem bad in a large one. We found that economic conditions and educational and cultural background are also related subtly to values of parents.

These findings should remind those trying to help parents that the ends parents seek with their children are related to the makeup of the family unit, the kind of home and neighborhood the family lives in, the family's economic security, and perhaps to other conditions of living as well. In general, the parents in this study who emphasized the influence of values on their child-rearing were not high seekers from communication sources. The professional person working with parents should realize that the parent who reads the leaflet given to him, or comes to the lecture, or joins the study group, or seeks help from the doctor is likely to be a man or woman who lacks strong commitment to values for guidance in the parental role. He is less conscious of his goals, of what he wants for his children, of what kind of child he wants to develop, of his aims or purposes as a parent. On the other hand, the parent who only rarely reads books for parents, or enlarges the lecturer's audience, or joins study groups, or visits the doctor's office is more likely to be a parent who has strong convictions concerning his goals and purposes as a parent. These may not necessarily be goals and purposes the professional worker would approve or recommend, but the parent has values that guide his behavior with his children to some extent.

Those concerned with the education of parents are faced with two problems: one, how to help the parents who contact them develop more conscious, clear-cut values to guide them in child-rearing; and two, how to reach those parents who do have strong values, but values that may not be in the best interests of the child.

Instrumental Beliefs

Closely related to values are the beliefs about how to obtain them. Instrumental beliefs constitute about one-third of the nearly 5,000 codings of beliefs analyzed. Such beliefs were reported in relation to all eleven major categories of values and to about 70 per cent of the 55 subcategories. Three conclusions stand out clearly in this analysis.

First, parents may have the same goal, but show wide variation in their beliefs about how to obtain the goal. For example, a high percentage of parents believed that obedience could be obtained if the parent exercised control, but the kind of control they believed to be efficacious varied greatly, both in level and method. Such variability in instrumental beliefs was found for each of the 38 subcategories of values mentioned.

Second, there is a discrepancy between the emphasis parents place on values and the emphasis they give to the beliefs implementing such values. Both parent groups were guided most by instrumental beliefs relating to three general categories of values—biological, emotional security, and moral—but of these only moral is among the values most highly influential on parents. Among the subcategories, similar discrepancies in emphasis are found between instrumental beliefs and values. For example, religious values (a subcategory under moral values) were stressed by almost 60 per cent of the parents, but only 8 per cent reported being influenced by beliefs about how to instill religion in children. For biological values, the discrepancy is in the opposite direction. Although over three-fourths of the parents mention such values, they are given little emphasis, especially by mothers. In contrast, beliefs about how to obtain such values stand first in emphasis. Parents give greatest emphasis to instrumental beliefs relating to the goals of nutrition, regulation of sexual behavior, mental health, obedience, morality, and health, only two of which (obedience and morality) are among their highest values. Morality is the value under which we coded goals for "good" children. It stands high both in values and in implementing beliefs, probably because of its nonspecific generalized connotation.

There are several explanations for the lack of correspondence between values and implementing beliefs. For one thing, parents may have goals that they really do not know (or only vaguely know) how to obtain. But parents are quite clear about the ways to obtain goals that are a matter of social concern (for example, health, nutrition, and mental health), probably because the techniques for obtaining these goals have been widely publicized. We also believe that some parents hold beliefs for which the end result is not clear in their minds. We sensed this in relation to beliefs concerning morality and regulation of sexual behavior.

Third, we found that these parents relied heavily on parental control and on child obedience as means of obtaining what they desired in their children. They laid considerably less stress on the usefulness of expressing affection for, and interest in, the child, and gave scant attention to the importance of parental example. They seemed almost unaware of the subtle influences a parent's behavior has through serving as a model for his child.

If we are correct in our analysis, some parents, and especially mothers, might be helped by being made to realize the importance of knowing what one wants to achieve with children, and of finding ways to obtain the goals in view. Techniques should be considered in relation to the values for which they are instrumental, rather than as ends in themselves.

Descriptive Beliefs

Descriptive beliefs were limited to those that parents discussed as influential in the rearing of their children. We coded over 3,000 beliefs on the characteristics of children, the effects of heredity and environment, learning, reward, punishment, and control. Here, too, we found wide variation in the beliefs that guide parents. However, it is possible to make a few generalizations that may offer suggestions to parents and to those professional workers and writers concerned with parents.

Characteristics of children. In spite of the fact that much of the material describing children and their development reported by child psychologists has gradually filtered through to parents by means of various communication sources (Brim, 1959, Chap. 6), we found parents in this study who evidenced little real understanding of children, and who had misconceptions concerning some of the fundamental aspects of child development. We shall discuss just a few of the areas in which parents' misconceptions occurred.

In spite of the vast amount of material available on individual differences, parents seldom emphasized beliefs in this area, mentioning only about a third as many beliefs as they mentioned for sex differences. In addition, their beliefs about the differences between boys and girls conform to the usual cultural stereotypes: noisy, aggressive, dirty boys; conforming, passive, underhanded girls. They had little realization of the variability within each sex, and of the overlap between the sexes in psychological characteristics.

Many parents are convinced that children go through "stages" in their psychological development that are universal, inevitable, and transient. As parents see these "stages," they are part of the growing-up process of every child, something the child "goes through." The parent can do little about such behavior; he must wait until the "stage" has spent itself. These parents were not concerned with stages in personality development, such as the theoretical formulations proposed by Freud (1949, pp. 89–99), or Erikson (1950, Chap. 7). Their beliefs referred to specific behaviors connected, for example, with eating, or independence, or language. Brim (1959, Chap. 6) has termed them "Gesellian" developmental stages, since they emanate from material presented in three widely read books for parents written by Arnold Gesell and his associates (Gesell and Ilg, 1943, 1946; Gesell, Ilg, and Ames, 1956). However, recent critiques have pointed out the inadequacies of the Gesell sample, and the lack of data to support the theoretical conception that behavior develops in chronological-age rhythmic stages (Senn and Wylie, 1955; Stolz, 1958).

Adolescence was of special concern to over two-fifths of the parents, even though only a few of the children in the families had reached this period of development. Parents see adolescence as a point in development identified by specific characteristics, rather than as a period extending from five to eight years during which marked changes occur in physical growth, in attitudes, and in personality (Stolz and Stolz, 1951). For them, adolescence refers to the latter half of the period, and they were uninformed concerning the onset of adolescence, and the changes that occur during the first part of the period in body, attitudes, and behavior.

The behavioral sciences have much to contribute to the beliefs of parents about individual and sex differences, adolescent development, and developmental stages—all areas of high interest to parents. Information in these areas should be transmitted to parents, not only to correct misconceptions and to increase understanding of children, but also to encourage parents to cope with situations which arise with their children.

Heredity and environment. There was little unanimity among these parents in assessing the role of heredity and environment in the development of personality and behavior of children. Parents are poorly informed about the interaction of heredity and environment. Their beliefs are often vague, confusing, and sometimes incorrect. The use of communication sources does not seem to have helped them clarify their ideas about the interaction of heredity and environment, but only to stress one or the other. The interaction of heredity and environment is a complex process, which scientists are continuing to explore, but enough is known to clarify some of the vague beliefs, and to correct some of the misconceptions of parents, if translated for them by writers, discussion leaders, or consultants.

Learning, reward, and punishment. Beliefs concerning the learning of children influenced all parents in this group. Parents who emphasized beliefs about learning were apt to be those who were high seekers from communication sources. The surprising fact is that despite exposure to various communication sources, most of these parents saw little connection between reward or punishment and learning, at least not in relation to learning new tasks. Beliefs about reward and punishment related primarily to the child doing what had been learned previously, i.e., obeying, or taking responsibility.

Beliefs about punishment were mentioned four or five times as much as beliefs about reward; and beliefs indicating approval of punishment outnumbered those indicating disapproval of its use. These findings are in line with Yarrow's (1963) report that mothers give scant evidence of positive techniques in interviews. Mothers who have larger families stress beliefs related to the use of punishment, especially physical punishment. The fathers of lower social position are likely to disapprove of physical punishment, perhaps because they suffered too much from it in their own childhood.

How children learn is the basis of the socialization process. Information concerning the effects of reward and punishment on learning, and on the consequent development of such personality characteristics as self-esteem, hostility, or submissiveness, if communicated to parents, could help them to evaluate more adequately their child-rearing practices.

Control. Socialization involves both teaching and control of children. If we combine the instrumental and descriptive beliefs about teaching and compare them with those about control, we find that both mothers and fathers appear to be influenced more by beliefs related to teaching than by beliefs related to control (mean percentage scores for mothers, 5.63 vs. 3.56; for fathers, 5.35 vs. 4.39).

Five levels of control—permissive, lenient, firm, strict, and authoritarian—were identified in the beliefs of these parents. The two extremes, permissive and authoritarian, were described, but not approved of, by parents, but some intimated that they had observed other parents using such methods. It seemed to us that parents use beliefs about extreme methods in order to clarify and justify the level of control they do use. Strictness goes with lower social position for both mothers and fathers. In addition, mothers with larger families believe in it. Parents of higher social position tend to believe in more lenient control. The parents who are strongly guided by beliefs about punishment and control are not those who make much use of communication sources. Their discussions lead one to think that they have learned from their childhood experiences, from watching other parents and their children, and from trial and error with their own offspring.

Our analysis of control suggests that parents could profit by a clarification of levels of control, the labels assigned to them, and their effects on learning and personality of children. Clarification of the differences between permissive and lenient control, and between strict and authoritarian control, as we have used the terms, seems especially important not only for parents, but for investigators of child-rearing as well.

Other Influences

If a parent always acted in accordance with his values and his beliefs, prognosis of parental behavior would be simplified, and the study of antecedents and consequents in the behavior of children might conceivably be more fruitful. The fact is, however, that other elements intrude to inhibit, modify, change, or, sometimes, to reinforce behavior that emanates from a parent's values and beliefs. We have analyzed several such intrusive influences: characteristics of the parent; characteristics and behavior of the child; husband-wife interaction; and the behavior setting in which the parent-child interaction takes place. There were over 7,000 codings of these kinds of influence.

Behavior of children. The fact that children's behavior influences parents' behavior has had little recognition in child psychology. Many studies since 1945 have focused on the effect of the practices of parents on the psychological development of the child (Yarrow and Yarrow, 1964), but rarely has attention been given to the effect that children have on parents. Here is an area which promises to be fruitful for investigation.

The interaction between a child and a parent, of course, becomes circular: child behavior instigates parent behavior; the parent behavior, in turn, influences the child; and then the cycle may begin again. Sometimes it is difficult to tell whether child or parent is the initiator of the sequence. The parents reported nearly 3,400 instances in which the parent perceived the behavior of the child as instigating the parent's behavior.

Although parents are not unresponsive to the behavior of their children they approve of, by far the strongest influence on parents is behavior they disapprove of and wish to change. This tendency seems related to the greater emphasis parents place on beliefs related to punishment, as opposed to reward, and to their strong concern with beliefs concerning control.

We have some indication of the systems of behavior that elicit the greatest response from parents: behavior related to aggression, to orderly living, to obedience, to eating, and to dependency. On the other hand, more subtle behavior—behavior expressing anxiety, guilt, or unhappiness—is mentioned only rarely as modifying the practices of either parent.

Parents today seem to be somewhat like the teachers in Cleveland and Minneapolis whom Wickman studied in the 1920's. After analyzing the kinds of behavior that the teachers considered problems in the classroom, Wickman (1929, p. 50) concluded: "Teachers are more sensitive to overt types of behavior and aggressive personality traits than they are to the personal problems of children which do not interfere directly with the purposes of teaching." If we replace the first word in the quotation with *parents,* and the last word with *family life,* the statement describes the parents in this study. We suggest that some parents may need help in identifying, understanding, and responding to children's behavior that is painful to the children themselves, but not disturbing or annoying to the family.

The age of children in the family may determine to some extent the kind of behavior to which the parent is likely to respond: dependency in younger children, aggression in older children. When families are larger, mothers stress their reactions to aggressive behavior in children, and fathers stress problems in obedience and problems relating to mealtimes—all behavior that increases the difficulties in managing a large family.

It is important to realize that a mother or a father is not a free agent who can change his ways of rearing his children overnight. The relations a parent has established with a child build within the child certain expectancies. He becomes confused and resistant if these expectancies are not confirmed. In addition, children are people, too, with goals, urges, and habits that must be taken into account by the parent. When a mother says, "I cannot do that with Bill, it won't work," she is reminding us that children influence the practices of parents. One of the great advantages of nursery schools or play groups that are run in conjunction with parent-education group meetings is the opportunity they create for the leader to know the child whom the parent discusses.

Husband-wife interaction. In the past, professional advisors to parents and parent educators, and those engaged in child-development research, have operated as if the child had only one parent —the mother. Moreover, it has often been assumed that if the mother can be convinced of the value of a certain child-rearing practice, she can readily introduce the new practice into the home. Since 1950, there has been an increasing realization, documented to some extent by research (Stolz *et al.*, 1954; Bandura and Walters, 1959; Nash, 1965), that the father plays an important role with children, both directly and through his influence on the mother.

Our data show that child-rearing is a two-way affair, with mothers influencing fathers, and fathers influencing mothers. And each parent seems to feel that the spouse influences him (or her) more than he (or she) influences the spouse. These influences come about in various ways. Parents are especially affected by the competency of the spouse in an area of child-rearing, but they are also influenced by the likes or dislikes of a spouse, or emotional pressures on the spouse. Criticism by a spouse seems particularly effective in modifying practices.

Mothers make use of communication sources much more than fathers, and often attempt to convince their husbands of some new practice or idea that they themselves have only begun to understand and digest. This is a difficult task to undertake with men who have strongly entrenched values and beliefs, as many of the fathers in this study seemed to have. It is evident that finding ways to reach fathers through communication sources is a job of first order.

Behavior Settings

Behavior settings within the home (getting-up time in the morning; parents' entertaining adult guests at dinner) and, to a lesser degree, those outside of the home (child's riding a bicycle on a busy street; visiting in other people's homes) were shown to modify what parents expect of children, how they respond to misbehavior, and what activities they initiate. All parents mentioned such behavior settings. The parents were much less conscious of the influence of behavior settings on their child-rearing than they were of the influence of the behavior of their children. There are at least two explanations for this. Barker (1960, p. 18) said that the persons who are influenced by a behavior setting need not be aware of the setting per se, and are sometimes not as able to see it as those on the outside. It is also possible that some behavior of children (for example, overt aggression) may strongly motivate parents whenever it occurs, no matter what the behavior setting.

Further studies are needed of the effect of behavior settings on child-rearing, and of the way parents respond to behavior settings in socializing children. It may be that these parents recognized the influence of behavior settings to a greater extent than they reported, and that the techniques of interview were at fault. However, if, as Barker maintains, parents are found not to recognize the influence of the behavior setting, then the method of direct observation should be used to obtain data—just as Barker and his associates have used it to obtain data regarding the influence of behavior settings on children's behavior. From our data we would expect settings within the home to be more influential than those outside the home.

The educational and social background of parents seems related to the effect of behavior settings. Mothers who have moved up the social scale appear to be particularly conscious of settings. Whereas fathers of lower educational level are responsive to dangerous settings, fathers of higher educational level stress the effect of the time element involved. There is also a tendency for fathers with larger families to stress behavior settings. It seems reasonable that parents with larger families should be more influenced by behavior settings. As the number of children increases, parents have more difficulty supervising the behavior of children, but they may be pressed to take action when a dangerous situation or valuable property is involved. By making rules about specific behavior settings, parents lessen the need for individual supervision of children.

The parents who emphasize the influence of behavior settings are not those who emphasize the influence of communication sources. It may be that material concerning the effect of behavior settings on the behavior of children and adults, such as that analyzed by Roger Barker and his coworkers, has not yet been incorporated into the content of parent education. If parents realized that behavior settings are "entities that regulate some aspects of the behavior of their human components" (Barker, 1965, p. 12), they might understand and appreciate better the social structure that contributes to their own behavior, as well as to the learning of their children.

Communication Sources

Every parent in this study had been reached by some source, individual or group, lay or professional, that had transmitted to him information or advice about the care and guidance of children. Sometimes these parents were critical of source or content, but for the most part they were accepting, and they felt that the rearing of their children had indeed been modified because of such contacts. The parents who were influenced most were those with smaller families, and with younger children. As might be expected, physicians were their greatest source of help.

Individual consultations with professional people, including those at clinics, were mentioned about as much as mass communication sources (primarily literature). These parents were helped more by acquaintances than relatives, only physicians being mentioned more often as an interpersonal source. Though nearly all parents mentioned the influence of some form of organized education (college courses, lectures, adult classes, nursery school participation, and the like), they stressed them much less than consultations with specialists, or the books, articles, and pamphlets they read. In addition, they were quite critical of their experiences at lectures, church groups, and adult education classes. Only the parent-education programs connected with nursery school participation won general commendation.

Comparison with other studies. There are several previous studies of the communication practices of parents with which some of our findings can be compared. Although the samples in the three previous studies that we will discuss differ from the sample in the present study both in characteristics and in size, and although the methods used in the investigations are different, comparisons of relevant findings may be enlightening. Littman, Curry, and Pierce-Jones (1957) conducted single interviews with fathers and mothers in 200 families in Eugene, Oregon. They asked the parents whether they had ever felt the need for help in raising their children, and were told by 30 per cent of the mothers, and by 60 per cent of the fathers, that they had never felt such a need. In contrast, every parent in our study reported that they had been influenced to some extent by communication sources, although mothers emphasized the influence significantly more than the family-matched fathers. Littman *et al.* suggest that the responses of fathers in the Oregon study may have been affected by the survey-type method of collecting data, and by the use of "strange female" interviewers. We are inclined to agree that methodological factors are somewhat influential, since our data were collected through a series of interviews, with indirect probing for the effect of communication sources, and with the interviewers for fathers being either men or older highly trained women. The Littman study also suggests that fathers may be more self-reliant with their children than mothers; we suggest that fathers' greater emphasis on values in child-rearing may be one reason for their greater confidence.

Our finding that physicians were more influential than other professional or lay sources is in line with the findings of Littman *et al.* that physicians led the list of sources parents used for help in raising children, or would use in the future. However, in the Littman study 30 per cent of the parents had used physicians for help, whereas in our study all mothers and 95 per cent of fathers had been influenced by physicians.

Differences also emerge in the findings regarding the use of mass media. Only 25 per cent of the parents in Littman's study (findings are not given for mothers and fathers separately) reported using mass media, where mass media include books, magazines, and health columns in newspapers. We find that books for parents are mentioned by 95 per cent of mothers and 82 per cent of fathers; magazine articles by 92 per cent of mothers and 74 per cent of fathers; newspapers (not limited to health columns) by 56 per cent of mothers and 54 per cent of fathers. An average of 81 per cent of mothers and 70 per cent of fathers were influenced by such mass media.

Friends and relatives were consulted by relatively few (18 per cent) parents in the Oregon study. In our study, 74 per cent of mothers and 49 per cent of fathers had received help from relatives, and 97 per cent of mothers and 90 per cent of fathers report help from acquaintances and friends, making an average of 85.5 per cent of mothers and 68.5 per cent of fathers receiving help from such personal sources.

These differences in findings of the two studies may be due to sample differences, but we are inclined to believe that differences in methods of data collection are more likely the cause.

In any case, we do know that the more intensive methods used in our study revealed a much higher incidence of use of communication sources than was found by the survey techniques used in the larger Oregon study. It is quite possible that parents cannot recall what sources they have used in answer to a specific question, but are reminded of these influences as they discuss at greater length the behavior of their children, and the problems they have faced.

Previous studies have been made of the sources used by parents in rural communities in Ohio (Hoeflin, 1954) and in North Carolina (Sperry and Garner, 1962). Hoeflin's study was based on single interviews with 100 families of preschool children (2 through 5 years old). The mother was interviewed in all but four cases. Hoeflin investigated the resources of child-care information that had influenced eight areas of child-rearing practices. The resources mentioned included four categories of what we term communication sources, emphasized as first or second choice in the following order: relatives and friends (37 per cent), printed material (25.5 per cent), professional aid (9 per cent), lay groups (5.5 per cent). We find differences between the Ohio mothers and the mothers in our study, not only in the order of preference of communication sources, but also in the percentage of mothers being influenced. All of the mothers in our study had been influenced by relatives and friends, by professional sources, and by mass media; and about 72 per cent had been affected by some kind of study group. Although our categories are not exactly comparable, 19 per cent of the Ohio mothers stressed as first or second choice their own past experiences with children, whereas 44 per cent of the mothers in our study were influenced to some extent by adult experiences in teaching or caring for children.

There is no question that the mothers in our study reported

many more influences of these communication sources than the Ohio mothers. Altogether the Ohio mothers mentioned the four resources 578 times, an average of six mentions per mother; whereas the mothers in the present study had 2,516 codings in these four areas, an overall average of 64 mentions per mother. Neither the Stanford nor the Ohio study found a consistent pattern between socioeconomic status and child-care resources used by mothers.

There are several factors that may account for the differences in the findings of the two studies. Rural mothers may have less access to communication sources, except relatives, than mothers living in an extension of a metropolitan community. Differences in the educational background of the mothers in the two samples may have also affected the results. Although the range of educational level was similar for the two groups, the percentage of mothers with more than high school education varied greatly: 17 per cent in the Ohio study, 64 per cent in the Stanford study. The difference in educational background may have affected the mothers' uses of communication resources, and also their ability to recall or to see meaningful relations between cause and effect.

The investigation of Sperry and Garner (1962) is based on single taped interviews with 239 white mothers, who had an only child between birth and 35 months of age, living in three Piedmont (North Carolina) counties. The source that these mothers reported most used was the doctor, as we also found. Next in order of emphasis were: the mother's mother, own experience, reading material, mother-in-law, and other relatives. Mothers who had attended college (10.4 per cent) named reading materials most frequently. We found no statistically significant relation between the educational level of mothers and their emphasis on communication sources, but our sample, as we have stated before, had a high percentage of mothers with some college education, whereas the North Carolina study had a preponderance of parents who attended or graduated from high school (76.1 per cent).

Following the interview study reported in this monograph, several experimental field studies concerning communication of child-care information were conducted at the Laboratory of Human Development at Stanford University. The one that seems most pertinent to our study investigated the receptivity of mothers to information concerning toilet training (Maccoby *et al.*, 1962). The results indicate that mothers for whom information is critically important (e.g., their child is developmentally ready for toilet training) are more active seekers of information, are harder to influence initially, but once influenced are more likely to stay influenced. We have some findings in line with this "critical period" notion: mothers of younger firstborns, and those with smaller families, are influenced more by communication sources; and these higher seekers stress beliefs about infancy and learning, and are concerned with dependency behavior of their children.

Our study indicates that a parent's readiness for information or advice from communication sources is determined by the parent's feelings of inadequacy to handle the situation with his child. From this point of view the impetus for seeking may emerge from a variety of conditions, of which the "critical period" is one. Such conditions include the following: initial experience in caring for an infant; the level of development of the child; physical defects; illness; mental retardation; school failures; emotional or behavior problems. In general, as parents become more experienced in rearing children, they depend more on themselves and seek less from communication sources; for example, parents of younger children concerned with dependency problems are high seekers, but parents of older children concerned with problems of aggression or disobedience make little use of communication sources.

Relation of Influences to Demographic Characteristics of Parents

In each of the chapters reporting findings, we included a section discussing the correlations between the categories of influence discussed and seven demographic characteristics of the parents. We did this because the sample of parents represented a rather wide range in such characteristics as age, number of children, age of oldest child, education, and social position. In addition to the five demographic indices noted above, we added a score indicating consistency in family religion for two generations and a score for social mobility. The size and non-randomness of the sample of parents limit the usefulness of the correlations with demographic variables. They serve as descriptions of these parents, and as suggestions for further investigations, rather than as a basis for generalizations regarding other more representative samples of parents.

The seven demographic characteristics were correlated with 171 categories of influences. Of the 1,197 correlations, 68 (5.7 per cent) of those for mothers, and 77 (6.4 per cent) of those for fathers, are significant at the level of .02 or beyond; 24 correlations for each parent group could be expected by chance at these levels. An analysis of these highly significant correlations indicates that about half of them are related to the number and age of the children in the family. The size of the family accounts for the largest number of *r*'s at the level of .02 or beyond (21 *r*'s for mothers; 20 *r*'s for fathers); the age of the oldest child accounts for a slightly smaller number (14 *r*'s for mothers; 19 *r* 's for fathers).

The demographic variables that show the next largest number of highly significant correlations are education of parents and social position of family. Social position and education are more often highly related for fathers than for mothers. With social position, 9 *r*'s for mothers and 15 *r*'s for fathers reach a significance of .02 or beyond; whereas with education, 9 *r*'s for mothers and 14 for fathers reach that significance.

The remaining demographic characteristics yielded fewer significant correlations. Only the relation of the age of parents might be useful to investigate in future studies. This variable yielded 9 *r*'s for mothers and 8 *r*'s for fathers at the level of .02 or beyond. Consistency in religion and social mobility of parents as we scored them yielded few significant correlations, and most of these are at a low level of significance.

Mothers and fathers have the largest number of significant correlations ($p < .02$) with categories of beliefs, values, communication sources, and behavior of children. However, the number of categories of influences that were correlated with demographic characteristics varied for each of the major areas of influence. Therefore, the percentage of correlations that reached a significance of .02 or beyond was obtained for each area. By this measure, mothers have their highest percentage, and fathers their second highest percentage, of correlations with communication sources (smaller family, younger children, and higher social mobility). Fathers have the highest percentage of correlations with parental characteristics (higher education and higher social position).

The relations with demographic descriptions summarized here indicate the strong tendency of the influences on child-rearing of parents to be related to the education and social status of parents, and the age and number of their children. Younger children, larger families, less education, and lower social position are the characteristics that show the strongest relations to the influences on parental behavior. In future research, the sample might well be limited to specific groups, such as parents of young children, or parents with four or more children, or parents with high school educations. By limiting the sample, more precise information might be obtained on the effect of certain variables on child-rearing.

Differences between Mothers and Fathers

When the influences on the child-rearing behavior of family-matched mothers and fathers are compared, strong differences emerge. Of the difference scores, an unusually high percentage reach statistical significance: 9.5 per cent at the level of .05 to .10; 9.1 per cent at .02 to .05; 6.7 per cent at .01 to .02; 7.1 per cent at .001 to .01; 8 per cent at $<$.001. Altogether 40 per cent of the differences between mothers and fathers are statistically significant. In general, fathers are influenced more by values and beliefs, whereas mothers are more likely to be affected by other influences, especially behavior settings and communication sources.

Fathers stress values more than mothers, both parental values and basic values. In their actions they seem more conscious of the ends in view. Of the eight subcategories of values for parenthood, two were emphasized most by both parent groups: to provide emotional security for children, and to help children learn. However, fathers emphasized both of these values more than mothers. The outstanding differences in basic values of mothers and of fathers are found in the fathers' greater emphasis on education, biological, and moral values, especially responsibility. The only value that mothers report significantly more often than fathers is freedom from anxiety.

Fathers are also more motivated by their beliefs. To some extent they have beliefs about how to reach goals more clearly in mind, primarily those related to moral values, economic values, and general goals. Mothers give greater emphasis than fathers only to beliefs relating to the family. Differences are quite outstanding in the instrumental acts in beliefs: fathers place much stronger emphasis on socializing agents other than parents, including the neighborhood, school, and television. In their beliefs, mothers do not stress the usefulness of agencies other than the home, perhaps because of an unwillingness to depreciate the importance of their own role. Fathers, much more than mothers, are influenced by descriptive beliefs. The most outstanding differences are in the father's greater emphasis on beliefs related to learning, to punishment, and to control of children.

Whereas fathers emphasize more than mothers the effect of their values and beliefs on child-rearing, mothers tend to stress the effect of circumstances that inhibit, modify, or change practices emanating from a parent's values or beliefs. Mothers are more likely than fathers to change their child-rearing practices because of their interests, physical condition, or anxieties. The behavior setting in which parent-child interaction occurs modifies the practices of mothers more than fathers, both within and outside the home. Mothers are decidedly more affected than fathers by all kinds of communication sources.

There are three areas in which mothers and fathers strongly differ. One area is education. Fathers seem much more concerned and more directed by factors relating to education. They stress more the parent's role in educating children. They emphasize values relating to education more than mothers, especially the importance of education and the usefulness of knowledge. In their instrumental beliefs, fathers stress the importance of formal education as a means to other values. They are more often guided by descriptive beliefs about learning: they stress maturity as an index of readiness for learning, and parental example and reasoning as ways of helping children to learn. Closely related to their emphasis on learning is their greater emphasis on beliefs about environment as a primary factor in development. (Mothers exceed fathers in only two areas concerning education: the influence of communication sources such as teachers and organized education; and the influence of previous experiences in teaching.) The fathers' greater concern with education may be due to the fact that the fathers were on the average more highly educated than the mothers. However, we are more inclined to believe that since the occupational success of men is strongly related to their educational level, fathers are more likely to be conscious of the values and rewards to be derived from learning and education.

The second area in which fathers quite consistently exceed mothers in emphasis relates to control and to punishment. Fathers are guided more strongly by beliefs concerning both control and punishment. Fathers are more critical and more disapproving of physical punishment than mothers, but they give greater emphasis to the positive effects of punishment in general. Beliefs concerning strict control are much more emphasized by fathers, as are beliefs about the use of inhibition or rules in control. A combination of beliefs related to reward, punishment, and control finds fathers believing in fewer rewards, more punishment, and stricter control than mothers. Mothers emphasize more than fathers only beliefs concerning the bad effects of social ostracism or rejection as a form of punishment.

In the third area that relates to the family, mothers have a tendency to exceed fathers in their emphasis, though for the most part the differences are not highly significant. Mothers appear to be guided somewhat more by goals relating to the family. They augment these goals by beliefs about how to reach them more than fathers do, especially beliefs about goals that relate to harmony in the family. Mothers appear to stress beliefs concerning the importance of parental behavior in obtaining values, whereas fathers are much more likely to stress the usefulness of other socializing agents, such as the neighborhood, the school, and television. We had expected that mothers would be more influenced by the behavior of their children; and there is a slight tendency for them to discuss the influence of family members as a whole more than fathers do ($p < .10$), but the difference in emphasis on the influence of children is not significant. Mothers do talk more about home settings, but they also stress settings outside the home more. They are more likely to be influenced by advice from relatives, but this seems only a manifestation of their more general susceptibility to advice from all communication sources.

From this summary we are inclined to believe that the fathers in this study are more predictable in their behavior, which is strongly guided by their goals and beliefs; whereas the mothers are more likely to be swayed by their own feelings at the moment, by activities or visitors in their own or other people's homes, or by the pressure of time. Our analysis does not tell us why fathers are more conscious of the influence of the good and the true on their actions. It is not that mothers do not have values or beliefs, but rather that they tend to give more emphasis to other factors as explanations of their behavior. Mothers are much more highly influenced by communication sources; their values and beliefs, therefore, may be less sure, may depend more upon outside authority than internal conviction, and be more subject to change. Fathers who use communication sources less may be less confused and more confident of the goals they wish to reach. It is possible that many forms of parent education or advising have failed in helping mothers to appraise their values or clarify what they want to achieve with their children.

Because beliefs constitute a large part of the content of parent-education programs (Brim, 1959, Chap. 7), one might reasonably expect mothers to emphasize beliefs more than fathers. The fact that they do not may be due to women's greater dependency. Mothers may need to bolster their confidence with the authority of a communication source; whereas fathers may incorporate the advice or information received into their system of beliefs.

It is not surprising that mothers are affected more by their own physical condition, interests, and feelings. They are with children more and have both a greater need to protect themselves from intrusions and more opportunity to share interests with their children. A similar explanation might be given for mothers' greater emphasis on behavior settings, although this also may be caused by the woman's greater sensitivity to appropriate behavior.

The findings reported here on differences in influences on mothers' and fathers' child-rearing are in line with those of other studies in which interview data concerning practices and attitudes of mothers and fathers were compared. In response to the problems of a first child born while the father was separated from his family because of war, fathers had less insight into problems, and were more annoyed and less worried about the behavior, than their wives (Engvall, 1954). Differences have been reported in the child-rearing of mothers and fathers of aggressive and nonaggressive boys, with less interparental consistency in the aggressive boys' families (Weide, 1962). In another interview study of children's aggression, little agreement was found between the reports of mothers and of fathers concerning either the child's behavior or the parent's interaction with the child (Eron, Banta, Walder, and Laulicht, 1961). As has been pointed out by Nash (1965), most research workers have considered fathers to be both inaccessible for research and unimportant in child-rearing. This study underscores the importance for child development research to be concerned with fathers as well as mothers, since the motivations underlying practices of mothers and fathers often differ.

The differences in influences on child-rearing between mothers and fathers that are suggested by this study also focus attention on the complexities which professional people meet when they try to influence the way children are reared. The mother is usually more available for conferences, attends more lectures or study groups, and therefore becomes the target for advice or education. It is easy for the advisor or educator to act as if the child has only one parent, or to assume that mother and father are really one in goals and methods of child-rearing, or to believe that the mother can easily convince the father that change in a certain direction is desirable.

The question of "how to reach fathers" is an old one in parent education. This research only underscores the need, it does not suggest solutions. Professional people who work with individuals (physicians, psychiatrists, psychologists, social workers) more and more tend to require or encourage both parents to come for conferences. Teachers who hold conferences in the evening can stress the importance of this, too. Some parent-education groups have been successful in enrolling both parents. Perhaps it will be possible to do more of this in the future. For some parents, separate groups or separate conferences for fathers and for mothers may be more appropriate, making it possible to adjust content to the differing needs of men and women.

Summary

From a series of individual interviews with mothers and fathers widely differing in demographic characteristics, an analysis was made of the influences that affect the rearing of children. A variety of influences are revealed, some coming from experiences of these parents during childhood, but intensified, modified, or drastically changed by later experiences. Although many values and beliefs guide the behavior of parents, there are other elements entering into any parent-child interaction that may often be critical in determining a practice. Within the family, the personal needs of parents, the influence of the spouse, and especially the characteristics and behavior of the child have strong effects on the way parents bring up their children. Even the behavior setting in which the parent-child interaction takes place may be a determining factor in the parent's behavior. Communication sources when used are on the whole influential, primarily in relation to beliefs, but their effect is limited by other variables that enter into the situation. To some extent the influences on child-rearing are related to the age and number of children in the family and, to a lesser extent, to the social position of the family—but the findings here are only suggestive for future investigations.

Probably the most noteworthy conclusion from this study is that any act of a parent with his child is the result of the interplay of pluralistic pressures, and that the degree of dominance of an influence is determined by elements in the total situation. The environment in which parents rear their children is, in Ashby's terms (1960, Chap. 16), "richly joined," in that "every variable is joined directly to every other variable," so that what happens to one member of the family may very well effect changes in each of the other members (mother, father, and each child) and in their interrelations with each other. Heider (1967, p. 26), who calls attention to these interlacings of causal connections in interpersonal relations, states, "not only do we find that there are influences from every part to every other part, but also that influences are specific to parts in such a way that the whole may become very complex."

The study reported here marks only a beginning in delineating the influences that determine the family environment in which parents and children live and develop. As we begin to understand the complex interaction of these influences, we shall gain more insight into why parents rear their children as they do, and in turn will understand more of the reasons why American children grow up to be the kind of people they are.

Appendix A

Tables for Chapter II

Table A.1. *Age and Sex of Children (54 Boys, 57 Girls)*

Age in years	*No. of boys*	*No. of girls*	*Total*	*Age in years*	*No. of boys*	*No. of girls*	*Total*
0–0.9	5	7	12	7–7.9	4	7	11
1–1.9	6	2	8	8–8.9	7	4	11
2–2.9	6	2	8	9–9.9	0	3	3
3–3.9	5	3	8	10–10.9	5	1	6
4–4.9	5	6	11	11–11.9	3	3	6
5–5.9	3	9	12	12–12.9	0	2	2
6–6.9	3	7	10	13–13.9	2	1	3

Table A.2 *National Origins of Respondents*

Birthplace of respondents' parents	*Number of respondents*		*Birthplace of respondents' parents*	*Number of respondents*	
	Mothers	*Fathers*		*Mothers*	*Fathers*
Both U.S.	23	23	Germany & Switzerland	1	0
U.S. & England	2	1	Both Italy	0	2
U.S. & Spain	2	0	Both Sweden	1	0
U.S. & Germany	1	1	Both Hungary	0	1
U.S. & Sweden	0	1	Both Spain	1	0
U.S. & Italy	0	1	Both Mexico	1	1
U.S. & Portugal	0	1	Both Japan	3	2
Both England	1	1	Japan & Hawaii[a]	0	1
England & Norway	0	1	Philippines & Hawaii	1	1
Both Germany	0	1	Portugal & Hawaii[b]	1	0
Germany & Spain	1	0			

[a] Japanese ancestry; [b] Portuguese ancestry.

TABLE A.3. *Education of Parents*

Highest level reached	*No. of mothers*	*No. of fathers*
1. Graduate professional training	3	7
2. College or university graduation	13	8
3. Partial college education	9	11
4. High school graduation	9	9
5. Partial high school	4	3
6. Junior high school (7–9 grade)	1	1
7. Less than 7 years of school	0	0

TABLE A.4. *Occupational Level of Fathers*

1. Executives and proprietors of large concerns and major professionals	7
2. Managers and proprietors of medium-sized businesses and lesser professionals	7
3. Administrative personnel of large concerns, owners of small independent businesses, and semiprofessionals	9
4. Owners of little businesses, clerical and sales workers, and technicians	5
5. Skilled workers	8
6. Semiskilled workers	2
7. Unskilled workers	1

NOTE: Scale from Hollingshead and Redlich, 1958, pp. 390–91.

TABLE A.5. *Scale for Rating of Residences*

Rating	*No. of houses*
1. Excellent	0
Very large single-family dwellings in good repair, well cared for and surrounded by large landscaped grounds. Somewhat ostentatious in size, architectural style, and landscaping.	
2. Very good	5
Large well-cared-for single-family dwellings in good repair. Not ostentatious, but attractive. Well-tended grounds, landscaped or planned.	
3. Good	8
Medium-sized single-family dwellings on lots of quarter acre or less (might be found in a small tract). First-class apartments. Large older houses that do not qualify for No. 2 rating because of poorer general condition and unfashionable architectural style. Yards not elaborate or professionally landscaped, but well cared for.	
4. Fair	18
Well-cared-for small houses, bungalows, and older two-story ("conventional") dwellings. Modest in appearance and may be in older sections of town or in new tracts. Less pretentious apartments than No. 3. Duplexes.	
5. Poor	6
Run-down single-family dwellings (may be in tracts). Apartments or duplexes that are old and somewhat shabby. Yards neglected or minimally kept.	
6. Very poor	2
Deteriorated and unrepairable houses. Shacks, buildings not intended for dwellings, overcrowded houses. Yards littered with junk. Perhaps outside toilet.	

Appendix B

Tables for Chapter V

Table B.1. *Order of Mean Percentage Scores for Basic Values—Mothers*

Values	Rank order	Mean percentage score	Per cent reporting	Values	Rank order	Mean percentage score	Per cent reporting
Independence	1	.65	62	Work	30.5	.16	31
Family unity	2	.61	79	Tolerance	32	.16	23
Obedience	3	.58	74	Money	33	.15	31
Manners	4	.56	72	Food	34	.13	31
Religion	5	.52	59	Self-respect	35	.13	28
Getting along	6	.49	72	Generosity	36	.12	33
Free from anxiety	7	.46	64	Achievement	37	.12	31
Family love	8	.41	59	Health	38	.12	23
Morality	9	.40	59	Physical activity	39	.11	23
Enjoyment	10	.39	64	Conformity	40	.10	21
Responsibility	11	.36	56	Citizenship	41	.10	15
Property	12	.33	51	Appearance	42	.08	23
Happiness	13	.32	38	Carefulness	43.5	.08	21
Family harmony	14	.31	51	Enthusiasm	43.5	.08	21
Knowledge	15	.26	51	Rest and sleep	45	.07	18
Level of education	16	.26	49	Nonconformity[a]	46	.06	15
Orderliness	17	.24	33	Religion (neg.)[a]	47	.06	8
Cooperation	18	.23	49	Punctuality	48	.05	15
Justice	19	.23	44	Privacy	49	.05	13
Nonaggression[a]	20	.23	41	Family location	50	.05	10
Safety	21	.22	46	Type of education	51	.05	8
Family democracy	22	.20	33	Nurturance	52	.04	10
Mental health	23	.19	38	Determination	53	.03	10
Creativity	24	.18	28	Obedience (neg.)[a]	54	.03	5
Friends	25	.17	41	Sex	55	.02	8
Educ. in general	26	.17	38	Affection	56	.02	5
Intelligence	27.5	.17	33	Aggression	57	.02	3
Interesting life	27.5	.17	33	Recognition	58	.01	5
Practicality	29	.16	33	Modesty	59	.00	3
Marriage	30.5	.16	31				

[a] Negative influences of aggression, conformity, religion, and obedience, respectively.

TABLE B.2. *Order of Mean Percentage Scores for Basic Values—Fathers*

Values	*Rank order*	*Mean percentage score*	*Percent reporting*	*Values*	*Rank order*	*Mean percentage score*	*Percent reporting*
Religion	1	.84	56	Practicality	31	.23	33
Independence	2	.81	69	Family harmony	32	.20	31
Responsibility	3	.75	59	Food	33	.17	33
Knowledge	4	.66	74	Punctuality	34	.17	31
Family unity	5	.65	67	Intelligence	35	.17	23
Manners	6	.59	69	Creativity	36	.15	26
Morality	7	.49	59	Rest and sleep	37.5	.15	23
Getting along	8	.45	49	Tolerance	37.5	.15	23
Obedience	9	.44	67	Work	39	.14	18
Safety	10	.42	62	Marriage	40	.13	28
Justice	11	.41	44	Nonconformity[a]	41	.13	15
Educ. in general	12	.38	54	Family location	42	.12	15
Happiness	13	.36	46	Enthusiasm	43	.11	21
Family love	14	.36	41	Religion (neg.)[a]	44.5	.11	13
Orderliness	15	.35	54	Friends	44.5	.11	13
Enjoyment	16	.35	46	Carefulness	46	.09	21
Property	17	.30	49	Conformity	47	.08	21
Level of education	18	.29	38	Type of education	48	.08	18
Physical activity	19	.28	36	Determination	49.5	.08	15
Free from anxiety	20	.27	51	Aggression	49.5	.08	15
Achievement	21	.27	38	Recognition	51.5	.08	13
Money	22	.26	49	Privacy	51.5	.08	13
Nonaggression[a]	23	.26	41	Citizenship	53	.06	13
Self-respect	25	.25	36	Obedience (neg.)[a]	54	.06	10
Family democracy	25	.25	36	Sex	55	.05	3
Health	25	.25	36	Nurturance	56	.04	10
Generosity	27	.25	33	Modesty	57.5	.03	5
Mental health	28	.24	46	Appearance	57.5	.03	5
Family cooperation	29	.24	41	Affection	59	.01	3
Interesting life	30	.23	36				

[a] Negative influences of aggression, conformity, religion, and obedience, respectively.

TABLE B.3. *Intercorrelations of 18 Basic Values*

(Father correlations are above the diagonal; mother correlations below)

Values	*(1)*	*(2)*	*(3)*	*(4)*	*(5)*	*(6)*	*(7)*	*(8)*	*(9)*	*(10)*	*(11)*	*(12)*	*(13)*	*(14)*	*(15)*	*(16)*	*(17)*	*(18)*
(1) Independence	*	–.05	.02	.00	.27^{a}	.19	.19	.08	.10	–.16	.26	.19	.12	–.09	.13	.20	–.29^{a}	–.11
(2) Family unity	.00	*	.15	.08	.08	.12	.47^{d}	.08	.19	.26	–.03	–.10	–.14	–.07	.15	–.20	.02	.44^{d}
(3) Obedience	–.21	.14	*	.58^{e}	.24	–.10	–.18	–.15	–.05	.14	.02	–.08	–.07	.18	–.07	.04	.28^{a}	–.03
(4) Manners	.21	.27^{a}	–.11	*	.25	.01	–.03	–.09	.00	.10	.03	–.11	.18	.11	.10	–.05	.35^{b}	–.17
(5) Religion	–.04	.19	.11	–.11	*	.13	.40^{c}	–.04	–.15	–.03	–.09	.32^{b}	.04	–.01	.42^{d}	.07	.25	–.17
(6) Getting along	–.05	.15	–.08	.38^{c}	.30^{a}	*	.49^{d}	–.19	.21	–.19	.23	–.08	–.04	–.05	–.08	–.05	.20	.00
(7) Responsibility	–.08	.40^{c}	.25	–.02	.29^{a}	–.02	*	.17	–.04	–.18	.15	–.02	.05	–.15	.29^{a}	–.28^{a}	.13	.04
(8) Morality	–.07	–.21	–.19	–.07	–.24	.06	.15	*	–.32^{b}	–.22	.05	.20	.25	.24	.07	–.23	–.16	.13
(9) Free from anxiety	–.19	.18	–.01	–.13	–.13	.10	.06	.16	*	.10	.07	.02	.05	–.05	.19	.12	–.24	.18
(10) Family love	.60^{e}	.08	.16	.04	.00	–.26	.15	–.13	.11	*	.12	–.12	.03	–.01	–.12	.29^{a}	–.03	.01
(11) Enjoyment	–.12	.00	–.15	.12	.07	–.06	–.24	–.08	.07	–.20	*	.24	.21	.24	.00	–.15	–.28^{a}	–.15
(12) Property	–.01	.00	.17	.20	.20	.45^{d}	.09	.01	–.08	–.09	–.14	*	.14	.14	.33^{b}	.03	–.25	.00
(13) Knowledge	–.10	–.09	.00	–.08	.31^{a}	.16	.43^{d}	.00	–.09	–.21	–.03	.19	*	.09	–.04	.17	.00	–.11
(14) Safety	–.19	.18	.00	.08	.17	.07	.05	–.25	.10	.07	–.27^{a}	.30^{a}	.00	*	.04	–.05	.11	.12
(15) Justice	–.16	.00	–.18	–.06	–.06	.10.	.30^{a}	.46^{d}	.41^{d}	.23	–.06	.04	.21	–.16	*	–.14	–.09	–.02
(16) Educ. in general	–.10	.08	.29^{a}	.09	.10	.14	.12	–.12	.10	.00	.07	–.02	.20	.13	–.15	*	.08	–.07
(17) Orderliness	–.13	.36^{b}	.10	.01	–.14	–.14	.33^{b}	–.12	.07	.12	–.08	–.24	–.21	.09	.00	–.12	*	.07
(18) Family harmony	–.17	.47^{d}	.21	.10	.09	.07	.24	–.05	.31^{a}	.07	.03	–.09	–.22	.11	.13	.19	.19	*

^{a} $p < .10$; ^{b} $p < .05$; ^{c} $p < .02$; ^{d} $p < .01$; ^{e} $p < .001$.

TABLE B.4. *Significance of Intercorrelations of 18 Basic Values*

Level of significance	Number expected by chance (153 r's)	Number observed Mo (153 r's)	Number observed Fa (153 r's)
<.001	.15	1	1
.001 to .01	1.38	5	4
.01 to .02	1.68	2	1
.02 to .05	5.97	2	4
.05 to .10	9.33	9	7

TABLE B.5 *Normal Varimax Factors for 18 Values—Mothers*

Values	1	2	3	4	5	6	7	8	Communality (h^2)
Independence	–.14	.06	.06	.91	–.02	–.01	–.21	–.05	.89
Family unity	.80	.19	–.22	.10	.06	.03	.01	.09	.75
Manners	.28	.67	.00	.32	–.30	–.14	.05	–.25	.80
Religion	.07	.20	–.43	.02	.68	–.12	–.03	.17	.74
Getting along	.06	.83	.04	–.11	.08	–.10	.00	.15	.75
Obedience	.16	–.08	–.12	.00	.06	.30	.75	–.21	.75
Honesty	.54	–.02	.26	.04	.65	.27	.18	–.05	.88
Morality	–.08	.05	.83	–.17	–.04	.01	–.03	.08	.74
Family love	.07	–.25	–.03	.81	–.01	.32	.07	.23	.88
Free from anxiety	.21	–.07	.22	–.13	–.17	–.01	.15	.79	.79
Enjoyment	.07	–.05	–.14	–.07	–.08	–.83	.00	.06	.72
Property	–.20	.70	–.03	–.07	.16	.35	.07	.03	.68
Knowledge	–.16	.16	.14	–.12	.80	–.10	.11	–.05	.75
Safety	.04	.23	–.50	–.18	.00	.56	–.08	.34	.76
Justice	.12	.03	.68	.20	.23	.01	–.12	.48	.83
Education	–.01	.11	–.19	.02	.09	–.15	.76	.13	.67
Orderliness	.70	–.28	–.02	–.08	–.09	.26	–.18	–.19	.72
Family harmony	.62	.02	–.07	–.03	–.14	–.03	.31	.37	.64

TABLE B.6 *Normal Varimax Factors for 18 Values—Fathers*

Values	*1*	*2*	*3*	*4*	*5*	*6*	*7*	*8*	*Communality (h^2)*
Independence	.38	−.09	−.10	.03	.38	.28	.30	−.20	.52
Family unity	.05	.12	.92	−.06	.01	.06	−.11	−.02	.88
Manners	.07	.83	−.01	−.01	−.05	.14	.00	−.08	.73
Religion	.67	.29	.05	.15	−.30	.28	.17	−.24	.81
Getting along	−.04	−.11	.06	−.25	.12	.87	−.03	.04	.85
Obedience	.04	.82	−.02	−.12	−.11	−.03	−.04	.05	.70
Honesty	.26	−.14	.50	.22	.02	.65	−.16	−.26	.90
Morality	.07	−.15	.15	.81	.12	−.10	−.14	.14	.77
Family love	−.27	.38	.38	−.16	.17	−.35	.39	−.21	.73
Free from anxiety .	.16	−.07	.22	−.65	.34	.05	.22	.23	.71
Enjoyment	.00	.19	−.06	.11	.82	.23	−.07	.06	.79
Property	.66	−.09	−.13	.20	.23	−.15	.15	.23	.66
Learning	−.08	.11	−.03	.50	.26	.16	.53	.08	.65
Safety	.05	.33	−.12	.25	.15	.00	−.09	.73	.74
Justice	.81	.02	.17	−.03	−.01	−.07	−.11	−.04	.71
Education	−.05	−.01	−.17	−.16	−.14	−.07	.86	.00	.82
Orderliness	−.16	.38	−.02	.06	−.68	.42	.05	.16	.83
Family harmony ..	−.06	−.20	.57	−.12	−.17	−.06	.02	.60	.77

TABLE B.7. *Correlations between Basic Values and Demographic Characteristics*

Values	*Age of parents*	*Number of children*	*Age of oldest child*	*Consistency in religion*	*Education level*	*Social position*	*Social mobility*
MOTHERS							
Moral	–.21	.33[b]	.04	.00	–.09	–.05	–.09
Family	.10	.18	.32[b]	–.11	–.10	–.02	–.17
Egoistic	.16	–.07	.13	–.15	.13	.05	–.23
Interpersonal	.08	.01	.07	.07	.00	.08	.04
Emotional security	–.11	–.21	–.22	–.19	.12	.24	–.04
Education	.18	.15	.21	.20	–.23	–.10	–.04
Orderly living	–.26	.39[c]	.05	–.13	–.44[d]	–.37[c]	–.24
Biological	.19	–.28[a]	–.32[b]	–.16	–.19	–.11	.13
Play	–.01	.01	.07	.00	.02	.16	.19
Economic	.02	.09	.27[a]	.15	–.22	–.12	.11
Σ Mothers' basic values	.14	.23	.17	–.03	–.27[a]	–.10	–.15
FATHERS							
Moral	.13	.37[c]	.39[c]	.10	.05	.04	.09
Family	.13	.00	.19	–.21	.12	.15	–.10
Egoistic	.18	–.15	.14	.17	.09	.06	.48[d]
Interpersonal	.25	.07	.18	.14	.00	–.16	–.11
Emotional security	.03	–.36[b]	.26	–.09	.26	.18	–.08
Education	–.01	–.06	.08	.18	–.22	.12	.02
Orderly living	–.13	.50[d]	.01	.13	–.05	.02	-.07
Biological	–.23	–.18	–.28[a]	–.15	–.24	–.20	–.07
Play	.17	–.18	–.05	–.21	.23	.38[c]	.10
Economic	–.21	.05	–.06	.24	–.22	–.43[d]	.00
Σ Fathers' basic values	.20	.04	.27[a]	.15	.00	–.02	.15

[a] $p < .10$; [b] $p < .05$; [c] $p < .02$; [d] $p < .01$.

TABLE B.8. *Correlations of 18 Subcategories of Basic Values with Demographic Characteristics—Mothers*

Values	Age of parents	Number of children	Age of oldest child	Consistency in religion	Education level	Social position	Social mobility
Independence	.16	−.07	.15	−.18	.12	.08	−.25
Family unity	−.02	.23	.22	−.04	−.22	−.25	−.23
Obedience	−.40[c]	.06	−.16	.18	−.27[a]	−.31[a]	−.20
Manners	−.17	.16	.08	−.02	−.29[a]	−.09	−.23
Religion	−.04	.20	−.03	.15	.06	.04	.07
Getting along	−.06	.26	.09	.10	−.07	−.01	−.03
Responsibility	−.01	.29[a]	.27[a]	.00	−.26	−.15	−.11
Morality	.07	.03	.02	.00	.17	.12	−.15
Free from anxiety	.19	−.22	−.26	−.33[b]	−.15	.19	.13
Family love	.02	−.10	.08	−.14	−.07	−.03	−.19
Enjoyment	.04	−.19	−.12	−.15	.12	.26	−.09
Knowledge	.20	.16	.37[c]	.01	.10	.29[a]	−.02
Safety	−.09	−.16	.01	−.08	−.20	−.20	.31[a]
Justice	.16	.03	.17	−.41[d]	.14	.36[b]	−.02
Property	−.06	−.10	.10	−.02	−.04	.08	.05
Education in gen.	−.26	.00	−.02	.17	−.18	−.05	.09
Orderliness	−.37[c]	.41[d]	−.06	.08	−.41[d]	−.58[e]	−.15
Family harmony	−.05	.33[b]	.11	.03	−.23	−.06	.15

[a] $p < .10$; [b] $p < .05$; [c] $p < .02$; [d] $p < .01$; [e] $p < .001$.

TABLE B.9. *Correlations of 18 Subcategories of Basic Values with Demographic Characteristics—Fathers*

Values	Age of parents	Number of children	Age of oldest child	Consistency in religion	Education level	Social position	Social mobility
Independence	−.03	.03	.08	.32[b]	−.10	−.11	.15
Family unity	.03	.06	.17	−.15	.09	.08	−.20
Obedience	−.32[b]	.18	−.08	.04	−.07	−.05	−.21
Manners	−.14	.50[d]	.03	.16	−.09	−.03	−.28[a]
Religion	−.10	.27[a]	.08	.01	−.04	−.08	.06
Getting along	.29[a]	−.05	.13	−.11	.22	.13	−.11
Responsibility	.43[d]	.16	.49[d]	.08	.09	.13	.05
Morality	.11	.16	.39[c]	.18	−.23	−.19	.18
Free from anxiety	−.16	−.17	−.20	−.01	.09	−.01	−.19
Family love	−.11	−.12	−.26	−.10	.22	.31[a]	.05
Enjoyment	.18	−.16	.12	−.04	.02	.16	−.04
Knowledge	.26	.05	.28[a]	.28[a]	−.11	.02	.06
Safety	−.16	.39[c]	.09	.06	−.43[d]	−.42[d]	−.10
Justice	−.03	.24	.07	.14	.14	.09	−.03
Property	−.24	−.13	−.17	−.03	−.19	−.31[a]	−.17
Education in gen.	−.36[b]	−.31[a]	−.40[c]	−.03	−.04	−.05	−.16
Orderliness	−.19	.41[d]	−.01	.08	−.01	.01	−.02
Family harmony	−.11	−.02	−.07	−.12	−.13	−.17	−.07

[a] $p < .10$; [b] $p < .05$; [c] $p < .02$; [d] $p < .01$.

TABLE B.10. *Significance of Correlations of Basic Values with Demographic Descriptions*

Level of significance	*11 Major categories* Number expected by chance (77 r's)	Number observed Mo (77 r's)	Number observed Fa (77 r's)	*18 Subcategories* Number expected by chance (126 r's)	Number observed Mo (126 r's)	Number observed Fa (126 r's)
<.001	.08	0	0	.13	1	0
.001 to .01	.69	1	4	1.13	3	6
.01 to .02	.77	2	2	1.26	3	3
.02 to .05	2.31	3	1	3.78	3	3
.05 to .10	3.85	3	2	6.30	7	8

TABLE B.11. *Significance of Differences between Mothers and Fathers in Basic Values*

Level of significance	*11 Basic values* Number expected by chance	Number observed	*18 Subcategories* Number expected by chance	Number observed
<.001	.01	3	.02	1
.001 to .01	.10	1	.16	0
.01 to .02	.11	0	.18	3
.02 to .05	.33	1	.54	1
.05 to .10	.55	1	.90	3

NOTE: The 18 value subcategories with the highest priority are given in Table 5.2, p. 73.

Appendix C

Tables for Chapter VI

Table C.1. *Beliefs Relating to the Attainment of Nutritional Values*

	Per cent reporting		*Number of codings*		*Mean percentage score*	
	Mo	*Fa*	*Mo*	*Fa*	*Mo*	*Fa*
Nutritional foods:	77	69	101	100	.95	1.16
Fruits, vegetables	44	46	25	26	.24	.30
Meat	26	36	11	15	.10	.16
Milk	23	33	14	16	.12	.22
Vitamins	13	23	5	10	.06	.11
Variety	46	33	25	17	.25	.18
Miscellaneous	36	31	21	16	.18	.19
Nonnutritional foods:	41	31	23	19	.28	.20
Sweets	31	21	16	13	.20	.14
Miscellaneous	15	13	7	6	.08	.06
Conditions for eating:	74	72	80	84	.75	.91
Appetite	51	59	32	32	.29	.38
Relaxed atmosphere	31	41	17	25	.17	.25
Family meal	39	18	17	10	.17	.09
Miscellaneous	23	31	14	17	.12	.19
Σ Beliefs about nutrition	85	82	204	203	1.98	2.27

Table C.2. *Beliefs Relating to Regulation of Sexual Behavior*

	Per cent reporting		*Number of codings*		*Mean percentage score*	
	Mo	*Fa*	*Mo*	*Fa*	*Mo*	*Fa*
Sex education	33	28	50	49	.40	.52
Masturbation	15	26	23	16	.17	.18
Sex experimentation	15	—	6	—	.05	—
Miscellaneous	10	5	5	2	.04	.02
Σ Beliefs about sex regulation	46	41	84	67	.66	.72

TABLE C.3. *Beliefs about Child-oriented and Adult-oriented Techniques Leading to Emotional Security*

Techniques	*Per cent reporting*		*Number of codings*		*Mean percentage score*	
	Mo	*Fa*	*Mo*	*Fa*	*Mo*	*Fa*
Child-oriented:	74	44	77	46	.66	.41
Expression of parental love	28	26	15	19	.12	.15
Unified, harmonious family	31	10	13	5	.11	.06
Requirements adjusted to needs of child	23	28	19	12	.16	.13
Freedom for emotional expression	46	8	22	6	.20	.04
Other practices	13	5	8	4	.07	.03
Adult-oriented:	33	28	19	19	.16	.17
Strict discipline, authority	21	13	11	7	.09	.06
Schedules, limits	18	23	8	12	.07	.11

TABLE C.4. *Instrumental Acts in Beliefs: Values Obtained from Child-oriented and Adult-oriented Parental Control*

Values obtained	*Per cent reporting*		*Number of codings*		*Mean percentage score*	
	Mo	*Fa*	*Mo*	*Fa*	*Mo*	*Fa*
From child-oriented control:						
Emotional security	67	36	49	22	.44	.20
Independence (egoistic)	44	36	26	23	.22	.23
Obedience (moral)	33	18	14	8	.12	.09
Family love	5	13	2	5	.01	.05
Sex regulation (biological)	5	8	3	3	.02	.04
Morality (moral)	3	5	1	3	.01	.04
Family cooperation	3	3	1	1	.01	.03
Self-confidence (egoistic)	3	5	1	2	.01	.02
Family harmony	8	—	3	—	.03	—
Religion (moral)	—	5	—	2	—	.03
Enjoyment (play)	—	5	—	2	—	.02
Creativity (play)	5	—	2	—	.01	—
Getting along (interpersonal)	3	—	1	—	.01	—
Family democracy	3	—	1	—	.01	—
Σ Child-oriented control	85	77	104	71	.90	.75
From adult-oriented control:						
Emotional security	33	28	19	19	.15	.17
Obedience (moral)	41	26	20	11	.18	.12
Nonaggression (egoistic)	23	18	9	9	.08	.10
Aggression (egoistic)	13	3	5	1	.05	.01
Morality (moral)	13	3	5	3	.05	.04
Punctuality (orderly living)	3	8	1	3	.01	.03
Property (economic)	5	3	2	1	.02	.01
Achievement (egoistic)	3	—	1	—	.01	—
Tolerance (interpersonal)	—	3	—	1	—	.01
Sex regulation (biological)	3	—	1	—	.01	—
Carefulness (orderly living)	3	—	1	—	.01	—
Σ Adult-oriented control	77	67	64	48	.57	.49

NOTE: Morality, obedience, religion, and getting along with others are among the 20 per cent highest values for mothers and fathers; family love, emotional security, and enjoyment are among the 20 per cent highest values for mothers.

TABLE C.5. *Instrumental Acts in Beliefs: Values Obtained from Parental Love and Interest*

Values obtained	*Per cent reporting* Mo	Fa	*Number of codings* Mo	Fa	*Mean percentage score* Mo	Fa
Emotional security	49	21	26	11	.23	.11
Education	15	21	10	15	.09	.14
Family unity	26	13	12	6	.10	.07
Morality (moral)	18	18	8	7	.06	.08
Family love	13	8	5	3	.06	.03
Self-confidence (egoistic)	13	5	5	2	.05	.02
Achievement (egoistic)	3	3	1	1	.01	.02
Health (biological)	3	3	1	1	.01	.01
Intelligence (egoistic)	—	5	—	2	—	.02
Work (economic)	—	5	—	2	—	.02
Σ Parental love, interest	82	62	68	50	.61	.52

NOTE: Morality and family unity are among the 20 per cent highest values for mothers and fathers. Values for family love and emotional security are among the highest 20 per cent for mothers; values for education are among the highest 20 per cent for fathers.

TABLE C.6. *Instrumental Acts in Beliefs: Values Obtained from Teaching Methods*

Instrumental act and value obtained	*Per cent reporting* Mo	Fa	*Number of codings* Mo	Fa	*Mean percentage score* Mo	Fa
Beginning early:						
Obedience (moral)	33	33	13	14	.09	.16
Morality (moral)	13	21	5	15	.05	.19
Sex regulation (biological)	10	15	6	8	.04	.08
Manners (orderly living)	10	—	4	—	.03	—
Family cooperation	5	—	2	—	.03	—
Beginning in adolescence:						
Sex regulation (biological)	5	—	2	—	.02	—
Giving allowances:						
Thrift (economic)	—	10	—	4	—	.03
Family democracy	—	3	—	1	—	.01
Teaching by parent:						
Sex regulation (biological)	21	13	16	13	.13	.15
Other methods:						
Sex regulation (biological)	30	26	23	23	.17	.22
Sports (biological)	5	3	2	1	.01	.02
General values	—	8	—	3	—	.03
Σ Teaching methods	69	67	73	82	.57	.89

NOTE: Morality, obedience, and manners are among the 20 per cent highest values for mothers and fathers.

TABLE C.7. *Instrumental Acts in Beliefs: Values Obtained from Feeding Techniques*

Instrumental act and value obtained	*Per cent reporting*		*Number of codings*		*Mean percentage score*	
	Mo	*Fa*	*Mo*	*Fa*	*Mo*	*Fa*
Requiring approved foods:						
Nutrition	82	69	101	85	.95	.94
Health	31	31	12	14	.13	.15
Forbidding disapproved foods:						
Nutrition	39	31	21	19	.28	.20
Eating as a family:						
Nutrition	39	18	17	25	.17	.25
Family unity	—	5	—	2	—	.02
Relaxed atmosphere:						
Nutrition	31	39	17	25	.17	.25
Breast-feeding:						
Emotional security	3	13	1	7	.01	.06
Health	10	5	4	2	.03	.03
Nutrition	—	3	—	1	—	.01
Demand-feeding:						
Emotional security	6	8	2	3	.01	.04
Nutrition	10	3	6	1	.03	.01
Health	3	3	1	1	.01	.01
Miscellaneous techniques:						
Health	3	—	1	—	.01	—
Physical activity	3	—	1	—	.01	—
Σ Feeding techniques	90	85	184	185	1.81	1.97

NOTE: Family unity is among the highest 20 per cent of values for mothers and fathers; emotional security for mothers.

TABLE C.8. *Instrumental Acts in Beliefs: Parent Behavior Affecting One Value Each*

Instrumental act	*Value obtained*
Father's demanding more effective	Obedience (moral)
Mother's demanding more effective	Obedience (moral)
Mother's staying at home	Family harmony
Mother's having outside interests	Family harmony
Father's providing economically	Family harmony
Father's caring for children	Family harmony
Father's assisting in housework	Family harmony
Not drinking to excess	Family Love
Not moving	Friends (interpersonal)
Father's teaching in child's school	Getting along with others (interpersonal)
Making no issue of differences	Tolerance (interpersonal)
Parent's ability	Education
Having few children in family	Education
Father's being head of family	Emotional security
Singing to children	Emotional security
Not calling attention to defects	Emotional security
Problems of parents	Emotional security (neg.)
General standards of living	Emotional security
Keeping things out of child's mouth	Safety (biological)
Fresh air	Health (biological)
Rooming-in	Health (biological)
Warm clothing	Preventing illness (biological)
Vitamins	Preventing illness (biological)
Isolation	Preventing illness (biological)
Limiting number of toys	Carefulness (orderly living)
Emphasizing money	Materialistic values (economic)
Talking about self-confidence	Self-confidence (egoistic)

NOTE: Obedience and getting along with others are among the highest 20 per cent of values for mothers and fathers. Family love and emotional security are among the highest 20 per cent for mothers; education and safety, for fathers.

TABLE C.9. *Instrumental Acts in Beliefs: Child Behavior Affecting One Value Each*

Instrumental act	*Value obtained*
Fatigue	Morality (moral)
Need to prove himself	Morality (moral)
A strong conscience	Obedience (moral)
Tolerance	Citizenship (moral)
Admitting wrong-doing	Responsibility (moral)
Concept of parent	Family love
Appearance	Getting along with others (interpersonal)
Going to school	Education
Liking variety of foods	Emotional security
Appetite	Nutrition (biological)
No conversation at meals	Nutrition (biological)
Cleanliness	Health (biological)
Elimination	Health (biological)
Not smoking	Health (biological)
Not lying in bed	Sex regulation (biological)
Paying for toys	Carefulness (orderly living)
Motivation	Achievement (egoistic)
Achievement	Enjoyment (play)

NOTE: Morality, obedience, and getting along with others are among the highest 20 per cent of values for mothers and fathers. Family love, emotional security, and enjoyment are among the highest 20 per cent for mothers; education, for fathers.

Appendix D

Tables for Chapter VII

Table D.1. *Beliefs about General Characteristics of Children*

	Per cent reporting		*Number of codings*		*Mean percentage score*	
	Mo	*Fa*	*Mo*	*Fa*	*Mo*	*Fa*
Intelligence	72	64	47	40	.43	.39
Impulse control	41	31	35	21	.29	.22
Problems	31	31	26	25	.19	.31
Intrinsic needs	38	38	25	20	.20	.25
Parent relations	33	49	19	28	.13	.31
Interests	31	31	20	19	.19	.18
Sibling relations	21	36	10	27	.09	.27
Other	33	31	17	14	.14	.14
Σ Beliefs, characteristics of children	90	95	199	194	1.66	2.07

Table D.2. *Beliefs about Age and Development of Children*

	Per cent reporting		*Number of codings*		*Mean percentage score*	
	Mo	*Fa*	*Mo*	*Fa*	*Mo*	*Fa*
Infancy (birth to 2 years)	33	36	44	26	.32	.33
Early childhood (3–5 years)	54	56	37	39	.29	.45
Late childhood (6–12 years)	38	28	25	16	.21	.22
Adolescence (12–16 years)	46	36	157	119	1.24	1.17
General	59	59	52	41	.23	.55
Σ Beliefs, age and development	95	97	315	241	2.29	2.72

TABLE D.3. *Beliefs about Sex Differences*

	Per cent reporting		*Number of codings*		*Mean percentage score*	
	Mo	*Fa*	*Mo*	*Fa*	*Mo*	*Fa*
None	44	23	19	15	.15	.15
Roles	36	28	34	16	.23	.16
Activities, interests	33	26	21	11	.16	.15
Conformity	28	26	12	11	.10	.15
Parent relations	28	15	15	8	.12	.08
Rate of development	15	15	9	9	.05	.12
Drives	15	13	7	6	.05	.08
Personality	8	13	7	6	.07	.05
Other	5	5	2	2	.01	.02
Σ Beliefs, sex differences	82	79	126	84	.94	.96

TABLE D.4. *Percentage of Parents Discussing Beliefs about Heredity, Environment, and Interaction*

	Percentage	
	Mo	*Fa*
Heredity only	23	18
Environment only	10	23
Heredity and environment	31	20
Heredity and interaction	10	8
Environment and interaction	0	8
Heredity, environment, and interaction	11	8
Σ Percentage parents reporting beliefs about heredity and environment	85	85

TABLE D.5. *Intercorrelations between Values (V) and Beliefs (B) about Reward, Punishment, and Control*

(Fathers' correlations above diagonal; mothers' correlations below)

	(1)	(2)	(3)	(4)	(5)	(6)	(7)	(8)	(9)	(10)	(11)	(12)
(1) V Lenient control	*	–.13	.26	–.20	–.19	–.02	.17	–.03	–.08	.04	–.05	–.09
(2) V Strict control	.03	*	–.13	.13	.36[b]	.22	.12	.25	.07	.20	.07	.05
(3) B Reward	.11	–.09	*	.47[d]	.06	–.03	–.04	–.17	.35[b]	.00	.34[b]	.31[a]
(4) B Reward (neg.)	.36[b]	–.01	.19	*	.03	.20	.14	–.09	.39[c]	.08	.42[d]	.41[d]
(5) B Punishment (pos.)	.11	.37[c]	–.17	.07	*	.21	–.26	–.07	.09	.11	.09	.11
(6) B Punishment (neg.)	.06	.28[a]	.03	–.12	.12	*	.04	.02	–.10	–.06	.18	–.14
(7) B Lenient control	.06	–.10	.13	–.09	–.20	.32[b]	*	.02	.05	–.23	–.05	.21
(8) B Firm control	–.29[a]	.11	–.19	–.18	.16	.07	–.14	*	–.18	–.09	–.25	–.16
(9) B Strict control	.12	.42[d]	–.16	–.10	.61[e]	.00	–.23	–.15	*	.02	.48[d]	.13
(10) B Child-oriented control	.11	–.16	–.07	–.03	–.27[a]	.12	.02	–.21	–.14	*	.00	–.16
(11) B Adult-oriented control	–.06	.47[d]	.19	–.09	.28[a]	–.11	.07	.18	.18	–.02	*	.11
(12) B Parental love	.11	.08	.41[d]	–.05	–.18	–.11	.04	–.01	–.12	.21	.37[c]	*
(13) B Parental example	.14	.03	–.09	.32[b]	–.05	–.04	–.14	.07	–.19	–.06	–.01	.09
(14) B Peer groups	–.30[a]	–.14	–.16	–.15	–.13	.11	.17	.01	.04	.42[d]	–.11	.01
(15) B Church, relig. groups	–.12	–.18	–.01	.00	–.02	.02	–.14	.07	–.11	.13	–.06	.23
(16) B Obedience	.08	.28[a]	.00	–.06	.08	.00	.25	.02	.07	.01	.46[d]	.22
(17) B Reasoning	.11	.16	–.01	–.02	.27[a]	.42[d]	.00	.32[b]	.04	.15	.22	.08
(18) B Consistency	–.13	.11	.27[a]	–.06	–.15	–.26	.08	–.02	–.08	.06	.26	.22
(19) B Inhibition (pos.)	–.18	–.10	–.04	–.16	.23	.28[a]	.21	.22	.02	–.14	–.06	–.20
(20) B Inhibition (neg.)	–.16	–.11	–.14	.00	–.06	.22	.32[b]	.13	–.14	.29[a]	–.27[a]	.07
(21) B Insistence (neg.)	–.03	.16	–.02	.11	.38[c]	.34[b]	–.04	.02	.31[a]	–.01	.15	–.23
(22) B Maturity of child	–.05	–.06	.14	–.02	–.02	–.07	–.15	.23	–.16	–.15	.00	.01
(23) B Immaturity of child	.11	–.07	.21	.12	–.09	.18	.50[d]	–.20	–.23	.07	.14	–.09

[a] $p < .10$; [b] $p < .05$; [c] $p < .02$; [d] $p < .01$; [e] $p < .001$.

TABLE D.5 (Cont.).

(Fathers' correlations above diagonal; mothers' correlations below)

	(13)	(14)	(15)	(16)	(17)	(18)	(19)	(20)	(21)	(22)	(23)
(1) V Lenient control	–.06	.44[d]	–.13	–.01	–.14	–.14	.17	–.08	.12	.00	.10
(2) V Strict control	.02	–.19	.02	–.12	.01	–.14	.28[a]	.12	.24	–.16	–.30[a]
(3) B Reward	.11	.21	.11	.29[a]	–.16	.18	.08	.02	.26	–.25	–.09
(4) B Reward (neg.)	.36[b]	.01	.26	.08	.07	.25	.01	.09	–.02	.00	–.04
(5) B Punishment (pos.)	.22	–.03	.21	–.14	.31[a]	–.10	–.19	.18	–.03	.17	–.37[c]
(6) B Punishment (neg.)	–.11	.45[d]	.10	–.21	.33[b]	–.06	–.13	.00	.29[a]	–.08	.10
(7) B Lenient control	–.05	.20	–.09	–.14	–.06	–.27[a]	–.03	.24	–.14	–.11	–.12
(8) B Firm control	.06	–.05	.05	–.11	.10	–.19	.07	.07	.11	–.17	.16
(9) B Strict control	.25	.02	.28[a]	.13	.05	.34[b]	–.08	–.10	.11	.01	–.15
(10) B Child-oriented control	–.01	–.19	.02	.10	–.05	.21	.35[b]	.05	–.14	.08	–.01
(11) B Adult-oriented control	.17	.31[a]	.39[c]	.20	.06	.41[d]	–.16	–.04	.12	–.13	–.03
(12) B Parental love	.33[b]	.12	.01	–.01	.10	–.14	.01	.01	.01	.10	–.03
(13) B Parental example	*	.02	.22	–.09	.20	–.02	–.05	–.06	–.02	.37[c]	.13
(14) B Peer groups	.03	*	.26	.13	.38[c]	–.10	–.11	–.19	.08	–.07	.09
(15) B Church, relig. groups	–11	.02	*	–.09	.03	.26	–.05	.01	–.07	–.12	–.12
(16) B Obedience	.15	–.11	.03	*	–.18	.48[d]	.14	–.06	.09	.02	–.08
(17) B Reasoning	.29[a]	.10	.02	.14	*	–.06	–.30[a]	.00	.00	.23	–.04
(18) B Consistency	–.06	.11	–.24	.13	–.17	*	.04	–.04	.03	.00	–.07
(19) B Inhibition (pos.)	–.19	.04	–.03	.05	.34[b]	.02	*	–.02	.17	.13	–.16
(20) B Inhibition (neg.)	–.18	.48[d]	–.11	–.22	–.05	.04	.00	*	.02	.01	–.20
(21) B Insistence (neg.)	.11	–.02	–.07	–.10	.26	–.05	.27[a]	–.16	*	–.09	–.10
(22) B Maturity of child	–21	–.29[a]	.15	–.18	–.12	.21	–.07	–.12	.00	*	.20
(23) B Immaturity of child	.38[e]	.12	–.24	.15	.40[e]	.13	.15	–.09	.13	–.09	*

[a] $p < .10$; [b] $p < .05$; [c] $p < .02$; [d] $p < .01$; [e] $p < .001$.

TABLE D.6. *Significance of Intercorrelations between Values and Beliefs about Reward, Punishment, and Control*

Level of significance	*Number expected by chance (253 r's)*	*Number observed* Mo (253 r's)	Fa (253 r's)
<.001	.25	1	0
.001 to .01	2.28	8	7
.01 to .02	2.53	5	5
.02 to .05	7.59	7	8
.05 to .10	12.65	10	7

TABLE D.7. *Combinations of Values and Beliefs about Reward, Punishment, and Control*

	Per cent reporting		*Number of codings*		*Mean percentage score*		*Percentage score difference*	
	Mo	*Fa*	*Mo*	*Fa*	*Mo*	*Fa*	*t*	*p*
V, B, lenient control[a]	62	51	46	68	.39	.59	—	n.s.
V, B, lenient control, IB, child-oriented control	95	87	150	139	1.29	1.34	—	n.s.
B, reward, neg. punishment, lenient control	100	95	155	176	1.34	1.71	1.74	<.10
V, B, strict control	82	82	101	108	.91	1.14	—	n.s.
V, B, strict control, IB, adult-oriented control	95	87	166	153	1.46	1.60	—	n.s.
B, neg. reward, punishment, strict control	85	95	111	181	1.01	2.10	4.13	<.001

[a] Value (V); Belief (B); Instrumental Belief (IB).

TABLE D.8. *Correlations between Demographic Characteristics and Combinations of Values and Beliefs about Reward, Punishment, and Control*

	Age of parent	*Number of children*	*Age of oldest child*	*Consistency in religion*	*Education level*	*Social position*	*Social mobility*
MOTHERS							
V, B, lenient control	.26	−.03	−.09	−.19	.31[a]	.41[d]	.16
V, B, lenient control, IB, child-oriented control ..	.06	.01	.07	.02	−.04	−.02	−.03
B, reward, neg. punishment, lenient control	.15	−.18	.05	−.35[b]	.36[b]	.32[b]	.02
V, B, strict control	−.26	.42[d]	.11	.05	−.19	−.39[c]	.01
V, B, strict control, IB, adult-oriented control ..	−.19	.55[e]	.10	.12	−.10	−.30[a]	.01
B, neg. reward, punishment, strict control	.09	.49[d]	.11	−.01	−.05	−.02	−.03
FATHERS							
V, B, lenient control	.10	−.13	.22	−.17	.20	.22	.28[a]
V, B, lenient control, IB, child-oriented control ..	.12	−.08	.13	.00	.25	.25	.25
B, reward, neg. punishment, lenient control	−.09	.04	.11	.09	−.19	−.15	.08
V, B, strict control	.32[b]	−.09	.28[a]	.24	−.21	−.11	.03
V, B, strict control, IB, adult-oriented control ..	.21	−.16	.29[a]	−.19	.05	.16	−.05
B, neg. reward, punishment, strict control	.04	.11	.20	.04	−.27[a]	−.29[a]	−.01

NOTE: Value (V); Belief (B); Instrumental Belief (IB).
[a] $p < .10$; [b] $p < .05$; [c] $p < .02$; [d] $p < .01$; [e] $p < .001$.

Appendix E

Tables for Chapter VIII

Table E.1. *Difference in Scores Related to Object of Children's Aggressive Behavior*

Object of aggressive behavior	Mothers			Fathers		
	>	*t*	*p*	>	*t*	*p*
Parent vs. children	Pa	3.28	<.01	Pa	—	n.s.
Parent vs. property	Pa	6.68	<.001	Pa	4.54	<.001
Parent vs. self	Pa	3.87	<.001	Pa	—	n.s.
Children vs. property	Ch	4.41	<.001	Ch	3.37	<.01

Table E.2. *Influence of Child's Motivations on Child-rearing*

	Per cent Reporting		Number of codings		Mean percentage score	
	Mo	Fa	Mo	Fa	Mo	Fa
Likes, wants, desires	100	92	274	192	2.30	1.98
Dislikes	90	69	114	70	1.00	.69
Lack of motivation	18	15	7	9	.05	.08
Σ Motivations of children	100	97	395	271	3.35	2.75

TABLE E.3. *Influence of Child's Abilities on Child-rearing*

	Per cent Reporting		Number of codings		Mean percentage score	
	Mo	Fa	Mo	Fa	Mo	Fa
Intellectual	39	49	29	32	.28	.31
Motor	41	44	24	31	.18	.28
Artistic	10	10	8	5	.06	.04
Σ Positive abilities	51	41	39	37	.30	.33
Σ Lack of abilities	31	49	22	31	.22	.30
Σ Abilities of children	62	64	61	68	.52	.63

TABLE E.4. *Correlations between Demographic Characteristics and Influence of Family Members*

	Age of parent	Number of children	Age of oldest child	Consistency in religion	Education level	Social position	Social mobility
MOTHERS							
Characteristics of parent	.02	.15	–.24	.17	–.01	.30[a]	–.01
Fatigued	.08	–.17	–.35[b]	.01	–.13	.00	.07
Angry	.03	–.05	–.03	–.30[a]	.23	.37[c]	.10
Anxious	–.04	–.11	–.32[b]	–.10	–.09	–.03	.11
Interests	.10	–.18	–.21	–.29[a]	.08	.13	–.09
Spouse interaction	.09	–.30[a]	.08	–.05	.15	.23	.10
Mo influences Fa	.11	–.15	–.07	–.16	.13	.08	.10
Fa influences Mo	.13	–.07	.14	–.07	–.04	.28[a]	.00
Mutual interaction	.01	–.26	.04	.11	.16	–.10	.14
Agreement	.03	–.19	.06	.10	.25	–.08	.11
FATHERS							
Characteristics of parent	.01	.05	–.08	–.15	.46[d]	.51[e]	–.14
Fatigued	.15	–.04	–.13	–.05	.33[b]	.31[a]	–.02
Angry	.21	.00	.25	–.22	.42[d]	.40[c]	.10
Anxious	.13	.06	.28[a]	–.03	–.03	.10	.19
Interests	–.06	–.17	–.15	–.17	.40[c]	.48[d]	.00
Spouse interaction	.24	–.27[a]	.17	–.21	.07	.18	.14
Mo influences Fa	.30[a]	–.32[b]	.10	–.17	.05	.09	.01
Fa influences Mo	–.10	–.28[a]	–.41[d]	–.20	.32[b]	.32[b]	.14
Mutual interaction	.17	–.08	.30[a]	–.13	–.03	.10	.16
Agreement	.28[a]	–.04	.43[d]	–.09	–.01	.11	.13

[a] $p < .10$; [b] $p < .05$; [c] $p < .02$; [d] $p < .01$; [e] $p < .001$.

TABLE E.5. *Correlations of Demographic Characteristics with Influence of Children—Mothers*

	Age of parent	*Number of children*	*Age of oldest child*	*Consistency in religion*	*Education level*	*Social position*	*Social mobility*
Characteristics of children	.02	.07	.17	–.01	–.40[c]	–.04	–.10
Motivations	.10	.10	.28[a]	.06	–.33[b]	–.10	–.04
Positive motivations	.14	.04	.19	.10	–.37[c]	–.15	.08
Negative motivations	–.05	.21	.32[b]	.01	–.12	.02	–.24
Maturity	.10	.00	.25	.10	–.17	–.02	.27[a]
Temporary condition	–.26	.05	–.33[b]	–.06	–.22	–.19	–.14
Abilities	–.08	–.09	–.12	–.06	–.09	.31[a]	–.12
Positive abilities	.06	–.17	–.08	–.11	.07	.13	.15
Physical characteristics	.30[a]	–.11	.23	–.01	–.06	.05	–.28[a]
Behavior of children	.20	.42[d]	.35[b]	.04	–.05	.02	.00
Problems (in general)	.08	.48[d]	.31[a]	.21	–.17	–.06	–.11
Eating	–.06	.15	–.03	.03	–.15	.21	–.12
Eating problems	–.07	.21	.02	.12	–.16	.18	–.11
Orderly living	.04	.02	.05	–.04	–.02	.13	–.04
Orderly-living problems	.00	.01	.00	.02	–.05	.08	–.08
Obedience	.14	.34[b]	.23	.35[b]	.07	–.17	–.11
Obedience problems	.13	.35[b]	.29[a]	.39[c]	.07	–.23	–.14
Dependency	.01	–.10	–.21	–.06	.11	.11	.13
Dependency problems	–.16	–.07	–.44[d]	–.07	.01	.00	.14
Aggression	.16	.44[d]	.44[d]	–.13	.02	–.05	.08
Aggression problems	.09	.45[d]	.38[c]	.02	–.02	–.13	–.05
Fear	.20	.10	.20	.05	–.26	–.07	.07
Curiosity	.07	.36[b]	.18	.22	–.19	–.48[d]	–.27[a]

[a] $p < .10$; [b] $p < .05$; [c] $p < .02$; [d] $p < .01$.

TABLE E.6. *Correlations of Demographic Characteristics with Influence of Children—Fathers*

	Age of parent	*Number of children*	*Age of first-born*	*Consistency in religion*	*Education level*	*Social position*	*Social mobility*
Characteristics of children	–.05	.02	.11	–.14	.38[c]	.40[c]	.14
Motivations	–.05	.02	.09	–.08	.26	.22	.26
Positive motivations	–.04	–.03	.05	.07	.20	.16	.26
Negative motivations	.05	.17	.17	–.25	.22	.25	.16
Maturity	.08	–.14	.20	–.06	.26	.37[c]	.05
Temporary condition	–.43[d]	.28[a]	–.25	–.02	.09	.04	–.01
Abilities	–.06	–.16	–.06	–.21	.17	.28[a]	–.08
Positive abilities	.05	–.23	–.02	–.03	.09	.20	–.03
Physical characteristics	.29[a]	–.08	.21	–.04	.20	.15	–.02
Behavior of children	.05	.34[b]	.30[a]	.06	–.04	–.01	.16
Problems (in general)	.16	.44[d]	.34[b]	.08	–.12	–.11	.15
Eating	–.25	.35[b]	–.06	.16	–.10	–.04	.05
Eating problems	–.19	.52[e]	.07	.18	–.14	–.07	.09
Orderly living	–.21	.08	–.03	–.19	–.09	–.17	.09
Orderly-living problems	–.22	.06	–.10	–.17	–.09	–.17	.08
Obedience	.06	.36[b]	.24	.18	–.03	–.15	–.01
Obedience problems	.05	.39[c]	.22	.20	–.06	–.16	.00
Dependency	–.02	.00	–.10	–.02	.13	.12	.35[b]
Dependency problems	.02	–.03	–.26	–.01	.18	.15	.30[a]
Aggression	.51[e]	.02	.52[e]	–.11	.10	.13	.04
Aggression problems	.48[d]	.09	.54[e]	–.03	–.07	–.02	.06
Fear	–.04	.14	.13	.05	–.21	–.23	–.02
Curiosity	–.24	–.02	–.20	.19	–.11	–.12	.05

[a] $p < .10$; [b] $p < .05$; [c] $p < .02$; [d] $p < .01$; [e] $p < .001$.

TABLE E.7. *Correlations of Demographic Characteristics with Influence of Parent-Child Interaction*

	Age of parent	Number of children	Age of first-born	Consistency in religion	Education level	Social position	Social mobility
MOTHERS							
Parent-child interaction	.02	.14	.00	.18	.04	.06	.07
With sibling	.12	.35[b]	.15	.06	.28[a]	.13	.09
Practice repeated	.14	.19	.06	.07	.08	–.11	–.06
Practice changed	.08	.31[a]	.14	.02	.28[a]	.21	.13
With child	–.06	–.21	–.18	.22	–.28[a]	–.20	.07
Practice changed	–.07	–.08	–.12	.32[b]	–.19	–.17	.08
Σ Repetition of practice	.09	–.11	–.11	.01	–.17	–.19	–.02
Σ Change in practice	.02	.20	.05	.20	.12	.06	.13
FATHERS							
Parent-child interaction	–.06	.05	.00	–.16	.13	.21	–.14
With sibling	–.01	.28[a]	.15	–.26	.18	.17	.10
Practice repeated	–.03	.25	.06	.02	–.02	–.06	–.15
Practice changed	.00	.19	.14	–.33[b]	.22	.23	.21
With child	–.07	–.32[b]	–.20	.12	–.07	.08	–.36[b]
Practice changed	.05	–.14	–.07	.19	–.08	.06	–.34[b]
Σ Repetition of practice	–.17	–.03	–.13	–.04	–.03	–.02	–.27[a]
Σ Change in practice	.03	.08	.07	–.17	.17	.26	–.02

[a] $p < .10$; [b] $p < .05$.

TABLE E.8. *Significance of Correlations between Influence of Family Members and Demographic Characteristics*

Level of significance	Number expected by chance (287r's)	Number observed: Mo (287r's)	Number observed: Fa (287r's)
<.001	.29	0	5
.001 to .01	2.58	7	8
.01 to .02	2.87	4	6
.02 to .05	8.61	13	12
.05 to .10	14.35	17	13

TABLE E.9. *Summary of Differences in Emphasis on Influence of Family Members by Mothers and Fathers*

(Level of significance .10 or beyond)

	Higher	*t*	*p*
Σ Characteristics of parents	Mo	2.60	<.02
Fatigued	Mo	2.11	<.05
Angry	Fa	1.73	<.10
Anxious	Mo	2.09	<.05
Interests	Mo	3.04	<.01
Σ Mo influences on Fa	Fa	1.73	<.10
Mo competent	Fa	3.06	<.01
Mo indisposed	Fa	1.82	<.10
Mo attitude toward Fa	Mo	2.33	<.05
Σ Fa influences on Mo	Mo	3.27	<.01
Fa competent	Mo	3.81	<.001
Fa attitude toward Mo	Mo	1.91	<.10
Motivations of children	Mo	1.97	<.10
Similarity of child to Mo	Mo	2.60	<.02
Similarity of child to Fa	Fa	2.75	<.01
Σ Parent-child interactions leading to change	Mo	2.03	<.05
Σ Influence of family members	Mo	2.01	<.10

TABLE E.10. *Significance of Differences in Emphasis on Influence of Family Members by Mothers and by Fathers*

Level of significance	*Number expected by chance (60 differences)*	*Number observed (60 differences)*
<.001	.06	1
.001 to .01	.54	4
.01 to .02	.60	2
.02 to .05	1.80	4
.05 to .10	3.00	6

Appendix F

Tables for Chapter X

Table F.1. *Attitudes toward Influences of Family of Orientation*

	Percentage of respondents reporting							
	only positive		*only negative*		*pos. & neg.*		*none*	
	Mo	*Fa*	*Mo*	*Fa*	*Mo*	*Fa*	*Mo*	*Fa*
Respondent's mother	26	5	13	8	46	28	15	59
Respondent's father	21	18	13	8	10	31	56	43
Respondent's "family"	18	21	15	13	57	51	10	15
Σ Influence of family of orientation	8	13	15	5	77	74	0	8

Table F.2. *Sources of Influence in Family of Orientation*

	Per cent reporting		*Number of codings*		*Mean percentage score*		*Percentage score difference*	
	Mo	*Fa*	*Mo*	*Fa*	*Mo*	*Fa*	*t*	*p*
Practices	97	92	256	196	2.20	2.08	—	n.s.
of mother	85	44	109	47	.92	.51	2.23	<.05
of father	31	49	20	42	.14	.40	—	n.s.
of "family"	85	82	127	107	1.14	1.17	—	n.s.
Values	39	39	32	26	.24	.23	—	n.s.
of mother	8	8	4	5	.03	.03	—	n.s.
of father	3	8	2	3	.01	.03	—	n.s.
of "family"	36	28	26	18	.20	.17	—	n.s.
Beliefs	26	28	19	17	.14	.16	—	n.s.
of mother	8	5	6	4	.04	.02	—	n.s.
of father	5	8	2	6	.02	.07	—	n.s.
of "family"	15	15	11	7	.08	.07	—	n.s.
Characteristics	62	39	59	39	.50	.34	—	n.s.
of mother	31	10	23	8	.18	.06	1.86	<.10
of father	21	26	11	22	.11	.20	—	n.s.
of "family"	44	18	25	9	.21	.08	2.96	<.01
Σ Influences in family of orientation	100	92	366	278	3.08	2.81	—	n.s.

TABLE F.3. *Summary of Differences between Mothers and Fathers in Influence of Previous Experiences* (.10 or beyond)

Influence	*Higher*	*t*	*p*
Family of orientation:			
Respondent's mother	Mo	2.33	<.05
Negative	Mo	2.49	<.02
Positive	Mo	2.23	<.05
Characteristics	Mo	1.86	<.10
Respondent's father	Fa	2.88	<.01
Positive	Fa	2.33	<.05
Negative	Fa	1.99	<.10
Respondent's family			
Characteristics	Mo	2.96	<.01
Other childhood experiences:			
In settings	Fa	1.75	<.10
Negative	Fa	2.59	<.02
Adult experiences:			
Teaching, etc.	Mo	2.77	<.01
Positive	Mo	2.40	<.05
Other	Fa	2.61	<.02
Positive	Fa	2.67	<.02

Appendix G

Tables for Chapter XI

Table G.1. *Direct Relations between Emphasis on Influence of Physicians and Other Influences* (*p* .10 or beyond)

	Mo	*Fa*
Values for parenthood		
Nurture	.39*	—
Economic provision	.31	—
Basic values		
Biological	.48*	—
Emotional security	—	.40
Instrumental beliefs		
Emotional security	—	.38
Parental love	—	.27
Descriptive beliefs		
Maturity	.46	—
Infancy	.64*	.44*
Environment	.39	.53*
Learning	.30*	.31
Process of learning	.33*	—
Child behavior		
Dependency	.35*	—
Dependency problems	.55*	.29*
Parent-child interaction	—	.43*
Leading to change	—	.30
Adult experiences		
With children	.27*	—
Parents and children	—	.31*
Positive	—	.41*

* Correlations also significant with sum of communications. See Table 11.9.
r .27, $p < .10$; r .32, $p < .05$; r .37, $p < .02$; r .41, $p < .01$; r .51, $p < .001$.

TABLE G.2. *Direct Relations between Emphasis on Teachers and Other Influences* (p .10 or beyond)

	Mo	*Fa*
Values for parenthood		
Control	—	.31
Control authoritatively	—	.41
Use community resources	.43	—
Basic values		
Family	—	.35
Economic	.44	—
Education	.27	—
Descriptive beliefs		
Infancy	.37*	—
Adolescence	—	.36
Learning	.41*	—
Learning readiness	.28	.28*
Permissive control (neg.)	.37	—
Strict control	.30	—
Spouse interaction	—	.32
Mutual interaction	—	.29
Child characteristics		
Abilities	—	.30
Child behavior		
Dependency	.35*	—
Dependency problems	.31*	—
Adult experiences	.28	—
With children	.32*	.35
With parents and children (pos.)	—	.30*
Other	.30*	—

* Correlations also significant with sum of communications. See Table 11.9.
r .27, $p < .10$; r .32, $p < .05$; r .37, $p < .02$; r .41, $p < .01$.

TABLE G.3. *Direct Relations between Emphasis on Acquaintances and Other Influences* (*p* .10 or beyond)

	Mo	*Fa*
Values for parenthood		
Nurture	.41*	.31
Economic provision	.35	—
Basic values		
Biological	—	.37*
Descriptive beliefs		
Infancy	.28*	—
Environment	.38	—
Process of learning	.38*	—
Spouse interaction	.27	—
Child characteristics		
Temporary condition	.39	.37
Parent-offspring interaction	—	.38
Leading to change	—	.29
With child	.35	—
With child leading to repetition	.27	—
Behavior settings		
Weather	—	.40
Childhood experiences with people	.27	—

* Correlations also significant with sum of communications. See Table 11.9.
r .27, $p < .10$; r .32, $p < .05$; r .37, $p < .02$; r .41, $p < .01$.

TABLE G.4. *Direct Relations between Emphasis on Influence of Organized Education Sources and Other Influences* (*p* .10 or beyond)

	Mo	*Fa*
Values for parenthood		
Rear well	—	.30
Basic values		
Emotional security	—	.36*
Instrumental beliefs		
Emotional security	—	.32
Regulation of sex behavior	.44	—
Child-oriented control	.44	—
Adult-oriented control	—	.32
Parental love	—	.36
Peer groups	.45	—
Descriptive beliefs		
Infancy	—	.44*
Development	.27	—
Environment	—	.28*
Learning	—	.34
Process of learning	.33*	—
Strict control	—	.33
Consistency	—	.32

* Correlations also significant with sum of communications. See Table 11.9.
r .27, $p < .10$; r .32, $p < .05$; r .37, $p < .02$; r .41, $p < .01$.

TABLE G.5. *Direct Relations between Emphasis on Influence of Mass Media and Other Influences* (p .10 or beyond)

	Mo	*Fa*
Values for parenthood		
Nurture	.44*	—
Basic values		
Emotional security	—	.30*
Instrumental beliefs		
Family values	—	.35*
Interpersonal values	—	.27
Regulation of sex behavior	.37	—
Play values	—	.27
Adult-oriented techniques	—	.27
Parental love	—	.29
Peer groups	—	.28
Obedience	—	.36
Descriptive beliefs		
Characteristics of children	.27	—
Maturity	.27*	—
Abilities (positive)	—	.35
Infancy	.48*	.44*
Adolescence	.29	—
Heredity	.46*	—
Environment	—	.39*
Process of learning	.29*	—
Inhibition	—	.55*
Child behavior		
Dependency problems	.27*	—
Adult experiences	—	.31
With children	.42*	—
Parents and children	—	.33*
Other (positive)	.37*	—

* Correlations also significant with sum of communications. See Table 11.9.
r .27, $p < .10$; r .32, $p < .05$; r .37, $p < .02$; r .41, $p < .01$; r .51, $p < .001$.

TABLE G.6. *Negative Correlations between Categories of Communication Sources and Other Influences (p .10 or beyond)—Mothers*

	Inter-personal	*Profes-sional*	*Physi-cian*	*Teacher*	*Acquaint-ance*	*Organized education*	*Mass media*	*Litera-ture*
Basic values								
Play	–.28	–.27	—	—	—	—	—	—
Instrumental beliefs								
Family values	—	—	—	—	—	—	–.33	–.34
Orderly living values	—	—	—	—	—	–.29	—	—
Interpersonal values	–.31	–.35	–.32	–.29	—	—	—	—
Biological values	—	—	—	–.27	—	—	–.31	—
Descriptive beliefs								
Intelligence	–.29	—	—	—	—	—	—	—
Early childhood	—	—	—	—	—	–.33	—	—
Punishment (positive)	—	—	—	—	–.32	—	–.35	–.37
Physical (positive)	—	—	—	—	—	—	–.30	–.33
Punishment (negative)	—	—	–.28	—	—	—	—	—
Physical (negative)	—	—	–.31	—	–.27	—	—	—
Control								
Permissive	–.28	–.28	—	–.35	—	—	—	—
Lenient	—	—	—	—	–.27	—	–.28	–.28
Firm	—	—	—	—	–.27	—	–.30	–.29
Strict	—	—	—	—	–.27	—	–.32	–.32
Authoritarian	–.29	–.30	–.28	—	–.33	—	—	—
Inhibition (positive)	—	—	—	—	—	–.35	—	—
Characteristics of parent								
Anxious	—	—	—	—	—	–.36	—	—
Interests	—	—	—	—	—	–.35	—	—
Characteristics of child								
Motivations	–.34	–.36	—	—	—	—	—	—
Motivations (positive)	–.27	—	–.34	—	—	—	—	—
Temporary condition	—	—	—	—	—	–.38	—	—
Parent-child interaction								
Leading to repetition	—	—	—	–.30	—	—	—	—
Characteristics of setting								
Occupational	—	—	—	—	—	–.35	—	—
Past experiences in family orientation								
Mother	—	—	—	—	—	—	—	–.30
Characteristics of parent	—	—	—	–.38	—	–.40	—	—

r .27, $p < .10$; r .32, $p < .05$; r .37, $p < .02$.

TABLE G.7. *Negative Correlations between Categories of Communication Sources and Other Influences* (p .10 or beyond)—*Fathers*

	Inter-personal	*Profes-sional*	*Physi-cian*	*Teacher*	*Acquaint-ance*	*Organized education*	*Mass media*	*Litera-ture*
Values for parenthood								
Community resources	—	—	–.29	—	—	—	—	—
Basic values								
Orderly living	–.44	—	—	—	—	—	–.31	—
Economic	—	–.27	—	—	—	—	—	—
Instrumental beliefs								
Orderly living values	—	—	—	—	—	–.29	—	—
Biological values	—	—	—	—	—	—	–.30	—
Parental example	—	—	—	—	–.33	—	—	—
Obedience	—	—	—	–.27	—	—	—	—
Descriptive beliefs								
Intelligence	—	—	—	—	—	—	–.32	–.38
Early childhood	—	—	—	–.30	—	—	—	—
Late childhood	—	—	—	—	—	—	–.30	–.27
Heredity	—	—	—	—	—	–.55	—	—
Punishment								
Positive	—	—	—	—	—	—	–.30	—
Social (positive)	—	—	—	—	—	—	–.47	–.44
Control (firm)	—	—	—	—	—	–.35	–.27	—
Settings								
Home								
Rooms	—	—	—	—	—	—	–.31	–.31
Furnishings	—	—	—	–.27	—	—	—	—
Outside	—	—	–.33	—	—	—	—	—
Neighborhood	—	–.31	–.32	—	—	—	—	—
Characteristics								
Occupational	—	—	—	—	—	–.33	—	–.29

r .27, $p < .10$; r .32, $p < .05$; r .37, $p < .02$; r .41, $p < .01$; r .51, $p < .001$.

References

Ackerman, N. W. 1958. *The psychodynamics of family life: diagnosis and treatment of family relationships.* New York: Basic Books.

Adorno, T. W., E. Frenkel-Brunswik, D. J. Levison, and R. N. Sanford. 1950. *The authoritarian personality.* New York: Harper.

Ashby, W. R. 1960. *Design for a brain.* New York: Wiley.

Baldwin, A. L., J. Kalhorn, and F. H. Breese. 1945. Patterns of parent behavior. *Psychol. Monogr., 58,* no. 268.

Bandura, A., and R. H. Walters. 1959. *Adolescent aggression.* New York: Ronald Press.

Barker, R. G. 1960. Ecology and motivation. In *Nebraska Symposium on Motivation.* 1960. Lincoln: University of Nebraska Press.

Barker, R. G. 1965. Explorations in ecological psychology. *Amer. Psychologist, 20,* no. 1.

Barker, R. G., and H. F. Wright. 1955. *Midwest and its children.* New York: Row, Peterson.

Block, J. 1955. Personality characteristics associated with fathers' attitudes toward child-rearing. *Child Develpm., 26,* no. 1.

Brim, O. G. 1959. *Education for child rearing.* New York: Russell Sage Foundation.

Engvall, A. 1954. Comparison of mother and father attitudes toward war-separated children. Chap. 8 in L. M. Stolz *et al., Father-relations of war-born children.* Stanford, Calif.: Stanford University Press.

Erikson, E. H. 1950. *Childhood and society.* New York: Norton.

Eron, L. D., T. J. Banta, L. O. Walder, and J. H. Laulicht. 1961. Comparison of data obtained from mothers and fathers on child-rearing practices and their relation to child aggression. *Child Develpm., 32,* no. 3, 455–72.

Fenichel, O. 1945. *The psychoanalytic theory of neurosis.* New York: Norton.

Freud, S. 1949. *An outline of psychoanalysis.* New York: Norton.

Gesell, A., and F. L. Ilg. 1943. *Infant and child in the culture of today.* New York: Harper.

Gesell, A., and F. L. Ilg. 1946. *The child from five to ten.* New York: Harper.

Gesell, A., F. L. Ilg, and L. B. Ames. 1956. *Youth, the years from ten to sixteen.* New York: Harper.

Heider, F. 1967. On social cognition. *Amer. Psychologist,* 22, no. 1.

Hoeflin, R. 1954. Child rearing practices and child care resources used by Ohio farm families with preschool children. *J. genet. Psychol., 84,* 175–85.

Hollingshead, A. B. Undated. Index of social position: Seven socio-economic scale positions. New Haven, Conn.: Yale University. Mimeographed.

Hollingshead, A. B., and F. C. Redlich. 1958. *Social class and mental illness.* New York: Wiley.

Littman, R. A., J. Curry, and J. Pierce-Jones. 1957. Where parents go for help. *The Coordinator, 6,* no. 1.

Lord, E. 1947. The use of range in place of the standard deviation in the *t* test. *Biometrica, 34,* 41.

Maccoby, N., A. K. Romney, J. S. Adams, and E. E. Maccoby. 1962. "Critical periods" in seeking and accepting information. *Paris-Stanford Studies in Communication.* Stanford, Calif.: Institute for Communication Research, Stanford University, pp. 47–57.

Miller, D. R., and G. E. Swanson. 1958. *The changing American parent.* New York: Wiley.

Nash, J. 1965. The father in contemporary culture and current psychological literature. *Child Develpm., 36,* no. 1, 261–97.

Robbins, L. C. 1963. The accuracy of parental recall of aspects of child development and of child rearing practices. *J. abnorm. soc. Psychol., 66,* 261–70.

Sears, R. R., E. E. Maccoby, and H. Levin. 1957. *Patterns of child rearing.* New York: Row, Peterson.

Senn, M. J. E., and E. M. Wylie. 1955. The epoch approach to child development. *Woman's Home Companion,* November 1955, pp. 40–42.

Sperry, I. V., and K. B. Garner. 1962. *Information and services obtained and desired by parents of young children.* Greensboro: North Carolina Agricultural Experiment Station in Cooperation with the School of Home Economics, Woman's College of the University of North Carolina.

Stolz, H. R., and L. M. Stolz. 1951. *Somatic development of adolescent boys.* New York: Macmillan.

Stolz, L.M. 1958. Youth: The Gesell Institute and its latest study. *Contemp. Psychol., 3,* no. 1. Also in J. F. Rosenblith and W. Allinsmith, eds., *The causes of behavior.* Boston: Allyn and Bacon, 1962. Chap. 2, pp. 52–58.

Stolz, L. M., *et al.* 1954. *Father relations of war-born children.* Stanford, Calif.: Stanford University Press.

Warner, W. L., M. Meeker, and K. Eells. 1949. *Social class in America.* Science Research Associates.

Weide, M. L. H. 1962. Parental relationships in the homes of delinquent and non-delinquent boys. Stanford, Calif.: Stanford University, master's thesis.

White, R. K. 1951. *Value-analysis.* Society for the Psychological Study of Social Issues.

Whiting, J. W. M., and I. R. Child. 1953. *Child-training and personality: a cross-cultural study.* New Haven: Yale Univ. Press.

Wickman, E. K. 1929. *Children's behavior and teachers' attitudes.* New York: Commonwealth Fund, Division of Publications.

Yarrow, L. J., and M. R. Yarrow. 1964. Personality continuity and change in the family context. In P. Worchel and D. Byrne, eds., *Personality change.* New York: Wiley.

Yarrow, M. R. 1963. The elusive evidence. Division Seven, American Psychological Association. Newsletter, Fall, 1963.

Index